W9-ATO-951

OF GODS AND MEN
NEW RELIGIOUS MOVEMENTS
IN THE WEST

OF GODS AND MEN
NEW RELIGIOUS MOVEMENTS IN THE WEST

Proceedings of the
1981 Annual Conference of the
British Sociological Association
Sociology of Religion Study Group

Eileen Barker
editor

ISBN 0-86554-095-0

All books published by Mercer University Press are produced on acid-free paper that exceeds the minimum standards set by the National Historical Publications and Records Commission.

LIBRARY OF CONGRESS CATALOGING IN PUBLICATION DATA

British Sociological Association. Sociology of Religion Study Group. Conference (1981: Lincoln, Lincolnshire)
Of gods and men.

Includes bibliographies.
1. Religions—Congresses. 2. Cults—Congresses. I. Barker, Eileen.
II. Title.
BL21.B74 1984 306'.6 83-23822
ISBN 0-86554-095-0 (alk. paper)

CONTENTS

DEDICATION

To the Memory of
Mary Helen Roxburgh

PREFACE

The British Sociological Association Sociology of Religion Study Group held its 1981 annual conference at Edward King House in the shadow of Lincoln Cathedral. The theme for the meeting was new religious movements. Most of the participants (who came from ten different countries) were academics currently involved in research into the movements, but also present, adding a bit of "data input" and some remarkably good-humoured spice to the proceedings, were two persons actively involved in the production of "anticult" literature and advice, and three representatives of the movements themselves.

The papers, not all of which are in agreement, cover a wide range of approaches to new religious movements. Some contributions are almost entirely theoretical, others contain empirical information that was, in certain instances, still being analyzed at the time of the conference. No attempt has been made in this collection to edit or to mold the contributions into any general theme. The aim is primarily to bring the proceedings together and to make available to a wider readership some of the latest thinking and findings of this international group of scholars.

The papers are arranged roughly according to the degree of generality with which they are concerned. We begin with the more abstract, theoretical themes and some of the wider issues raised by the new religions before moving on to a discussion of phenomena that might be termed "movements" rather than groups. Next there are papers in which several groups are compared, and these are followed by papers describing studies of specific aspects of specific groups.

John Lofland and Norman Skonovd open the volume with a model for the comparative analysis of patterns of conversion. They also consider some of the social, psychological, and organizational implications of the different motifs which they isolate in their model. Next David Snow and Richard Machalek challenge the view that unconventional beliefs are necessarily inherently fragile or that they must owe their persistence to the power of "plausibility structures." It is, they argue, disbelief rather than belief that we should consider problematic, belief being the "natural attitude."

An analysis of the relationship between politics and religion is to be found in Carroll Bourg's comparison of participants in current new religious movements with the left-wing activists of the 1930s in the United States and the youth movements in Germany both before and after the First World War. Bourg sees the primary political task of the new religious movements being internal—the movements are the testing ground for "new" human capacities. This brings him to raise the issue of ways in which religious movements can be studied and he joins Touraine in advocating a sociology of action, or "sociology as participation."

Drawing on the data collected from a number of studies, James Richardson charts ways in which movements and communes can support themselves, public solicitation being only one of the many means employed. Most groups, he argues, go through a period of experimentation to see which methods are most successful and most acceptable to the group's ideology. Richardson also offers us a "data frame" for gathering information on the economic policies of new religious movements.

One of the largest movements in recent years has been the rise of neo-Pentecostalism within the Christian churches. Andrew Walker traces three phases of this phenomenon which he sees as an essentially twentieth-century movement. He believes, however, that an increasing number of new charismatics, displaying the sectarian form of classical Pentecostalism, are now in the process of shifting away from the mainline churches, either into the growing House Church movement or by following charismatic leaders into schismatic groups. The next two papers look at another, to some extent overlapping, phenomenon of modern America—the popularly labeled "Moral Majority." In a not altogether dissimilar argument from that of Samuel Hill, Paul Schwartz and James McBride describe ways in which the Christian New Right differs from nineteenth-century Fundamentalism in the United States, and how these differences permit an accommodation to the rest of society, allowing modern Fundamentalism to move from the periphery to the center of American life. Doubts are expressed in both papers about the success the new religious-political right (the NRPR as Hill calls it) might have in achieving its goals, but it is generally agreed that the movement both reflects and has led to some important changes in the functioning of religion and politics in contemporary America.

Jean Burfoot examines what she calls the "fun movement" in California. This contemporary emphasis on pleasure, happiness, and play has much in common, she suggests, with what, in a less secular milieu, would be an outbreak of religious ecstasy. It provides a pool of individuals who are open to the kinds of new systems of meanings to be found in new religious movements. Not perhaps entirely unrelated is Geoffrey Ahern's discussion of the extent to which the prospering of esoteric movements will be dependent upon the existence of a macrocultural plausibility structure for an esoteric cosmology.

The next two papers consider the reactions of a society to the new religious movements it "hosts." Anson Shupe, Bert Hardin, and David Bromley compare the "anticult movements" in the United States of America and in the Federal Republic of Germany. James Beckford further compares the anticultists in those two countries with anticult activity in the United Kingdom, France, and Japan. These contributions clearly illustrate that the ways in which a society responds to new religious movements can give us a not inconsiderable amount of information about that society, its beliefs, its values, and its institutions.

The paper by Frederick Bird and William Reimer reports on participation rates in new religious and parareligious movements in Montreal. The findings are compared with those of Wuthnow in California and we are given brief profiles of the sorts of people most likely to become associated with the groups either as committed members or (as in the vast majority of cases) on a casual, temporary basis.

Christine King compares the different ways in which five sects fared during the period of the Third Reich, the Jehovah's Witnesses suffering the most extreme opposition with half of their membership ending up in prison or in a concentration camp, and a quarter of their number being executed. It was, King argues, not belief per se but the way in which a group was willing to *amend* its beliefs that was the crucial factor under the Nazi regime.

The data presented by Wolfgang Kuner arise from his administration of a personality test to German members of the Unification Church, the Children of God, the Ananda Marga, and to a control group of nonaffiliated students. He was unable to find any evidence of a general mental disturbance in terms of clinical psychology among the members of the three movements.

Steven Tipton's paper looks at the way in which *est* (Erhard Seminars Training) has supplied an ethic which, among other things, justified for some of the dropouts of the 1960s a dropping back into middle-class economic and social life. Burke Rochford's research has been with the Hare Krishna. He illustrates how factors external to the movement can shape its structure and recruitment strategies. Frans Derks and Jan van der Lans show how changes in the type of people who join the Divine Light Mission have coincided with organizational and ideological changes in the movement itself. And finally, Eileen Barker, through a comparative analysis of those who attend Unification Church workshops and do *not* join, with those who *do*, attempts to isolate factors that could, on the one hand, predispose people toward conversion or could, on the other hand, "protect" them from joining.

—Eileen Barker
London School of Economics
1983

ACKNOWLEDGMENTS

Heartfelt gratitude is due to Canon Rex Davis who was our most genial host at Lincoln. Jim Richardson was a constant source of inspiration in the preparation of the conference and it was largely due to his initiative that so many of the participants came from overseas. Jean Ridyard and Cindy Celant have given invaluable secretarial assistance. And my thanks to Peter Barker who, as always, just helped.

PATTERNS OF CONVERSION

by John Lofland
and Norman Skonovd

THE STUDY OF religious conversion has undergone a research renaissance in recent years. In the wake of the worldwide wave of "new religions" and the resurgence of traditional religions, social-scientific and journalistic inquiry into this phenomenon has blossomed. As is to be expected, investigators have stressed different aspects of the conversion process. Focusing on how organized group activities can induce conversion, some employ such concepts as "affective bonds," "programming," or even "mind control." Others highlight the individual convert's subjective life and what is seen as the "self-guiding" and "self-induced" side of conversion. Yet others attempt to encompass all these aspects and point to various additional facets. Indeed, the literature on the topic is becoming so rich and diverse in these and other ways that we believe a pause and provisional stocktaking is now in order.[1]

Such a stocktaking is prompted, moreover, by a sense that the differences among conversion experiences which investigators are reporting with increasing frequency are not merely a matter of the "theoretical goggles" worn by the researchers—or, in a pejorative view,

---

[1]The research outpouring is rich and a comprehensive bibliography by Lewis Rambo (1982) has recently been published. Limitations of space unfortunately force us to draw quite selectively on what is, in fact, an enormous body of literature. This paper is an elaborated and in-depth treatment of a set of ideas presented in brief and truncated fashion in Lofland and Skonovd, 1981.

their conceptual blinders, as some are wont to argue. Rather, such differences are inherent in the central or key features of conversions themselves. Therefore it is our goal to explore the usefulness of the analytic supposition that there are several major "types" of conversions or even "conversion careers." Given this assumption, our yet more restricted aim is to isolate what we may think of as key, critical, orienting, defining, or "motif" experiences as they vary among conversions. The notion of a "motif experience" in conversion is, on one side, an effort to attend to accounts of conversion that describe the subjective perceptions of the convert. What converts stress in their accounts varies markedly and we suspect that the differences are not simply artifacts of the "accounting" process (Beckford, 1978), biases elicited by researchers, or the result of selective perception in the construction of conversion accounts. Instead, we are suggesting that holistic, subjective conversions actually vary in a number of acute, qualitatively different ways that are best differentiated by their respective "motif experiences." "Motif experiences," then, are to be defined as those aspects of a conversion experience that are most memorable and orienting to the person "doing" or "undergoing" personal transformation—aspects that add a tone to the experience, to its importance in time, and to its positive or negative affective content.

However, in so attuning to the convert's subjective experience we do not elect to be bound entirely by it. We want also—on the other "side"—to "bracket" that subjective experience in more objective terms than the convert might do. We need particularly to look at the objective ways in which it is clear that the social organizational aspects of the process differ. Our approach, therefore, strives to blend phenomenological fidelity with some distance from that to which we are faithful. Both sides together—salient thematic elements and key experiences combined with objective situations—may be thought of as making up the "motif" of a conversion.

By such an approach we hope both to incorporate and to go beyond the kind of problems James Beckford (1978) poses in his seminal thoughts on "accounting for conversion." Beckford points out that among Jehovah's Witnesses, at least, there is a rather formal, public, or even official conception of appropriate features of the conversion experience. The organization provides, in effect, a paradigm that converts use to pattern their conversion accounts; some aspects are stressed, others de-emphasized or altogether deleted. In the case of the Jehovah's Witnesses, conversion is expected to be slow, progressive, extremely cognitive, and something that one achieves. Experiences "which smack of sudden or idiosyncratic illumination/revelation [are not] reconcilable" with Witness theory (Beckford, 1978:254).

Some investigators take such molding to pose an insurmountable problem that confines us forever and only to the study of "molds." We, however, do not consider such molding or structuring a problem. Instead, we recognize that the conversion experience *itself* is partly molded by expectations of what conversion is about or "is like" and that there is therefore the probability of a relatively "good fit" between the "real" experiences and paradigmatic accounts. Because it is probable that they reflect "raw reality"—the *first level* of social reality—it is our intention here, in part, to delineate the variety of conversion accounts—the *second level* of social reality.

The efforts of analysts may be thought of, indeed, as a *third level* of social reality—one that tries to keep pace, often unsuccessfully, with the ever-changing character of the first two levels.

Following tradition, we use the term "conversion" to refer to, in the oft quoted words of Richard Travisano (1970:660), "a radical reorganization of identity, meaning, life." Or in Max Heirich's felicitous phrases, conversion is "the process of changing a sense of root reality" or "a conscious shift in one's sense of grounding" (Heirich, 1977:674). Conversions, further, may involve a number of different types of changes in organizational terms. From the careful analysis of Lewis Rambo (1980:4-5), it is apparent that there are at least five of these: (1) transitions from one religious tradition to another, (2) transitions within major components of a single tradition, (3) movement from no or minimal participation to a state of high commitment and participation, (4) the reverse (that is, defection), or (5) significant "intensification" within an existing affiliation. Any such movements can and quite often do display the qualities suggested by Travisano and Heirich.

In overview, we believe it worthwhile to distinguish six "motifs" of conversion. These and the major variations that distinguish them are depicted in chart 1. The five major dimensions along which they vary should not be construed as exhaustive profiles of features of each type. Instead, they are only *major* aspects that serve to locate each in a very large field of possibilities.

The five major dimensions or variations that appear most salient in the "raw reality" of conversions, in the conversion accounts, and in our

	CONVERSION MOTIFS					
	1. Intellectual	2. Mystical	3. Experimental	4. Affectional	5. Revivalist	6. Coercive
1. Degree of Social Pressure	low or none	none or little	low	medium	high	high
2. Temporal Duration	medium	short	long	long	short	long
3. Level of Affective Arousal	medium	high	low	medium	high	high
4. Affective Content	illumination	awe, love, fear	curiosity	affection	love (& fear)	fear (& love)
5. Belief-Participation Sequence	participation-belief	belief-participation	participation-belief	participation - belief	participation - belief	participation - belief

CHART 1. CONVERSION MOTIFS

"bracketing" of those accounts encompass the traditional trinity of the intellectual, physical, and emotional. The first dimension measures the degree to which the actor is subjected to external social pressure to convert. The second inquires into the subjective and objective duration of the conversion experience. The third and fourth dimensions focus on affect: the former seeking to gauge the degree of emotional arousal accompanying the experience and the latter concerned with its content. The fifth dimension seeks to determine the sequential order in which individuals adopt a religion's cognitive framework and actually participate in its ritual and organizational activities. As chart 1 illustrates, it appears rather common for people to participate actively in their new roles as converts well in advance of their cognitive assent to their new religion's theological implications. In fact, this is a conscious, conspicuous, and significant aspect of some conversion motifs.

We need to stress that we are *not* discussing "causes" of conversion, processes or phases of it, functions it may serve, or any other aspect save that of "what it is like" or "what kinds are there?" Our task is exclusively that of constructing a more refined, precise "dependent variable." Explaining why the dependent variable happens at all or assumes different forms is an altogether separate task. We need especially to underscore this point because some of the motifs draw on what have been considered (historically in the literature) as key causal factors in conversion—for example, intensive interaction in the case of experimental conversion, affective bonds in the case of affectional conversion, joyous crowds in the case of revivalist conversion. We do not quarrel with assertions that these and other variables may and do figure in the causes of conversion. Such factors are beyond dispute. They are *also* irrelevant, as such, to the present purposes except insofar as they enter to "set the tone"—the motif—of the conversion itself. Their role as causal factors is simply a separate question, one not attended to here.

INTELLECTUAL CONVERSION

The first motif we want to single out is as yet relatively uncommon, though we expect it to become increasingly important. The intellectual mode of conversion commences with individual, private investigation of possible "new grounds of being," alternative theodicies, personal fulfillment, and so forth, by reading books, watching television, attending lectures, and other impersonal or "disembodied" ways in which it is increasingly possible sans social involvement to become acquainted with alternative ideologies and ways of life. In the course of such reconnaissance, some individuals convert themselves in isolation from any actual interaction with devotees of the respective religion. A prototypical case is that of sociologist Roger Straus who, while an undergraduate, substantially converted himself to Scientology through extensive reading. His first contact with an actual Scientologist was for the predecided purpose of attaining full membership.

> Although I was highly suspicious of any organized group, after several months I concluded that the only way to check the whole thing out was to take the plunge: I walked into New York Org and asked the receptionist what I had to do to "go Clear" and become an auditor (Straus, 1979a:7).

In the literature, this pattern is spoken of as the "activist" model of conversion (Lofland, 1977; Straus, 1976, 1979b; Richardson, 1979). In terms of the major variations mentioned, there is little or no external social pressure; the events defined as making up the conversion appear to be drawn out over a number of weeks or months—a period we might characterize as "medium" in length. The convert-in-process is affectively aroused, but the emotional level is far from ecstatic. The emotional tone of the experience seems best characterized as one of "illumination." Furthermore, and most importantly, a reasonably high level of belief occurs prior to actual participation in the religion's ritual and organizational activities.

The intellectual or self-conversion motif is obviously a new and contemporary mode of entry into a religious community or movement. Its incidence as a conversion mode is probably on the increase due to the "privatized" (Luckmann, 1967) nature of religion in Western society, the smorgasbord of religions competing for members, and the ever-increasing presence of disembodied modes of religious communication: books, magazines, specialized newspapers, movies, television, video and audio cassettes, and so forth. The so-called "electronic church"—the television-production-oriented Christian Fundamentalist groups whose "congregations" are essentially television viewers—is a particularly good example of this current trend. It has become very easy for people privately to control their own decisions about religious beliefs, organizations, and even ways of life, quite apart from any physically embodied social contact, support, or inducement of an affect-laden sort. In such a situation people in search of "truth," community, identity, salvation, and so forth, can calmly and privately elect to "go for it," as people in the seventies often expressed their adoption of a new "trip."

It is important to recognize that this conversion motif is not confined to the more "profound" transformations of cosmic or religious consciousness. In studying old-car enthusiasts, for example, Dale Dannefer has discovered that well more than half of his sample of adult males developed their passion for antique automobiles quite apart from social support and, indeed, often apart from even knowing of "the existence of a world of car people" (Dannefer, 1980:7). A significant portion of males who make up the old-car world—a world of high commitment, incidentally—"present an impressively consistent picture of a process of independent *individual* commitment that leads to social participation and commitment rather than the reverse" (Dannefer, 1980:8).

In conceptualizing his findings Dannefer draws on ideas developed by Berger and Luckmann (1967) that may clarify the study of intellectual conversions. With the shrinking of the "sacred canopy" in contemporary society, the social environment is "underinstitutionalized." This signifies a "decline in the organization of individual consciousness and activity by social and cultural forces." Increasingly, "the individual must decide how to organize his or her activity" (Dannefer, 1980:15; Berger, et al., 1973). In the process which Berger and others (1973) label "subjectivization," individuals can internalize social and cultural images *directly,* "bypassing interpersonal relationships that might cushion its effects" (Dannefer, 1980:16). Because they are legitimized as worthwhile by their very presence in the media, we see such subjectivization of mass-culture objects on a grand scale, as witness the organized worlds of devotion around stamps, coins, bottles, and a host of similar material objects. In fact, it would be strange if we did *not* begin to find the pattern of intellectual conversion associated with religious devotion—such devotion being among the myriad of devotional outpourings available to modern people.

MYSTICAL CONVERSION

Historically speaking, the best known conversion motif is probably the one we here label "mystical"—a term that is not entirely accurate but which is better than its alternatives such as "Damascus Road," "Pauline," "evangelical," and "born again." The term mystical at least has the virtue of signaling the common feeling among converts that "the experience cannot be expressed in logical and coherent terms," that "clear characterizations . . . miss its depth" (Jules-Rosette, 1975:62). The prototypical instance within the Christian tradition is, of course, the conversion of St. Paul in a dramatic incident on the Damascus Road in the first century A.D. In fact, St. Paul's conversion, as recorded in Acts 9 and elsewhere in the New Testament, has in a sense functioned as the ideal in the Western world of what conversion should be.

It is of note that the earliest scholars of conversion—William James (1911), Edwin Starbuck (1911), and E. T. Clark (1929)—focused heavily on mystical conversion. The reason for this might have been its more widespread incidence in late nineteenth- and early twentieth-century America. It seems to have attracted less interest among converts and scholars (who simply follow converts) in the middle third of the twentieth century except as a minor topic in psychoanalysis. In fact, our contemporary definitions of mystical conversion are provided by psychoanalytically oriented scholars such as Carl Christensen who describes it as

> An acute hallucinatory episode occurring within the framework of religious belief and characterized by its subjective intensity, apparent suddenness of onset, brief duration, auditory and, sometimes, visual hallucinations, and an observable change in the subsequent behavior of the convert (Christensen, 1963:207).

It is characterized, further, by seeming "not to be wrought by the subject but upon him" (Coe, 1916:152, quoted in Christensen, 1963). This "feeling of submission—of giving up or giving to" is preceded by "withdrawal from others with a sense of estrangement and often in feelings of unreality" and the outcome is

> a sense of sudden understanding accompanied by a feeling of elation and by an auditory and sometimes visual hallucination. . . . There is a feeling of change within the self . . . associated with a sense of presence (Christensen, 1963:214).

In terms of our "major variations," there is little or no social pressure; the convert is even likely to be alone at the time of the actual event. What the convert defines as the most critical period of the conversion is quite brief—perhaps on the order of minutes or hours—although a period of stress preceding the critical event may stretch back some days or weeks. Its very brevity functions, indeed, to heighten the meaning, as was stated by an anthropologist who was converted to an African Apostolic church: "In my case the initial shift from one set of interpretations to another was dramatic, resulting in a moment of shock in which even the physical terms of existence seemed to alter" (Jules-Rosette, 1963:62-63).

The level of emotional arousal is extremely high—sometimes involving theophanic *ecstasis*, awe, love, or even fear. And the event signals the onset—or active intensification—of belief which is then followed by participation in the ritual and organizational activities of the religion with which the conversion experience is associated.

There is some suggestion that mystical conversions have been making a cultural comeback—so to speak—within the last few years. At the very least, the mass media have paid considerable attention to the surprising conversions of various infamous individuals who have not hesitated to have detailed accounts of their mystical conversions appear in books and/or magazine and newspaper articles. Such publications speak of "miraculous rebirth" (Atkins with Slosser, 1977: cover) and express astonishment regarding the event: "the . . . most shocking conversion in this century" (Oliver, 1977: cover). The conversions of Charles Colson, Eldridge Cleaver, and Susan Atkins are among the most noted of these. In claiming a profound and transforming moment of cosmic contact, this kind of conversion functions better than other means to legitimize and to give credibility to what might otherwise be seen as mere connivance or as a cynical shift of allegiance for personal gain or respectability. One may ask, for example, how plausible the professions of personal change made by Colson, Cleaver, and Atkins would be in the *absence* of their detailed, public claims to have been spiritually "born again" in a moment of profound emotion and saving "grace"? The mystical experience is latently, at least, a strategic way of saying "I have changed and have become a new, better person." That message is especially important to convey if one is of doubtful moral character and particularly if one's personal history includes convictions for such felonies as obstruction of justice, rape, flight to avoid prosecution, and first-degree murder.

It has recently become almost fashionable in the United States to say one has been "born again." This is, of course, a rather ambiguous term, but it often refers to mystical conversion. In fact, the three major candidates running for president of the United States in 1980 all claimed to be "born again." A poll of Californians in the same year showed about a quarter of them claiming this experience also (Field, 1980).

EXPERIMENTAL CONVERSION

As observers of social life we are prone to commit the *fallacy of the uniformly profound.* If someone makes a dramatic change of life-orientation ("a radical reorganization of identity, meaning, life," as Travisano puts it), we are likely to feel that there must be equally dramatic, deep, and strong forces which have brought it about. In the eyes of analysts, one strong event must be "balanced" by some other strong event or events. Accounts of mystical conversion, for example, often display such a balancing of cause and effect in the reports of both convert and analyst—as in the crescendo of personal guilt that culminates in the mystical experience.

That imagery often seems, indeed, to fit the "first" and "second" level of reality we have mentioned—but not always; thus we have the fallacy of the uniformly profound. Specifically, recent research is uncovering the surprising degree to which—and the frequency with which—a transformation of religious identity, behavior, and world view can occur quite tentatively and slowly and yet be identified by the convert-in-process as happening in that manner. This motif has been scrutinized most closely by Robert Balch and his associate David Taylor. Studying followers of the Process—a group in which one gives up all possessions and becomes an itinerant—they have found a "pragmatic 'show me' attitude, ready to give the Process a try, but withholding judgment" for a considerable length of time after taking up the life-style of the fully committed participant and making significant sacrifices (Balch and Taylor, 1977:5). Attuned to similar themes proposed by Bromley and Shupe (1979) and Straus (1976), Balch concludes "the first step in conversion . . . is learning to *act* like a convert. . . . Genuine conviction develops later . . . after intense involvement" (Balch, 1980:142). Referring to this as an "*experimental* rationale" Roger Straus provides a vivid illustration:

> A beturbaned Kundalini Yoga instructor remarked at the end of our interview: I'm interested how long I'll stay with Yogi Bhajan. I always told myself if it gets too weird I can always quit, walk away—and I still keep that idea in my mind (Straus, 1976:260).

The research that has revealed this conversion motif has focused on "new age," metaphysical types of groups. However, experimental conversions do not appear to be confined to them. Groups that might appear to be poles apart in their authoritarianism and organizational structure such as the Jehovah's Witnesses and Scientology typically insist that the prospective convert take an experimental attitude toward—and *participate* in—the group's ritual and organizational activities. This is quite clearly brought out in James Beckford's analysis of Jehovah's Witnesses' "talk about conversion." He outlines four characteristics of conversion that are central in conversations among Witnesses concerning their conversions: (1) it is thought to involve a "progression of mental states"; (2) it is considered to be "predominantly cognitive" in nature; (3) it is "framed as something they *achieved*"; and (4) it follows a policy to involve the neophyte immediately "in practical work alongside more mature Witnesses" (Beckford, 1978:253, 255, 257). Regarding Scientology, Roger Straus reports that

> There are no discrete points of self-conscious conviction or conversion. Rather, we see a series of highly structured actions and interactions each of which, if well managed by both the group and the subject, leads to a more positive definition of the situation, acceptance or internalization of some portion of the collective language and perspective . . . and promotes agreement to initiate further interaction with Scientology . . . without ever having to commit self, the person—so long as they remain an "active" Scientologist taking services and associating with other group members . . . [they come] to progressively accept and then take for granted the cognitive, behavioral and organizational institutions of Scientology. Every effort is made to keep the person "moving up the Bridge to Total Freedom." As he or she does so, it becomes more and more natural to redefine one's personal goals and interests in terms of the group's collective definition of the situation (Straus, 1979a:9).

In terms of our list of major variations, experimental conversions involve relatively low degrees of social pressure to participate since the recruit takes on a "try-it-out" posture. The actual transformation of identity, behavior, and world view commonly called conversion takes place over a relatively prolonged period—often months or even years—and does not appear to be accompanied by high levels of emotional arousal in most instances. The effective content of the experience appears to be that of curiosity.

This motif of change is, of course, not unique to religious or other highly ideologized contexts. In fact, it resembles the ubiquitous manner in which people learn new social roles and are more ordinarily assimilated into groups. The social mechanism of such socialization processes has long ago been identified by Howard Becker as *situational adjustment*—*commitment* being the end result of increasing adaptation and the making of *side-bets* (Becker, 1964). The notion of situational adjustment provides for us a "picture of a person trying to meet the expectations he encounters in immediate face-to-face situations," thus encouraging us to "look to the character of the [micro and immediate] situation for the explanation of why people change as they do. We ask what there is in the situation that requires the person to act in a certain way or to hold certain beliefs" (Becker, 1964:44). Once we assume that, for whatever reasons, a person wants to continue in a given situation, subsequent behavior can then be understood in terms of ordinary situational requirements.

It is in such terms that we can hope to shine new light on the consistent finding that "intensive interaction" is a significant feature of many conversion experiences. Indeed, one recent study of Nichiren Shoshu asserts that intensive interaction is "the key to . . . transformation" (Snow and Philips, 1980:444). Reformulated, "intensive interaction" is an abstract and rather crude way in which to talk about opportunities for progressive situational adjustments and the consequent development of committing side-bets in Becker's (1964) terms.

AFFECTIONAL CONVERSION

As alluded to at the outset, there is a continuing interplay of three levels of reality in the study of conversion. At the first level—that of "raw reality"—the conversion process involves "actual," "out-there" occurrences or situations. That level is, however, ambiguously and imperfectly available to us. The second level—that of the convert's experience and interpretation—is structured by the first level and by any particular paradigm found useful to the convert to interpret the former. The third level—that of analytic interpretations—provides, in its own right, a screen through which we attempt to perceive the social-psychological reality of the transformation. However, we must keep in mind that the prominence of any particular conversion motif is likely to vary over time and geography, partly as a function of shifting fashions at the second level, but mostly as a consequence of more weighty factors such as the prevalence and content of mass communications. And, of course, the third level changes in order to keep up with the first two.

We reiterate these ideas because they are especially pertinent in understanding the dominance of the "affectional conversion" motif over the past two decades in social science theory and research. The identification of this motif dates back to John Lofland's and Rodney Stark's 1965 analysis of positive affective bonds in the conversion process. The notion was widely adopted and rapidly documented during subsequent years (see, for example, the literature reviewed in Gerlach and Hine, 1970, ch. 4; Richardson, ed., 1977; Hierich, 1977; Robbins, Anthony, and Richardson, 1978; Snow and Philips, 1980). By 1980, the motif was formulated in such phrases as "interpersonal bonds are the fundamental support for recruitment" (Stark and Bainbridge, 1980:389)—a more formal rewording of the original phrase that becoming "one" was "coming to accept the opinions of one's friends" (Lofland and Stark, 1965:871). Critical causal efficacy implied here aside, the experiential or motif thesis is that personal attachments or strong liking for practicing believers is central to the conversion process. Such sentiment has the same defining importance or central significance in the process of affectional conversion as intellectual illumination, mystical encounter, or experimental immersion have in the motifs already described.

We would like to believe that the popularity of the affectional motif in social science in recent years has been more than mere intellectual faddishness. Rather, during that period, investigators were uncovering—however fitfully and imperfectly—a new central meaning in conversion—one that was both there in "raw reality" (our first level) and to a reasonable extent in the convert's own perceptions and accounts (the second level).[2]

As a motif, the cognitive element is de-emphasized (in decided contrast to intellectual conversion). Reflecting the reality constructionism of the sixties (which was itself a reflection of a broader relativism of the time), there is stress on the strong degree to which all systems of social knowledge and beliefs are sustained by an underlying "sentimental order" (Shibutani, 1961; Berger and Luckmann, 1967). Truth is a function of what is defined as such in the individual's social and emotional milieu. "Social pressure" is certainly present but exists and functions more as "support" and attraction than as "conducement" to convert. Analysts are somewhat vague on the point, but one gets the impression that the process is relatively prolonged—a matter of at least several weeks. Despite the central experience being affection, the ordinary level of emotional arousal seems more in the range of "medium" intensity rather than the more extreme states we find in the revivalist or mystical motifs. As in experimental conversions, belief arises out of participation.

---

[2]This is not to imply that affectional conversions are new in history. Indeed, the story of Ruth provides a biblical prototype. After the death of her husband, readers may recall, she refuses to return to her own ethnic group and insists on accompanying Naomi, her mother-in-law, as she prepares to return to Judah. Surprised that Ruth does not follow her other widowed daughter-in-law in returning to her family, Naomi questions Ruth and learns that she is determined to return with her to Judah and become a Jew because of her affection and commitment to her:

> And she said, "See, your sister-in-law has gone back to her people and to her gods; return after your sister-in-law." But Ruth said, "Entreat me not to leave you or to return from following you; for where you go I will go, and where you lodge I will lodge; your people shall be my people and your God my God (Ruth 1:15-16, RSV).

REVIVALIST CONVERSION

In several studies since World War II, the phenomenon of revivalist conversion has been debunked by the finding that the most famous of revivalist preachers and their organizations appear merely to simulate or stage quite mild conversions rather than bring about the kind of dramatic occurrences asserted to have been common in the eighteenth and nineteenth centuries (e.g., Lang and Lang, 1960; Altheide and Johnson, 1977; Wimberly, et al, 1980). We have thus become cynical about the idea that there can be true revivalist conversions, and the abundant literature documenting their occurrence in earlier centuries has been ignored or at least neglected. However, that neglect is combined with the probability of an actual decline in the incidence of revivalist conversions in modern societies—or at least a decline in the incidence of their more extreme versions, representing a decline of experiential acuteness at what we have called the "first level of reality."

It is particularly incumbent on those of us who work at "level three reality" to "keep alive" in human consciousness the broad spectrum of possibilities in all areas of social life, including that of conversion. Even though it appears to be in decline in contemporary industrialized societies,[3] conversions whose central feature consists of profound experiences that occur within the context of an emotionally aroused crowd are far from absent in most societies throughout the world. Probably due to a rationalist tendency to retreat from emotionalism, however, scholars of crowd behavior—or collective behavior—have generally lost sight of the very real fact that crowds *can* be brought to ecstatic arousals that have a critically transforming effect on some people. The "social pressure" and

---

[3]The Western prototype of the revivalistic conversion is, of course, the biblical account of the conversion of 3,000 people on the day of Pentecost. The biblical author claims that there was a massive response to Peter's sermon (which occurred immediately after the reported experience of the descent of the Holy Spirit) in which he preached the passion of Jesus and accused his audience of guilt in his crucifixion:

> Now when they heard this they were cut to the heart, and said to Peter and the rest of the apostles, "Brethren, what shall we do?" And Peter said to them, "Repent, and be baptized every one of you in the name of Jesus Christ for the forgiveness of your sins; and you shall receive the gift of the Holy Spirit. For the promise is to you and to your children and to all that are far off, every one whom the Lord our God calls to him." And he testified with many other words and exhorted them, saying, "Save yourselves from this crooked generation." So those who received his word were baptized, and there were added that day about three thousand souls (Acts 2:37-41, RSV).

"contagion"—albeit brief—can produce fear, guilt, and joy of such intensity that individuals may obediently go through the outward and inward process of a fundamentalist or evangelical conversion (Lofland, 1982).

There are, however, apparent revivalist "waves" of recurrence in spite of the long-term decline of this conversion motif in Western societies (McLoughlin, 1978). Some people have even argued that we witnessed a relatively mild wave of revivalist conversions during the early seventies concomitant with the coming of the "new religions." For example, a member of the International Society for Krishna Consciousness relates a conversion experience that is not unlike the revivalist conversion experience of earlier centuries:

> The room was brightly lit, and I'd never seen devotees dressed in their robes before. They were dancing. . . . I saw that the guy playing the drum had this big grin on his face—it was so ecstatic, and it immediately made me enthusiastic. And I started to dance, and I felt real ecstasy, which was a completely new experience. . . . It was natural, this feeling of joy that was coming from within. . . . It was a more powerful happiness than any I had ever felt before—my first real religious experience (Dasa, 1979:26).

Another of the new religions, the Unification Church, appears to have resurrected the revivalist experience in highly effective modern garb. Prospective converts recruited literally off the streets are taken on weekend retreats that involve a whirlwind round of singing, chanting, hand-holding, preaching, and diffuse, loving camaraderie. In the apt terminology of its closest participant-observer, David Taylor, the effect is "enthralling" for many. There is a marked "transition from a relatively mundane world to a dynamic environment of ecstatic youth" (Taylor, 1978:107):

> Events and activities have an exciting quality. Participants experience emotional heights without suffering subsequent letdowns. The exceptional nature of collective joy lies in . . . members' ability to create events [that] have natural endings, yet the stimulation produced is seemingly inexhaustible. There is the promise of more—the next event, the next day, the coming week.
>
> All aspects of the training session blend together with exhilarating momentum. [The members'] enthusiasm requires prospects to invest their entire beings in the participatory events. Jumping up to sing tumultuous songs; running from place to place hand in hand with a buddy; and cheering, chanting, and clapping in unison with dozens of others inevitably make a deep impression on prospective members.
>
> Even the most reticent . . . find it difficult to resist being swept into this performance of continual consensus. One may remain intellectually unsympathetic to [the members'] . . . beliefs and goals, but he [or she] will be in some way moved by the intense revelry. Possibly no participant escapes feeling intense

excitement, even if he regards the performance as inauthentic (Taylor, 1978: 153-154).

The effect of such an experience is all the more potent because it is *novel* to the youths who ordinarily undergo it. Unacquainted with crowd arousal as a generic and powerful human experience known throughout history—modern American society being statistically deviant in this respect—prospects easily construe a special and causal relation between the experience of emotional contagion and the religion producing it. The understandable, though erroneous, belief is that the particular religion has a special power to produce crowd joy and the credibility of the religion's doctrines are thus enhanced.

COERCIVE CONVERSION

We come, finally, to a conversion motif that takes place only in extremely rare and special circumstances but which has been alleged by some to be rampant among the new religions of the Western world. Our reference is to what has been labeled, variously, "brainwashing," "programming," "mind control," "coercive persuasion," "thought reform," and "menticide," among other names.

Even though we believe it virtually never occurs, it is nonetheless a possibility, and in the interest of theoretical comprehensiveness it needs to be included in our treatment. The relatively widespread fear that it is a common phenomenon also necessitates its consideration. (A Gallup poll of 1978 found, for example, that seven percent of the American people thought individuals in groups such as Peoples' Temple were brainwashed.)

The accusations surrounding this topic make it especially important to form a very clear conception of the "nature of the beast" under discussion—a step that seems noticeably neglected in the leading literature (e. g., Delgado, 1977). Toward that clarification, we want to draw on what we believe to be the best single and most accurate summary of "brainwashing." It appears under that title in the *International Encyclopedia of the Social Sciences* (1968) and was written by Albert Somit. An extremely cogent treatment that has been inexplicably ignored, Somit's vision may have been clear because he wrote *after* the 1950s fears of Communist brainwashing and *before* the 1970s fears of "cult mind control."

The two key features of brainwashing—or as we prefer, coercive persuasion (Schein, 1961)—are (1) the *compulsion* of an individual (2) *sincerely* to confess guilt or to embrace an ideological system. The process of brainwashing individuals was independently invented in the early twentieth century by European Communists extracting simple confessions of guilt and by Chinese Communists striving for systematic ideological conformity.

While practices differed somewhat in Europe and China, Somit delineates seven "measures" that characterize both traditions:

- *total control* of the prisoner's round of life "down to the most intimate needs"
- *uncertainty* of the charges against one and of one's entire future
- *isolation* from the outside world
- *torture* in the form of "mental and physical torment"
- *physical debilitation and exhaustion* achieved by a "diet . . . planned to ensure rapid loss of weight, strength, and stamina" and induced by the "constant interrogation, tension, and terror" associated with the other measures
- *personal humiliation* associated with denial of "any previous claim to personal dignity or status"
- *certainty of the captive's guilt*—"the unyielding assumption that he will confess and change"—which, when displayed by the captors, "justifies even in the prisoner's mind the stringency of the measures applied" (all quoted phrased from Somit, 1968:139-40).

Although these are the fundamental, social interactional aspects of brainwashing, the process is not entirely negative. As the subject begins to capitulate—or to "see the light"—"living conditions improve . . . [and] even . . . interrogators become more friendly and less impersonal" (Somit, 1968:140).

A variety of psychological mechanisms or processes have been posited as operative in coercive persuasion. Somit (1968:141-142) lists ten—among which are heightened suggestibility, identification with the aggressor, and generalized activation of guilt feelings. Identification with the aggressor is of special note, involving as it does the anomaly that captives of many sorts often become quite fond of their captors. The title Brian Jenkins gives to an article (1975) about a generically similar situation sums up this aspect of the phenomenon: "Hostages and Captors—Friends and Lovers."

Whatever the psychological mechanisms, the "measures" listed do seem to work. As a strategy, however, coercive conversion has two serious problems that limit its usefulness even by ideologues who hold state power. First, if allowed to return to a more or less open society, subjects "backslide,"—the results achieved are not permanent" (Somit, 1968:142). Something very similar to this may well have happened to Patricia Hearst who, after being converted to the radical Marxist doctrine of the Symbionese Liberation Army, appeared to return to her earlier sociopolitical beliefs relatively easily and quickly once she was removed from the influence and control of her abductors. Second, an inordinant amount of personnel, space, time, and other resources is required to achieve sincere ideological change. At best, a relatively large staff must be marshaled to "process" a single person or, at most, a small group. Compared to other motifs, this is likely the "most expensive and uneconomical" of possibilities (Somit, 1968:142).

It is currently common to summarize chapter 22, entitled "Ideological Totalism," of Robert Lifton's *Thought Reform and the Psychology of Totalism* (1961) in characterizing "brainwashing." The eight "psychological themes" he so skillfully evokes have become, indeed, a kind of litany on the topic. We also think it is a litany that is off the mark and that misses the point even though it is *also* probably accurate as a characterization of certain aspects of the settings he studied and in its generalizations about the abstract features of certain ideologies. Indeed, *by definition,* ideological totalism is constructed from the eight items he enumerates: milieu control, mystical manipulation, the demand for purity, a cult of confession, a sacred science, loading the language, doctrine over person, and dispensing of existence. Such features are surely found in brainwashing settings but *not confined to or definitive of them.* Instead, we must go on to *add* the kinds of considerations that Albert Somit makes so explicit but which are muted in Lifton's treatment. And we must appreciate that we can find totalistic settings (in the sense that they display Lifton's eight features) that are *not* brainwashing settings (in the sense that they do not have Somit's seven features), as for example the Bruderhof as reported by Zablocki (1971). Thus, with regard to contemporary controversies over the degree to which some of the new religions use brainwashing, we would agree with Thomas Robbins and Dick Anthony (1978:79) that "brainwashing divorced from physical restraint is generally in the eye of the beholder." When new religions are observed carefully, virtually no physical restraint is discovered, much less the kind of social organization for conversion resembling the features Somit describes. A small minority of the new religions may tend in that direction, but the bulk do not (Robbins and Anthony, 1979).

The possibility of *social-psychological* coercion, however, cannot be ignored; interactional affective pressures and fears resulting from theological precepts could conceivably function as coercively on some individuals as actual physical restraints and threats. For example, some evidence of such pressures is apparent in Taylor's (1978:153-54) description of revivalism quoted in our discussion of revivalist conversion. Future treatments will have to deal with the crossovers between revivalist and coercive conversion as well as the question of what "legitimately" constitutes coercion.

Summarized in terms of our five major variations, coercive conversion entails an extremely high degree of external pressure over a relatively long period of time, during which there is intense arousal of fear and uncertainty, culminating in empathetic identification and even love. Belief, of course, follows participation.

IMPLICATIONS

We want to conclude by pointing out two classes of implications of this kind of endeavor. The first concerns the social psychology of conversion per se. (1) Differentiating "motifs," "careers," or "styles" should allow us to sharpen our understanding of the phenomenon of conversion. Irrespective of the merits of the present formulation, we feel that efforts of this kind are very much in order and we urge others interested in the subject matter to join us in improving on schemes of conversion types. (2) The present effort is, of course, quite narrow in the specific sense that it adduces types but does not go on to delineate steps, phases, or processes within each type. In further more refined schemes that will render this one obsolete, we hope that the specification of process will receive prominent attention.

A second class of implications is sociohistorical and organizational. (1) As previously mentioned, we suspect that conversion motifs differ significantly from one historical epoch to another, across societal boundaries, and even across subcultures within a single society. There are probably trends and subtrends in the prevalence of particular conversion motifs and in the social conditions with which such trends are correlated. Among other possibilities, we have suggested that in the media-drenched ("advanced") societies, intellectual and experimental conversions are on the increase and revivalist conversions are in relative decline. A wide variety of other conjunctions of social circumstances and conversion motifs are likely to be discernible. (2) Such broader trends in motif actually occur in specific organizational settings, being concretely situated in history and society. In other words, particular conversion motifs fit certain organizational trends and ritualistic practices and not others; and, of course, motifs and practices which "fit" a particular organization and ritualistic practice may not "work" in a subsequent era as the wax and wane of the several "Great Awakenings" in America aptly illustrates. An appreciation of objective social conditions and existing drifts in conversion motifs can thus better inform practical decisions about the kinds of conversion motifs that can be successfully fostered. (3) Following in part from such considerations, it may be fruitful to explore ways in which certain religious ideologies and organizations have an affinity with some, rather than other, conversion motifs. The classification of religious systems is itself a complex and contention-ridden task. Nevertheless, one recurrent dimension of difference appears to be the degree to which a religion absorbs and reorders an adherent's life. We might expect that those religious systems that least affect an individual's life would be characterized by conversions that are the least arousing (for example, intellectual and experimental conversions), and that those that affect an individual's life the most would be characterized by the more dramatic (for example, revivalist) conversions. The picture is obviously far from simple, partly because converts to any single religion do not all experience the same kind of conversion and because the dominant motif (if there is one) of any one religion sometimes changes over time (for example, the Unification Church's move from affectional to revivalist conversions, as reported by Bromley and Shupe, 1979).

In any event, the topic of religious conversion is among the most active, challenging, and exciting in social science at the present time and we invite others to contribute to our understanding of this complex and evolving body of materials.

REFERENCES

Altheide, David and John Johnson
1977 "Counting Souls." *Pacific Sociological Review* 20:323-48.

Atkins, Susan with Bob Slosser
1977 *Child of Satan, Child of God.* Plainfield NJ: Logos International.

Balch, Robert
1979 "Two Models of Conversion and Commitment in a UFO Cult." Paper presented at the annual meeting of the Pacific Sociological Association.

1980 "Looking Behind the Scenes in a Religious Cult: Implications for the Study of Conversion." *Sociological Analysis* 41:137-43.

Balch, Robert W. and David Taylor
1977 "On Getting in Tune: The Process of Making Supernatural Contact." Paper, University of Montana.

Becker, Howard S.
1960 "Notes on the Concept of Commitment." *American Journal of Sociology* 64:32-40.

Beckford, James A.
1978 "Accounting for Conversion." *British Journal of Sociology* 29:249-62.

Berger, Peter and Thomas Luckmann
1967 *The Social Construction of Reality.* Garden City NY: Doubleday.

Berger, Peter L., B. Berger and H. Kellner
1973 *The Homeless Mind.* New York: Random House.

Bromley, David G. and Anson D. Shupe
1979 *"Moonies" in America: Cult, Church, and Crusade.* Beverly Hills: Sage Publications.

Christensen, Carl W.
1963 "Religious Conversion." *Archives of General Psychiatry* 9:207-16.

Clark, Elmer
1929 *The Psychology of Religious Awakening.* New York: Macmillan.

Coe, G. A.
1916 *The Psychology of Religion.* Chicago: University of Chicago Press.

Dannefer, Dale
1980 "Socialization, Social Influence and Subjectivization: The Avocational Careers of Old Car Enthusiasts." Paper.

Dasa, Bahudaka
1979 "How I Came to Krishna Consciousness." *Back to the Godhead* 14:1 (February): 25-34.

Delgado, Richard
1977 "Religious Totalism: Gentle and Ungentle Persuasion Under the First Amendment." *Southern California Law Review* 51:1-110.

Field, Marvin D.
1980 "California Poll: Politics and 'Born Again' Christians." *San Francisco Chronicle*, 21 August.

Gallup, George
1978 "Jonestown Story Riveted the Public" *San Francisco Chronicle*, 29 December.

Gerlach, Luther and Virginia Hine
1970 *People, Power, Change: Movement of Social Transformation.* Indianapolis: Bobbs-Merrill.

Heirich, Max
1977 "Change of Heart: A Test of Some Widely Held Theories About Religious Conversion." *American Sociology Review* 83:653-80.

James, William
1902 *The Varieties of Religious Experience.* Garden City NY: Doubleday, Dolphin.

Jenkins, Brian
1975 "Hostages and Captors—Friends and Lovers." The Rand Paper Series. Santa Monica CA: The Rand Corporation.

Jules-Rosette, Bennetta
1975 *African Apostles: Ritual and Conversion in the Church of John Maranke.* Ithaca NY: Cornell University Press.

Lang, Kurt and Gladys Lang
1960 "Decisions for Christ." *Identity and Anxiety.* M. R. Stein, A. Vidich, and D. White, eds. Glencoe Il: Free Press, 415-27.

Lifton, Robert Jay
1961 *Thought Reform and the Psychology of Totalism.* New York: Norton.

Lofland, John
1977 "Becoming a World-Saver Revisited." *American Behavioral Scientist* 20:805-18.

1982 "Crowd Joys." *Urban Life* 10 (January): 355-81.

Lofland, John and Norman Skonovd
1981 "Conversion Motifs." *Journal for the Scientific Study of Religion* 20 (December): 373-85.

Lofland, John and Rodney Stark
1965 "Becoming a World-Saver." *American Sociological Review* 30:862-74.

Luckmann, Thomas
1967 *The Invisible Religion: The Problem of Religion in Modern Society.* New York: Macmillan.

Oliver, John A.
1977 *Eldridge Cleaver Reborn.* Plainfield NJ: Logos International.

McLoughlin, William G.
1978 *Revivals, Awakenings, and Reform.* Chicago: University of Chicago Press.

Rambo, Lewis R.

1980 "Toward a Holistic Theory of Conversion." Paper, San Francisco Theological Seminary, San Anselmo CA.

1982 "Current Research on Religious Conversion." *Religious Studies Review* 8 (April): 146-59.

Richardson, James T.

1978 *Conversion Careers.* (ed.) Beverly Hills: Sage.

1979 "A New Paradigm for Conversion Research." Paper presented at the annual meeting of the International Society for Political Psychology.

Robbins, Thomas and Dick Anthony

1978 "New Religions, Families and Brainwashing." *Transaction* (May/June): 77-83.

1979 "The Limits of 'Coercive Persuasion' as an Explanation for Conversion to Authoritarian Sects." Paper presented at the annual meeting of the International Society for Political Psychology.

Robbins, Thomas, Dick Anthony and James Richardson

1978 "Theory and Research on Today's New Religions." *Sociological Analysis* 39:39-122.

Schein, E. H.

1961 *Coercive Persuasion.* New York: Norton.

Shibutani, Tomatsu

1961 *Society and Personality.* Englewood Cliffs NJ: Prentice-Hall.

Snow, David A. and Cynthia Phillips

1980 "The Lofland-Stark Model: A Critical Reassessment." *Social Problems* 27:430-47.

Somit, Albert

1968 "Brainwashing." Vol. 2, *International Encyclopedia of the Social Sciences.* David Sills, ed. New York: Macmillan, 138-43.

Starbuck, Edwin

1911 *The Psychology of Religion.* New York: Scribners.

Stark, Rodney and William Bainbridge

1980 "Networks of Faith: Interpersonal Bonds and Recruitment to Cults and Sects." *American Journal of Sociology* 85:1376-95.

Straus, Roger

1976 "Changing Oneself: Seekers and the Creative Transformation of Experience." *Doing Social Life.* J. Lofland, ed. New York: Wiley, 252-72.

1979a "Inside Scientology." Paper presented at the annual meeting of the Pacific Sociological Association.

1979b "Religious Conversion as a Personal and Collective Accomplishment." *Sociological Analysis* 40:158-65.

Taylor, David

1978 "The Social Organization of Recruitment in the Unification Church." Master of Arts Thesis in Sociology, University of Montana.

Travisano, Richard
1970 "Alienation and Conversion as Qualitatively Different Transformations." *Social Psychology Through Symbolic Interaction*, G. P. Stone and H. Faberman, eds. Waltham MA: Ginn-Blaisdell, 594-606.

Williams, Emilio
1967 *Followers of the New Faith*. Nashville: Vanderbilt University Press.

Wimberly, Ronald C., T. Hood, C. Lipsey, D. Clelland, and M. Hay
1980 "Conversion in a Billy Graham Crusade." *Collective Behavior: A Source Book*. M. D. Pugh, ed. St. Paul MN: West, 278-85.

Zablocki, Benjamin
1971 *The Joyful Community*. Baltimore: Pelican.

SECOND THOUGHTS ON THE PRESUMED FRAGILITY OF UNCONVENTIONAL BELIEFS*

by David A. Snow
and Richard Machalek

ABSTRACT

Upon encountering an unconventional belief system, people are often heard to exclaim, "How could anyone in their right mind believe such nonsense?" This sentiment is not restricted to the layperson. A more subtle version of it is featured in some of the social-scientific literature on religious cults and movements. As such, it gives rise to explanations of cult or movement viability that are premised on an assumption that unconventional religious beliefs are highly vulnerable to everyday experience and therefore inherently fragile. This assumption prompts some sociologists to propose the existence of elaborate "plausibility structures" that are presumably required to maintain the tenuous beliefs and to protect their respective adherents from cognitive dissonance. Drawing on a number of secondary data sources, our research on the Nichiren Shoshu Buddhist Movement, and on the work of Borhek and Curtis (1975), we challenge the view that unconventional belief systems are necessarily inherently fragile and owe their persistence primarily to the power of plausibility structures. We also contend that such assumptions can function as barriers to the understanding of contemporary religious movements and other unconventional beliefs.

INTRODUCTION

Two couples stand in line outside of a Los Angeles restaurant. A neatly dressed Caucasian female, in her early twenties, approaches and asks if they have ever heard of *Nam-Myoho-Renge-Kyo*. They look at her in puzzlement, as

---

*This is an expanded version of "On the Presumed Fragility of Unconventional Beliefs" that appeared in the *Journal for the Scientific Study of Religion* 21:1 (March 1982).

if to say, "What are you talking about?" Noting their confusion, the proselytizer asks if they want to be happy and fulfill their dreams. They immediately indicate that they are quite content. At this point, the proselytizer emphasizes that they could get whatever they want—materially, physically, or spiritually—if only they chanted. And then, so as to objectify this claim, she indicates how chanting has provided her with greater meaning and purpose, enabled her to get better grades in school, and improved her relationship with her parents. Their response is still one of disinterest. Sensing that she is not making much progress in luring them to a meeting, the proselytizer moves on in search of other prospects. One of the members of the party then remarks to another that it is hardly worth getting excited over, especially since what is being promoted is just another of the "many strange and fanatical religious groups" that grace the Los Angeles scene. "No question about it," scoffs another member of the party, "those people are really strange, if not downright sick." "Yea," adds another, "how else could anyone believe such crap?"[1]

THERE IS NOTHING unusual about the preceding scenario. Not only have hundreds of thousands of people been solicited by religious enthusiasts during the past decade, but they have often dismissed categorically the various movements and philosophies encountered. Indeed, such a response constitutes a common form of verbal exorcism that is typically employed when our taken-for-granted world, or what Schutz (1971) referred to as our "paramount reality," is breached and challenged by an alternative reality. As Lofland (1966:193) observed during the course of his study of the early American devotees of Sun Myung Moon, the common sense response to members of such groups "is, in effect, 'My God, how can they believe such obvious nonsense?' "

Such sentiments are not restricted to the layperson. They are also prominent in some of the social-scientific literature on religious cults and movements and on the carriers of other unconventional beliefs.[2] Bain-

[1]This vignette is excerpted from the senior author's field notes based on his ethnographic study of the Nichiren Shoshu movement in America. Also known as Nichiren Shoshu Academy or just NSA, Nichiren Shoshu is a Japanese-based, culturally transplanted, proselytizing Buddhist movement that seeks to change the world by changing individuals. It was formally introduced into America in 1960 and claims to have since attracted more than 200,000 members, most of whom are Occidental, since the mid-1960s. For a detailed examination of the movement's beliefs, goals, and operation in America, see Snow (1976, 1979).

[2]The term unconventional beliefs is used broadly to refer to beliefs that depart from and/or challenge culturally dominant beliefs. Within the sociology of religion, for example, this would distinguish the beliefs of cults and sects from those of denominations. Although we do not use the term "deviant beliefs," others have used it in lieu of unconventional beliefs (Lofland and Stark, 1965; Lofland, 1966; Simmons, 1964).

bridge and Stark (1980), for example, have argued recently that the beliefs and claims of Scientologists are "impossible" to validate and therefore seemingly incredible. They thus raise for investigation "the question of how thousands of individuals could be seriously mistaken about their own" claims and beliefs (Bainbridge and Stark, 1980:128). Though few other students of unconventional beliefs, religious or otherwise, are as bold about their observations as Bainbridge and Stark, most seem to subscribe to the assumption that unconventional beliefs are highly vulnerable to everyday experience and therefore inherently fragile. Given this presumed fragility, it is further assumed that believers are continuously confronted with the problem of salvaging their beliefs in the face of disconfirming evidence. This discrepancy between belief and experience is assumed to induce cognitive dissonance that must be resolved if belief is to persist. As such, much of the literature rests on the additional assumption that the viability of unconventional beliefs and their organizational carriers is contingent on the existence of elaborate plausibility structures and strategies (Bainbridge and Stark, 1980; Bittner, 1963; Festinger, et al., 1956; Prus, 1976; Simmons, 1964; Wallis, 1977).

This paper challenges the aforementioned assumptions. It is our contention that they impede rather than facilitate understanding of the new religious movements and other unconventional beliefs. We begin with a critical examination of the relation between unconventional beliefs and plausibility structures. We then assess the fragility assumption by examining the nature of belief systems in general and unconventional beliefs in particular. Here we argue that variation in some of the characteristics of belief systems accounts in part for their differential viability. Next, we evaluate the dissonance assumption. Finally, we contend that the credibility of unconventional beliefs is also attributable to the impulse to believe or to what phenomenologists refer to as the "natural attitude." This discussion turns the focus of much of the literature on its head by suggesting that perhaps it is disbelief rather than belief that is problematic and in need of attention. Throughout the paper we present illustrative data drawn from a number of secondary sources and from the senior author's research on the Nichiren Shoshu Buddhist movement in America.[3]

---

[3]The data pertaining to Nichiren Shoshu were gathered by the senior author over the course of a year and a half of association with the movement as a participant observer. For discussion of the research, see Snow (1976:1-39; 1979).

PLAUSIBILITY STRUCTURES AND UNCONVENTIONAL BELIEFS

Premised on the assumption of the fundamentally tenuous nature of unconventional beliefs, research about such beliefs has typically sought to elaborate various organizational devices that are presumed to account for their maintenance. For example, Bittner (1963:934), in his work on radicalism, argued that since radical beliefs are contradicted by practical experience in the everyday, commonsense world, "radical action groups must have some way to reduce the horizon of possible encounters and cause the remaining contingencies of potential embarrassment to be seen as either not pertaining, or, when 'correctly' seen, further boosting the doctrine." In examining the belief system of a small group of "mystics" located in the southeastern United States, Simmons (1964:250) similarly focused on "the means through which (such) divergent beliefs are maintained in the face of a disbelieving larger society." More recently, Wallis (1977:226) has argued that belief in Scientology is maintained by a set of organizational strategies and processes that functions to protect believers from the conventional world, which, from Wallis's standpoint, constitutes "a major challenge to the legitimacy or validity of their definition of reality." Bainbridge and Stark (1980:128), who similarly see Scientologists' beliefs and claims as "highly subject to empirical disconfirmation," also attribute the persistence of those beliefs to the existence of a number of elaborate organizational strategies and mechanisms.

Taken together, such work suggests that the credibility of unconventional beliefs depends upon the existence of various reality-maintaining structures and processes that function to manage, eliminate, or accommodate the omnipresent challenges that presumably emanate from the everyday commonsense world. At first glance, such a view seems quite reasonable. As students of the sociology of knowledge have long noted, acquiring a particular set of beliefs, whatever their substance, provides no assurance of their persistence (Berger, 1967; Berger and Luckmann, 1966; Borhek and Curtis, 1975; Schutz, 1971). Not only is there a multitude of realities, but realities that compel conviction in one setting may appear embarrassingly transparent and insubstantial in another. Consequently, sociologists have generally argued that maintenance of belief in a particular configuration of ideas is contingent on involvement in interaction networks that are simultaneously based on and devoted to sustaining those very ideas. Berger and Luckmann (1966:154) refer to such social infrastructures as "plausibility structures." They contend that "subjective reality . . . is always dependent upon" such structures.

> One can maintain one's self-identification as a man of importance only in a milieu that confirms this identity; one can maintain one's Catholic faith only if one retains one's significant relationship with the Catholic community; and so forth. Disruption of significant conversation with the mediators of the respective plausibility structures threatens the subjective realities in question (Berger and Luckmann, 1966:154-55).

Given this established emphasis on the role of social processes in validating and sustaining beliefs, it is hardly surprising to find that focus reflected in the work on new religious movements and on other unconventional beliefs. Unfortunately, however, that focus, if overworked, can yield a truncated understanding of unconventional beliefs and their organizational carriers. We think that some of the research on the beliefs and claims of new religious movements reflects such a debilitating reliance on the idea of plausibility structures. There are several reasons for this contention. First, in attempting to account for the persistence of unconventional beliefs in terms of elaborate plausibility structures, many students of such beliefs have tended to ignore the fact that all belief systems, whether deviant or conventional, secular or sacred, rest in part on plausibility structures. Wallis (1977:225-41), for example, indicates that Scientologists have minimized the threat of challenge to their world view by, among other things, strategically compartmentalizing and segregating their beliefs and behavior, and by developing a specialized language that functions "to render Scientological conversation and internal documentation all but unintelligible to the uninitiated." We have no quarrel with Wallis's observations, especially since they have been documented by others (Bainbridge and Stark, 1980). However, it is important to emphasize that there is nothing particularly unusual about the kinds of reality-maintaining devices observed by Wallis. Not only are beliefs and behaviors routinely compartmentalized and segregated in the modern bureaucratic world, but all conventional religions, professions, and academic disciplines, including sociology, have their own specialized languages that function in a manner similar to Scientology's argot. That is, they help to distinguish between insiders and outsiders, they function to establish and maintain the boundaries of the system, and they support the validity of its claims and practices.

Such observations suggest that there may be little qualitative difference between the plausibility structures that have been enumerated in support of unconventional beliefs and those associated with conventional or dominant realities. If so, then it follows that the differential viability of belief systems cannot be accounted for merely in terms of underlying plausibility structures. To argue otherwise begs the initial question; for it treats as exceptional or unique to some groups that which is, in fact, commonplace. It also deflects attention from other possible sources of validation, thereby precluding a fuller understanding of the appeal and credibility of unconventional beliefs.

THE SELF-VALIDATING NATURE OF UNCONVENTIONAL BELIEFS

That most sociological examinations of unconventional beliefs have sought to account for their viability primarily in terms of plausibility structures is due only in part to the sociologist's interest in social forces and processes. As noted earlier, much of the literature on unconventional beliefs seems to be premised on the assumption that such beliefs are highly vulnerable to everyday experience and therefore inherently fragile. There are, however, a number of studies of religious movements that strongly suggest that this fragility assumption is ill-founded. Zygmunt's (1970) research on Jehovah's Witnesses indicates that even though the movement experienced a succession of prophetic failures between 1878 and 1925, neither the belief system nor its following has dissolved. Zygmunt attributes the movement's resilience partly to the self-fulfilling nature of its belief system. He notes that the prophecies were phrased in such a manner that they were open to chronological but not substantive disconfirmation. As such, group members believed that "unfulfilled prophecies . . . would surely come to pass in the proximate future" (Zygmunt, 1970:944). Moreover, the belief system was flexible enough to allow believers to convert retrospectively the prophetic failures "into partial successes, sustaining chiliastic sentiment and providing a basis for renewed prophesying and evangelization" (Zygmunt, 1970: 944-45).

Lofland's (1966) research on the Unification Church during the early days of its operation in America suggests that its belief system was even less assailable than the Witness world view. Lofland (1966:195) reports that the movement's belief system was "logically impossible to confront with disconfirming or negative evidence" because it "was designed so that all experience, all counter-arguments, would only produce confirmation." Though the movement's beliefs were supported by various plausibility structures, it was the belief system's "enormous explanatory scope and confirmational" capacity that Lofland (1966:196) found most interesting and impressive.

Our findings regarding the Nichiren Shoshu belief system indicate that it is also a formidable interpretive scheme that is not highly vulnerable to contradiction and challenge. Not only does it protect believers from negative evidence, but it defines virtually all events and experiences as confirmation of the system. Two major elements of the belief system perform this validation function and provide members with a handy rationale for everything that occurs. On the one hand, anything that is perceived as negative, undesirable, or that impedes members' progress and interferes with Nichiren Shoshu activities is attributed to three obstacles and four devils *(Sansho Shima)* that stand in the way of members' practice and prevents them from attaining enlightenment.[4] On the other hand, anything that is beneficial to the member or the movement is attributed to the power of chanting *Nam-Myoho-Renge-Kyo* to the *Gohonzon* (sacred scroll). Thus, whatever happens, whether good or bad, intended or unintended, is explained in terms of *Sansho Shima* or chanting. The system cannot fail, for the very occurrence of an event provides its confirmation.

The foregoing observations indicate that some unconventional belief systems are amazingly resilient and apparently invulnerable to disconfirmation. Such findings not only render questionable the fragility assumption, but they suggest that perhaps a thorough understanding of the differential credibility and viability of beliefs requires that we attend to the features of belief systems themselves.

This line of inquiry has, in fact, been suggested by Borhek and Curtis (1975:111-34) in their important attempt to develop a general theory of belief. Though Borhek and Curtis (1975:112, 133) are most concerned with the social processes that validate and sustain commitment to beliefs, they emphasize that "validation is not simply a matter of organizational devices" or plausibility structures, but that "the characteristics of the

---

[4]*Sansho* refers to three obstacles; *Shima* refers to four devils. *Sho* of *Sansho* literally means impediment or interference. The three obstacles are : (1) *Bon'no-sho*—hindrance due to early desires caused by the three life impurities of avarice, anger, and stupidity; (2) *Go-sho*—interference in the form of opposition from spouse and children; and (3) *Ho-Sho*—obstacles caused by one's sovereign, parent, teachers, or other superiors, *Ma* of *Shima* refers to life-denying force. The four devils or life-denying forces are: (1) *On-ma*—hardships deriving from physical illnesses or weaknesses; (2) *Bon'no-ma*—delusions caused by confusion that arises from earthly desires; (3) *Shi-ma*—death by accident or from illness; and (4) *Tenji-ma*—oppression by national authorities.

belief system itself, a nonsocial element, are of critical importance." Borhek and Curtis claim that nonsocial elements play an important role in the validation process because social supports alone cannot effectively neutralize, deflect, or accommodate all of the challenges that belief systems may encounter from within and from without. Threats from within derive from the perception of logical or normative inconsistencies and from lacunae of various sorts. Challenges from without derive from what Borhek and Curtis (1975:112) call the "pressure of events," that is, from "happenings in the real world that may bring pressure on believers to relinquish a belief." Such events may vary drastically in scope and momentousness, ranging from unfulfilled prayers and chants to prophetic failures, from the death of a loved one to the extermination of millions. But however they vary, they illustrate the potential challenge to belief system validity.

That some belief systems and their carriers can fend off what appear to be challenges from within and without is clearly illustrated by Jehovah's Witnesses, the Unification Church, and Nichiren Shoshu, not to mention Scientology and other contemporary religious cults and movements. The question thus arises as to the specific features of some belief systems that enable them to persist in the face of contradictory evidence.

Borhek and Curtis (1975:113) identify two variable characteristics of belief systems that "directly affect the ease with which a given belief system can be validated, or invalidated, as it confronts the continual pressure of events." They refer to these characteristics as the "degree of system" and "empirical relevance." The first pertains to the logical interrelatedness of a belief system's substantive components; the second to its testability or direct pertinence to the empirical world. Belief systems can vary considerably in terms of both characteristics, ranging from those that are tightly integrated (high system) to those that are loosely coupled (low system), and from those that are directly empirically pertinent (high empirical relevance) to those for which the empirical world is almost totally irrelevant (low empirical relevance). The cross-classification of these two dimensions yields four general and distinct types of belief systems. Figure 1 schematically portrays these alternative perspectives, each of which is distinguished by the interrelatedness of its parts and by its empirical relevance, and each of which is differentially vulnerable to challenge from within and disconfirmation from without.

Among these types of belief systems, the most vulnerable are those that are highly systematic and directly empirically relevant. Perhaps the

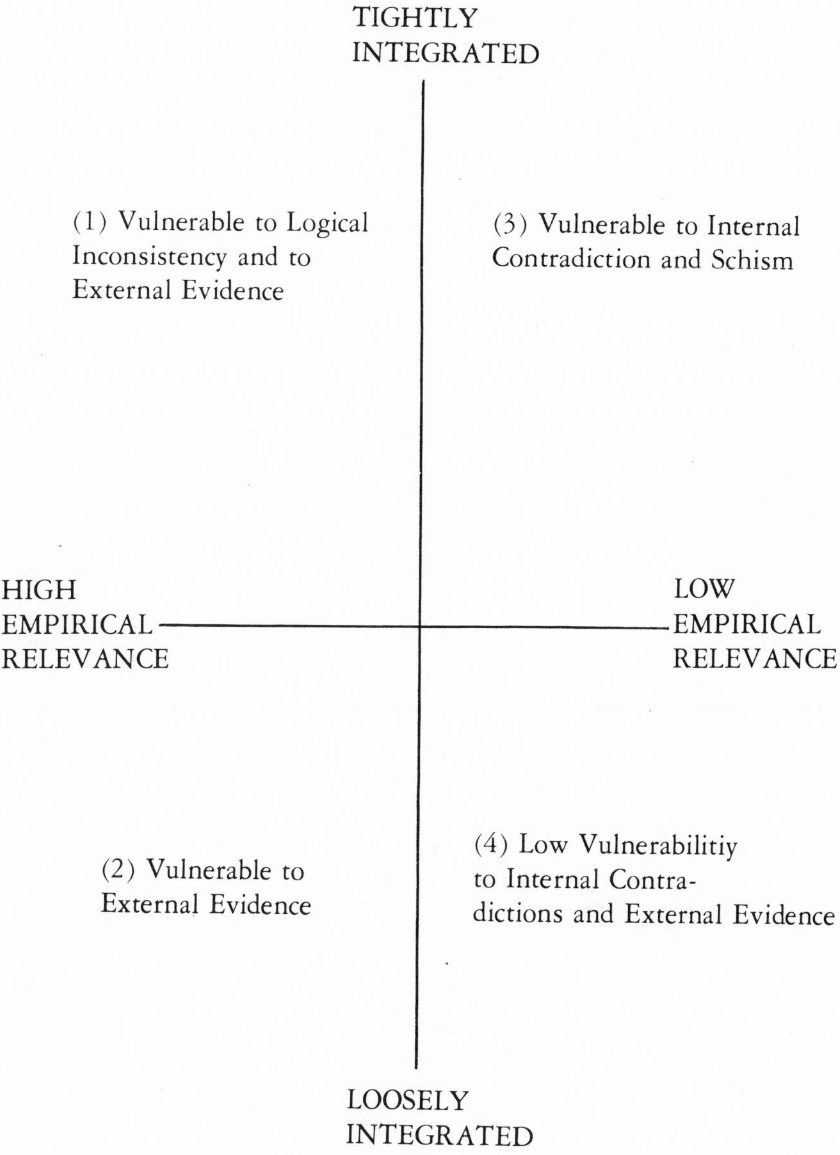

FIGURE 1:
Classification of Belief Systems According to Degree of Interrelatedness, Extent of Empirical Relevance, and Vulnerability to Challenge

best example is deductive scientific theory. The vulnerability to disconfirmation in this case, of course, is a matter of design. The scrupulous theorist actually hopes that logical fallibility or predictive inaccuracy will force a modification if not outright abandonment of the proposed theory. Deductive scientific theory is intended to be falsifiable, even if the theorist privately indulges in the hope of proposing a theory that successfully resists falsification. Systematization exposes the entire corpus of a belief system to internal flaws in any of its parts, and empirical relevance subjects it to the pressure of events.

At the other extreme are belief systems that lack empirical relevance and internal logical consistency. They are the least vulnerable to falsification. It is evident enough that belief systems that fail to make precise claims about the empirical world are unlikely to be disconfirmed by empirical events. It is less clear that the very ambiguity, generality, and even inconsistency of poorly systematized belief systems help protect their integrity. According to Borhek and Curtis (1975:114), however, such a belief system may "have so many possible interpretations, or so few *necessary* connections between beliefs, that neither empirical events nor text book logic can contradict the system itself." In other words, the very lack of internal interrelatedness and empirical relevance protects the overall integrity of the belief system. Individual elements of the overall system may be chipped away, one at a time, by the discovery of logical inconsistencies, but the remainder of the system may remain firmly intact. This is vividly illustrated by the resilience of the belief system of a Jamaican cult called the Rastafarians (Barrett, 1977). The Rastafarians adhere to a highly syncretic but loosely articulated system of beliefs that derive from Marcus Garvey's teachings, Old Testament Christianity, and African tribal cultures. The movement promises repatriation of Jamaican blacks, the "true" lost tribe of Israel, to Ethiopia. The late Haile Selassie, Emperor of Ethiopia and the "Lion of Judah," was regarded as God incarnate and was to have led the repatriation. Selassie, of course, died in prison, and the belief that he personally would lead his exiled "Israelites" home was radically disconfirmed. Nevertheless, the Rastafarian belief system survived Selassie's death. The rather loosely articulated, unsystematized nature of Rastafarian theology protected the belief system from total collapse in the face of the invalidation of the apparently crucial belief in Selassie as Messiah. A much more highly systematized theology would likely have been more severely shaken if not destroyed by the sudden discovery of the "savior's" disconcerting mortality.

In between the extremes of cells 1 and 4 are those belief systems that are loosely integrated but empirically relevant (cell 2) versus those with little empirical relevance but considerable integration (cell 3). Superstitions, and folk sciences and medicines, such as curanderismo and witchcraft, are illustrative of the former; whereas Communism and perhaps Catholicism are illustrative of the latter. Although it is an empirical question as to how the various new religious movements might be classified in terms of the foregoing typology, we think that most would probably fall into cells 3 and 4. If so, then most of them enjoy an immunity to disconfirmation that is similar to Jehovah's Witnesses and the Rastafarians. As indicated earlier, this is certainly the case with the Unification Church, at least in its formative years (Lofland, 1966), and with Nichiren Shoshu (Snow, 1976); and we suspect that it is also the case with most of the other contemporary religious movements.

In addition to the self-validating nature of some belief systems, Borhek and Curtis (1975:126-133) suggest that all belief systems have built into them various validation logics or strategies that also provide immunity from the pressure of events. These validation logics often take the form of invoking a belief from one end of the empirical relevance continuum in order to protect a belief or claim at the other end that has been called into question.[5] Borhek and Curtis mention two such validation logics that we think play an important role in protecting and maintaining unconventional beliefs. The first of these validation logics involves the use of "an empirically nonrelevant belief to protect an empirically relevant belief" (Borhek and Curtis, 1975:127). In other words, an unfalsifiable claim is used to support a falsifiable claim. This protective tactic is commonly invoked when prophetic claims or revelations are called into question. The typical response to such challenges is that the prophecy will *eventually* materialize. To assert that a prophecy or revelation will eventually occur is, of course, unfalsifiable in principle. The very indeterminate nature of the supportive claim thus immunizes the challenged claim from empirical disconfirmation. The persistence of Christianity and other millennial movements seems to rest in part on this interpretive strategy.

---

[5]Such protective tactics are possible because no matter how much a specific belief system is skewed in the direction of either greater or lesser integration and greater or lesser empirical relevance, it is never totally one-sided. All belief systems contain at least some beliefs from the subordinate sides of the two dichotomies (Borhek and Curtis, 1975:126).

The same is also true with Scientology. Practitioners are promised attainment of an almost superhuman level of mental functioning known as "clear." Yet, as Bainbridge and Stark (1980) note, there is no clear evidence that any Scientologists have attained such a state. However, Scientologists do not necessarily interpret failure to achieve "clear" as disconfirmation of the movement's claims. Instead, the individual Scientologist is more likely to emphasize that he or she has not yet attained the "appropriate mental level" that is a prerequisite to "clear." As Bainbridge and Stark (1980) report, those mental levels are continually expanding while the goal of perfect mental functioning is receding. Nonetheless, the Scientologist, like the devoted Christian, the Jehovah's Witness, and other millennial enthusiasts, can maintain faith in unfulfilled claims by invoking the unfalsifiable belief that "ultimately all the promised benefits (will) be provided" (Bainbridge and Stark, 1980:134).

This tactic is also employed by Nichiren Shoshu Buddhists. As noted earlier, *Sansho Shima* is regularly invoked to account for both personal or movement setbacks and for the failure of chanting to produce anticipated benefits. If, for example, a member has been chanting to attend a movement event, but becomes ill and is unable to attend the activity, the illness is not seen as evidence of the failure of chanting; instead, it is attributed to *Sansho Shima.* Belief in an unfalsifiable force thus protects belief in the power of chanting, the results of which are claimed to be empirically discernible. But belief in *Sansho Shima* does not do this alone. It is also supported by a number of subsidiary beliefs. First, it is believed that though *Sansho Shima* is constantly lurking along the road to enlightenment, it is most likely to surface when the member has lengthened his stride, hastened his pace, and strengthened his determination. As one member put it,

> it seems that obstacles or devils become stronger the harder we practice. Just like the airplane, the faster our life is moving, the greater the resistance will be.

Lest this resistance be interpreted as reason for frustration and despair, there is the additional belief that the surfacing of *Sansho Shima* is a sign of devotion and progress. As another member explained,

> it should be the cause for great joy and renewed determination. After all, how else would we know that chanting is having a profound effect on our lives?

Thus, not only is *Sansho Shima* anticipated, but, ironically, it is even welcomed on occasion; for its very appearance is interpreted as confirmation of the power of chanting. All of this was personally illustrated to the senior author one evening toward the end of his association with the Nichiren Shoshu movement.

> My group leader called around dinner time . . . to remind me that there would be a meeting tonight. . . . Having decided that the time had come to curtail my involvement as a participant observer, I indicated that I wasn't planning to attend the meeting and that I had become disenchanted with the practice. . . . No sooner had I finished telling the group leader about my growing disillusionment than he congratulated me, indicating that such feelings were good signs. He went on to suggest that . . . something is really happening in my life, that it is the stirring of "human revolution" (profound change within). Rather than getting discouraged and giving up, I was told to chant and participate even more. . . . Even though I had seen this sort of "rallying" around other backsliding members, my reaction was still one of puzzlement. Here I had indicated my growing disenchantment and the factors in which it was grounded, and what does my group leader do? He takes what I had proposed as indicative of the failure of the practice and grounds for disillusionment, and turns it around by offering a different interpretation. Thus, what I saw as constitutive of failure and reason to defect, he interprets as the surfacing of *Sansho Shima*, the stirring of "human revolution," and as reason for greater participation.[6]

A second logic for protecting beliefs from disconfirmation is the obverse of the one just discussed. Rather than using an unfalsifiable belief to support a falsifiable one, empirically relevant beliefs are used to validate empirically nonrelevant ones (Borhek and Curtis, 1975:129). We think that this tactic is also a salient characteristic of the belief systems of many of the new religious movements. The proponents of many of those belief systems seem to be at no loss to produce "empirical evidence" that supports their claims and prophecies. That the "evidence" assumes the form of selected examples rather than vigorously generated data is of no concern to the believer. Such examples provide all the empirical grounding for belief that is required.

The doomsday prophecies of countless millenarian movements dating from early Christianity to the Unification Church have relied upon this tactic for validating beliefs (Cohn, 1957; Festinger, et al., 1956; Lofland, 1966; Wilson, 1973; Worsley, 1968; and Zygmunt, 1970). This is not all that unreasonable, however, given that many societies contain ample imperfections that can easily be defined as "evidence" of impending catastrophe. For example, both domestic and international economic,

---

[6]For a discussion of this particular incident in relation to the problem of disengagement from Nichiren Shoshu and other such groups, see Snow (1980).

energy, and military problems, as well as natural catastrophes, provide rich repositories of events from which to draw inferences of doom. A particularly vivid case in point is Hal Lindsey's *The Late Great Planet Earth* (1970). Not only does Lindsey adduce "evidence" confirming long-standing prophecies, but that "evidence" was used by various strands of the Jesus movement to support their claims and efforts in the early 1970s. Again the efficacy of such a tactic is enhanced by social discourse; but, as before, the logic of the belief system itself meets the conditional requirements for its existence and persistence. Plausibility structures operate to enhance that which is logically self-perpetuating.

COGNITIVE DISSONANCE AND UNCONVENTIONAL BELIEFS

Since the publication of *When Prophecy Fails* (Festinger et al., 1956), social scientists have often assumed that those who subscribe to unconventional beliefs consistently face the problem of reconciling discrepancies between belief and experience. As often as not, this is said to create cognitive dissonance. Understandably, social scientists have devoted considerable effort toward identifying various mechanisms for resolving dissonance (Abelson, et al., 1968; Dunford and Kunz, 1973; Festinger, 1957; Prus, 1976). However, our earlier observations as well as recent research suggest that cognitive dissonance may be less of a problem for the believer than for the researcher. In a series of three experiments on occult belief, Benassi and others (1980) demonstrated the remarkably durable nature of belief in psychic phenomena. These researchers found that even in the face of strong disconfirming evidence their subjects persisted in attributing psychic powers to a magician. Furthermore, it was discovered that despite the availability of contradictory information and alternative explanatory hypotheses, belief in psychic power remained undisturbed. It is worth noting that some of the contradictory evidence was produced by the subjects themselves. Nonetheless, the persistence of belief was not due to personal strategies for reducing dissonance. Rather, the subjects apparently never experienced dissonance because they "simply failed to absorb the fact that these beliefs were being challenged" (Benassi et al., 1980:347). In the words of Benassi and others (1980:347), "the pattern, then, was of subjects blandly ignoring input rather than resisting it."

This pattern was also frequently observed among Nichiren Shoshu converts. Before proselytizing in city streets, for example, members would chant collectively for the success of the recruiting expedition. More often than not, however, the recruiting forays into public places were failures; members typically returned empty handed (Snow, et al., 1980). The senior author assumed that such experiences constituted a disconfirmation of the power of chanting, and that members would as a consequence experience dissonance. However, as the following field notes indicate, that was not the case.

> Upon arriving at the meeting this evening I was surprised to find only a handful of members present. I had anticipated a much larger gathering. At last night's meeting we chanted for a large turnout this evening. We were expecting around forty people; only ten showed up, most of whom were the old faithfuls. I expressed my surprise to one of the assistant leaders. I commented that "this seemed to represent a defeat of sorts." I added that "we had all chanted so hard for a large turnout, and nobody showed up." She advised me that we "just ran into some heavy *Sansho Shima* and that we shouldn't despair or feel depressed." To the contrary, she emphasized that the low turnout was "a good sign." It shows that we are making the "right cause" and reflects "hard work." The leader thus interpreted as a good sign what I took to be a basis for dissonance.

The implications of such findings are crucial for understanding the persistence of unconventional beliefs. They suggest that, unlike belief in science, many belief systems do not require consistent and frequent confirmatory evidence. Beliefs may withstand the pressure of disconfirming events not because of the effectiveness of dissonance-reducing strategies, but because disconfirming evidence may simply go unacknowledged. Unlike social scientists such as Bainbridge and Stark (1980), Scientologists, for example, may not keep their antennae up for signals of falsification. And if, in fact, the signals are transmitted, they are by no means necessarily received. Perhaps social scientists should be counseled not to project their own criteria for belief onto their subjects. The canons of science that require consistent, predictable, and frequent evidence to justify belief in a system of ideas do not extend to all belief systems. If we treat the incidence of confirmatory empirical evidence as a reinforcer, the lessons of behaviorism suggest that beliefs based on inconsistent (variable ratio or interval) reinforcement may be the most persistent (have the longest extinction periods). As Skinner (1969) has noted, the persistence of belief in the efficacy of prayer and magic may owe much to such reinforcement schedules. In summary, we do not deny that the mechanisms for reducing dissonance such as those identified by Prus (1976) and Wallis (1977) are inoperative in maintaining belief. Rather, we argue that belief is often maintained because disconfirming evidence, however compelling to the nonbeliever, goes unnoticed by the believer.

CONCLUSIONS AND IMPLICATIONS

We have challenged the assumption that unconventional beliefs are inherently fragile. While not denying that plausibility structures are important in validating beliefs, we have explained how characteristics of belief systems themselves contribute to their perpetuation. Furthermore, we have demonstrated how belief systems may feature validation logics that help insure their persistence. Finally, we suggest that evidence that is discrepant with belief does not necessarily create cognitive dissonance. Instead, believers often appear to be under no constraints even to acknowledge evidence capable of inducing dissonance.

How is it, then, that many sociologists have come to presume the inherent instability of unconventional beliefs? Part of the answer may lie in their socialization. The norms of science require a highly developed sensitivity and receptivity to the "pressure of event." As the "official" arbiter of scientific belief, empirical evidence is assigned the final responsibility of justifying belief or mandating disbelief. As is well known, however, a given empirical event may allow tremendous variability of interpretation. Predictive science is extraordinary in the requirement that the interpretation of an event precede its actual occurrence. Many nonscientific belief systems are not so constrained. To the contrary, the decision as to whether an event confirms or falsifies belief is often not made until after the event has occurred. In many cases, this allows the believer great interpretive discretion. Furthermore, as taught by sociologists of knowledge, one's social position is a powerful determinant of the meanings that are ascribed to events. Simply put, "insiders" to a religious group may believe that the suffering of children is evidence of the visitation of God's wrath on the sins of their parents, while "outsiders" may interpret the same event as compelling evidence against the very existence of God.

With this basic proposition in mind, it is a bit puzzling to learn of Bainbridge's and Stark's surprise at the persistence of Scientologists' belief in the authenticity of "clear." For Bainbridge and Stark (1980:128), "outsiders" to Scientology, four kinds of events are decisively interpreted as evidence of the inauthenticity of clear. Yet, by their own definition as "outsiders," Bainbridge and Stark should not expect their strategies for interpreting events to coincide with those who are "inside" Scientology. If an event is an event for both "insiders" and "outsiders," it does not follow that evidence is evidence for all involved. Borhek and Curtis

(1975:127) explain clearly that "logics and proofs are just as much social products as the beliefs they validate." The logics according to which events are translated into evidence are thus variable and socially contingent. The logic of evidence shared by Scientologists is apparently not that shared by Bainbridge and Stark.

Perhaps another reason for sociologists' presuming the fragility of unconventional beliefs is that they have tended to be more concerned with accounting for belief than for disbelief. The persistence of belief can, of course, be approached from at least two assumptions: (1) believing is natural; doubting requires an "unnatural" exertion of will in order to overcome the inertia of taken-for-grantedness; (2) doubting is natural; believing requires an "unnatural" exertion of will to overcome the inertia of skepticism. Given the amount of research devoted to explaining how people maintain beliefs, it seems that most social scientists subscribe to the second assumption. Nevertheless, there is sound theoretical reasoning on which to assume that people are typically inclined toward belief rather than disbelief. Schutz (1971), for instance, drew a sharp distinction between the "natural attitude" and the "scientific attitude." The "scientific attitude" is one in which "nothing is to be taken as what it appears without evidence" (Schwartz and Jacobs, 1979:202). In daily existence, however, it is doubt, not belief that is typically suspended. As, Schwartz and Jacobs (1979:202) note in their interpretation of Schutz, "we assume that things are in fact what they appear to be unless we have reasons to do otherwise."

The scientist is called upon, then, to do something quite unnatural: to suspend belief in the paramount reality of the life world. That is, "the scientist must leave aside all presuppositions about what is *of course* real and 'true' to examine the subject matter indifferently and objectively" (Morris, 1977:19). It is thus entirely possible that sociologists have projected the assumptions of the "scientific attitude" onto those whose unconventional beliefs they would explain. As such, they regard as curious the persistence of belief in the face of disconfirming evidence. If the "natural attitude" is more pervasive than the "scientific attitude," then perhaps social scientists should rephrase Borhek's and Curtis' question to ask: How does doubt emerge in spite of the "natural attitude" to believe?

Popper (1964) commented on the peculiar cultural feature of science that institutionalizes skepticism. For Popper, this trait distinguishes science from other belief systems. Bloch (1973) noted the persistence of the belief, despite centuries of failure, that kings could cure skin disease by touch. Similarly, Evans-Pritchard commented on the self-confirming character of the Zande belief in poison oracles: "In this web of belief, every strand depends on every other strand, and a Zande cannot get out of its meshes because it is the only world he knows" (Burke, 1980:76). Perhaps, then, the theoretically interesting question may require that we try to explain how doubt emerges. The "natural attitude" encourages the suspension of doubt. The disposition to believe is compelling. It is as if the faithful have taken to heart William James's (1979:16) paraphrase of Pascal's wager: "Go, then, and take holy water, and have masses said; belief will come and stupefy your scruples—Cela vous fera croire et vous abêtira. Why should you not? At bottom, what have you to lose?"

REFERENCES

Abelson, Robert P. (ed.)
1968 *Theories of Cognitive Consistency: A Sourcebook.* Chicago: Rand-McNally.

Bainbridge, William S. and Rodney Stark
1980 "Scientology: To Be Perfectly Clear." *Sociological Analysis* 41:128-36.

Barrett, Leonard
1977 *The Rastafarians: Sounds of Cultural Dissonance.* Boston: Beacon Press.

Benassi, Victor A., Barry Singer and Craig B. Reynolds
1980 "Occult Belief: Seeing is Believing." *Journal for the Scientific Study of Religion* 19:337-49.

Berger, Peter L.
1966 *The Social Construction of Reality.* New York: Doubleday.

Bittner, Egon
1963 "Radicalism and the Organization of Radical Movements." *American Sociological Review* 28:928-40.

Bloch, Marc
1973 *The Royal Touch.* London: Routledge and K. Paul.

Borhek, James T. and Richard F. Curtis
1975 *A Sociology of Belief.* New York: John Wiley.

Burke, Peter
1980 *Sociology and History.* London: George Allen and Unwin.

Cohn, Norman
1957 *The Pursuit of the Millennium.* New York: Essential Books.

Dunford, F. and Phillip Kunz
1973 "The Neutralization of Religious Dissonance." *Review of Religions Research* 15:2-9.

Festinger, Leon
1957 *A Theory of Cognitive Dissonance.* Palo Alto CA: Stanford University Press.

Festinger, Leon, Henry Riecken and Stanley Schacter
1956 *When Prophecy Fails.* New York: Harper and Row.

James, William
1979 *The Will to Believe.* Cambridge MA: Harvard University Press.

Lindsey, Hal
1970 *The Late Great Planet Earth.* Grand Rapids MI: Zondervan.

Lofland, John
1966 *Doomsday Cult.* Englewood Cliffs NJ: Prentice-Hall.

Lofland, John and Rodney Stark
1965 "Becoming a World-Saver: A Theory of Religious Conversion." *American Sociological Review* 30:862-74.

Morris, Monica B.
1977 *An Excursion into Creative Sociology*. New York: Columbia University Press.

Popper, Karl E.
1964 *The Poverty of Historicism*. New York: Harper Torchbooks.

Prus, Robert C.
1976 "Religious Recruitment and the Management of Dissonance: A Sociological Perspective." *Sociological Inquiry* 46:127-34.

Schutz, Alfred
1971 *Collected Papers I: The Problem of Social Reality*. The Hague: Martinus Nijhoff.

Schwartz, Howard and Jerry Jacobs
1979 *Qualitative Sociology*. New York: The Free Press.

Simmons, J. L.
1964 "On Maintaining Deviant Belief Systems: A Case Study." *Social Problems* 11:250-56.

Skinner, B.F.
1969 *Contingencies of Reinforcement: A Theoretical Analysis*. New York: Appleton-Century-Crofts.

Snow, David A.
1976 *The Nichiren Shoshu Buddhist Movement in America: A Sociological Examination of its Value Orientation, Recruitment Efforts, and Spread*. Ann Arbor MI: University Microfilms.

1979 "A Dramaturgical Analysis of Movement Accommodation: Building Idiosyncrasy Credit as a Movement Mobilization Strategy." *Symbolic Interaction* 2:23-44.

1980 "The Disengagment Process: A Neglected Problem in Participant Observation Research" *Qualitative Sociology* 3:100-22.

Snow, David A., Louis A. Zurcher, Jr., and Sheldon Ekland-Olsen
1980 "Social Networks and Social Movements: A Microstructural Approach to Differential Recruitment." *American Sociological Review* 45:787-801.

Wallis, Roy
1977 *The Road to Total Freedom: A Sociological Analysis of Scientology*. New York: Columbia University Press.

Wilson, Bryan R.
1973 *Magic and the Millennium*. New York: Harper and Row.

Worsley, Peter
1968 *The Trumpet Shall Sound*. New York: Schocken Books.

Zygmunt, Joseph F.
1970 "Prophetic Failure and Chiliastic Identity: The Case of Jehovah's Witnesses." *American Journal of Sociology* 75:926-48.

THE POLITICS OF RELIGIOUS MOVEMENTS

by Carroll J. Bourg

SEVERAL QUESTIONS about the new religious movements stem from the general inquiry: what do the New Religious Movements[1] add up to? One set of questions has to do with what is "new" about them. Do they constitute a new form of religion? Do they contain evidence of new manners and modes of being religious? Is theirs a way of being religious that is especially related to the characteristics of contemporary society and in that respect different from earlier modes of being religious? A second set of questions has to do with their being "movements." In what sense are the New Religious Movements indeed movements at all? Do they constitute a challenge to the existing political order in the various societies in which they are flourishing? Are they developing a new

---

[1]The new religious movements cover a wide range of current religious ferment among collectivities that are attempting to pursue religious and spiritual objectives in some regular fashion. The variety of movements in the San Francisco area was analyzed by a Berkeley group and reported on in Glock and Bellah, 1976. In the report of a survey among the Bay area religious collectivities, Wuthnow (1976) had distinguished three types: the countercultural, personal growth and neo-Christian. Robbins, Anthony and Richardson (1978) had discussed several typologies of new religious movements in their comprehensive review of the literature about them. Robertson (1979) attempted to analyze the ensemble in identifying a new problematic in regard of what was considered to be legitimate individuals, and thus legitimate groups for the fostering of those individuals. Wuthnow has recently defended his identification of four types of consciousness among the participants in new religious movements (Wuthnow, 1976, 1981).

cultural model? Or are they merely enjoying a place in the rather wide berth afforded voluntary associations of whatever persuasion? In brief, what kind of movements are they? So I will discuss the ways in which the New Religious Movements are *new,* and the ways in which they might constitute a movement in contemporary society. However, I do not pretend to offer more than preliminary reflections on these topics, both of which seem central to our current deliberations.

ARE THEY NEW?

As an aid in addressing the question about how new the NRMs actually are, I propose to make some comparisons with other movements in the twentieth century. While there has been an enormous growth of movements in industrialized societies during the current century, I have chosen to compare the characteristics of selected youth movements for the purpose of identifying some common themes.

YOUTH MOVEMENTS IN THE TWENTIETH CENTURY

In the 1960s I did a study of participants in the civil rights movement in the United States (Bourg, 1967). For many of them participation in that movement included a deliberate involvement in the ecumenical movement, meaning by the latter, joint religious activities among members of different denominations. While cooperation had often begun in projects within the civil rights efforts, they soon recognized religious divisions that made little sense, and sought to ignore or bypass them.

In an effort at understanding the characteristics of the participants in those movements of the 1960s I made a comparison with youth movements earlier in the twentieth century. Here I will present a summary of those similarities and differences as a prelude to the question of what is new about the new religious movements. The movements include the *Wandervogel* and *Bunde* in Germany before and after World War I, the political movements of the 1930s in the United States, and then the movements in the 1960s.

The *Wandervogel* appeared in Germany between 1900 and 1914 at a time when industry was beginning to be developed on a large scale. Many attracted to the movement came from the cities where the growing industrial effort had its greatest impact. According to Walter Laqueur, the youth movement became "an unpolitical form of opposition to a civilization that had little to offer the young generation, a protest against its lack of vitality, warmth, emotion, and ideals" (Laqueur, 1962:4).

The *Wandervogel* took a mode of protest that tended to be romantic and preliberal, providing a partial liberation from the control of parents and teachers, but they were unclear about aims and objectives. It was a return to nature and the simple life. The Middle Ages became the ideal which included the romanticized life styles of knights and vassals, and the corporate organization of guilds. The members relied on collective experiences through folk-singing, walks in the countryside, and prolonged conversation. They stood for "revival and reform, not merely in one particular section of life but in life, whole and entire" (Laqueur, 1962:480). The leaders were preoccupied with questions of philosophy and religion rather than with an involvement in political realities. Laqueur sees them as part of "rightwing nationalism" with its anti-Semitism and its championing of the nationalistic aims of Germany. Still there was a high regard for the development of personality.

A later phase of the German youth movement was the *bundische* phase (1920-1933). There developed among the participants collective efforts, often with a sense of mission to German society. Howard Becker (1946) claimed that the personal qualities of the leadership were important factors in attracting and keeping members. Whereas the *Wandervogel* did not attend to the social critics of their time they certainly felt, according to Laqueur (1962:232), "some deep disquiet about the society." After World War I, the members of the *Bunde* were more aware of political problems and thus became nationalist because of a common conviction that Germany had been excessively humbled at Versailles. While the vagrant scholar might be said to have been the ideal for the ramblers before the war, the ideal of the youth after the war was the soldier.

In the 1930s in the United States, the depression had brought economic collapse and widespread poverty; and it also brought a sense of aimlessness among the young. The economic situation at home was coupled by the growth of fascism abroad, and these two issues stimulated students to take stands with regard to general social conditions and political issues. Some universities became centers for debate of the issues and for recruitment of members to particular political persuasions (Bell, 1952).

Three political groups achieved importance in the 1930s: the Socialists, the Communists, and the Trotskyists. The Socialists considered themselves to be intellectuals who attempted to argue within an ethical framework for what they considered to be constructive political action.

They sought improvements within the existing system. The Communists tended to identify with a larger political involvement. The experiment in Russia seemed exciting, especially in comparison with what appeared to be the collapse of capitalism in the United States. Intense commitment to programs which were part of the larger Communist struggle in the world made them less concerned about intellectual argument (Howe and Coser, 1962). The third group, the Trotskyists, were opposed to Stalin and the student Communists. In disagreement with the others' interpretation of Marx, they were prepared for intellectual argument. In general, the ideological stances the students took stemmed from affiliations with non-students. They were participating in issues that directly challenged the entire society.

Unlike the *Wandervogel*, who also rejected the life-styles of their parents and teachers, those in the 1960s movements did not seek a return to nature. While rejecting the highly administered urban style of life, they still wanted to act within it. Moreover, there was a search among them for a psychic community just as in the *Bunde* of the 1920s. In the 1960s movement the scope of concern extended beyond national boundaries. Unlike the nationalistic character of the *Wandervogel* and the *Bunde*, and more like the Communists and Trotskyists in the 1930s, those in the 1960s movements felt they were part of a much larger movement which was stirring in many parts of the world. But there was rejection of the rhetoric which moved the activists in the 1930s.

Those in the 1960s tended to identify primarily with the movement. They did not seek the quasi-permanent *Bunde* as the German youth of the 1920s; nor were there intellectual disputes among factions as in the 1930s, although there were lengthy arguments about strategies. While small groups were important and there was much talk of community, as event and experience, the actors did not feel tied to a particular small group. They were part of something bigger that manifested itself in the smaller group experiences of conversation, song, argument, planning. Allegiance was more to the happening and to events generally than to the formal credentials of membership.

Unlike the *Wandervogel* whose prospects were less hopeful, or the political activists of the thirties who felt aimless, the actors in the movement of the 1960s more consciously rejected career patterns which they could actually pursue. While the German youth tended to look to the past in search of values they felt were lost, and the political students of the 1930s looked ahead to the realization of some revolution and project, the movement members in the 1960s tended to look at the present possibility without much deliberate thought about the past or future.

The movements in the 1960s included many organizations. But there were large numbers of supporters and participants who were not affiliated with any organization. The unaffiliated supporters comprised by far the largest number who considered themselves part of the movement. Indeed, one of the characteristics was to shy away from organization. The movement in the 1960s was characterized by a functional use of organizations: Let it occur when necessary; let it disappear at the first sign of its uselessness.

TYPE OF ACTOR IN THE 1960s MOVEMENT

In the analysis of the actor in the movements of the 1960s, I constructed a type with the following attributes: historical and critical (Bourg, 1967; 1974). The historical attribute was further specified into particularizing and participatory. As actor, he was participatory in the events and programs which he recognized as part of the movement, for he was involved with others in the "making of history." He was also participatory because of a growing desire to be responsible, that is, to be able to respond to the issues, and to be accountable to do something about them. The particularizing aspect of the actor was noetic rather than activist, for it indicated the way in which knowledge emerged from the participation. Through participation the actor discovered both anticipating and conserving characteristics which were united in his action.

The other attribute of the actor was critical, a note that had two further meanings: socially critical and revelatory. The actor was socially critical in terms of many different standards of excellence, challenging the status quo as inadequate. The actor was revelatory, which involved the noetic element. Knowledge found through participation was revelatory of both the actor himself and the events in which he participated.

The attributes of the actor in the 1960s movements have been constructed from the materials gathered in studying the changes in consciousness among the participants. They served as another mode of comparison among the German youth movements and the political activists in the 1930s. With the attributes of being historical and critical, the actor in the 1960s was both like and unlike youth in other social movements.

The *Wandervogel,* for example, was critical in reaction against the developing industrial society in which he lived. But his criticism led him to flee contemporary society in a return to nature and the simple life. The romantic character of his rebellion pointed backward to the Middle Ages with its stylized patterns of life. He sought to recapture what was being lost, and he did so by seeking what he considered to be the better values of German culture. The nationalistic orientation did not lead him to be critical of social life in order to reform it; he tried instead to find the organic qualities of life in isolation from the developing cities. The companionship of the ramblers served as an end in itself; and their collective ventures in song and conversation did not point outwards to current problems. The *Wandervogel* chose what Laqueur (1962:234) calls "der Weg nach Innen." They were basically ahistorical in approach for they withdrew from the historical situation in Germany for the cult of the private. The cult of personality carried with it aristocratic attitudes because the ramblers looked upon themselves as the elite of the young who would rediscover in themselves the more significant cultural values which were being lost in contemporary society.

The *Bunde* which formed after World War I had a more deliberate political orientation. In the aftermath of Germany's defeat, the youth in the *Bunde* became critical of the conditions imposed by the peace treaty at Versailles. The members of the *Bunde* did not seek a return to nature, as the *Wandervogel* had done, but they pursued the ideal of the soldier with all the discipline and group control which go with it. They were critical of whatever accentuated the inferior position of Germany, and they tried to create in their own groups a sense of pride and dignity in themselves and in their country.

The members of the *Bunde* were historical in the sense that they considered themselves to be part of the historic mission of Germany. Their nationalistic orientation, however, limited their perspective to the restoration of their country's greatness. But these youth were intent on influencing large groups of the young in Germany. They may have had elitist ideas, but unlike the *Wandervogel* who considered themselves to be the elite, the *Bunde* wanted to make an impact on others for the sake of the entire country.

The political movements of the 1930s in the United States comprised different kinds of reactions and attitudes. All of them were critical of American society in terms of some criterion of analysis or evaluation. Although there were differences among them, according to the interpretation of Marxist doctrine and according to the understanding of what was appropriate political action, the youth in the political movements were arguing for changes in economic and political life. Moreover, they were historical in orientation inasmuch as they had a keen sense of participating in the significant political events of their time. With the emphasis on the political, the students engaged in all sorts of protest and discussion by which they sought to be effective participants in the improvement of American society. Often their more ideological bent led them to accent the plan which had been formulated outside their circles. They participated in American society by becoming part of movements which included many more adults than either the German youth groups or the movement in the 1960s.

The actor in the movement of the 1960s identified less with a particular group such as the *Wandervogel, Bunde,* Socialists, Communists, Trotskyists, and more with the general orientation that included more unaffiliated than active members of organizations. He was as romantic in orientation as the *Wandervogel,* but with greater concern for the group, as in the *Bunde.* He had greater political interest than the *Wandervogel,* but less clearly so than the political youth of the 1930s. Hence the actor often appeared politically naive. He referred less to historical realities, but was more intent on the events and their consequent personal and social meaning than the earlier youth.

The type of actor in the 1960s, then, seemed to have his own combination of the personal and the political which was unlike the personal and political emphases of the earlier youth. To some critics, the political understanding often seemed utopian and too romantic, and the personal approach too delicate, too public. His effort to combine the political and the personal circumvented the expected distinctions between the public and the private. For the actor neither had nor wanted any radical separation of the two. He tended to avoid the more aggressive expressions which were often the sources of violence and creativity in the past. His concern for nonviolence, either as tactic or as philosophy of life, persuaded him to share his sentiments rather than to impose them. The actor tended to concentrate his energies and his attention on the present events in which he was involved; unlike the *Wandervogel* and their penchant for the past, unlike the political youth of the thirties and their push towards the future, the actor in the sixties wanted to linger in the present events so that the fuller personal and social meaning might be discovered. What distinguished him from his predecessors was, among other things, the concern for the revelatory character of his knowing. Any rupture of the personal and the political, of self and society, was considered false and unfaithful to the experiences he had had and to the revelations, both personal and social, to which he testified. Furthermore, by particularizing the phenomena he confronted, even though at times cursorily and superficially, the actor intended to accent the human agency of those involved in the activities of the movement. He was more certain of the contingent than the necessary character of contemporary society, and he saw himself as part of a larger movement which was stirring below the surface throughout the world.

These, then, were the elements which comprised the consciousness of a type of actor which had emerged through participation in the civil rights and ecumenical movements of the 1960s in the United States. Involved in the politically relevant experiences of current history, the consciousness that emerged in him manifested some anticipatory elements which point to more inclusive identities in a world grown smaller and more available to human awareness.

RELIGIOUS MOVEMENTS—1970s AND 1980s

Meredith McGuire has identified four themes among the new religious movements. While the precise ways in which these themes are manifested vary, McGuire finds that the new religious movements emphasize religious experience, access to power, a sense of order implying authority, moral norms and judgment, and, finally, a theme of unity through communalism or some redefinition of family (McGuire, 1981:136-137). I will compare these themes across the movements previously indicated.

Religious experience and the experiential mode of knowing was a central attribute of the actor in the civil rights and ecumenical movements of the 1960s, a note I have analyzed as participatory and revelatory. Knowledge that did not emerge from direct experience or could not be verified through direct experience was either suspect or inadequate. The emphasis on experimental knowledge is surely consistent with the romantic mode of the German youth movements, especially before World War I but also to some degree after the war.

The second note common to the new religious movement was power to which "new religious movements offer their adherents access" (McGuire, 1981:136). The power may be described as spiritual but it is expected to have effects in other spheres of life. The concern about access to power is not altogether new to the current religious movements but the emphasis on spiritual power as the basic matrix from which empowerment in other areas of life would stem may be a new emphasis among movements in the twentieth century. The German youth before the war felt aimless and withdrew by seeking a more genuine existence in a natural mode of living. The German youth after the war sought empowerment but in a nationalistic and militaristic mode for the purpose of redressing perceived wrongs. Those in the 1930s were attracted to the Russian experiment because of their powerlessness in the face of a collapsing capitalism. But they first sought the power of ideas as a guide toward the reform they thought to be necessary. The actor in the movements of the 1960s sought a merged political-personal stance insisting that power become a personal attribute consistently manifesting itself in both the spiritual and the political realm. But among them there was no priority given to the spiritual because religious traditions were judged to be in need of reform as much as the extant political forms. While the actor in the 1960s sought an integrated view of power, and access to power, those in the religious movements of the 1970s have given priority and primacy to spiritual power as the fundamental empowerment that must precede and support any other.

The third theme is order. According to McGuire, while some groups emphasize order that includes authority and precise moral norms, others think of order as harmony and tranquility. Among the movements under review, the German youth before the war were ramblers, fleeing the organized life of the cities, seeking the freedom of natural habitats; the German youth after the war gradually developed a strong sense of moral purpose which would require the authority of military discipline and the mission of the soldier. While the actor in the 1960s movement did not seek organization and authority but sought direction through reflection on events of the moment, the activists in the 1930s argued about the appropriate order of events by which the then current crisis would be resolved. The contemporary religious movements seek an ordered life that is the result of obedience to the rule or to the leader. They are in that regard similar to religious collectivities in earlier centuries but unlike the romantic and intellectual movements of this century.

The fourth theme, that of unity, seems to be a continuation of the unitary thematic of the civil rights and ecumenical movements of the 1960s. The theme of unity was not merely an intellectual ideal as an offshoot of a political ideology, like the arguments of the activists in the 1930s. It was something to be lived. For the contemporary movements it would take the form of communalism or some new idea of family. Unity was first to be lived in the groups to which one belonged.

In summary, the contemporary religious movements, many of them with members of varying ages, have continued some of the religious emphases emergent among the actors in the civil rights and ecumenical movements of the 1960s. While there is considerably less emphasis on a direct political agenda, and more direct cultivation of personal attributes that characterize the religious agenda, there is an integrated view of the personal and political. By cultivating personal qualities and virtues, one becomes empowered spiritually and thus has the basis for exerting power in other realms. In comparison with the activists of the 1930s in the United States, the participants in the current religious movements are quite short on political ideology and argument. But there is a romantic dimension to the religious effort, a sense of being able to construct new worlds of meaning, much like the youth movements before and after World War I, in Germany.

The religious work that the current religious groups are engaged in is continuous with the efforts of the earlier movements. Whatever the precise differences among them, the current religious movements share the ambiguities of a romantic dimension in the cultivation of the self and they participate in a basic dilemma in the relation between politics and religion in our time. The romantic element is found in the emphasis on the individual, on the self, on the acquisition of skills, abilities and capacities for engaging in pursuits of spiritual development. The difficulty in the romantic quest is the dilemma between a mode of candor, self-expression, and search for the authentic and the opposite impulse toward narcissism and self-preoccupation. While pursuing the one there is the attendant danger of falling into the other. But that dilemma has frequently characterized spiritual quests and is not peculiar to the contemporary movements.

The dilemma confronting both politics and religion today is in my view that between privatization and what I call pluralization (Bourg, 1980). By the latter I include the idea of publicizing, but with something added. Given that one's spiritual quest is not in isolation from the rest of the world, it must necessarily entail the experience of multiple traditions. Indeed I find that participants in the contemporary religious groups do not feel compelled to abandon the tradition of their earlier years while undertaking a quest within some new religious matrix. To the extent that the participants are nourished by more than one religious tradition, they experience a pluralization of consciousness and conscience, and thereby may find a new experience of becoming plural. That means that while they are nurtured by more than one religious tradition, they are not bound to any one of them. The religious search moves beyond preexisting boundaries among established religious collectivities to whatever makes sense in the current religious tasks.

It is the quality and character of the plural experience that I think best characterizes the participants in contemporary religious movements. While for some multiple belonging may be fearful and confusing, for others it is liberating. In my view, it may well pose the basic religious task in our time, the task of finding out, indeed of inventing in some detail, what manner of living together is indeed possible on the occasion of the multiplication of religious traditions in one's own immediate experience. These participants are migrants in an unsettled world, some fleeing the complex invasion of alien modes of life, others experimenting with diverse human and religious traditions by embracing several of them and testing them all in the light of personal criteria.

The testing of one's plural consciousness in matters of traditional importance to religion is taking place in the regimen and rules by which the participants attempt to live and be faithful. All of these dimensions of the religiously collective life admit of corruption and deformation, that is, forms of manipulation and control in sexual relations, in economic matters and in religious authority. But there is some evidence that the experiments among the contemporary religious groups include novel ways of addressing the issues of sexual relations, economic dependencies and political authority. What the new religious movements may add up to, then, is a testing ground for "new" human capacities, not now widespread, but surely necessary if we are to have diverse human populations that are both empowered and unified. Their primary political task, then, is internal. It is the development of a political economy in which multiple religious traditions contribute to new modes of human community, now more diverse and varied than previously known or previously cultivated.

THE STUDY OF RELIGIOUS MOVEMENTS

The second issue I am raising concerns what kind of movement the current religious ferment might be. While the rather loose use of the term "movement" is surely legitimate in indicating that something seems to be happening which is different from the established or institutionalized way of proceeding, there are more precise ways in which movements are ordinarily analyzed. There are three modes of analysis, of which the first two are more familiar because they have already been used in studies of particular religious collectivities (Wuthnow, 1981).

The first is based on the assumption that shared grievances and the beliefs about the causes and means of reducing the grievances are important preconditions for the appearance of a social movement in some form of collectivity. Discontent of some kind, then, would be a prerequisite to the development of social movements. The focus in this mode of analysis would be on the grievances and the deprivations of the participants.

In using such an approach for the study of religious movements, one finds that the characteristics of the participants are central. The religious collectivity often becomes a haven for those discontented with their prior way of life, or it is the locus of rehabilitative efforts. Neil Smelser (1963) and Turner and Killian (1972) have codified the elements of this analytical procedure.

McCarthy and Zald (1973, 1977) report on a second approach to the study of social movements which has been developed in reaction against the emphasis on members and their grievances. The approach called "resource mobilization" is based on the recognition of the increased affluence and leisure in the United States which has enabled growing numbers of persons to become involved in social movements by supplying resources. Moreover, there has also been a growth of professional careers in social movements where both part-time and full-time staff are supported by regular budgets. A major example is the National Council on the Aging in the United States which recently held its thirty-first annual meeting. The major topics of conversation were the proposed cuts in the federal budget. The concern centered as much on the anticipated reduction in support for programs as it was on the expected reduction in support for their very large staff of full-time professionals.

McCarthy and Zald argue for the resource mobilization approach because of the declining importance of the membership base with a consequent separation of funding and leadership from the base. Moreover, the increased role of the mass media requires persons capable of using them effectively. These developments have resulted in "professional social movements" with full-time leadership, large amounts of resources originating outside the aggrieved group, often a small membership base and the need for spokespersons for a potential constituency.

A major emphasis in the mode of analysis suggested by McCarthy and Zald draws attention to the organizational characteristics of what is still called a "social movement." While some of these movement organizations have become quite large and well-endowed, there are many others with temporary staff, some letterhead, a telephone, a mailing address and an office with a desk and a few chairs. One leader of the Sierra Club in Tennessee, an environmental group, reported to me that its press releases always included the adjectives "power" or "well-organized protest" although the membership is small and the annual meeting draws only some of the members.

The resource mobilization approach has great usefulness in raising the issue of resources and support. These issues are particularly important in the second generation of movements, after the "original" leader has moved on or died, and the successors attempt to "organize" for the future, issues that Kanter (1972) has analyzed for the religious experiments during the 19th century in the United States. The items of professional staff and public relations capabilities for the effective use of the media are particularly relevant in the light of the "electric church" movements in recent years. The direct mailing procedures for contact with members, adherents and supporters have been used as effectively by the Republican Party in the 1980 elections in the United States as they have been used by the media preachers.

The thesis of McCarthy and Zald is that there has been a general growth in the availability of resources to the social movement sector (SMS) and that social movement organizations compete among one another for those resources. They argue further that "conscience adherents" would tend to support movements that promoted change. Their general conclusion is that "the resource mobilization model . . . emphasizes the interaction between resource availability, the preexisting organization of preference structures and entrepreneurial attempts to meet preference demand" (McCarthy and Zald, 1977:1236). For the study of new religious collectivities, I would expect that the issue of resource availability is critical. If the local unit must husband resources for itself and also supply a portion to a headquarters or larger unit, then it may well be part of a network that requires accounting and accountability. Moreover, the more a religious movement is indeed a confederation of different settlements, the more there would be staff review and perhaps control from above. The maintenance of resource availability would be both internal among the member units and external from potential donors and supporters, whether through gifts or purchases.

In the study of the new religions, there are two limitations to the resource mobilization approach. One is the continuing emphasis on grievances to be redressed by the social movement for some potential beneficiaries. I do not think that the new religious collectivities of the 1970s can be adequately understood in terms of coping with the grievances of members. For many religions, the participants have unexpectedly found new experiences and new enthusiasms that were unavailable in their prior circumstances or in their normal participation in social and economic activities. The other limitation is that while religious movements may attract adherents and supporters in ways quite similar to social movements, they do not show much evidence of "preference structures" (to use McCarthy and Zald's term) or clearly expressed social or political objectives. The spiritual quest is primarily interior and personal with an emphasis on the cultivation of personal qualities. Yet the internal organization of the new religious collectivities often includes the staffing and marshaling of resources that are the major emphasis in this mode of analysis.

A third approach to the study of social movements is quite different from the other two and has been developed by Alain Touraine in his book *The Self-Production of Society* (1977) and in the recently translated book called *The Voice and The Eye, An Analysis of Social Movements* (1981). While Touraine has a great deal to say about social movements in general and in particular, I find it most helpful to emphasize his search for the social movement that may potentially reside in some collective behavior. Rather than presume that every collective conduct is a social movement, Touraine claims that it is a task of sociology to enable the social movement to appear, to become evident, to be recognized, even by the participants themselves. A social movement, in this scheme, is society at work on itself; it is the self-production of society itself. The production of society is a work of historicity which Touraine contrasts to society as mere functioning or reproduction of itself.

Giddens (1976:21; 1977:123) has criticized Touraine for drawing too sharp a distinction between production and reproduction, arguing as he does that even reproduction is itself a mode of production of society. The reasons why Touraine insists on a fundamental difference between production and reproduction become clearer in his recent work *The Voice and the Eye.* There he describes the increased encroachment of the state in social life, approaching a near absorption of civil society, most evidently in socialist societies but also to a more limited extent in capitalist societies. As a contrast and corrective to statism, he posits social movements at the heart of society's production of itself. To the extent that the state takes over social life, the society is reduced to mere functioning, and thus to mere reproduction of itself. To the extent that society's historicity is still operative then the fundamental work of its own self-production continues apace. The social movement takes place in that realm of historicity.

For Touraine, social movements are "socially conflictual behavior but also culturally oriented forms of behavior." Moreover, a social movement is a "class action, directed against a truly social adversary." But it is not part of an evolutionary scheme, the seedbed as it were to a more advanced society than the one it is contesting. It is rather "within a given cultural and historical field, . . . defending another society" (Touraine, 1981:80). He would expect then that in a particular society there would be relatively few major social movements but more specific conflicts and struggles may embody some elements of the social movements. If the field proper to social movements is class relations and historicity then particular conflicts may approach these principal stakes of society. A social movement is "not an affirmation, an intention; it is a double relation, directed at an adversary and at what is at stake" (Touraine, 1981:80).

This idealist model of social movement may seem too distant from the empirical reality of the wide range of behaviors that are designated social movements or new religious movements. As a corrective to mere description of the diversity of collective conduct, I find Touraine's notion helpful because it urges us to raise the question of what various movements portend for the society as a whole. In the matter of new religious movements, what do they add up to? Are they merely collective behavior at the institutional level, or at the organizational levels, perhaps conflictual behavior but within narrower social fields? Or are they showing evidence of social struggles over the basic stakes of the society's production of itself, its modes of knowing, its manner of accumulation, its model of creativity? I think it would be useful to study the new religious movements in these dimensions.

Yet Touraine's approach to the study of social movements is as novel for the level of reality to which he assigns it as it is for the method of grasping it. In the former, Touraine seems to make social movements quite singular, insisting there may be only one, or at most a few, social movements occurring at one time, because the movement comprises the basic struggle over the historicity of society itself, that is, its own self-production. Whatever the refractions into particular struggles or conflicts they are not manifestations of the singular social movement at the heart of society's work unless they indeed participate in the basic venture.

By refusing to limit social movements to a "peripheral phenomenon of deviation or outright conflict" Touraine urges the opinion that each societal type has a characteristic social movement which occupies a central role. Thus he is searching for the social movement which will be as central to post-industrial society, an emergent societal type (Touraine, 1977), as the workers' movement was to industrial society and the movement for civil freedom was for mercantile society (Touraine, 1981:95).

But the analysis is synchronic rather than diachronic. It is not the case that the social movement is the embryo of a next phase of societal development. It is rather the situation that the central social movement will emerge and disappear with the societal type for which it embodies society's historicity or production of itself. Thus the social movement will share the "decadence" of the society of which it is a part even while retaining a political importance far greater than that which the fledgling movements have.

Were one to utilize this notion of social movements in the study of new religious movements, one would indeed be searching for evidence of what kind of movement these religious collectivities happen to be. While they can surely be in conflict at the institutional level of organized religion or at the organizational level of particular denominations, the perspective here points toward discovery of evidence as to the level of social struggles which may be at the center of society's production of itself.

Touraine's method of studying social movements as he has identified them requires a sociology of action, a style of sociology that emerges to accomplish the task of grasping the potential movements. To carry out a sociology of action entails the researcher's intervention into the collective conduct that he is studying. The participants in the movement may be able to identify particular grievances or objectives for their common efforts. The researcher assists them in recognizing the elements of the movement, if they are there. One element is the adversary, the components of the opposition in the struggle.

In the study of the participants in the civil rights and ecumenical movements in the 1960s, reported above for comparing the characteristics of other movements, I developed a method of inquiry to grasp what was happening to the actors as a consequence of their experiences in the movements. I called it "sociology as participation" because I had to serve as midwife to the components of consciousness reported on by the actors (Bourg, 1967; 1974). While less activist than Touraine's intervention, there was similarity in recognizing that the sociologist's task had to be participatory in the movements themselves if one expected to uncover the levels of meaning that they carried. In Touraine's methods, through the active intervention of the sociologist, the social relations governing the situation are brought to the surface, are made evident, are revealed. Once revealed, these social relations become the object of analysis (Touraine, 1981:139-40).

Through the intervention the researcher "causes the stakes to emerge" and thus they become available for the analysis. As a result, the group can then enter into self-analysis. For the actors the analysis is to provide greater knowledge of their situation and thus to identify the strategies and even tactics for further action. For the analyst, the sociological inquiry continues for the purpose of understanding to what extent the movement, the adversary and the stakes are indeed elements of the society's historicity and thus part of society's production of itself.

All these components of Touraine's sociology of action and sociological intervention require more detailed description. He has promised to illustrate the stages of this procedure in a series of books about various movements in which he has intervened. Here I am recommending it as a third approach to the study of movements, one that may yield understanding of new religious movements unavailable in the approaches described above which focus on the deprivations of participants and the issues of resource mobilization.

CONCLUDING REMARKS

In searching for what might be new about the current religious ferment, I would recommend all three modes of analyzing social movements. Thus the politics of the religious movements would not be limited to the organizational level or to the institutional level, but it would also be found both in the internal political economy of the group and in the political work of society's self production, to use Touraine's language.

The current dilemma of privatization versus pluralization is particularly prominent among the new religious movements. Given the freedom of movement and the relatively simply procedures of establishing settlements in new locations, the religious collectivities can become havens of escape for the cult of the private. Or they could be undertaking a religious work of importance for the current or emergent phase of societal development.

REFERENCES

Becker, Howard

1952 *German Youth: Bond or Free.* London: Kegan Paul, Trench, Trubner & Co.

Bell, Daniel

1952 "The Background and Development of Marxian Socialism in the United States." In *Socialism in American Life.* Donald Drew Egbert and Stow Persons, eds. Princeton NJ: Princeton University Press, 213-405.

Bourg, Carroll J.

1967 "Sociology as Participation: A Critical, Historical Orientation." Doctoral dissertation, Brandeis University.

1974 "Contemporary Religious Consciousness among Some Young Adults." *The Human Context* 6:632-41.

1980 "Politics and Religion." *Sociological Analysis* 41:297-315.

Giddens, Anthony

1976 *New Rules of Sociological Method: A Positive Critique of Interpretive Sociologies.* New York: Basic Books.

1977 *Studies in Social and Political Theory.* New York: Basic Books.

Glock, Charles Y. and Robert N. Bellah

1976 *The New Religious Consciousness.* Berkeley CA: The University of California Press.

Howe, Irving and Lewis Coser

1962 *The American Communist Party.* New York: Frederick Praeger.

Kanter, Rosabeth

1972 *Commitment and Community: Communes and Utopias in Sociological Perspective.* Cambridge MA: Harvard University Press.

Laqueur, Walter Z.

1962 *Young German, A History of the German Youth Movement.* New York: Basic Books.

McCarthy, John D. and Mayer N. Zald

1973 *The Trend of Social Movements in America: Professionalization and Resources Mobilization.* Morristown NJ: General Learning Press.

1977 "Resources Mobilization and Social Movements: A Partial Theory." *American Journal of Sociology* 82:1212-41.

McGuire, Meredith B.

1981 *Religion: The Social Context.* Belmont CA: Wadsworth.

Robbins, Thomas, Dick Anthony, and James Richardson

1978 "Theory and Research on Today's Religions." *Sociological Analysis* 39:95-122.

Robertson, Ronald

1979 "Religious Movements and Modern Societies: Toward a Progressive Problemshift." *Sociological Analysis* 40:297-314.

Smelser, N.

1963 *Theory of Collective Behavior.* New York: Free Press.

Touraine, Alain

1977 *The Self-Production of Society.* Chicago: University of Chicago Press.

1981 *The Voice and The Eye: An Analysis of Social Movements.* Cambridge: Cambridge University Press.

Turner, R. N. and L. Killian

1972 *Collective Behavior.* 2d ed. Englewood Cliffs NJ: Prentice-Hall.

Wuthnow, Robert

1981 "Two Traditions in the Study of Religion." *Journal for the Scientific Study of Religion* 20:16-32.

1976 *The Consciousness Reformation.* Berkeley CA: University of California Press.

FINANCING THE NEW RELIGIONS: A BROADER VIEW*

by James T. Richardson

INTRODUCTION

MOST OF THE SCHOLARLY literature concerning new religions does not attend adequately, if at all, to the question of how the new religions support themselves and use their financial resources, partly because many scholars studying the new religions are not addressing the problems from an organizational point of view. They instead focus on why and how people join such groups, or on the beliefs and individual behaviors propounded by such groups. Questions such as these are important, but they cannot be answered properly without understanding the economic policies and practices of the groups, and noting the interaction of important elements of group life with fund-raising and internal allocation schemes.

Many historical and contemporary religious groups have made financial contributions and participation in fund raising and other "investments" in the group an integral part of the recruitment, commitment, and resocialization process (see Kanter, 1972, 1973; Richardson, et

*This paper is reprinted, in slightly revised form, from the *Journal for the Scientific Study of Religion* (Fall 1982). The paper was written during a Fulbright Fellowship spent at the Psychologisch Laboratorium of Katholieke Universiteit, Nijmegen, The Netherlands. Grateful acknowlegment is made for this support. Appreciation is also expressed for valuable comments by Frans Derks, Jan van der Lans, David Bromley, Anson Shupe, Jr., and Tom Robbins on an earlier draft.

al., 1979; Bromley and Shupe, 1979b; Bainbridge, 1978; Beckford, 1975; Rigby, 1974; Nordquist, 1978, among others). Some groups have allowed their theology or beliefs to develop in ways that justify what have been found to be successful fund-raising techniques. Bromley and Shupe (1979b:120) discuss how the Unification Church members justified, after the fact, the successful street solicitation methods they developed almost accidentally. Richardson and others (1979:100-101) quote some of the scriptural justification for a totally different approach to financing developed by the group they studied (a large Jesus movement group the authors call Christ Communal Organization—CCO). That approach entailed raising much of their own food, selling agricultural products, and working for others for salaries which were given to the organization to be redistributed as needed by the members. Johnston (1980) describes how financial considerations have been nearly totally determining in the way that the Transcendental Meditation (TM) movement organized itself, affecting both the interpretation of the ideology and recruitment practices of the movement.

If researchers on new religions would routinely take such economic factors into account, as is regularly done in studies of communes (see for examples, Rigby, 1974; and Kanter, 1972; 1973; Stein, 1973; Richardson, 1977a; Abrams and McCulloch, 1976; Shey, 1977; Zablocki, 1971; Kephart, 1974; Mowery, 1978) then the literature produced would be of more value in helping inform other scholars and the general public about the new religions. This latter point is important because there is such public controversy about the new religions. The controversy in the popular literature seems to swirl about two major issues: (1) recruitment tactics used by the new movements, and (2) methods which are used to finance the new movements (and the ways they use their resources). The area of recruitment has been addressed at considerable length by scholars in the field of new religions (see, for example, Richardson, 1978) although some works have not been fully informed of organizational variables.

The area of economic policies and practices of new religions has, however, been relatively neglected as a research area and few studies have dealt in any depth with the topic (see Nordquist, 1978; Bromley and Shupe, 1979b; Lofland, 1977; Davis and Richardson, 1976; Messer, 1976, Johnston, 1980; Richardson, et al., 1979; Bainbridge, 1978; Lester, 1978; Welles, 1978; for a few examples that incorporate substantial discussion of economic matters). What solid research there is has usually focused on one particular group instead of on more broad questions, and seldom has there been any kind of comparison made between groups on the question of economic policies and practices. This has meant that discussions of this issue have usually been less than fully informed.[1]

Therefore the recent contribution by Bromley and Shupe (1980) on one method of financing the new religions was a valuable addition to the area of new religious studies. Their paper does an excellent job of discussing the development of street solicitation as a major tactic of fund raising by two of the newer groups—the Unification Church (UC) and the Hare Krishna (HK). Their use of the "resource mobilization" approach from the literature of social movements aids understanding of how this high-profit tactic of fund raising became so central particularly to the UC for a time. Further, the paper offers a valuable social psychological analysis of the solicitation episode, helping us grasp why UC and HK members were so phenomenally successful at gathering funds this way.

There are some problems with the paper, however, and there are some other economic issues of import that could not be addressed by Bromley and Shupe in one article. One problem area is conceptual and concerns the use of "world-transforming movement" as a major explanatory device by Bromley and Shupe. Another problem is that the paper may inadvertently be subject to overgeneralization, because the uninformed reader may get the impression from the article that public solicitation is the major way that new religions raise funds. Such is not the case. In fact, public solicitation was not used as the major method of support for the HK and the UC during most of their history. Public solicitation was the major method used by the UC to finance their large property purchases and other activities in recent times, but, as will be discussed, other methods of support have also been important.

---

[1]It must be admitted that the growing literature about conversion processes clearly showing that nothing like classical brainwashing occurs in the new movements has not deterred a number of people and groups from assuming that such is the case and using that assumption in their efforts to get people out of the new groups and to affect the groups in various ways. See Robbins and Anthony (1979) for a good discussion of this problem that puts the situation in a historical perspective. It should be noted that some studies of "less new" religious groups have taken economic matters into consideration (see Klassen, 1964; Leone, 1979; Barclay, 1969; Hostetler, 1963, 1974; Bennett, 1967; Beckford, 1975; Zablocki, 1971; Andrews, 1963, for examples). However, the popular literature in particular has treated new religions as "something new under the sun," and has not referred to this material.

This paper will address the issues mentioned and will also attempt to relate economic policies and practices of the new religions to broader theoretical questions, deriving mainly from the literature of commune studies.[2]

CONCEPTUAL PROBLEMS

Bromley and Shupe did not set out to discuss all the fund-raising tactics and economic policies of all new religious groups over their entire history. They were not even trying to give a complete fund-raising history of the two groups discussed in their paper. Instead they were trying to analyze one major tactic of fund raising used by a general type of group they call "world transforming." But the title of their paper is very general, and uninformed readers could be misled. This problem is compounded by a seeming lack of conceptual clarity regarding the notion of "world-transforming" movements. Bromley and Shupe define world-transforming movements (1980:228) as those which "seek to institute *total* rather than limited change (either societal or personal) and at the same time rely on a strategy of persuasion rather than coercion to bring about that change."[3]

Given this definition, some scholars might disallow the designation of the UC and HK as world-transforming movements, and others would perhaps expand the category to include different communal groups, or even some noncommunal ones. It would have been useful for the writers to have characterized some of the major new religions, especially those that have received much attention from scholars and popular writers alike. Bromley and Shupe mention the Children of God (COG) along with

---

[2]A later paper will address other key economic issues, such as how funds are used by the groups, the level and type of support for individual members, the relationship of economic policies and practices to government agencies (especially taxing authorities), and the impact of spending policies of new religions on the general economic activity in society and in certain locales.

[3]One reason why this would have been useful is that Bromley and Shupe are unclear on whether they consider movements intent on radical individual change to be "world transforming." As indicated, they include total change of society *or* the personality structure as part of their definition (1980:228). But in their recent book (1979b:22) they define world-transforming movement as "one which seeks permanent structural change of societies across all institutions," a definition they also employed in their latest book (Shupe and Bromley, 1980:14). They also distinguish between movements which seek to restructure institutions and those "whose goals are to transform individuals" (1979b:24), which raises a question of how they would apply their definition.

the UC and the HK in the opening sentence of their paper, but there is no systematic relating of their dichotomy to the general field.

The point about the classification of the UC can be illustrated from Bromley and Shupe's book on the UC (1979b) and from the work of Lofland (1977) in his "Epilogue" section which summarizes the history of the UC since the original edition of *Doomsday Cult* was published in 1966. Both of these works, particularly the Bromley and Shupe book, indicate considerable accommodationist activity by the UC, in an effort to "clean up its act" and gain more public support and a better image. Thus the degree of adherence to their "world-transforming" ideology may be less than suggested by UC rhetoric, and even the rhetoric may be lessening. Similar comments can be made about HK, which operates what is reputed to be the largest incense company in the world, producing a line of shampoos, oils, incense, soap, and similar products with millions of dollars (see Judah, 1974:43; and 1975). The HK are quite skilled at soliciting money from peddling books at airports and other places, but this is not their only way of gathering money. Their involvement in the world of commerce with their publishing and the incense company also suggests some degree of accommodation to the world.

On the other hand, there are some newer groups which are or have been at least partially communal in nature and that may fit the definition of world-transforming that Bromley and Shupe offer, yet they are not and have not been involved to any great extent in street solicitation for funds. Three well-documented examples of this type of group are the Ananda "Cooperative Village" (ACV) studied by Nordquist (1978), the Divine Light Mission (DLM) studied by Messer (1976) and Pilarzyk (1978a), and CCO, the group studied by Richardson and others (1979). The first and second of these examples are well known Eastern-oriented new religious groups, and the third has been one of the major groups in the Jesus Movement (JM).[4] In the following section the fund-raising methods of these three groups will be briefly described, after first discussing whether or not such groups could be considered "world transforming."

---

[4]"Degree of communalness" might even be considered a variable of importance since the three groups mentioned in the paragraph are only partially communal. ACV is a cooperative village with many communal aspects. CCO was initially completely communal, but changed within a few years to a situation in which a majority of the members lived noncommunally, mainly because they could then afford to live as nuclear families. DLM has varied in the proportion who live communally, but the best estimates seem to be that about twenty-five percent usually live communally.

Some might argue that the DLM and other Eastern-oriented groups such as ACV are not really world transforming because they lack a "radical ideology." The individualistic experiential orientation of the DLM (Messer, 1976) and of the ACV (Nordquist, 1978) might even suggest to some that the groups are supportive of the political and economic structures of society. Further evidence for such a characterization might come from the involvement of ACV and to some extent the DLM in small capitalistic enterprises to furnish sustenance to the organizations. However, others would suggest that the heavy emphasis on the experiential is itself radical. Certainly the way of interpreting the experiences of DLM and ACV members differs radically from traditional Christian interpretations of peak experiences. Also, Bromley and Shupe say (1979b:93) that the DLM is viewed as one of the "extreme" movements in the field of new religions, and as indicated (footnote 3) they also state (1980:228) that world-transforming movements can seek total change in "either societal *or* personality structure" (emphasis mine).

Groups and movements that seek to change the world by first changing individuals can be considered radical, especially if they aggressively press their ideas on society. This point would seem to hold for both the Eastern-oriented groups such as DLM and ACV, and it would also seem applicable to some communal groups within the Christian tradition. CCO has been very aggressive in promoting a utopian kind of lifestyle and an apocalyptic ideology during its history (see Richardson, et al., 1979:82-89). Thus it can be viewed as somewhat radical, even if it has obvious ties with the dominant religious culture.

The question of the necessity of living communally to the world-transforming definition must also be raised. Some groups that might be considered rather radical (especially if societal reaction to them is any measure) are not communal or are only involved in communal living in a limited way. Scientology and TM are two such cases that are both financially successful, but which have evoked considerable controversy (particularly Scientology). Also, as indicated, some groups may be communal at the start, and evolve in a noncommunal way (or vice versa). Thus it seems that the communal nature of new religious groups, while plainly of significance, should be treated independently of overall characterizations of such movements.

FUND-RAISING IN PARTIALLY COMMUNAL GROUPS

Messer (1976) goes into some detail about DLM finances, and her findings are substantiated by Pilarzyk (1978a) and Stoner and Parke

(1977). Messer notes that the DLM receives many donations from outsiders, but that most funding comes from donations by members who work outside the ashrams (communes) or who live noncommunally and work at outside jobs of one type or another. Funds are also received from service-like businesses (such as janitorial services) operated by individual ashrams. The only solicitation used by the DLM seems to be sometimes asking merchants or other people for old possessions to sell in rummage sales and small secondhand stores. This method can be lucrative, of course. For example, the former DLM leader in The Netherlands claimed that the group gathered and sold over five hundred thousand dollars of goods in their most fruitful year. Also, this same informant claimed that a high-level decision was made by DLM leadership in America several years ago to have fewer ashrams and more festivals, because the festivals, which are the major ritual events for members of the DLM, are money-making events. The participants, most of whom are members, must pay large amounts of money (fifty to one hundred dollars) to participate, and sometimes the festivals attract thousands of followers.[5]

Nordquist's (1978) study of the Ananda group (ACV) located in the foothills of the Sierra Nevada mountains in California reveals another pattern of support that has not incorporated public solicitation in any large degree (also see Kriyananda, 1972). A large amount of financial support for the first few years of this more inwardly focused cooperative came directly from the founder, Swami Kriyananda, who spent a great deal of time giving courses to people in order to raise needed funds. Other founding members worked at outside jobs and contributed earnings to the group. Sizable membership fees are now charged to new members and a monthly fee is also expected. The money is usually earned by working in the "cottage industries" that the group has established and which operate on a capitalistic basis and pay salaries to worker-members. Most of the property of the group is owned collectively and community building projects are funded by the collective.

The Jesus Movement group, CCO, (Richardson, et al., 1979) has been very aggressive at spreading its message of fundamentalism in a number of different ways and, as indicated, might also seem to qualify for the category of world-transforming. But even if CCO is not included in the world-transforming category the group is of interest as a large communal

---

[5]This information on the Netherlands was furnished by Jan van der Lans and Frans Derks, from their research on the DLM in the Netherlands, (see Derks, 1978, and Derks and van der Lans, 1981, for reports from this research).

organization which has *not* used street solicitation as a support method, even though it might have found more support for such tactics than the UC and HK because of the more acceptable fundamentalist Christian ideology of the group. Instead of depending on public solicitation the group evolved fairly quickly from a situation of dependence on others to a "mixed" economy that depended not only on outside agencies and other assistance, but also on the work of members at jobs outside the group. CCO adopted a scripturally-justified "work motif" that led them to a situation of nearly total independence of others (see Richardson, et al., 1979:100-101). They developed large work teams in several agricultural enterprises and sometimes the teams were hired out to private individuals and firms or to government agencies. Large amounts of money were generated in this way, and none was raised through public solicitation such as was done by the UC.

FUND RAISING IN SOME NONCOMMUNAL GROUPS AND MOVEMENTS

As indicated, it can be argued that some noncommunal movements are world transforming. That point will not be pressed here because the thrust of these comments is not so much definitional as it is to illustrate that public solicitation, while it is the most visible and controversial of the fund-raising techniques used by the new religions, is not the general mode of support for most of the groups, whether they be communal or noncommunal. There are a large number of noncommunal newer religious groups and movements and their financial methods usually differ considerably from those of groups which are communal. There is generally less overhead cost for noncommunal groups because the groups are not required to care for members and participants on a twenty-four-hour basis. But some such groups may develop elaborate services to offer affluent constituencies, and they can successfully charge sizable fees for the services offered.

A good case in point is the Scientology movement that generates considerable money through its course fees (Wallis, 1976:179; Straus, 1979; and Bainbridge and Stark, 1980:132, for some discussions of the cost associated with becoming "clear"). The organization is not communal, although during one period of its history it operated a fleet of ships known as Sea Org, which, of course, meant that those on the ships were living communally. Straus's (1979b) informative analysis of life on Sea Org reveals that approximately 1,000 people were involved in this operation at one time, and he also says that some Scientologists live together "on land" but only because they share common interests and world view, and not because the organization requires it. The organization itself is a large network of Scientology churches which sells services to interested members of the public and to regular participants in the auditing the organization offers. This service organization is the major source of funds for this organization and estimates of gross income range up to 100 million dollars a year in the U.S. alone (see Weldon, 1975:420).

TM is also a well-known but noncommunal organization which has become financially strong. Johnston (1980) insightfully discusses how the organization has become a "marketed social movement" because of the willingness of its leaders to orient the movement totally toward the selling of TM techniques to the general public.[6] The deliberateness of those leading TM's development seems to be a contrast to the accidental and unplanned nature of the development of funding mechanisms in some of the other groups discussed. The very rational tactics used to attract members of several target populations have been successful and, apparently, large amounts of money have been generated. Weldon (1975) claims that more than 60 million dollars was collected by TM in the U.S. alone during 1970-1975.

Groups such as Scientology and TM seldom get involved in direct street solicitation but may use various advertising techniques and make use of personal contacts for recruitment. Apparently because of considerable interest in techniques for self-improvement there is a very large market for groups like Scientology, est, TM, Silva Mind Control, and other such groups that offer courses for a fee (see Westley, 1978, for a discussion of functions served by such groups). Thus some such groups have been able to amass large sums of money through this approach to financing.

Gerlach and Hine (1970:50-55) have a brief discussion of fund raising for the Neo-Pentecostal movement (NPM), which differs significantly from TM or Scientology, but is mainly noncommunal. However, again we find that public solicitation is *not* a primary means of gaining funds. Perhaps the NPM should not be considered here on the grounds

---

[6]New religious groups are not alone, of course, in their use of modern marketing techniques. See the interesting and revealing discussion of this issue in Ashton (1977) of Mormon concerns with their public image and their efforts to do something about that image.

that it is not "world transforming," but many members of the movement would argue about such a designation, citing ideological factors and growth rates to counter the idea that they are not engaged in something world transforming. Gerlach and Hine point out that the NPM is funded mostly through internal sources. Tithing (giving ten percent of income) is the chief source of money, although special "love offerings" provide money for special causes. People involved in the movement also sometimes make large personal financial sacrifices to promote the cause of which they are a part.

OTHER FUND-RAISING METHODS OF THE UC, HK, AND SIMILAR GROUPS

As indicated, the Bromley and Shupe paper, because of its focus on public solicitation, may inadvertently mislead about the history and variety of fund-raising methods used by the HK and UC. Other discussions of the UC's public solicitation in particular may contribute to this partial picture of UC fund-raising methods (see Welles, 1978; Lester, 1978; and Underwood and Underwood, 1979). However, Lofland points out (1977:282) that for the first twelve years the UC depended nearly totally on contributions from members who had outside jobs. The group also started a few small businesses, but these were not major elements in UC funding at that time. After 1971 money was received from a number of sources (Lofland, 1977:289-91). Some apparently came from Moon himself (his business enterprises), or from other branches of the movement, particularly in Japan. There were also some allegations that the Korean and American CIAs were involved in some funding (see U.S. Government, 1978), although this has not been proven and the allegation has been scoffed at by one UC critic (see Welles, 1978:246). Lofland suggests that the largest amounts came through the street peddling of handcrafted items made or obtained by the UC, but he allows that some funds still came from the many small business ventures operated by the local UC groups (restaurants, janitorial services, gas stations, and so forth, and that new members and the parents of members still contributed significant amounts of money. This general picture of the diverse history of UC fund-raising is also supported by Bromley and Shupe's book on the UC (1979b), by Welles (1978), by Mickler (1980—a member of the UC who did a master's thesis on the early history of the group) and by information on UC development in England. Some comments about the other funding sources for the HK have already been mentioned (publishing and incense). Besides these the HK has apparently also been the recipient of some donations of land, buildings, and money that have been used to develop temples and ashrams in various parts of the world (Judah, 1974:44-45).

The fund-raising history of a group most like the UC and HK in its use of public solicitation—the COG—has, with a major exception, followed a similar pattern to that of the UC and HK (see Davis and Richardson, 1976; and Richardson and Davis, 1982). Funds and donations of property and other support have been received from members and sympathetic outsiders. Some methods of obtaining support have been quite ingenious—"house-sitting" for financial institutions in England, for one example. But many of its operations such as its music businesses and special youth-oriented "night clubs" have not usually been money making. These have been a drain on the coffers of the group because they were developed primarily as efforts at evangelism. The COG has realized most of its money in recent years from its "litnessing" (street distribution of literature), but public solicitation has by no means been the only source of support for all the COG's colorful history.

Another group that might be considered "world transforming," even though it is a "psychotherapy cult," is the Power described by Bainbridge (1978). This satanist group used public solicitation (referred to as "donating") during part of its history, but it also experimented with several different ways of supporting the organization. New members were required to give up their possessions and inheritances and all members of this mainly communal group were required to turn over a tithe of their outside income if they were working. The group also begged for food and other things (referred to as "retrieving"). The group charged fees for psychic readings and similar activities. But earlier in its history, during its formative years in England especially, the Power practiced a variant of psychotherapy and was able to support itself in this way. The public solicitation phase was developed later, once the group had come to America.

This history of many different fund-raising methods being tried by the HK, the COG, the Power, and the UC is probably similar to that of other communal organizations that must find a way to support their life-style. Zablocki's thorough discussion of Bruderhof economic matters indicates such a pattern of experimentation for them. It was only after they received the toy business as a part of absorbing a smaller group that they oriented themselves completely in the direction of this profitable industry (see Zablocki, 1971:130-138). Ofshe (1980) discusses similar patterns for an "old" organization, Synanon, which has made a deliberate effort to become accepted as a new religion in recent years. Experimentation was the key to Synanon economics, and sometimes that meant massive street solicitation (that is, raffle ticket sales) but often it did not.

Thus we see that public solicitation is just one of many ways to secure funding for communal religious and quasi-religious groups, and it may not even be the most important. It does gain considerable attention and even notoriety, however, as the history of the UC, the COG, and the HK demonstrates.

THEORETICAL CONSIDERATIONS

The Bromley-Shupe paper is informative, but it does not relate to relevant theoretical ideas of some commune theorists (see earlier citations). Here a few selections from the commune theory literature will be discussed in brief to offer ideas for those studying new religions. Also, it is hoped that these works will demonstrate the need for researchers of new religious groups to gather data on financial considerations.[7]

Kanter offers a lengthy introduction to the section on "Work and Property" in her edited volume *Communes: Creating and Managing the Collective Life* (1973:223-30), in which she proposes a three-part classification scheme for communes in terms of their "primary economic stance." Economic *generalists* attempt to be economically self-sufficient and are often "comprehensive villages;" economic *specialists* develop one or more "specialized enterprises" which allow them to sell something for the public for needed funds; and economic *dependents* do not develop internal methods of support and must depend on participation in "external enterprises."

---

[7]This section does not mean to imply that the ideas from the literature on communal groups can only be tested and applied to communal new religious groups. Certainly some of the ideas are specifically applicable to communal groups, but a great number of the ideas (and the general questions about raising and allocating funds) plainly are applicable to *all* of the new religious organizations. As Richardson, and others (1979:94-97) note, commune theorists could also benefit from paying more attention to religious groups instead of following tendencies in the commune literature which lumps all "religious" communes in a residual category that is not dealt with in depth. This tendency derives from the fascination of some commune theorists with the hippie or left-oriented communes that have proliferated recently. Particularly the commune literature is deficient in explaining much about *federations of communes* or organizations such as those developed by the COG, CCO, HK, and the UC. Kanter's (1972) discussion of Synanon is a major exception to this comment.

This seems a useful way to categorize new religious groups. For instance, the HK seems now to be more of a specialist organization, especially when one considers its emphasis on the incense business. The ACV group seems to be an effort at a generalist approach, as does CCO during most of its history. The UC focus in recent years on public solicitation may make it a dependent organization now, but it is making some efforts to become a specialist group that can live off its own businesses (see Bromley and Shupe, 1979b:237, and Welles, 1978). DLM, the Power, and COG have been mainly dependent (with some qualifications), an orientation also found by Pilarzyk and Jacobson (1977) in their study of the Milwaukee Jesus People. The classification scheme of Kanter would classify groups like Scientology and TM (and the Power, at first) as specialist organizations which sell something to the public.

Just classifying the organizations is not enough, of course, and the Kanter scheme suggests more. For instance it might be fruitful to examine the *patterns of change* from one category to another in such groups. CCO moved from being a dependent organization initially to become more of a generalist and specialist group, but then evolved into a dependent one again, but at a different level of support and affluence (see Richardson et al., 1979). Why and how such changes occur are important questions. It might also be possible to discern propensities for certain types of groups to become any one of the three types and to examine reasons for such tendencies. For instance, Kanter suggests that contemporary rural hippie communes and urban communes are usually dependent. She also notes (1973:225) that religious groups frequently get involved in "group enterprises" because their theology can give a special meaning to work as a part of the commitment process, a finding of Richardson, and others (1979), who also cite social-psychological reasons for the "team" approach.

Kanter's comments on the social meaning of work and the various practices developed by some of the groups she studied are also suggestive. She mentions several schemes that have been used to insure the contribution of work to the social aspect of communal life, including such things as job rotation, the development of dual specializations to allow variety, and using a team approach to much work. She discusses the way that children have been integrated into work patterns in communes, and the general reintegration of work and life that takes place in communes, and she claims that communes deliberately choose certain types of work to further social and spiritual goals and thereby make a statement to their members and the world about "what they are."

In her discussion are a number of testable ideas that could be examined in new religious groups. Her ideas on the meaning of work and how that relates to group goals are significant notions demonstrating that we need research on the various ways that group goals are implemented in the new religious groups. The relationship of work to ideology can be examined, and the meaning of rituals surrounding work (including fund raising) ought to be more carefully studied. Questions about the relationship of life and work and the integration of children into the occupational and social life of the organization can be examined in the new groups as well, both to use the groups as a "testing ground," and in order to find out more about the groups themselves.

Abrams and McCulloch (1976:173) indicate that some deliberately choose asceticism when they do not have to and collectively decide *not* to earn as much as they could if desired (Zablocki's study of the Bruderhof illustrates this point—see Zablocki, 1971:35). Why and how such decisions are made can and should be investigated in the new religions, if for no other reason than the fact that some people and groups have been so critical of the economically deprived life-style alleged to be the norm in such groups. Also, since public solicitation is, as Bromley and Shupe point out, so "easy" and so fruitful a method of support, we are left to explain why *all* new religious groups do not choose to use the tactic. Some (probably most) of the groups decide not to use public solicitation and thereby apparently choose to live a somewhat more ascetic (or at least different) life-style by virtue of the decision. The circumstances of such "vows of comparative group poverty" and radically different approaches to the world are of both theoretical and practical significance. For instance, explaining why and how the two Jesus Movement groups—CCO and the COG—chose different approaches to group support is of interest. CCO chose the route of physical labor and self-support (see Richardson, et. al., 1979) whereas the COG chose a path that emphasized public solicitation through aggressive distribution of their literature, known as "Mo letters" (see Davis and Richardson, 1976) and more recently, the use of sex as a way of gaining at least some support.[8] Both

[8]Both CCO and COG derived from fundamentalist Christianity, and both are glossolalic and evangelical. However, there are significant differences, including the liberal

groups achieved considerable economic strength, but the support methods chosen seemed to contribute to making them very different organizations, even though both were communal and shared a somewhat similar ideological base.

Abrams and McCulloch offer other intriguing ideas on financing that could be examined with newer religious groups. They suggest (1976:173) that the real economic efficiency of the commune is not realized unless some of the members *are* earning low incomes, an idea that seems counter to common sense. They also suggest, in their analysis of internal allocation schemes (1976:171-73), that perceived equity is more important than formal equality in any resource allocation scheme, an idea that raises questions about how such perceptions are developed and managed within the group. They mention that all communes have implicit or explicit notions of an internal wage paid to members who do a disproportionate share of the domestic chores, a notion that could be tested and extended to incorporate implicit wage rates for *any* member or leader doing *any* special task (including fund-raising) assigned by the collectivity or its leadership. How such implicit and explicit wage rates are developed within the group would be significant information to compare with perceptions of outsiders. Since some, especially Delgado (1979), have in all seriousness raised the issue of whether or not members of the new religions fit a legal and constitutional definition of a slave, more attention to internal allocation schemes, questions of equity, and implicitly accepted wage rates seems to be needed.

Stein (1973) relates the type of distribution system in communes to the level of affluence, and also suggests that economic success can lead to tension and possibly to group schism. He says that this tendency toward schism with increased affluence develops because of pressures to move back to a more capitalistic mode with the increased material affluence. He says communes usually are forced to start as *socialistic* ventures out of necessity, but that increased affluence allows the adoption of a form of *humanism* in allocation of rewards, and that this evolution can then continue (if more affluence develops) to bring back some elements of *capitalism*, such as differential rewards. His analysis suggests that communes (or new religions) that are less than completely successful on the economic

---

approach to sexual matters that seems to be the case in the COG (see Wallis, 1979; Davis, 1981; Richardson, 1982), and the fact that the COG developed such a large international organization (see Davis and Richardson, 1976).

front may well have a better change to survive because the pressures to return to capitalistic economic arrangements are lessened. He mentions efforts of groups like the Bruderhof and the kibbutzim movement to deal with increased prosperity and says that any economically successful group must attend to this crucial problem of the effects (unintended) of affluence.

Stein's analysis is replete with ideas that can be applied to both communal and noncommunal new religious groups and his work also seems related to the classical question from Weber (1930) about the relationship of religious ideas to economic practices. The interesting study by Barclay (1969) of a communally organized group of Mennonites which was able to suppress the tendency toward capitalism suggests, at least, that Stein's ideas are in need of some qualification. Some of the new religious groups, especially those related to the Judeo-Christian tradition, would seem to offer excellent contexts in which to address this important issue.

The case of CCO seems instructive in this regard. Richardson, and others (1979) described in detail the rapidly developing affluence in CCO and the reasons for it, and stated (p. 64), "A most interesting question concerns the ability of the group to withstand the pressure of the newfound prosperity—pressures that might well lead to dramatic but as yet unforeseen changes in the organization." Since that comment was written there have been difficulties within CCO, and the group has apparently divided into at least two major segments over issues related to the increased rationality of the group. One segment has reaffiliated with the large youth-oriented and "hip" church from which CCO initially came, and one remains in charge of much of the property amassed by the group. Full details are not yet available on what led to this schism, but Stein's ideas are suggestive.[9]

Stein's ideas also offer some interesting questions to pose about some of the other groups. For instance, one would expect that the tendency Stein posits would reinforce the anticommunist ideology of the UC (and vice versa), whereas in some other groups trying to live a communistically oriented life (based, say, on early Christianity, as with

---

[9]Information is being gathered about this division in an effort to relate it to the issue just raised and to factors on which data has already been obtained; we also want to test some notions from the small literature on schisms in religious groups (see Wilson, 1971, and Wellis 1979, for instance).

CCO) the tendency toward capitalism and group ideology might conflict. It would indeed be ironic if members of the Jesus Movement communes who joined at least in part to flee the contradictions of capitalism could get so easily drawn back into a capitalistic way of life through the very success of their communal ventures.

CONCLUSIONS

The thrust of this paper has been to build on the good beginning by Bromley and Shupe (1980) on research concerning economic policies and practices of the newer religious groups. Their work is valuable, particularly in offering more understanding of public solicitation as a method of financing. However, their paper may have implied a greater reliance on public solicitation by such groups than is actually the case, and thus may have left the impression that public solicitation is the most prevalent and significant method of financing such groups. This is probably not the case. Also, there seemed to be some conceptual problems with their paper in its use of the "world-transforming movement" idea.

In the present paper an effort has been made to elucidate the conceptual difficulty of the Bromley and Shupe paper and also to demonstrate that public solicitation is only one of many ways that new religious groups support themselves. Most groups go through a multistep history of experimentation with support methods and select the ones that seem most successful and acceptable to the group ideology.[10]

Also in this paper an effort has been made to tie the study of new religions into the related area of commune studies. Plainly, many of the same issues confound scholars in both areas and sharing information could very well result in a cross-fertilization of ideas. This paper has presented a few specific ideas that have developed out of the considerable study that commune theorists have made of economic policies and practices in communal groups in order to demonstrate both the applicability and testability of such ideas within the new religions.

An appendix to the paper offers a modification of the "economic" part of an earlier-presented "data frame" for the study of communal groups (Richardson, 1977a). The modifications incorporate several

---

[10]This does not mean that ideology determines fund-raising methods, of course, but it does mean that any fund-raising method used must eventually be integrated into the belief system of the group, something that may not be difficult to do, given the flexibility of most large systems of thought.

issues that have developed in the study of new religions and also attempt to insure that the proposed data frame will be useful for groups that are noncommunal or which have only some communal segments. It is hoped that researchers will find this data frame valuable and that further improvements in the proposed approach can be offered. If this approach is found to be useful, then it will help redress the pervasive problem of lack of information about the economic policies and practices of the newer religious groups which have caught the interest of the public, government agencies, and scholars.[11]

[11]This "data frame" is also designed to incorporate the issues alluded to in footnote 2, above, which will be developed in a later paper.

APPENDIX

The following is a suggested "data frame" for gathering data on economic policies of the new religions. Detailed information on the considerations listed would be useful in dealing with the theoretical questions mentioned and also in helping government officials and the general public to understand better the economics of the new religions. This data frame is a modification of part of the data frame suggested for commune studies in Richardson (1977a).

ECONOMIC CONSIDERATIONS IN STUDIES OF NEW RELIGIOUS GROUPS

A. Organizational or Federation Level (if a "federation" of communes or of branches of a noncommunal or partially communal organization)
   1. *Method(s) of economic support for organization as a whole*
      a. "Entrance fees" and/or regular "dues" or fees for individual members and/or clients and/or special communes or groups
      b. "Welfare" (public and private largesse)
      c. Gathering or scavenging for goods and food
      d. Working for nonmembers (by individual members, teams of members, or even entire specific communes or branches)
      e. Producing goods, services and/or agricultural/livestock products for sale and/or barter to nonmembers
      f. Producing goods, services, and/or agricultural products for use within the organization
   2. *Degree to which organization is self-supporting*
      a. Totally self-supporting
      b. Partially self-supporting (to what degree and type of support)
      c. Totally dependent on outside "unearned" income
   3. *Level of support available, for the organization as a whole, from all sources*
   4. *Variations (if any) in level and type of support for specific communes or branches*
   5. *How economic support is administered and how such decisions are made*
      a. More centralized system
      b. Specific communes or branches autonomous and more self-supporting
      c. Mixed system
   6. *Division of economic functions by commune or branch*
      a. Involving all communes or branches
      b. Involving some communes or branches
      c. Not present
   7. *Organization's position (and variations) on private ownership by specific communes or branches, and by individual members, and members and/or families*
   8. *Organization's economic priorities, including way in which leaders are supported*
   9. *Effects of economic considerations on other facets of organization life, and vice versa (ideology, recruitment and resocialization and organizational structure, especially)*
   10. *Ways in which "surplus funds" available to group are invested, and information on economic impact of such investments on locale or specific industry (or area of investment)*
   11. *Tax status of organization, and description of relationship the organization has had with tax and/or other governmental agencies*

12. *Changes in (or plans to change) any of above considerations over time*
13. *Other economic considerations of import*

B. SPECIFIC COMMUNE ON BRANCH LEVEL (see section A for details)

1. *Method(s) of support*
2. *Degree to which commune or branch is self-supporting*
3. *Level of support available for commune or branch from all sources*
4. *Variations (if any) in level and type of support for individual members (or families), by commune or branch*
5. *How decisions about economic support are made for commune or branch*
6. *Division of economic functions within commune or branch*
7. *Commune or branch position on private ownership (and any variations by class of member) for members and member families*
8. *Economic priorities of commune or branch, including economic support for leaders and "investment policy"*
9. *Interplay of economic considerations with other aspects of commune or branch life*
10. *Any problems with government agencies that affect economic life of commune or branch*
11. *Change in (and plans to change) any of the above over time*
12. *Other economic considersations of import*

C. INDIVIDUAL LEVEL (and family level, if "families" allowed)

1. *Method(s) of support both direct and indirect, for members (and families), by category of membership (if differentiation exists), and tax status of support*
2. *Degree to which each member (and family) is self-supporting, and any within-commune or branch variations*
3. *Level of support available from all sources for individuals (and families), and variations by marital status, leadership status, or other variables*
4. *Methods of administering economic support and making such decisions within commune or branch, and any relationship this has to level of support*
5. *How much private property is allowed for individuals (and families)*
6. *How economic considerations affect a person's life in the commune or branch*
7. *What skills are taught to members or clients that are of possible economic benefit to members in the future?*
8. *What is "refund policy" for members or clients who leave organization or no longer participate in its activities?*
9. *What economic alternatives are available to members or participants outside the group?*
10. *Changes in (or plans to change) any of the above considerations over time*
11. *Other economic considerations of import*

REFERENCES

Abrams, Philip and Andrew McCulloch
1976 *Communes, Sociology and Society*. Cambridge: Cambridge University Press.

Andrews, E. D.
1963 *The People Called Shakers*. New York: Dover Publications.

Ashton, Wendell J.
1977 "Marketing the Mormon Image: An Interview with Wendell J. Ashton." *Dialogue* 10 (Spring): 15-20.

Bainbridge, William S.
1978 *Satan's Power: A Deviant Psychotherapy Cult*. Berkeley CA: University of California Press.

Bainbridge, W. S., and Rodney Stark
1980 "Scientology: To Be Perfectly Clear." *Sociological Analysis* 41:2:128-36.

Barclay, H. B.
1969 "The Protestant Ethic versus the Spirit of Capitalism." *Review of Religious Research* 10:3:151-58.

Beckford, James A.
1975 *The Trumpet of Prophecy: A Sociological Study of Jehovah's Witnesses*. Oxford: Basil Blackwell.

Bennett, J. W.
1967 *Hutterite Brethern*. Stanford CA: Stanford University Press.

Bromley, D. G., and A. D. Shupe, Jr.
1979 *Moonies in America: Cult, Church and Crusade*. Beverly Hills CA: Sage.

1980 "Financing the New Religions: A Resource Mobilization Approach." *Journal for the Scientific Study of Religion* 19:3:227-39.

Davis, Rex
1981 "Where Have the Children Gone?" Paper presented at British Sociological Association Sociology of Religion Study Group Conference on "New Religious Movements," Lincoln, England.

Davis, Rex, and J. T. Richardson
1976 "The Organization and Functioning of the Children of God." *Sociological Analysis* 37:4:321-39.

Delgado, Richard
1979 "Religious Totalism as Slavery." *Review of Law and Social Change* 9:1:51-68.

Derks, Frans
1978 "Differences in Social Isolation between Members of Two New Religious Movements (Ananda Marga and Divine Light Mission)." *Proceedings of the Colloquy of European Psychologists of Religion at Nijmegen*. Department of Psychology of Culture and Religion, Catholic University, Nijmegen, The Netherlands.

Derks, Frans, and Jan van der Lans
1981 "Subgroups in Divine Light Mission Membership." Presented at British Sociological Association Conference on "New Religious Movements," Lincoln, England.

Gerlach, Luther, and Virginia Hine
1970 *People, Power, Change: Movements of Social Transformation.* Indianapolis: Bobbs-Merrill.

Horowitz, I. L., ed.
1978 *Science, Sin, and Scholarship.* Cambridge MA: MIT Press.

Hostetler, J. A.
1963 *Amish Society.* Baltimore: John Hopkins Press.
1974 *Hutterite Society.* Baltimore: John Hopkins Press.

Johnston, Hank
1980 "The Marketed Social Movement: A Case Study of the Rapid Growth of TM." *Pacific Sociological Review* 23:3:333-54.

Judah, Stillson
1974 *Hare Krishna and the Counter Culture.* New York: Wiley.
1977 "Attitudinal Changes among Members of the Unification Church." Presented at the annual meeting of the American Association for the Advancement of Science, Denver, Colorado.

Kanter, R. M.
1972 *Cambridge and Community: Communes and Utopians in Sociological Perspective.* Cambridge MA: Harvard University Press.
1973 Editor. *Communes: Creating and Managing the Collective Life.* New York: Harper and Row.

Kephart, W. M.
1974 "Why they Fail—A Sociohistorical Analysis of Religious and Secular Communes." *The Journal of Comparative Family Studies* 5:2:130-40.

Klassen, Peter J.
1964 *The Economics of Anabaptism—1525-1560.* The Hague: Mouton.

Kriyananda, Swami
1972 *Cooperative Communities—How to Start Them, and Why.* Nevada City CA: Ananda Publications.

Lester, Marianne
1978 "Profits, Politics, Power: The Heart of the Controversy." In *Science, Sin, and Scholarship.* I. L. Horowitz, ed. Cambridge MA: MIT Press.

Leone, Mark
1979 *Roots of Modern Mormonism.* Cambridge MA: Harvard University Press.

Lofland, John
1977 *Doomsday Cult: A Study of Conversion, Proselytization, and Maintenance of Faith.* New York: Irvington Press.
1978 " 'Becoming a World-Saver' Revisited." In *Conversion Careers.* J. T. Richardson, ed. Beverly Hills CA: Sage. Pp. 10-23.

Messer, Jeanne
1976 "Guru Maharaji-ji and the Divine Light Mission." In *The New Religious Consciousness.* C. Glock and R. Bellah, eds. Berkeley CA: University of California Press. Pp. 52-72.

Mickler, M. I.
1980 "A History of the Unification Church in the Bay Area: 1960-1974." Master of Arts Thesis, Graduate Theological Union, Berkeley CA.

Mowery, Jeni
1978 "Systemic Requisites of Communal Groups." *Alternative Lifestyles* 1:2:235-61.

Nordquist, Ted
1978 *Ananda Cooperative Village: A Study of the Values and Attitudes of a New Age Religious Community:* Monograph series, no. 16. The religionshistoriska institut. Uppsala University, Uppsala, Sweden.

Ofshe, Richard
1980 "The Social Development of the Synanon Cult: The Managerial Strategy of Organizational Transformation." *Sociological Analysis* 41:2:109-27.

Pilarzyk, Thomas
1978 "The Origin, Development, and Decline of a Youth Culture Religion: An Application of Sectarianization Theory." *Review of Religious Research* 20:23-43.

Pilarzyk, T. J., and C. K. Jacobson
1977 "Christians in the Youth Culture: The Life History of an Urban Commune." *Wisconsin Sociologist* 14 (Fall): 136-51.

Richardson, James T.
1977a "A Data-Frame for Commune Research." *Communal Studies Newsletter* 4:1-13.

1978 Editor. *Conversion Careers: In and Out of the New Religions*. Beverly Hills CA: Sage Publications.

Richardson, J. T. and Rex Davis
1983 "Experiential Fundamentalism: Revisions of Orthodoxy in Jesus Movement Groups. *Journal of the Academy of Religion*, forthcoming.

Richardson, J. T., M. W. Steward, and R. B. Simmonds
1979 *Organized Miracles: A Study of a Contemporary Youth, Communal, Fundamentalist Organization.* New Brunswick NJ: Transaction Books.

Rigby, Andrew
1974 *Alternative Realities: A Study of Communes and Their Members.* London: Routledge and Kegan Paul.

Robbins, Thomas and Dick Anthony
1979 "Cults, Brainwashing, and Countersubversion." *The Annals* 446 (November): 78-90.

Shey, Thomas H.
1977 "Why Communes Fail: A Comparative Analysis of the Viability of Danish and American Communes." *Journal of Marriage and the Family* 39 (August): 605-13.

Stein, Barry A.
1973 "The Internal Economics of Communes." In *Communes*. R. Moss Kanter, ed. New York: Harper and Row. Pp. 264-76.

Stoner, C., and J. Parke
1977 *All God's Children: The Cult Experience—Salvation or Slavery?* Radnor PA: Chilton.

Straus, Roger
1979 "Inside Scientology: Everyday Life in a Societally Deviant World," unpublished paper.

Underwood, Barbara, and Betty Underwood
1979 *Hostage to Heaven.* New York: Clarkson N. Potter, Inc.

U.S. Government
1978 *Investigation of Korean-American relations: Report of the Subcommittee on International Relations, U.S. House of Representatives.* Washington DC: U.S. Government Printing Office.

Wallis, Roy
1976 "Observations of the Children of God." *Sociological Review* 24:4:807-28.

1975 "Societal Reactions to Scientology." In *Sectarianism.* R. Wallis, ed. New York: Halstead.

1979 *Salvation and Protest: Studies in Social and Religious Movements.* New York: St. Martin's Press.

Weldon, John
1978 "A Sampling of the New Religions: Four Groups Described." *International Review of Mission* 67:268:407-26.

Welles, Chris
1978 "The Eclipse of Sun Myung Moon." *Science, Sin, and Scholarship.* I. Horowitz, ed. Cambridge MA: MIT Press. Pp. 242-58.

Westley, Frances
1978 " 'The Cult of Man': Durkheim's Predictions and Religious Movements." *Sociological Analysis* 39:2:135-45.

Wilson, John
1971 "The Sociology of Schism." *A Sociological Yearbook of Religion in Britain.* M. Hill, ed. London: SCM Press. Pp. 1-20.

Zablocki, Benjamin
1971 *Joyful Community.* Baltimore MD: Penguin Books.

PENTECOSTAL POWER: THE "CHARISMATIC RENEWAL MOVEMENT" AND THE POLITICS OF PENTECOSTAL EXPERIENCE

by Andrew Walker

ONE OF THE JOYS of critical rationalism, it seems to me, is that one does not have to be afraid to admit mistakes. Indeed, it is almost a moral imperative to rework previous research material in the light of present experience. Recently, sociologists have been forced into a major rethinking and a clearer understanding of the phenomenon of Pentecostalism. What has happened, in a way, is that it has gotten out of hand: what was once thought by many social scientists to be a sectarian expression of economic and social deprivation[1] has turned out to be a massive social movement beyond sectarian boundaries and incorporating the middle classes and the intelligentsia.

In this paper I attempt to chart the emergence of this new Pentecostalism, highlighting its distinguishing features and demonstrating its similarities and differences with the old Pentecostalism. In particular, I want to identify three stages, or phases, of its growth. This identification will concentrate on the power struggles between the Pentecostalists and their opponents within the mainstream churches. Finally, I shall discuss Pentecostal understanding of Christian practice, the attitude to the secular world, and the Pentecostals' future in Christendom.

---

[1]Some writers still think the same way. Cf. Anderson's *Vision of The Disinherited* (Oxford University Press, 1980).

To begin sensibly a caveat is needed, for the phenomenon of the new Pentecostalism has been worldwide and has involved between one and a half to two million people. No one paper can hope to capture the diversity of practice, the differing theological interpretations by participants, and the national and regional differences that together constitute the movement of charismatic renewal. For the sake of clarity and expediency, therefore, I shall concentrate on the growth of Pentecostalism in the Western world[2] with particular reference to Britain. This affords me not only a manageable package, but allows me to rely on participant observation, personal interviews, and informants.[3] Although it can be argued that this is not the most scientific of methodologies, I contend that it is far more desirable and dependable than having to rely on the idealized versions of Pentecostalism to be found in apologist literature. (For readers who are not familiar with earlier Pentecostal nomenclature or sociological jargon concerning Pentecostalism, I have added a short glossary rather than burden the text with endless definitions.)

CLASSICAL PENTECOSTALISM AS FORERUNNER TO THE CHARISMATIC MOVEMENT

Modern charismatics often tell you that Pentecostalism is as old as the New Testament and that *glossolalia* is to be found throughout church history. Such statements are contestable as truth statements, but are undeniably powerful as legitimating devices whereby charismatics can demonstrate that Pentecostal experience has always been the lot of the saints of Church history. It is true, in fact, that tongue-speaking—the distinguishing feature of Pentecostal spirituality—has played some part in the life of the historic church. It is more true to say, however, that it mainly was featured among heretical groups, or was an epiphenomenal aspect of the lives of certain saints and a few Protestant sects. Neither the great Methodist upsurgence nor the Evangelical and/or Holiness move-

---

[2]This is not meant to imply that the Third World Pentecostal movements are less significant. On the contrary, I believe with Prof. Walther Hollenweger that these groups probably have more to contribute to theology and to Christendom as a whole than do Western Pentecostals.

[3]This work is in three stages: (1) participant observation among classical Pentecostal and Roman Catholic groups from 1970 to 1975; (2) consultant and/or representative to Renewal consultations from 1978 to 1980; and (3) consultation, research, and reporting for British Broadcasting Corporation—television and radio—and London Weekend Television from 1980 to 1982.

ments of the nineteenth century exhibit tongue speaking in any major way. The Irvingites stand out as a distinctive, although small, Pentecostal movement of the nineteenth century, but they prefigure what I believe to be a fascinating yet unexplained fact: Pentecostalism is essentially a twentieth-century phenomenon.

Before the Great War had begun in 1914, classical Pentecostalism had emerged in both Europe and the United States of America. The Holiness movements, on both sides of the Atlantic, were the primary crucible for the new sects: their belief in and commitment to the "second experience" soon became the "second blessing," and eventually the more specific Pentecostal doctrine of the "Baptism of the Holy Spirit." In America the leadership of the fast-growing sects came from all classes and races, but the bulk of the new ranters and enthusiasts were black or poor urban and rural working class. European Pentecostalism grew from inside Lutheranism and Anglicanism as well as Holiness and Free-Evangelical churches. In Britain, particularly, the role of the aristocracy and the upper classes is far more important in the rise of classical Pentecostalism than is usually realized.[4]

Many Pentecostalists, even after the Great War had given way to the "roaring twenties," wished to remain in their own churches and denominations. They faced great hostility, however, from both the leaders and consumers of mainstream Christianity. Outbursts in tongues or prophecy and the practicing of "divine healing" combined with wildly enthusiastic services, exorcisms, and adventist eschatology, were too much for traditionalists. Many Christians interpreted this Pentecostalism as blasphemous, demonic, or heretical. Driven out from the mainstream churches, and driven on by the ever-urging Spirit, Pentecostalists soon became "The Pentecostals," forming in groups behind the enclaves of increasingly world-rejecting sects.

The great revivals of classical Pentecostalism continued in bursts throughout Europe and America until the Second World War. Much of the original fervor gave way to ritualized chorus singing and stereotyped extempore prayer and preaching. Standards of education rose, and although classical Pentecostals have remained firmly rooted in fundamentalist Evangelicalism, they look more and more (with their professional pastorate and Bible schools) like established sects and

---

[4]Walther Hollenweger rightly insists on this.

denominations. In the United States, and increasingly in Britain, it is no longer accurate to classify Classical groups as disinherited working-classes; like the Methodists before them, Pentecostals have achieved considerable social mobility. (It is also true that Pentecostalism remains a powerful influence among those sections of our society that Marx designated *lumpenproletariat*.)

It was often said by the leaders of Pentecostalism in Britain—notably Jeffreys and Gee—that the essence of Pentecost was experience not denomination. They looked forward to a time when the Pentecostal experience of the "baptism of the Spirit" would become the birthright of all Christians in the mainstream churches. The classical mode of Pentecostalism would wither away—would become redundant—if and when there should be an outpouring of God's Spirit upon the whole church. Their notion of church may have been theologically vague, but they hoped and believed that the *pneuma* of God would revitalize the dying body of Christianity.

Today many classical Pentecostals are faced with what appears to be the fulfilment of the dream. A vibrant Pentecostalism faces them and assails them from nearly every nook and cranny of Christendom. It is a threat to their very existence, and fear and "sour grapes" are as much part of their reaction as the wonderment and excitement. For many of them, the fact that Pentecostalism has taken root in Catholicism and what they would regard as "modernist" churches is more a cause for concern than for rejoicing.

THE PEOPLE OF THE CHARISMATA

Stage 1: Anarchic Pentecostalism. I think it is important that we do not see the origins and growth of Neo-Pentecostalism in terms of crude diffusionism. It is simply not the case (as some charismatics have claimed) that it started in the Church of the Redeemer in Houston, Texas; from whence it spread to the rest of America and Europe. Neither is it the case that it started first in one denomination or one particular country. From the early 1960s—with a noticeable acceleration after mid-decade—here and there, country after country began to experience a form of Pentecostalism similar experientially to the classical mode but among groups of people within the historic churches and mainstream denominations.

Certainly it was the case that once this unplanned and unorchestrated movement gained momentum, not unnaturally fellow Pentecostals would meet together (often cutting across denominational boundaries), form informal groups, and establish newsletters and journals. It is a well-known phenomenon in science that new discoveries and theories emerge in different parts of the globe even though some of the scientists know nothing of each other's work. I fail to see why it should be so different in the field of religious experience. Once the news is out for all to see, of course, then collaboration and mutual sharing of information and experience take place. As the charismatic movement began to spread many observers wished to write it off as a fad.[5] Such a flimsy judgment looks less than convincing after twenty years of rapid growth.

A more sophisticated and empathetic view of Neo-Pentecostalism came from a Catholic professor, who attempted to see the new religious movement in the context of the counterculture of the mid and late 1960s.

> These movements belong to a post-literary culture which is experience-oriented, unstructured, spontaneous, inward, almost atomistic in its concern for the now at the expense of history, pursuing illumination, dominated by a sense of presence, sure that somewhere there is ultimate worth. To a greater or lesser degree the movement represents a turning back to recapture the original unstructured experience of the meaning of life at a level which, like tongues, is unutterable.[6]

The period from 1965 to 1975 (which roughly encapsulates what I have called "anarchic Pentecostalism") was a time of old-time revivalism in a new, sometimes alien, setting. Catholics, Episcopalians/Anglicans, Lutherans, the Greek Orthodox Church in America, the Church of Scotland, Baptists, Methodists, Presbyterians—and many other smaller groups—were having to come to grips with a Pentecostalism not burning in some extreme sect but in their very midst. Many church leaders were pretending nothing was happening; more strange was the fact that neither the national papers nor the trade press really grasped the extent or the fervor of the charismatic renewal movement.

The Neo-Pentecostals had three major problems, which in my opinion, they never really overcame. Their first problem was to demonstrate to their fellow denominationalists that they were not merely Pentecostals, and certainly not classical Pentecostals. They distanced

---

[5]The religious correspondent for *The Times* told me in telephone conversation that he saw the Renewal as a kind of self-induced therapy.

[6]Kilian McDonell, quoted in E. Sullivan, *Can The Pentecostal Movement Renew the Churches?* (B.C.C. Publication, 1972) 5.

themselves from the latter in a number of ways. First, they preferred the term "charismatic" to the more common substantive, "Pentecostal." For my part, I have yet to be persuaded from the position voiced to me at the World Council of Churches headquarters by a West Indian woman: "Charismatic is just a posh word for Pentecostal." Furthermore, many of the new Pentecostals were middle-class and certainly not fundamentalist in doctrine; for them the classical Pentecostals were admittedly related, but they were either afforded the status of poor cousins or relegated to the undesirable position of skeletons in the closet. The adoption of the word "renewal" as opposed to the more strident "revival" was a further attempt at distancing.

The second problem was more acute and cut across the first problem. What did the Pentecostal experience mean, and how should the new blessing influence worship and liturgy? This was a particularly difficult problem for Roman Catholics who had no ready made-to-hand theology to explain Pentecostalism; nor were they accustomed to the conversion effect of the new experience. I am convinced that Pentecostalism had a strong evangelical and personal appeal to Catholics, more so than to any other denomination. In any event, although it is often forgotten now, many Neo-Pentecostals attended (either openly or surreptitiously) classical Pentecostal services. Some fundamentalist theology was adopted and adapted while much of the ritual was taken over. Testifying to conversion and healing remains to this day, but many of the old hymns and choruses have been revamped into a more contemporary style. (Many of the young Catholic and Episcopalian charismatics who pray with their hands uplifted, sing endless repetitions of short choruses, and utter what traditionalists might think to be sentimental phrases about "Je—sus," have no idea that much of their "natural and spontaneous" behavior in the Lord comes directly from American classical Pentecostalism.)

The third problem for the Neo-Pentecostals was to demonstrate to their fellow denominationalists who were not charismatics that they were not heretical, psychologically unstable, or dangerous. This was not an easy task. Many of the Pentecostals—in the first flush of their experience—were both lax in their church discipline, and unformed in their theology. They were opposed not only by many hierarchs, but by ordinary laypersons who wanted to remain simply Catholic, Baptist (or whatever) without having to take on what appeared to them to be an alien creed and irreverent liturgy. The charismatics responded in two ways: (1) They demonstrated through apologist literature that Pentecostalism belonged to the tradition of their churches, whether Catholic, Protestant, Low, or High.[7] (2) Great emphasis was placed on the renewal of the traditional faith. Catholics, for example, insisted that they had a new love of the mass, a greater desire for the Eucharist, and more time for their rosaries. On the whole, during this phase (despite the very real opposition) the charismatics won more friends than enemies: their enthusiasm, commitment, and a certain "controlled wildness" was contagious. The mainstream Pentecostals maintained their denominational commitment, and showed no sign of forming a new sect, or trying to overturn the conventional wisdom. They emerged (and still remain) Catholics, Anglicans, Methodists, Presbyterians, Baptists, who also happen to be Pentecostal by experience.

During this ten-year period, however, there were many experiments which rarely received mention in apologist literature. In America and England, for example, many charismatic groups dabbled in occultism; there are practices which remain today such as the holding of hands in a circle which seem to owe more to Spiritualism than classical Pentecostalism. Astrology was popular with some groups, and a general intellectual permissiveness seemed part, for some, of the new freedom in the Spirit. Not all permissiveness was intellectual: in England, as in America, touching, hugging, and kissing were widespread. Some groups adopted the secular methods of sensitivity training. In England I know of one community that was closed by the diocesan bishop because of illicit sexual relations. Indeed, wife swapping and reneging on vows of chastity by priests and nuns were by no means that rare. Weird practices of exorcism and excessive emphasis on demonology were the side effects of anarchic Pentecostalism. Leaders were often made aware, sometimes painfully, that when the personality is opened up to its nonrational side, it can reveal the irrational and the dark-shadow side of life as well as authentic and transfiguring experience.

Stage 2: Consolidation, Broadened Horizons, Official Recognition. By 1975, the charismatics had won even the grudging respect of their antagonists. They had not left the denominations for new cults or sects.

---

[7]For example: E. D. O'Conner, C.S.C., *The Pentecostal Movement in the Catholic Church* (Ave Maria Press, 1971); M. Harper, *None Can Guess* (Hodder and Stoughton, 1971).

Many of the more embarrassing fellow travelers had left or been forced out. Furthermore, new, freewheeling forms of liturgy were acceptable to many of the noncharismatics who objected to the content rather than the form of Pentecostalism. Guitars, dancing, challenging drama were becoming commonplace in secular-oriented parishes as well as charismatic congregations.

Both in Europe and America, the charismatics had shown that being Pentecostal meant more than speaking in tongues: for many it was a new dimension of spiritual and psychological life. There was a freeing of guilt and inhibition, an acceptance of the nonrational side of life, and a passion for new experiences. Unlike their classical counterparts, many Neo-Pentecostals were free of fundamentalism: they drank alcohol, went to the theatre, took an active interest in politics, and in the case of Catholics, still smoked tobacco. Gradually, even classical Pentecostals became less antagonistic despite differing cultural and class traits.[8]

Ecumenists began to imagine that Pentecostalism might be an important noninstitutional force for church unity. (In fact, Pentecostalism continues to be interdenominational rather than truly ecumenical.) Church leaders, including two popes, held meetings with charismatics. Encouraging noises were made, and much was said during this time not only by apologist writers but also by sympathetic churchmen that the new Pentecostalism was the third force in Christendom.[9]

Charismatics did not realize it at the time, but they were enjoying the peak of the renewal movement. England, for example, could boast tens of thousands who could lay claim to the Spirit experience. The mainstream charismatics shared a common life together through conferences, retreats, interdenominational prayer groups, and conventions. Periodicals and tapes sold were everywhere proclaiming the Pentecostal message. The American Catholic journal, *New Covenant,* was so widespread that it could be found in nearly every Neo-Pentecostal group in Europe. The English magazine, *Renewal,* and the interdenominational organization, the Fountain Trust, not only kept charismatics in touch, but helped

---

[8]See, for example, Alfred Missen's enthusiastic speech delivered at the united conference of Elim and Assemblies of God, "The Pentecostal Movement in the Eighties," 16-19 Nov. 1979. (Missen is the former General Secretary of the Assemblies of God in Britain.)

[9]The other two being Catholicism and Protestantism. The Eastern Orthodox churches were hence removed from Christendom by a stroke of the pen.

to disseminate Pentecostal teaching within the context of traditional Christian practice. Throughout Britain such work—and particularly the leadership of Tom Smail, John Richards, and Michael Harper—did much to calm the fears of anxious Christian leaders.

There was cause for anxiety. The growing number of exorcisms, and an increasing emphasis on demonology was permeating the most respectable of charismatic circles. The American practice (stemming from the maverick side of classical Pentecostalism) of "slaying in the Spirit," with its dramatic effect of Spirit recipients swooning to the ground, was becoming established as normal behavior within the Renewal. On the whole, however, the people of the charismata with their clapping, singing in the Spirit, tongue speaking, healings, and unmistakable enthusiasm, had become part of the mainstream of Christian life. They had arrived to such an extent, that around the world all the major denominations were gathering to prepare reports on the charismatics.

While denominational leaders were gathering in their separate consultations, major changes were taking place in the Renewal Movement. Michael Harper claims in his booklet *Charismatic Crisis* (1980), that 1975 was a watershed in the Movement because of what he calls the discipleship issue. By the end of that year, the Renewal was established throughout the Western world. Many of the fringe groups had fallen away, and yet the anarchic spirit was still at work: people refused to do theology, or move beyond the initial Spirit experience. They were prepared to discuss wholeness, Harper claims, but were little interested in traditional notions of holiness. Discipleship became an issue in an attempt to instill order and seriousness into the Movement. Emphasis was placed on growing and maturing in the Christian life. For some, this necessitated living in a community or group under the leadership of "elders,"[10] or spiritual superiors. Catholics in America started their covenanted communities, and in Britain, particularly through the teaching of Harper, there was a growing mood of piety. This mood was not to everybody's taste. Some decided that the "party was over" and left their

---

[10]Orthodoxy was readmitted to the Christian fold by charismatics when they discovered the Eastern tradition of "elders." These men and women were leaders due to their spiritual authority, and were often lay people; their relationship with the official hierarchy was often problematic. Sociologically, the parallel with the modern charismatics is very interesting (and merits serious study) but it is a mistake to make too much of it in religious terms: the spirituality of Orthodox elders is not Pentecostal.

charismatic congregations; others maintained their links but with a noticeable cooling off towards the Renewal.

Although the discipleship issue can be seen as the first real split within Renewal, its initial effects were marginal to the Movement as a whole. Many charismatics were now looking to new horizons not only in terms of evangelism, but also in terms of welfare and social work. Particularly among Catholics and Anglicans (and Presbyterians in America) stands were taken against racism and social injustice. There was a growing interest in ecumenism, and a real desire for the renewal of churches that would lead to the unity of Christendom.

Many of the denominational consultation reports tended to underestimate the extent of charismatic involvement in activity other than "tongues talking," prophetic pronouncing, and hand clapping. Between 1974 (the Church of Scotland), and 1981 (the Church of England), all the major denominations of Britain pronounced on charismatic renewal. There was not a single report that could be considered to be really hostile; there were some harsh criticisms, but on the whole they were lukewarm or even favorable.

For me, the 1980 consultation of the World Council of Churches, marks the end of the second stage of charismatic renewal. The very fact that the consultation was held at all is witness to the sheer size and significance of worldwide Neo-Pentecostalism. Many charismatics were convinced that the leaders of the World Council of Churches would never take notice because of their predilection for social and political concerns. When the general secretary of the WCC (a self-confessed Methodist Socialist) stood up at the consultation and told the assembled company that he had been personally blessed by the charismatic nature of the enquiry, many Neo-Pentecostalists thought (without irony) that this was a miracle. Michael Harper saw it as official recognition; in his words, "an historic occasion."

The supreme irony of the event was this: by the time the consultation was held, the Charismatic Renewal Movement had peaked.[11] Its zenith was from 1974 to 1976. By 1980 it had consolidated, become more

[11]This is not merely my opinion. Tom Smail, former director of the Fountain Trust, has said as much. So too has Emmanuel Sullivan, *Can the Pentecostal Movement Renew the Churches?* See also Arthur Wallis of the House Church Movement, *Restoration* (Summer 1981).

respectable, serious, and outreaching, but had entered decline. Official recognition was not the cause of the decline, but not only was it the case that many charismatics predicted that official recognition would be the "kiss of death," but it is a well-established convention in sociology that decline in enthusiasm and increase in official support are often correlated. *Stage 3: Factions and Fractions—1980 to 1985.* Projection, it seems to me, is a reasonable compromise between prediction and prophecy. What follows, therefore, is an informed guess as to the likelihood of future events as well as a description as to what is happening now.[12]

The seeds of stage three were sown between 1975 and 1980. As the renewal movement consolidated, so it began to lose its fervor. Many charismatics left the Renewal once the experiential side of the baptism in the Spirit began to wane; even *glossolalia* for some was becoming "vain repetition." Although some denominations were still strong in Pentecostals (the population of Catholics, in Ireland, grew quite rapidly during this time), the overall trend was either static or slow decline. From its earliest days the Renewal had spawned its itinerant evangelists officially loyal to their denomination but in reality increasingly loyal to themselves and their organizations. These evangelists maintained an uneasy relationship with the ordinary priests and pastors who were responsible for the day-to-day spirituality of parish life. Sometimes the evangelists (called by one Baptist pastor "professional charismatics") had considerable commercial interests in the charismatic movement; this included their own publishing houses, records, tapes, and videos.

In 1980 the Fountain Trust collapsed. It had rapidly become functionless as the charismatic fire began to lose its sparkle. There was also increasing tension between some of its leaders. The end of what had been the major organization for promoting the renewal message in Britain, came as a great shock to many charismatics, particularly those in the Church of England. Some of the itinerant charismatic leaders began moving away from the mainstream denominational structures. Some formed new "communities" and independent organizations. The fastest growing religious phenomenon in Britain over the last few years is a new classical Pentecostal sect in the making—the House Church Movement. The Restoration Church, which is the largest and most structured of these

[12]No sociologist worth his salt, these days, makes scientific predictions, but I think it a matter of "bad faith" if we are not prepared "to put our money where our mouth is."

house churches, has been recruiting from the mainstream charismatics. Some of the itinerant evangelists have become increasingly involved in this movement. Furthermore, quite large sections of the Elim and Assemblies of God Pentecostal sects have been defecting to Restorationism. It is now clear that a realignment of Pentecostalism (involving both classical and Neo-Pentecostals) is taking place in Britain.

The above events signify the growing strain and confusion in the Neo-Pentecostal camp. This was highlighted by the debate, in November 1981, of the Church of England's report on the Renewal, which was held during the General Synod's annual assembly. The report was bland and seemingly noncontroversial, but to most people's surprise the debate was so vicious and venomous that it had to be abandoned because of heated uproar: the old charges of schism, "triumphalism," and the evils of enthusiasm were back in full force.

From now until 1985, I believe the following will happen to the Charismatic Renewal Movement in Britain. (Similar forces—although not identical—are at work in America and Canada, so I expect the pattern to be repeated in those countries.) First, the Renewal will continue to decline in numbers and in fervor. As it does so it will fractionalize or split up around new emerging factions. There will be attempts (it has already started in the Church of England) to form new organizations to replace the Fountain Trust; their purpose will be to "gee-up" the flagging Renewal. Many of the mainstream charismatics will support these ad hoc bodies and will remain loyal to Pentecostalism that will be of a more muted and less revivalistic nature. (Many charismatic leaders are already admitting that tongues and prophecy have declined in the movement.)

Other charismatics will follow the itinerant evangelists who will look to new pastures in order to keep what is for them both their life and their livelihood. What I call the "spiritual nomads" (those who always go "where the action is") will split up and follow their favorite leader into his self-appointed exile. At the moment, I believe that the evidence suggests that many mainstream Pentecostals will forsake their denominations and become involved with the House Church Movement. Some of its leaders have called to the charismatics to "Come Out . . . ," and already whole congregations have seceded from the Baptist Union.[13]

---

[13]This was the thrust of my report on the Restoration churches: *The Dales Bible Week,* "Sunday" programme, Radio 4, BBC; 8 August 1982.

The House Church Movement, which sociologically speaking belongs to classical Pentecostalism, will have little appeal to Catholic charismatics. They will cohere around their own charismatic leaders more than any other mainstream Pentecostal grouping. Indeed, I think that alone of the new Pentecostals, the Catholics will resist fractionalism (so many of their leaders are priests that they will eventually weld the new charisma onto the old structure). Catholicism will survive revitalized. Its Pentecostalism will be tamed, or channeled, into other spiritual directions.

Part of the problem for the Neo-Pentecostals is that they are having to face the reality of all revivals (even with a "posh" name like renewal): church history shows that they always come to an end. Perpetual Pentecost was unknown in the early Church. By the fifth century A.D., St. John Chrysostom knew nothing of Pentecostalism. Continual Pentecost also veered away from the classical Pentecostals. When Pentecost goes, it leaves in its wake memory, nostalgia, and the faint stirrings of the nascent experience. Using Pentecostal terminology, I have referred to this, elsewhere, as a "time of blessing."[14] It is difficult to recapture the full excitement and feelings of a lost love: remembered glimpses, hints, and shallow sentimentality are usually the best we can muster. When Pentecost leaves (and I believe that sociologists would do well to understand it experientially and not organizationally) like the beloved, you can invoke the *Paraclete* with noise, clapping, choruses, or tongues, but too easily the machinations are ritualistic responses: outward forms to clothe the inner nakedness. Many classical Pentecostals have had to face this truth often with great honesty and dignity. Sometimes, they settle for "going through the motions" in what becomes a quite developed though restless liturgy. For those who do not become trapped in Pentecostal nostalgia, which is itself embedded in outworn yet cherished rituals, they must look forward to a new Pentecost, a new awakening, another revival.

The new charismatics will have to learn how closely they are related, after all, to their older cousins. Their immediate future is to undergo (with their movement) change, mutation, and perhaps even cessation.

---

[14]With J. S. Atherton, "An Easter Pentecostal Convention: The Successful Management of a 'Time of Blessing'," *Sociological Review* (August 1971).

CHARISMATICS' VIEW OF CHRISTIAN LIFE, THEIR ATTITUDE TO SECULAR SOCIETY, AND THEIR FUTURE IN CHRISTENDOM

The new Pentecostals have underscored the essential component of experience in religious life. For them, belief and liturgy grow out of an encounter with a "God who is alive." While the "fire in the bones" burns deeply, not only for the individual Pentecostal but also for groups who share together—and hence reinforce—a common life, the experiential takes precedence over theologizing and the establishment of the parameters of belief and conduct. In the anarchic first phase of Neo-Pentecostalism, Christian life was reinterpreted as "Living in the Spirit"; "entering into freedom" was understood to mean not only experiencing the power of God in the form of ecstatic experiences, but also release from formal (charismatics see this as synonomous with "dead") Christianity. Traditional liturgies were not forsaken, but they often became forms of worship that were less well attended than the newer freewheeling services.

At the same time, for many charismatics, their personal Pentecost often went beyond the restrictions of classical Pentecostalism. They would talk about the gifts of helping, teaching, and administration, and they were concerned with psychological wholeness as well as the traditional sins.

During the second phase of the Renewal Movement, the emphasis on experience and individual piety (which shared the sentimentality if not the narrow morality of their charismatic cousins) gave way to more outward expressions. Evangelization, social concern, and the need for community were interests that dominated charismatic literature. An attempt was made to see the Christian life in terms of duties and responsibilities, as well as of experiencing joy and exercising spiritual gifts. In America, particularly by Catholic Pentecostals, there was talk of "liberating structures" as well as saving individuals from sin. To some extent, in the same sense that "hippies" gave way to "yippies" in the 1960s, so the 1970s saw a politicization of Pentecostals. On the whole, however, this did not lead to a major new development within the Renewal. It certainly did not lead to political activism. There were greater political awareness, avowed stands against racialism and social injustice, and a marked interest in ecological problems. These primarily remained epiphenomenal to the Charismatic Renewal, and can really be seen as a passive liberalism that led to no radical change of direction.

By the end of the second stage, many charismatics saw their Christian life in fairly traditional terms of piety, faithfulness, and discipleship. The Pentecostals had not radically altered denominational practices. (It could be argued that even the freewheeling liturgies stem as much from secularization as charismatic fervor.) They had certainly not threatened the hierarchical structures of the ecclesia. Little was contributed, by them, either to conservative and traditional theology, or to liberation and process theologies. Although, undoubtedly, hundreds of thousands of Christians had entered into new spiritual experiences, the institutional structure of the historical and mainstream churches remained unchanged. Pentecost may have changed lives, but it blew over the organizational structure leaving everything exactly as it was before.

This lack of innovation and change from within the Renewal explains why the movement did not become significant, sociologically, in terms of social movements.[15] Why it did not become so can partially be understood by looking at the charismatics' view of the secular world. On the one hand, many Pentecostals engaged in secular activities just as they did when they were traditional Catholics, Presbyterians, or whatever. After 1979, however, with the switch from wholeness to holiness, from freedom to discipleship, there was a noticeable sectarian attitude to the secular world. There was increasing suspicion against the World Council of Churches, which some saw as entirely secular in orientation if not demonic. Although no responsible observer of the Renewal would go so far as to say that it was so "otherworld-affirming that it was this-world-denying," nevertheless, there are two ways in which Neo-Pentecostalism has been closer to sectarianism than mainstream religion.

---

[15]See J. A. Banks: *The Sociology of Social Movements* (Macmillan, 1972). Banks improves greatly on earlier functionalist views of social movements. On the whole, however, his secular usage and insistence on innovation and social change, shows that social movement is not a particularly useful tool to explain Neo-Pentecostalism.

My use throughout this paper of such phrases as "social movement," "Renewal," "Charismatic Movement," and Charismatic Renewal Movement," should not be seen as attempts at sociological definition. On the contrary, they are self-consciously applied folk-model terms. I prefer not to operationalize a term unless it clearly can be shown—empirically, if it is possible—to explain satisfactorily disparate data. Indeed, strictly speaking (as I hinted in my introduction) there is no such thing as a "charismatic renewal movement" that can be simply labeled "this" rather than "that": in reality, we are faced with multifaceted charismatic movements. That basically is why I feel that John Moore's adoption of "craze" to explain the disparate phenomena is not very useful. See his article: "The Catholic Pentecostal Movement," *Sociological Yearbook of Religion*, Mike Hill, ed, (S.C.M., 1973).

First, among many of the Evangelical sections of the Renewal, classical Pentecostalism's piety and eschatology has been adopted. Second, throughout all sections and factions of the movement, there has been a tendency to withdraw from secular life. This inwardlookingness certainly characterizes Neo-Pentecostalism during its first phase; the new inner life and its outward expression (shared only with other charismatics) had little time for worldly pursuits. During phase two there was a greater concordat both with the secular world and ecumenism. By phase three, however, not only was "worldliness" increasingly rejected, but so also was there decreasing emphasis on involvement in the secular theatres of government, and social and political protest. This trend will continue as the factional and fractionalized Renewal retreats behind new borders. (If we were to drop the rather dubious use of sect, in sociology, as some form of religious organization, and see it in terms of ideological constructs adhered to by collectivities, then it would be the case that Neo-Pentecostalism is, after all, sectarian.)

Pentecostal power has not, by itself, led either to the humanitarian and reformist activities of nineteenth-century Evangelicalism, or produced the radicalism of Welsh Nonconformity at the beginning of the twentieth century. The revolutionary possibilities of a millenarian utopianism, such as the seventeenth-century Levellers espoused, finds no echo in Neo-Pentecostalism.[16]

Pentecostalism entered the twentieth century as a major new development of Protestant sectarianism. It appealed to—and presumably met the needs of—both the urban and rural masses. In its classical development, Pentecostalism remained imprisoned behind Fundamentalism. In Christian mythology, Noah, having failed with the raven, sends out the dove from the safety (yet enclosured world) of the ark. At first she returns because there is no land. She is sent out again and this time she brings back with her an olive leaf (itself, as the church fathers used to say, a symbol of anointing and power). The dove is then sent forth again, and she never returns. The *Paraclete,* which both Western and Eastern iconography always depicts as the Dove, seems to have left the imprisonment of the sect. If I may follow my analogy strictly (though I am not speaking theologically), I think the immediate future of the liberated bird is to return to the Classical Ship with the new anointing.

---

[16]It has, of course, cropped up in classical mode both in North and South America.

In America, the phenomenal rise of the new Fundamentalism is taking the steam out of the charismatic movement. The Church of God and Assemblies of God Pentecostal sects are not doing wonderfully well out of Neo-Pentecostalism, but the new independent organizations look increasingly like a new form of classical Pentecostalism.[17] In Britain, the House Church Movement is benefiting greatly from the decline of main-stream Pentecostalism. Many of its members were in the Renewal, and it has successfully integrated its worship from newer free styles of contemporary music with the old-style Pentecostal revivalism.

In short, the factionalism and fractionalism of Neo-Pentecostalism is not only leading to the partial disintegration of Charismatic Renewal, as it has existed over the last fifteen years, but it is aiding and abetting the rise of a new classical Pentecostalism.

But to return to our analogy: will the Dove ever get away? In one sense, of course, she has already left. Having spread her wings, she will never be content simply to return to the ark. She has many new places to go: there are many areas of the Third World as well as Western Europe that have not yet received a visitation. The Eastern Orthodox Church and Catholic Poland may be high on the list for future arrivals. In another sense, however, there is no evidence that the Dove will be free from the ark forever; she will keep visiting from time to time. Thus, classical Pentecostalism will undoubtedly continue causing the same disruption and controversy that it has for most of this century. So too will Neo-Pentecostalism flourish in new countries and old denominations (even though the present Charismatic Renewal is now slowly coming to a halt).

If we keep in mind all forms of Pentecostalism as experience rather than institution, then we would be foolish to imagine that it will simply go away. Perhaps *glossolalia* is the cry from the heart that rational speech represses. In our churches in the English-speaking world religious life has become secularized, radicalized, and rationalized: sacred language has given way to common nomenclature, mystery has been replaced by social concern, while miracles have been demythologized. Should we really be so surprised at such "revolts of the soul"?

Certainly, it seems to me, sociologists have learned a great deal from Neo-Pentecostalism: they have learned that they know very little about Pentecostalism. It has turned out to be a phenomenon capable of muta-

[17]Church Growth ministries, for example.

tion and change, and against conventional wisdom it has taken root in the most unlikely of classes and denominations. Maybe we misrepresented it in its classical mode when we saw it as group response to societal disinheritance. We were too eager to adapt it to spurious doctrines of "false consciousness," and in our Procrustean manner insisted that it stay locked behind sectarian typologies of our own making. At the beginning of this paper I contended that Pentecostalism had "gotten out of hand." It has certainly gotten out of our hands: this is another sense in which the Dove is free. In its freedom although it has not yet demonstrated that it has the Pentecostal power to radically destroy societal or denominational structures, it clearly has had enough explosive force to shatter sociological shibboleths.

GLOSSARY

BAPTISM OF THE HOLY SPIRIT. The phrase so often used to describe the Spirit-filling experience. Still popular among many Renewal devotees, but now rejected by many Catholics and sacramentalists as inconsistent with Catholic theology. Its usage gained popularity and sanctity in classical Pentecostal circles. Church history has seen this terminology before. In the Christian East, for example, St. Simeon the New Theologian used it in a manner similar to modern charismatics. He did not see tongue-speaking as the legitimate Spirit seal, however; he thought tears were the correct sign of the Baptism.

CHARISMATIC RENEWAL MOVEMENT. The usual terminology to index the present wave of Pentecostalism. Renewalists do not understand the term "movement" in sociological or organizational terms: it denotes a pneumatic, or Spirit motivated, movement. Renewal is understood as renewing the churches in their traditional faiths and people in their personal commitment to God.

CLASSICAL PENTECOSTALISM. Sectarian, fundamentalist, and evangelical; the elder denominational form of modern Pentecostalism.

DIVINE HEALING. Neither classicals nor charismatics like the term "faith healing": they believe that physical and mental healing is a result of direct intervention by God.

EXORCISM. Catholics have resorted to traditional formulas and rites, but often they (and most Protestant groups) lean on methods derived from classical Pentecostalism. Often, it is the direct method of the "laying on of hands" and shouting "In the name of Jesus, come out." Usually, the demonology owes more to the Bible Belt than to traditional and Patristic understanding of "principalities and powers."

GLOSSOLALIA. The Greek transliteration for "tongues of ecstasy." Tongues is the distinguishing feature of Pentecostal spirituality. It must not be confused with the phenomenon of *xenolalia*—or speaking in foreign languages—which is rarely reported in charismatic circles. It was this phenomenon which was the feature of the day of Pentecost, not the ecstatic utterance per se.

NEO-PENTECOSTALISM. This is the "new wave" Pentecostalism belonging to groups within existing churches; it is neither necessarily sectarian nor necessarily evangelical in doctrine.

PROPHECY. There is little use of either the biblical warnings to the nation, or foretelling. (David Wilkerson's *Vision* comes close.) Usually, prophecy is understood as "forthtelling." In practice this means offering homilies to the faithful.

RENEWAL. Simply the shorthand version favored by most charismatics of charismatic renewal.

REVIVAL. This terminology belongs to classical Pentecostalism. It denotes an outpouring of God's Spirit resulting in mass conversions, healings, prophecies, tongues, and so forth.

SINGING IN THE SPIRIT. Common phenomenon in charismatic circles—much seen at conventions—where the congregation sings together in tongues. Need not be a group phenomenon; it is not clear if this practice is always endorsed in classical circles (though the House Church Movement practices it). It does not, after all, receive mention by St. Paul—except in I Cor. 14:15, Eph. 5:19, Col. 3:16—nor does it appear in the charismatic stories of the New Testament.

A "TIME OF BLESSING" OR "TIMES OF REFRESHING." A short period—meeting/convention—where God is felt to have been present in some special way. This often includes Pentecostal phenomena, but may be simply a "good time had by all."

NRPR: THE NEW RELIGIOUS-POLITICAL RIGHT IN AMERICA*

by Samuel S. Hill

THE RECENT emergence of the "New Religious-Political Right" (the NRPR) in America, the movement popularly referred to as the "Moral Majority," must be puzzling to Europeans; it certainly is to a great many Americans. Whether or not this phenomenon properly qualifies as a "New Religious Movement" (NRM), it is new and it is a significant social force.

Reliable figures are hard to come by. Who can say what percentage of America's more than 226 million people actually combine religious convictions and political preferences as to candidates and issues in some way that qualifies them as belonging to the NRPR? Certainly not a majority of the reputed forty million "Evangelicals" in America. Certainly not all—perhaps not a majority—of the voters in the fewer than ten million households in which the television set is tuned (was, in November 1980) to programs featuring syndicated television preachers.[1] For, by no means is it true that these preachers are agreed on political

---

*The theme of this article is more fully developed in *The New Religious-Political Right in America,* by Samuel S. Hill and Dennis E. Owen (Nashville: Abingdon Press, 1982).

[1]Two sources of data in summary form are available: William Martin, "The Birth of a Media Myth," *The Atlantic* 247:6 (June 1981): 11; Jeffrey K. Hadden and Charles E. Swann, *Prime Time Preachers* (Reading MA: Addison-Wesley, 1981) 51-60.

matters; in fact, some of them take no public stand on political questions and others openly oppose the NRPR. In varying ways, this latter company includes Billy Graham, Robert Schuller, Oral Roberts, and Pat Robertson.[2]

But what we are talking about is a "significant social force," nevertheless. A specified list of Christian television preachers and local pastors, with Jerry Falwell as the figurehead, is visible and effective. Various well-developed, lobbying, and electorate-organizing groups flood the mails, turn out the voters, and work assiduously to court legislators; Christian Voice and Moral Majority, Inc., are the most prominent. In the elections of 1980, NRPR efforts were probably decisive in one senatorial election in Iowa and in one House of Representatives contest in Alabama. Their role was notable in many others, including the presidential race, but almost certainly not decisive. At present their greater success (threat?) may consist in getting certain kinds of bills before legislative bodies, state and national, and laboring to translate them into law—on issues like abortion, prayer in the public schools, and the teaching of creationism in high school biology classes.

When the statistical data do become known, one large sector of NRPR participation is very likely to be shown as coming from nonreligious people. There are in America millions of citizens who rarely or never attend church but who are devoted to one version of "civil religion." That is, these link certain moral positions with "what is best for America," with "what the Almighty intends for America." They take conservative political stands and affirm these to be "right," "holy," "godly"—in a word, the path of righteousness for God's American Israel. The moral preachments of a Jerry Falwell thus "sound right" to a constituency that does not subscribe to his theological foundations. The size and formidability of the NRPR are due to this expansive company of moralists made up perhaps of as many doctrinaire people outside the churches as zealots within.

The American social context sets the scene for the NRPR. It must be remembered by Europeans and American home folks as well that the United States of America has no formal unifying symbols, neither mon-

---

[2]A profile of Evangelical/Fundamentalist varieties on social ethical positions may be found in Robert E. Webber, *The Moral Majority: Right or Wrong?* (Westchester IL: Cornerstone Books, 1981), chs. 8, 11.

archy nor established religion. This helps explain the fascination with each president and the presidency. But there are informal symbols that provide the people with a sense of the common, of shared unity. Prominent among them are ideas, slogans, and value systems such as covenant, new Israel, and special destiny, all having a religious base. American society is self-conscious; that is, it rarely takes itself for granted and it is capable of arrogance and ethnocentrism. Unifying symbols thus are present, and they are lofty, in any event referring to reality that transcends the ordinary and in some cases elevating this nation to a high if not superior perch. The NRPR fits; its emergence and popularity are predictable. Americans are a "religious" people and "civil religion" of one sort or another is widespread.[3]

Even so, religious issues and rhetoric were more conspicuous in the 1980 elections than they usually are. Something is indeed astir in the national life that has not been present recently. In 1928, Alfred E. Smith's Catholicism was a dominant issue and cost him the presidency. In 1960, John F. Kennedy's Catholicism was an issue that had to be dealt with; it was, successfully. In 1968, George Romney's Mormonism would have been an issue had he received the Republican Party nomination. In 1976, Jimmy Carter's Southern Baptist "born-again" religion was cause for concern to some people, but it was not especially significant either in the election or in his conduct of the nation's highest office. Ronald Reagan's general tone and political posture "sounded right" to a society with an NRPR component in 1980, even though he was himself: (a) not a demonstrably pious person; (b) no more extreme than a right-centrist, and a genuinely "political animal"; (c) not preoccupied with the specific agenda of moral causes so dear to NRPR hearts. Here it bears repeating that the NRPR did not elect Reagan; but the typical voter was *politically* within range of the moral convictions and religious vision of the NRPR.

Quite a lot has been said about the relation of the NRPR to the American constitutional principle of the "separation of church and state." Many fear that, despite assurances to the contrary, this cadre of Americans would establish conservative Protestantism if they had the chance—a chance they are salivating to have. Perhaps something of that

---

[3]Robert N. Bellah, "Civil Religion in America" in *American Civil Religion,* eds. Russell E. Richey and Donald G. Jones (New York: Harper and Row, 1974); several other essays in this collection also are pertinent.

sort would develop if a massive groundswell of popular sentiment were to emerge. But any such eventuality (a) is highly unlikely in so diverse (and secularized) a society, (b) raises Constitutional issues, and (c) is not the stated goal of the NRPR (nor its hidden agenda, as far as this analyst can ascertain).

Nevertheless, this concern points to an issue that deserves attention. On the separation of state and church—"church" meaning any particular religion or denomination of that religion—the NRPR has a commendable American record. It is not plumping to make Christianity the official American faith, certainly not Baptistism. But acknowledgment of that should not blind us to some matters calling for vigilance. Is the NRPR hopeful of linking the state with specified moral positions? The answer is "yes" with respect to abortion, traditional roles for women, and the "quality of life" in public school classrooms. The answer may be "yes" with respect to state and religion, that is, turning conservative Protestantism or even "fundamentalism" into the societal norm, the national political-moral-ideological consensus. One wonders if the NRPR wants more than "equal time," that is, its "fair share" of representation and success at engendering its perspective(s) in the life of the society. Drawing the distinction between state and church, moral positions and religion, is difficult at best. Yet the point can and should be made that the conscious program of the NRPR is not to establish a church. Its constituency is too affirmatively American to do that. At the same time, one senses a passion to convert America into Christendom. When the issue is posed this way, we begin to gain some insight into why "secular humanism" is the unmistakable enemy of the NRPR. To Secular Humanism we shall soon return.

We must interject a qualifier about the NRPR and the state or government, especially the federal government. The NRPR stands foursquare against "big government." It opposes the role of government as dispenser of funds and services. On the other hand, it affirms the action of government as enforcer of laws and regulations and as conduit for values and traditions that it associates with the true America, the state and society that God has intended all along and that used to exist. For most of its history, this form of conservative Protestantism has exemplified sectarian behavior, that is, it has remained withdrawn from public life and involvement in the general society for reasons of indifference or hostility or inexperience and ineptitude. One of the most noteworthy features of the NRPR's visibility is how new that visibility is. This is not a sector of American society that we have been accustomed to seeing in political action. There is nothing new about the negative and positive assessments of government's roles, but until quite recently those have not been expressed in organized political action.

One suspects that three factors are prominent in NRPR's "going public." The first is simply the availability of television technology and the growth of such Christians' capability for taking full advantage of it. A second is the combination of distress over the moral state of affairs in America with a freshly discovered power to do battle with those forces of decay, a capacity that accompanies their rise from economic impotence to a greater purchase on power. The third is simply the size and responsiveness of the not-very-religious political-economic conservatives who find the NRPR a saving strength for an America gone wrong. No one can be exactly sure why these historic "sectarians" have "gone public;" but we cannot overlook the fact and importance of their doing so.

Mention of two paradoxes will have to suffice for completing this discussion of American society as context for the NRPR. The first is that the "most arresting fact" about the contemporary religious situation is the concurrent growth of secularization and conservative religion, not one but both. Secularism—the "practice of the absence of God," and to be distinguished from agnosticism or atheism—grows larger day by day. Furthermore, it shows no signs of containment or abatement through the influence of conservative religion. The latter is expanding apace, especially in its expression as authority-mindedness and high-intensity piety. Here there is little more to be said; curiously, religion is doing both "better" and "worse" in the America of the 1980s.

The second has to do with the place of the public schools in the life of Americans. Comprehensively considered, there is no doubt that the public schools are one of the two or three central institutions in the society, so much so that they are regarded as virtually "sacred." They forge a national unity and generate a social consensus as no other agency does. At the same time, a critical attitude toward public schools now prevails among those great lovers of all things American, the NRPR, a people who typically support such central agencies for the promotion of loyalty and identification. This leads to prophetic action in some cases: for example, opposition to classroom features such as the absence of prayer and the teaching of evolutionary theory in biology. In other cases it results in forthrightly separatist activity: the establishment of "Christian schools." In the more than 12,000 Christian schools now operating children are protected from evil and guided in a highly disciplined and doctrinaire fashion toward the goals of single-minded devotion to "pure Christianity."

These two paradoxical conditions confirm the curious state of religious political-social affairs in the United States today. Some funny things are happening on the way to the twenty-first century.

The New Religious-Political Right is a coalition of Americans who want to set the nation on its God-ordained course. An old political slogan runs, "Let's get this country moving again." The NRPR replaces that with keynotes like: "Let's turn this country around"; or, "Let's restore this nation to sanity, to the Lord's way"; or, "Let's be a righteous people as God intends." The sweeping takeover of lives and institutions by secularism must be checked. Especially deplorable to the NRPR is the supposed moral and spiritual sabotaging of the public schools, a hitherto sacred unit of American public life. This dire development is symbolized by the absence of (public) prayer in the classrooms, promoted by the teaching of evolutionary theory, and taken to the breaking point on occasion by the hiring of homosexual teachers.

This NRPR coalition is organized; it is exceedingly well organized. Its principal leaders and figureheads are television preachers, the stars of the "Electronic Church"—in particular, Jerry Falwell of "The Old-Time Gospel Hour" out of Lynchburg, Virginia, and Jim Bakker of the "PTL Club" (for "Praise the Lord" or "People That Love"), based in Charlotte, North Carolina.

There are other television ministries that promote the cause, and, as we shall see, some that sound like they might be promoting it but are not. Falwell is the real luminary. His congregation and ministry have spun off Moral Majority, Inc., the best known of several Christian political organizing operations. (Two others are Christian Voice and the Roundtable.) They are in turn tied in with some massive direct-mail businesses, enabling them to send out millions of pieces of mail to a multitude of citizens believed to have conservative leanings, political, religious-moral, or, desirably, both. Through the twin media of television appeal and mail-outs, they establish contact with several million Americans toward the goal of exposing evil, advocating particular positions and candidates, urging the right-hearted to vote, and raising enormous sums of money to expand their mission.

This phalanx of the pure in heart is composed largely of conservative Protestants. Typically the greatest support comes from independent

Baptist congregations. At this writing, not a single organized denomination has voted to endorse the NRPR, not even the "fundamentalist sects," and certainly not "mainline denominations." To be sure, some ultraconservative and dissident Methodists, Southern Baptists, and Roman Catholics lend their support, as do also some Mormons. But the NRPR is an independent church phenomenon, by and large; perhaps its greatest outside support comes, as we have surmised, from the politically conservative people who would be members of such churches if they were members at all. As to geographical distribution, all data gathered so far point to the South and the Midwest as the heartland of NRPR strength. These are "the folk" who have always been politically conservative, who stand for a strong America both militarily and morally, who like local and detest central governmental power. These two regions have been the most homogeneous areas of the United States; in the Midwest a historically diverse ethnicity has melded into a vigorous Americanism. As for class stratification, NRPR draws heavily from the ranks of the "working class," the sector of people who are not long removed from economic and political marginality but who now enjoy reasonable standards of living facilitated by jobs calling for skills in the moderate range.

It helps to see who does not belong to the NRPR. Many conservative Christians do not. One such group would be those descended from the left wing of the Reformation—the Mennonites, Amish, and Brethren, for example—where convictions run deep and identity is clear, most emphatically concerning the right of all others to live by their own convictions. Another is a curious medley of Roman Catholics, Southern Baptists, and Mormons who share certain outlooks with the NRPR but whose vision is largely limited to and whose loyalities lie with their own communions; these too in odd and varied ways practice a basic live-and-let-live policy. A third group is those conservative Protestants in "sects" and "denominations" alike who believe in minding the church's own spiritual business and steering clear of involvement in worldly affairs. The final mention is of a cadre of Evangelicals who are, if anything, more active in the political arena than the NRPR and whose agenda is sharply differentiated: instead of abortion, public schools, pornography, national defense, and homosexuality, these people focus on war and peace, social justice, and radical Christian life-style. The list of prominent conservative Protestant individuals and institutions that are disaffiliated from the NRPR is impressive: Billy Graham, Carl F. H. Henry; Wheaton and Calvin Colleges; Fuller Theological Seminary; the Southern Baptist Convention. In disclaiming membership in the NRPR, Dr. Graham, the foremost evangelist of this century, has been quoted as saying, "I don't wish to be identified with them . . . morality goes beyond sex to human freedom and social justice . . . Evangelists can't be closely identified with any particular party or person . . . it would disturb me if there was a wedding between the religious fundamentalist and the political right." Dr. Henry, the nation's most influential Evangelical theologian, is similarly skeptical and critical: "It does . . . reflect adversely upon the Evangelicals when many show less interest in getting biblical truth and right into national life than in promoting a born-again candidate or in getting prayer back into the public schools . . . the Christian fails his nation if he permits the evangelistic imperative to eclipse political duty. . . . To take the route of a Christian party is, in my view, a mistake."

The causes taken up by the NRPR have been alluded to several times. One whole cluster of them centers about the values of traditional family life. Abortion—unabashedly referred to as murder—is highest on the list. A great deal of NRPR energy being expended on Capitol Hill is poured out on legislation to make abortions illegal and to prevent any public funds from being used for that pupose. Opposition to the passage of the Equal Rights Amendment and all measures having to do with feminist causes is keen; the NRPR claim is that women already possess the right rights. Moreover, their biblically guided roles would be perverted were values of the ERA sort to become law. Similarly, vigorous attacks are leveled against pornography and against legal recognition of the rights of homosexual persons to express openly their sexual preferences.

As we have noted earlier, a second bastion of defense is the public schools. The NRPR is working zealously to overturn a 1963 Supreme Court decision which outlawed the scheduling of set times in classrooms for voluntary prayer. It is also lobbying in many state capitals and with hundreds of local school boards to require the teaching of the Genesis view of creation—Creationism, as it is called—alongside Evolutionism, the biological theory which has informed most scientific instruction for nearly a century. Actually, those family concerns and school concerns are rather closely related. Both uphold standards that are called "traditional values," "old-fashioned virtues," those alleged to have been normative before the corrosive acids of Secular Humanism commenced to do their destructive work. Both are affirmed to be the biblical way, the morality of a godly people. At a deeper level, both point to a disciplined, serious, strong, principled manner of living.

Secular Humanism, cosmic enemy number one, the destroyer of all things good, the subtle force that threatens to undermine biblical religion and theocratic society—what is it? As some observers perceive it, it is a value system that professes to follow a right road, but is devoid of transcendence and any sturdy, ethical principles; it caters to relevance and responsiveness to historical change, and is committed to social consensus on what rights and needs human beings truly have. For certain, it acknowledges no god. Equally clear is its positive attitude toward shifting positions. In its most extreme expressions it is relativistic; more fundamentally it adjusts, adapts, alters as times change, as specific human needs change, as perceptions of prescriptions change. But what makes Secular Humanism so perverse and pernicious on its positive side is precisely that it is "humanistic." It claims to care about people, to uphold the highest standards of morality, to foster good will, brotherhood, a firm moral basis for a noble civilization. Alas, it misleads, is a bastard, deceives. Thus, the NRPR does well to fear it and attack it, this unorganized but self-insinuating force in our culture. First, it ignores God. Second, it is the great moral impostor, sounding loud its trumpet of righteousness, but in fact destroying the only true permanent and ultimate foundation for righteousness, namely duty to an objectively real God, in favor of a supposed concern for people's rights, within a setting of constantly shifting relevance. If Secular Humanism is allowed to infect American society, the NRPR argues, then all is lost. God would not be honored. A high moral road would be forsaken. All standards would be abandoned. Truth and right would be whatever the ruling class thought it was. Weakness and sickness would ravage the body politic and lead to its death and destruction.[4]

So the NRPR stands foursquare for God, biblical righteousness, an ethical America, and the traditional family and school. It is ranged against the normless, man-made, ephemeral, and modernistic force of ethical humanism, amorphous and unorganized but powerful and pervasive as it is. But the NRPR itself is not a monolith; it is somewhat amorphous and unorganized. It aspires to being one body but, in the language of its

---

[4]Jerry Falwell, *Listen America.* (Garden City NY: Doubleday, 1980); Tim LaHaye, *The Battle for the Mind* (Old Tappan NJ: Fleming H. Revell Co., 1980)

beloved New Testament, that body has many members—alas, they do not necessarily pull together. In a word, the NRPR is diverse. Having noted that fact already in several references, we need only to underscore it now. (One reason for doing so is the evidence available now of "dissension in the ranks" or rivalry between constituent companies, and the possibility of fallings out and serious ruptures in the future.) In the first place there are several quite separate organized efforts: Moral Majority, Christian Voice, National Christian Action Coalition, and Roundtable. These groups often make common cause with another group of organizations: the Richard Viguerie direct-mail company, Conservative Caucus, NCPAC (National Conservative Political Action Committee), and the Committee for the Survival of a Free Congress. In addition there are Electronic Church ministries that claim a piece of the action but are less pointedly organized: James Robison of Texas, Oral Roberts, and Rex Humbard.

The existence of a complex of organized efforts and, not least, of strong personalities with loyal followings is enough to portray diversity of outlooks. There would appear to be other differences as well. Observers have noted that the Moral Majority is especially attractive to independent Baptists; that NCAC appeals to the hard-line Fundamentalists typified by Bob Jones University's sphere of influence; and that Christian Voice is dominated by charismatic Evangelicals.

Another impressionistic design for depicting the diversity within the NRPR follows Christian trinitarian doctrine. Some—such as Jerry Falwell—emphasize God as judge, governor, and commandant. Others—exemplified by Bill Bright and Campus Crusade for Christ, and such events as "Washington for Jesus" kinds of rallies—are oriented to God the Son, the Savior, and the agent of conversion. A third cluster—the Holy Spirit party, so to speak, associated with Pat Robertson and the 700 Club—magnifies empowerment, answer to prayer, healing through faith. While any such analytic device can be suggestive at the most, this one does help us see a subtle, informal way in which diversity develops and is identified.

More needs to be said somewhat more precisely about the theological position and setting of the NRPR. It is, after all, a religious movement, no matter what else it may be. In fact the spokesmen for the cause acknowledge the Bible, Christian teaching, and God's will and revelation as the sole reason for their energetic activities. We may begin by asking how this development is related to American Fundamentalism.

That outlook and cause dates back to the 1880s, a time of rapid change and real stress in American society. As thousands moved from rural to urban locations to live in an industrial society made possible in part by emerging views of science and the world that challenged traditional religious convictions, some reaction was inevitable. Summarized, some Evangelicals became Fundamentalists. Actually in the decades before the great conflict of 1861-1865, Protestantism of the Evangelical family was mainline religion. This way of looking at Christian meaning and responsibility emphasized individual regeneration and devotional piety, based itself solidly on biblical authority, and stressed personal morality—though sometimes it did extend its concerns to address social evils and corporate health.

Beginning in the 1880s, one cadre within this army of the Lord columned right. Aghast at developments in society and in religion and deeply alienated from what was happening, the Fundamentalists set themselves in opposition to culture. They became classic separatists or sectarians, belligerently set against a perverse world and militantly withdrawn from it. George M. Marsden's recent study, *Fundamentalism and American Culture,* describes this tradition of American religion in detail.

Marsden concludes that these Fundamentalists "experienced profound ambivalence toward the surrounding culture. . . . These American Christians underwent a remarkable transformation in their relationship to the culture. Respectable 'evangelicals' in the 1870s, by the 1920s they had become a laughing-stock, ideological strangers in their own land." This offspring group shared Evangelicalism's "complete confidence in the Bible" and preoccupation with the "message of God's salvation of sinners through the death of Jesus Christ."[5] But its strident opposition to "modernism" soon marked it off from such loosely related traditions as revivalism, the holiness movements, millenarianism, and Reformed confessionalism. They went their own way—the Lord's, they were convinced—as a "patchwork coalition." The common enemy was "modernist attempts to bring Christianity into line with modern thought." They would have nothing to do with political attempts to ameliorate conditions in the social order, espousing instead a Christianity that was "individualist, culture denying, soul rescuing." Also characteristic of this

[5]George M. Marsden, *Fundamentalism and American Culture* (New York: Oxford University Press, 1980) 3-8 *et passim.*

modern American Fundamentalism was its anti-intellectualism. Trusting only in biblical and theological perspectives on questions of truth and falsity, it rejected the "principal assumptions and conclusions of recent science and philosophy." (At the same time, its epistemology, its religious mode of knowing, was rationalistic in the manner of Bacon and "Scottish Common Sense Realism.") "Separatist" and "sectarian" then do typify Fundamentalism's posture vis-à-vis culture; its positive program amounted to biblical authority and personal salvation.

The NRPR of the 1980s is a descendant of modern American Fundamentalism. But the offspring has acquired a fresh gene pool in the transmission of generations. On the basal questions of biblical authority and personal redemption, any differences are negligible. There are some: for example, a less scholastic use of the biblical text by most NRPR supporters than is true of much Fundamentalism (which is traditionally Northern, by the way). The real departures occur at other points and are often complex. The most obvious is in the attitude toward culture. The NRPR criticizes American culture from a standpoint squarely within it. The tunes it sings are far more reformist than abrasive. It wants to change things, no doubt about that. But these troopers mount their message through well-dressed representatives from well-heeled religious or political organizations by means of the most sophisticated electronic equipment available today, in the process employing the ultimate in modern production techniques. "Separatist" does not apply; neither does "sectarian" in the old sense. "Reformist" and "dominant" come closer. While the NRPR ideology wages war with prevailing cultural norms, especially those emanating from Secular Humanism, it can hardly be described as alienated from culture or belligerent in its rejection thereof. Both the Reverend Jerry Falwell and Senator Jesse Helms are very much at home in the fast company of the halls of Congress, the National Press Club, and television talk-shows; both have "class" and basic good manners. Falwell, among others, has a rather pleasant and responsive demeanor.

A second departure of the NRPR from classic Fundamentalism comes at the point of the life of the mind. It is not really anti-intellectual. While mainstream scientific culture might be inclined to accuse it of such a stance, it is really more accurate to define its position as "counter-intellectual." It draws upon substantial resources in political and economic theory, biological science, biblical criticism, and historical understanding. This catalog of theories and theorists is either unknown to or viewed with some contempt by mainline culture, but is a considerable corpus. The heroes are Tim LaHaye (of LaJolla) and Francis Schaeffer (of Switzerland) in theology; the Creation Research Group (of La Jolla) in biology; Robert J. Ringer and Milton Friedman (not themselves of the NRPR) in economics; the Plymouth Rock Foundation and the Foundation for Christian Education in political theory and history; and born-again common sense in biblical criticism.

We may summarize the NRPR divergence from its Fundamentalist parentage by emphasizing its positive nature. It is set against the Secular Humanism of mainstream culture. Yet its identity is not formed decisively by what it is against; it is for a great deal and works hard to formulate its philosophy. While the old Fundamentalism was paralyzed by its depreciation of all and everyone else, the NRPR is proud, out-in-the-open, confident, aggressive. Moreover, it is proculture; that is to say, it advocates the American public order when that conforms to NRPR notions of what is right and good and best for America. Its nose is in the tent. Should the majority of the dwellers reject its views on what is "best for America," what then? It would remain to be seen whether the NRPR would withdraw to a separatist purity or persist in the righteous struggle to bring about God's kingdom (or make some other response). At the present, it is determined and active, far from sour or bitter.

On another theological question, we may describe the NRPR approach to life, social as well as individual, as following a problem-solution form. It interprets history as an endless series of failures and redemptions, of apostasies and recoveries. At the individual level, each person is lost until he or she is saved; the ministry of NRPR-type Christians to all people is determined by that sharply focused vision of the nature of the human condition. So it devotes more energy to inaugurating the Christian life than to enlarging or deepening it. Similarly, in the public realm, the NRPR looks at the moral-spiritual condition of the nation and concludes that it is deficient—nay, more, sick in fact, on the verge of a death and destruction mostly self-inflicted.

There isn't anything new or surprising about this approach, or so it seems at first. For a long time preachments have proclaimed mankind's evil ways and the imminent disaster a wrathful God will visit upon his wayward people. The NRPR variation on this problem-solution theme is a bit different. Predictions of grim things to come are matched by political programs for preventing them. Conversion of wayward souls must be accompanied by the transformation of the body social. It is not simply a matter of the second resulting from the first, according to NRPR strategy. The second goal is as specifiable and urgent as the first. America must be cleansed, restored to sanity, set on God's course. Moreover, the NRPR is glad to welcome as colleagues and fellow travelers people from any quarter who subscribe to their moral spiritual priorities list: antiabortion; a proreligious atmosphere in the public schools; traditional family values; and a strong national defense. Anyone is welcome—Mormons, even Jews, or irregular church-goers—anybody except Secular Humanists. Putting the point this way enables us to see that it is usually a morally "relativist" philosophy that places one outside the NRPR pale. Strong religious convictions as such are not requisite to inclusion in this rather diverse company of Americans; holding to eternally valid positions on key moral questions is. Situationism and temporizing are rejected; so are errant moral convictions. This is in no way to suggest that the leadership of the NRPR forsakes Evangelicalism's classic commitment to the evangelization of the lost. Even so, a good many evangelism-minded Christians, among them Billy Graham, fear that the NRPR will sidetrack Christians from their main ministry. They perceive correctly that the NRPR will settle for good politics, even though it prefers having things both ways.

Things are indeed in a bad way. Devout conservative Protestants and those who see eye-to-eye with them on the singled-out issues are called to be God's agents for rescuing America from its dash toward destruction. And they can be his effective agents for that purpose. Indeed, little about this entire effort is as surprising as how readily so cataclysmic a crisis can be resolved. All the literature and speeches emanating from NRPR circles picture in lurid tones the disaster toward which America is plummeting. They also "shout from the housetops" that this awful eventuation can be averted, and quickly. In other words, a buoyant optimism pervades the soul of the NRPR. The message is that God will heal our land, and quickly, if we will submit to his leading in the moral-spiritual depths of our national life. This is apocalyptic thinking—a new day is dawning, a new world is coming. This is eschatological thinking—the end-time is coming. All those termini of the historical process are seen as congruent with traditional Christian teaching concerning Christ's Second Coming. But this is more in tune with postmillennial interpretation than premillennial. It is indeed optimistic. The decisive event in God's governance of the world's future could occur soon. We are not given a clear analysis of the relation between this foreshortened eschaton in America and the ultimate eschatological event. It is plain, however, that the former has eschatological significance, that it is the energizer, and that Christians must work to bring it about. Something great must happen, can happen; we are called to make it happen, we as consecrated persons and as a political-moral force. It is illuminating to consider this view alongside some others that have been prominent in the Christian tradition: (a) Calvinism with its clear claims that God's actions are those of a Sovereign whose conduct of cosmic affairs may or may not jibe with righteous human efforts; (2) Luther's vigorous eschatology that rendered all human efforts, indeed all historical events, of secondary importance when viewed in the context of God's mysterious guidance of history toward Eschaton; (3) premillennial theology that is exceedingly modest in its estimate of the good that can be done by political means this side of God's reversal of history's slide by his return in Christ.

To the NRPR, the Kingdom of God can be realized—in America at any rate. If the Eschaton cannot be realized, it can be anticipated by an America that submits itself to God. America's role is central and critical. The return of godly ways must commence here. Indeed, in the NRPR vision—one that is sharply at variance with the worldwide ministry of many Evangelicals, not least that of Billy Graham—America is spotlighted. This nation is called to be a "light to the nations." Accordingly, the likelihood that the Lord is acting similarly in the life of other nations is small. In point of fact, the divine eschatological activity is understood as occurring in a special time-place dialectic: the place is the USA (Israel occupies a secondary position); the time is soon—when the American people repent and restore a righteous decorum, in both private and public spheres.

One has to suspect that this rather provincially American view of how the Lord plans to bring about his purposes is correlated with foreign policy positions the NRPR advocates. It is amiss as well as unbecoming to accuse the NRPR of an *über alles* posture; the NRPR is not even aggressively militarist. Rather, it wants a strong America because this nation is the chosen vessel of the divine energy and because the enemy—Communism, especially in its Soviet form—must be held in check. While extremist measures are not promoted and not even secretly desired, so far as we can ascertain, a means-ends philosophy does tend to heighten aggression more than formal policy declares. That is, some policies might well be advocated that presume the necessity of elevating America's moral-spiritual perceptions over others at the others' expense.

The mid-1981 Senate committee hearings on the nomination of Ernest W. Lefever to be Assistant Secretary of State for Human Rights illustrate the point. Lefever was opposed by most Senators within both parties because he took the stand that America could justify giving aid and support to friendly nations that were guilty of violating the basic human rights of some of their citizens; whereas it would withhold any such from unfriendly, philosophically alien nations without regard to its practice of prohuman-rights policies. Means-ends ways of thinking are prominent within the NRPR mentality.

One highly suggestive approach to interpreting the NRPR is provided by Revitalization Theory. This mode of analyzing social movements, formulated by anthropologist Anthony F. C. Wallace, can be given only the briefest sketch here. A Revitalization Movement is defined as a "deliberate, organized, conscious effort by members of a society to construct a more satisfying culture." It is said to occur under such conditions as high stress for individual members of the society, and disillusionment with a distorted cultural Gestalt. In its religious manifestations, it may be revivalistic, millenarian, or messianic. In all cases, a religious revitalization movement seeks escape from a stale or distorted or alienated social condition in favor of a radically new social condition that is "more satisfying."[6] An impressive similarity links the New Religious-Political Right in America with Revitalization Theory. A hitherto powerless, largely unnoticed segment of "little people," a "silent minority," has surged into the national scene to remedy a stale, sick, alienated, and perverted society. It has already moved through some of the stages Wallace describes: (a) acquiescence in a cultural steady state; (b) a period of increased individual stress; (c) the culture is seen as distorted so that stress rises; (d) revitalization is undertaken. In this fourth stage the plateau to which the NRPR as a revitalization movement—if it is such—has moved, leadership emerges, communication networks are established so as to create an incipient community, and organization is developed. (Later, other stages follow, such as adaptation, cultural transformation, routinization, and a new steady state.)

NRPR looks for all the world like a revitalization movement. It diverges from most examples, however, in its passion to exceed the creation of a satisfying subculture for itself. It yearns instead for the conquest of the entire American society. The transformation of all our

[6]Anthony F. C. Wallace, "Revitalization Movements," *American Anthropologist* 58:2 (1956): 265-81.

laws, policies, and values into conformity with God's will—as received by Jerry Falwell, Jesse Helms, Tim LaHaye, Donald Howard, Gary Jarmin, and the like—is the sure goal. Nothing less than conquest will suffice. This is a political-religious struggle toward a specified end.

Whether the NRPR will be successful of course remains to be seen. Its ranks comprise a minority of Americans. Its values strike home for a much larger segment, but it is not clear how many people will be able to buy the whole NRPR package. Moreover, the rhythms of NRPR activity may not be suited to large-scale, long-term change in a huge, complex, highly diverse society that is governed by a rule of law. It is instant- or quick-success oriented. It lives by some such strategy as: catch a vision, promote the cause, raise the money, lead out, and DO IT. The American political process is hardly cadenced that way; it lumbers along, never static, hardly ever stable, and certainly not committed to any specified program or list of concerns for long.

But the NRPR is on the contemporary scene and it is a significant social force. The best bet would be that it will not become the dominant religious or moral or political force in America. Nevertheless, it is making some changes. Many "modern" people are being reminded that old-fashioned virtues and traditional religion are far from passé. Some are even being challenged to reflect on values they have been quite glib about. Others are taking up the cause of defending America against NRPR incursions. It is hard simply to sit by and watch the New Religious-Political Right in America. It is a force to be reckoned with. While not quite an NRM in the ordinary sense, it reflects a new configuration of religious and political forces, one that commands our attention.

THE MORAL MAJORITY IN THE U.S.A. AS A NEW RELIGIOUS MOVEMENT

by Paul Anthony Schwartz and James McBride

> Christians are fed up. We are not going to take it anymore. Christians are tired of a school system that has taken God out and replaced him with anti-God humanism, amoral value systems, sex, drugs and illegitimate babies and crime. We as Christians are simply not going to sit back any longer and watch our families being destroyed.[1]

THESE SENTIMENTS of rage and anger at the betrayal of "Christian" values in an America turned from God are at the heart of the challenge thrown down by the Christian New Right to a radically pluralist American society. Preoccupied with the assault of "secular humanism" on the family, political institutions, and the military establishment, this coalition of "Bible-believing" Christians[2] sees itself as "the only hope for changing the present moral stance of the White House, Congress, and State Houses" where our elected representatives "are leading the nation into immorality."[3] Linked both historically and theologically with traditional Fundamentalism as it emerged in the United States following World War I, this neo-Fundamentalist revival takes place under radically changed social circumstances. Like its antecedent expressions, this movement

---

[1]Colonel Doner of The Christian Voice on CBS News, "60 Minutes," 21 September 1980.

[2]See appendix A for a listing of the major elements in this coalition.

[3]Jerry Falwell, *Moral Majority Report* 1:9 (14 July 1980): 5.

defines itself in the struggle with modernism—in fact, with modernity itself. Unlike them, it appears to have achieved an accommodation with modern society which may permit it to play a more significant role in the legitimation of very specific social interests. If this rapprochement has in fact occurred, it is due to a reformulation of Fundamentalism's previously total hostility towards autonomous reason and its role in the formation of culture.

Fundamentalism as a religious movement emerged as a result of the impact of secularization upon religious culture; that is, in the confrontation between the affirmation of the absolute authority of religious tradition and the critical self-reflection of modern thought. Richard Hofstadter speaks of a "union of social and political reaction" resulting in

> the emergence of a religious style shaped by a desire to strike back at everything modern—the higher criticism, evolutionism, the social gospel, rational criticism of any kind.[4]

Particularly annoying to the early Fundamentalists was the intrusion of secular culture upon the religious definitions of "man's" place in creation (the evolutionist controversies) and its rejection of the epistemological status of Christian scripture as literal truth (the development of higher biblical criticism).[5] According to Hofstadter's analysis, the Fundamentalists appeared to have lost this struggle due to the spread of secularist notions beyond a minority of intellectual elites following the development of a secularized mass culture.[6] This resulted in the political and cultural marginalization of Fundamentalism, enhancing the sectarian character of its religious beliefs and practices.

The liberal Protestant denominations, in contrast, were able to make peace with the increased secularization of mass culture by ceding the autonomy of critical reason in the social world and attempting to work out its implications in the churches. This acceptance encompassed both terms of the modern expression of critical thought. The accommodation with technical reason left undisputed the authority of "science" to describe the reality of the material universe. Beyond this, liberal religion also granted legitimacy in varying degrees to the autonomy of a "substan-

---

[4]*Anti-Intellectualism in American Life* (New York: Vintage, 1963) 121.

[5]See ibid., 55-144.

[6]Ibid., 118.

tive reason" growing out of the secular culture of the Enlightenment.[7] The two elements of the liberal religious accommodation are apparent in the latitude of the authority granted by liberal Protestantism to critical reason vis-á-vis the Christian scriptures. It not only accepted the archaeological and historical evidence developed from the physical sciences regarding the dating and authorship of biblical texts, but it also granted legitimacy to the autonomous development of a critical hermeneutic expounding the *meaning* of these texts for the believer.

The early Fundamentalists, of course, originally rejected the authority of critical reason in both its forms. They "held that the Bible was absolutely reliable and precise in matters of fact, that its meanings were plain, and that whenever possible it should be taken literally."[8] The evidence of paleontologists and other natural scientists used to construct a theory of evolution was rejected out of hand as contrary to the word of God expressed literally and without error in the scriptures.[9] A fortiori, any form of historical criticism applied to the interpretation of biblical texts was seen as an even clearer example of the incursion of an illegitimate modernism into the domain of sovereign religious truth. In the words of Billy Sunday, "When the word of God says one thing, and scholarship says another, scholarship can go to hell."[10]

The emergence today of the Christian New Right as a conspicuous political phenomenon suggests that Fundamentalism in the United States has undergone a historical change in its attitude toward the secular forces of modernity. This change becomes apparent when we consider the new attitude of Fundamentalists toward the two elements of an autonomous critical rationality.

---

[7]See the extended discussion of the two types of reason below. Cf. Charles Davis, *Theology and Political Society* (Cambridge: Cambridge University Press, 1980) 28-50.

[8]George M. Marsden, *Fundamentalism and American Culture* (New York/Oxford: Oxford University Press, 1980) 51.

[9]It is interesting to consider to what extent this stance already represents an interpretation by Fundamentalists of a kind of scientism in which the reduction of religious myth and parable to the epistemological status of "scientific formula" parallels a secular tendency to treat empirical "facts" as the uninterpreted truth of an objective material reality. See the discussion provoked by Thomas Kuhn's *The Structure of Scientific Revolutions*.

[10]Found in William McLoughlin, *Billy Sunday Was His Real Name*, cited in Hofstadter, *Anti-Intellectualism*, 122.

The new Fundamentalists still maintain a self-conscious critique of secular culture, inveighing against "godless humanism" as the antithesis of all morality and the fruit of a tainted lineage. Rated as one of five most pressing problems of the day by Jerry Falwell, "humanism" is described as

> the contemporary philosophy that glorifies man as man, apart from God [; it] is the ultimate outgrowth of evolutionary science and secular education. . . . Ultimately, humanism rests upon the philosophy of existentialism, which emphasizes that one's present existence is the true meaning and purpose of life. . . . Applied to psychology, it postulates a kind of moral neutrality that is detrimental to Christian ethics. In popular terminology it explains, "Do your own thing," and "If it feels good, do it!" It is an approach to life that has no room for God and makes man the measure of all things.[11]

At the same time, in place of the wholesale rejection of secular reason one would expect on the basis of repeated denunciations of "secular humanism," a reformulation of Fundamentalist theology emerges that in fact appropriates one element of the modern dyad—technical reason—while continuing to reject the other. On the basis of his own experience with televangelism (the Old Time Gospel Hour now grosses upwards of fifty million dollars a year), Moral Majority President Falwell is quite at home with modern technical operations, believing that "television, radio, and the printed page are things we must not destroy but that we must redirect."[12] In short, Fundamentalists appear to have learned something during their exile from the mainstream of American society, and they appear ready to apply that lesson to their battle for political power. If the neo-Fundamentalist understanding of truth as revealed in scripture is by itself *ineffective* in challenging mainstream American culture, the movement can take advantage of the benefits of technical rationality to promote its message through televangelism and computerized mass mailings. At the same time, this technical reason is seen as itself *insufficient* for the reestablishment of "Biblical morality," although it can be used in a limited way to demonstrate the truths expressed in an inerrant Bible.

This new marriage of convenience between the technical aspect of modern rationality and the eternal truth of biblical morality represents a historical shift in the theological content of Fundamentalism in the United States. It occurs within a historical context which enables a departure from the traditional absolutist rejection of autonomous reason

---

[11] *Listen America*! (Garden City, NY: Doubleday, 1980).

[12] Ibid., 195.

and allows Fundamentalism's return from the margins to the center of religious and political activity. To understand this development, we must investigate further the interaction in this instance between theological ideas on the one hand and changes in the social and political environment in which these ideas are formulated and expressed on the other.

The nature of the change in Fundamentalist thought can best be understood by a discussion of the distinction introduced above between the two sides of modern rationality as these have emerged in modern technological society. On the one hand, modern reason can be seen as embodied in the triumph of technical method (itself a derivative of properly "critical" rationality), the result of a "proliferation of theoretical knowledge without a reflexive relationship to human social action or practice, and consequently objectivistic and individualistic in its structure and amoral in its use."[13] This description characterizes the "empirical," "physical," and other "hard" sciences, and is usually the meaning given in everyday speech to the term "science." On the other hand, there is the existence of another type of modern rationality variously referred to as "substantive" or "holistic" reason. Often it is referred to *tout court* as "critical reason"; Charles Davis links it to

> the tradition of criticism in Western culture, which goes back to the Enlightenment, passes through the critical philosophy of Kant, Fichte and Hegel to the Marxist critique of ideology and is represented most clearly today by the critical theory of the Frankfurt School.[14]

In contrast to technical reason, substantive reason uses critical reflection as a means of understanding the physical and social universes primarily in their relation to human beings, not merely in terms of their value to the exercise of instrumental volition.

As Max Weber points out in his work on the Protestant ethic, the establishment of early capitalism and the rise of the Protestant work ethic in the United States is closely linked to a focus on the world as a sphere for the exercise of human instrumentality, a result of the Calvinist belief in the Christian's role as the instrument of God's will in creation. This development at the same time provides the basis in American culture for the bifurcation of reason into its technical and substantive elements, as Bellah has demonstrated in his work on American civil

---

[13]Davis, *Theology*, 109.

[14]Ibid., p. 104.

religion.[15] In Calvinist terms, the "world" was seen as the domain of purely instrumental rationality, while the substantive elements of value were projected into an absolutely transcendent—that is, absent—God. Bellah notes that Americans have been ambiguous about the degree of allegiance they have been willing to grant each of these two forms. From the start, there has been a close link between humane reason and American biblical religion in the articulation of a public theology centered on republican virtue, although it was biblical symbolism which has had by far the greater impact:

> The public theology provided a sense of value and purpose without which the national community and ultimately even the liberal state could not have survived, but it was never entirely clear what that value and purpose was. On the one hand it seemed to imply the full realization of the values laid down in the Declaration of Independence but certainly not fully implemented in a nation that among other things still legalized slavery. On the other hand it could imply a messianic mission of manifest destiny with respect to the rest of the continent.[16]

A later development in American culture was the liberal cultivation of a "utilitarian individualism" which Bellah sees embodied in the language of the Constitution. In many ways this strain of thought is sharply antagonistic to the humane beliefs he sees interacting with the biblical tradition; it possesses, however, the virtue of being able to legitimate entrepreneurial interests in a way not open to its predecessor.

Many observers have noted the disproportionate role of purely technical reason in contemporary American society. As Davis notes, modern science and modern society are here experiencing a crisis with roots in the emergence of modernity itself:

> the distinction between *poiesis* and *praxis* has been lost. *Poiesis* is making, and to it belongs *techne*, the rational adaptation of means to pregiven ends. *Praxis* is distinctively human doing, constituted by the deliberation and choice of ends. If all human action is conceived as *poiesis*, controllable by *techne*, so that *praxis* is ignored or eliminated, there is no freedom and no political discussion of ends. The experts become technocrats, ruling with an authority that cannot be challenged, except by other experts on technical grounds. Modernity is thus leading to the unfreedom of a society unable to question the expertise of bureaucrats and technocrats.[17]

---

[15]Robert N. Bellah and Phillip Hammond, *Varieties of Civil Religion* (San Francisco: Harper & Row, 1980). See especially Bellah's chapter on "Religion and the Legitimation of the American Republic."

[16]Bellah, ibid., 14-15.

[17]Davis, *Theology*, 30.

The countercultural and youth movements of the 1960s have been seen as a direct challenge to the technocratic domination of American life, as the attempt to reassert the autonomy and precedence of humane reason in the life of institutions and the formation of public policy. Theodore Roszak's *The Making of a Counterculture* first put forward this thesis in 1969, applying it to the primarily political outbursts of the middle and late 1960s. Others since then have attempted (for the most part, successfully) to extend his thesis to the new religious movements of the late 1960s and the 1970s, seeing in them the legitimate heirs of the counterculture, the "surviving institutional remnants" of that earlier period.[18]

It is in this perspective that we see the current upsurge in conservative Christian activity as paralleling that of the other new religious movements, although it does so in a fashion which tends to occlude the similarities between the two sets of phenomena. The countercultural and the neo-Fundamentalist movements have arisen as a result of keenly felt dissatisfaction with the effects of modern secular culture upon the lives of their adherents and the life of the nation in general. Observes Robert Grant, Director of The Christian Voice:

> There's a tremendous tidal wave of unrest and frustration sweeping the Christian community. . . . We did not create that wave; rather, it created us. We seek to guide its power so [that] it has massive impact on Washington, rather than dissipating aimlessly.[19]

The expressions of concern by the Moral Majority and similar groups with the decline of the family as an institution, with changing sexual mores, with the growth of bureaucracy, and with uncertain economic and political developments all touch on areas that have undergone radical change in the past two decades as a result of the dominance of technical reason in American economic, political and social life. But this is a point that the Christian New Right is not willing to grant; instead, like other nativist movements it "mistakes symptoms for causes,"[20] and insists on its interpretation of the present difficulty as a result of the nation's wholesale abandonment of biblical standards. Indeed, biblical morality is

---

[18]See, most recently, Thomas Robbins and Dick Anthony, eds., *In Gods We Trust*, a collection of essays upon this subject.

[19]Interview with Roland R. Hegstad, "Down the Road to a Christian Republic," *Liberty* (May/June 1980): 4.

[20]McLoughlin, William, *Revivals, Awakenings, and Reform* (Chicago: University of Chicago Press, 1978).

viewed as *supporting* the effort to reassert the legitimacy of traditional American political and economic structures:

> The free enterprise system is clearly outlined in the Book of Proverbs in the Bible. Jesus Christ makes it clear that the work ethic was a part of His plan for man. Ownership of property is biblical. Competition in business is biblical. Ambitious and successful business management is clearly outlined as a part of God's plan for His people.[21]

Fundamentalists, already predisposed to a deep distrust of modernity, grow more frustrated in their failure to control changes affecting their daily existence. Unable to effectively combat federal intrusions into the enclaves of the Christian Schools, threatened by the limited legal acceptance of civil rights for ethnic and sexual minorities, and, most significantly, powerless in the face of radical change in the family itself, they have been pushed to develop a rationale for attempting to alter the direction of social change by forcing a change in political leadership. Nourished still by the notion of individual salvation as normative, in 1976 they thus supported the election of a born-again Christian whose personal faith would carry biblical morality into government and turn the tide of moral degeneration.

Of course, Jimmy Carter—the nuclear engineer—was more than willing to continue the government's emphasis upon technical solutions to human problems, using the values from his religious tradition only as a technical means of motivating public compliance with his program of "lowered expectations." Moreover, in an attempt to shore up his own political support, he granted legitimacy to liberal attempts to preserve some notion of humane progress in the purely formal recognition of the "rights" of various minorities attempting to mitigate the inhuman effects of a technocratic system.

But it was precisely this *formal* legitimation of the inevitable course of the utilitarian and technical juggernaut that evangelicals and Fundamentalists could not bear. While liberal social policy demands the formal equality of citizen/consumers for the efficient utilization of a skilled labor pool and the promotion of consumption, the increased public visibility of those bearing the sign (and legitimation) of the beast could only incite the "Bible-believing" Christians to political action to reverse the course of this "politicization of immorality."

---

[21]Jerry Falwell, *Moral Majority*, 13.

The historic change in Fundamentalist beliefs which enables participation in a political system wholly dominated by technical reason, in the effort to reverse the effects of that very same domination, required a basic change in the theological understanding of the status of human reason. This reconceptualization has been provided by the religious mentor of the movement, Reverend Jerry Falwell, who has—at least temporarily—recast the Fundamentalist critique of modernity to allow at least a limited role for secular reason in Fundamentalist theology.

Cast in terms of the traditional Fundamentalist concern with the inerrancy of scripture, Falwell's innovation involves the implicit legitimation of at least some aspects of technical rationality which is now seen as providing some basis for the understanding of eternal scriptural verities. Unlike his forebears, Falwell is not willing to grant the *literal* truth of scriptural statements regarding the creation of the world, for instance. The world, he now admits, is as old as carbon-14 tests say it is; when questioned about his acceptance of the physical evidence for the age of the planet, he allowed that he has

> no problem at all with that. I thoroughly, totally agree with all of these findings. And the Bible is in no way contradicted, nor does the Bible contradict that. In the beginning, God created the heaven and the earth. If you'll read the first three chapters of Genesis, carefully, there's a very clear, unlimited time span there. It could have been millions of years; it could have been hundreds of millions of years.[22]

To this extent, then, we must be willing to change our imperfect understanding of scripture to accord with the "factual knowledge" of the scientists. But God—as Scripture says—*created* the world; this fact is not open to scientific investigation or verification. "Scripture is not subject to change," but "the interpretation of Scripture" is very subject to change.[23]

Where modern critical reason has no authority to question or change biblical norms is in the realm of moral injunctions which Falwell claims to find in scripture. It is apparent that here Falwell is rejecting the legitimacy of the eclipsed form of reason—humane, substantive, holistic reason—to further human self-understanding:

> Humanism is man's attempt to create a heaven on earth, exempting God and His law. Humanists propose that man is in charge of his own destiny. Human-

[22]*Penthouse Magazine* (March 1981): 151.

[23]Jerry Falwell, *San Francisco Chronicle,* "This World" section, 22 March 1981, 9.

> ism exalts man's reason and intelligence. It advocates situation ethics, freedom from any constraint, and defines sin as man's maladjustment to man.[24]

As technical reason is to operate in the world of "facts" without the need for the self-reflection of a knowing human subject, so morality operates in the theological realm as a kind of eternal calculus by which some are counted saved, others damned:

> I think that you could say that science is simplistic because it's exact. I was studying mechanical engineering before I became a Christian. . . . You come to exact, simplistic answers if you follow the proper equations and the proper processes. . . . Theology, to me, is an exact science. God is God. The Bible is the inspired, inherent [sic] word of God. And if everyone accepts the same equations, they will arrive at the same answer.[25]

Critical self-reflection—not scientific rationality—is thus seen as the essence of "secular humanism" and is condemned as a rejection of God's absolute authority in every non-technical matter. The Fundamentalist antipathy to the Satanic forces of modernity still stands in its rejection of what the Christian New Right instinctively recognizes as the modern soul—the twice-beleaguered forces of humanistic culture.

This basic change in the theology of the "Fundamentals" has enabled the participation of the Christian New Right in the 1980 Reagan campaign at a level of technical expertise never before seen in American political life. Guided by the organizational experts of the secular new right, and relying on the most technologically advanced media now available, the Christian New Right mobilized to produce an estimated sixty-six percent of Ronald Reagan's margin of victory in the Presidential election. Its effect upon other national and local elections is also viewed as significant. As a member of the Washington, D.C., Christian Action Council describes it,

> We gained nine seats in the Senate . . . and 20 seats in the House of Representatives. There's no question about it now, we are in the driver's seat.[26]

For their efforts, Christian New Right groups have been rewarded with posts in the Reagan administration; Robert Billings of the Moral Major-

---

[24]Falwell, *Listen America!*, 65-66.

[25]Falwell, *Penthouse Magazine* (March 1981): 150.

[26]*The Presbyterian Journal* 26 November 1980: 4.

ity and the Committee for the Survival of a Free Congress held the post of religious liaison during the transition and now occupies a position in the Department of Education. It is not unlikely that figures from the Christian New Right will continue to exert some influence in government as long as the present administration continues. Warnings from the right have already been issued:

> Ronald Reagan appealed for the votes of prolifers, born-again Christians, opponents of business, blue-collar workers and those patriotic Americans who want an America militarily superior to anyone—and they responded with their contributions and votes.
>
> These people understood that he was a man who honestly shared their deepest values.
>
> They were right. But holding those values is one thing. Implementing them is another.[27]

What is the nature of that influence likely to be? In posing this question, we are asking whether the New Fundamentalism—or any religious ideology—can in any way restrain the exercise of technical rationality in this society. We are also implicitly posing a question about the future of a critical reason predicated on a self-reflective search for humane values in the face of the new alliance between forces aggressively antagonistic to its survival.

There was a point in the development of the new religious movements—of which the Christian New Right is the latest and perhaps the most energetic example—when analysts could imagine the wholesale rejection of technical domination and the mass adoption of the values of the counterculture as institutionalized in these groups. And perhaps it is still possible to hope for such an outcome, as Bellah pensively suggests in his latest thoughts upon the phenomenon.[28]

But with many this possibility has never been given much chance of success; even for the most committed, it appears to have suffered a symbolic death with the nine hundred at Jonestown in Guyana. A "revolutionary alternative" based on a utopian vision is, as Bellah himself admits, the most unlikely of possible resolutions of the current crisis.

What is more likely is the failure and concomitant co-optation of the social critique obscured in the Christian New Right's challenge to modernity. Out of their critical ignorance of the causes of the current social

---

[27]Richard A. Viguerie, *Oakland Tribune: Eastbay Today*, 9 January 1981.

[28]Bellah, *Varieties*, 185-86.

disorder, the new Fundamentalists treat only its effects, chasing the bogeymen of "atheistic conspiracies" and moral failure in the American will. Meanwhile, in the centers of power, the new "experts" serving at the corporate temples of technical domination will both promote the latter's sovereign reign and use the new theology to legitimate their seizure of political power.

APPENDIX

(Source: *A Resource Packet on the Christian New Right.* Compiled by James McBride. February, 1981.)

CHRISTIAN NEW RIGHT

Christian Voice

Headquarters	Washington, D.C. and Pacific Grove, California
Officers	Executive Director: Reverend Robert Grant President (and Vice-Chairman of Christians for Reagan): Reverend Richard Zone Chief Strategist: Colonel V. Doner Legislative Liason: Gary Jarmin Legislative Assistant: David Troxler
Membership/ Mailing List	190,000 (45 Protestant denominations and the Roman Catholic Church represented including 37,000 pastors
Publications	Family Voting Issues Index, Report Card on Fourteen Key Moral Issues
Affiliates	Christians for Reagan, Moral Government Fund (Christian Voice Political Action Committee—PAC)

Moral Majority

(Moral Majority, Inc., Moral Majority Foundation, and Moral Majority Legal Defense Foundation)

Headquarters	Washington, D.C.
Officers	President: Reverend Jerry Falwell (Former) Executive Director and Board Member: Reverend Robert Billings Vice President of Operations: Dr. Ronald Godwin Vice President of Communications: Cal Thomas

Board of Directors	Reverend Greg Dixon, Indianapolis Baptist Temple Reverend Curtis Hutson, editor, *Sword of the Lord* and former president of the Baptist University of America Reverend James Kennedy, Coral Ridge Presbyterian Church, Fort Lauderdale, Florida Reverend Tim LaHaye, Scott Memorial Baptist Church and Chancellor of Christian Heritage College, El Cajon, California
Membership/ Mailing List	Mailing list runs about 400,000 with membership estimates ranging as high as 4 million. Includes over 70,000 ministers and 10,000 Christian schools.
Publications	The Moral Majority Report
Affiliates	Family America

National Christian Action Coalition

Headquarters	Washington, D.C.
Officers	Executive Director and Chairman: Reverend Robert Billings Executive Director of Christian Voters Victory Fund: Dale Silvers
Membership/ Mailing List	1200 Churches, Christian Schools, and Christian Associations
Publications	Congressional Scoreboard
Affiliates	Christian Voters Victory Fund (PAC)

Religious Roundtable†

Headquarters	Arlington, Virginia
Officers	President: Edward McAteer Vice President: Reverend James Robison

†Present at the founding session of the Religious Roundtable were such right-wing figures as:

John Beckett, Intercessors for America
Dr. George Benson, Harding College

	Executive Director: H. Edward Rowe Executive Vice President: William Chasey
Membership	Council of 56. Estimated mailing list of 15,000-20,000
Affiliates	Religious Roundtable Issues and Answers

SECULAR NEW RIGHT

Committee for the Survival of a Free Congress (CSFC)

Headquarters	Washington, D.C.
Officers	Executive Director and Chairman: Paul Weyrich Vice Chairman: Reverend Robert Billings Treasurer: Charles Moser
Membership/ Mailing List	Unknown
Publications	Political Report, Family Protection Report
Affiliates	CSFC Training School, Free Congress Research and Education Foundation, Heritage Foundation, National Congress for Educational Excellence

Conservative Caucus

Headquarters	Boston, Massachusetts
Officers	Chairman: Meldrim Thomson National Director: Howard Phillips Executive Director: Andy Messing National Field Director: Edward McAteer

---

Major Edgar C. Bundy, Church League of America
Clay Claiborne, Black Silent Majority
Dick Dingman, Republican Study Committee
Robert Dugan, National Association of Evangelicals
John Fisher, American Security Council
Peter Gemmma, National Pro-Life Political Action Committee
Howard Phillips, Conservative Caucus
Gary Potter, Catholics for Christian Political Action
Edward Rowe, Anita Bryant Ministries
Phyllis Schlafly, Eagle Forum (StopERA)
Richard A. Viguerie, RAVCO
Rus Walton, Third Century Movement
Paul Weyrich, Committee for the Survival of a Free Congress

Membership/ Mailing List: 300,000-400,000

Affiliates: American Legal Advocates; Conservative Caucus Research; Analysis and Education Foundation; National Defeat Legal Services; Wake Up, America

National Conservative Political Action Committee (NCPAC)

Headquarters: Rosslyn, Virginia

Officers: Chairman and Executive Director: John Terry Dolan
Vice Chairman: James Carbaugh
Secretary: J. Curtis Herge
Treasurer: Roger Stone

Membership/ Mailing List: 150,000

Affiliates: Conservatives Against Liberal Legislation (CALL), "Kennedy Truth Squad," National Conservative Research and Education Foundation, Washington Legal Foundation

Richard A. Viguerie Company (RAVCO)
(Directech, Viguerie Communications Corporation)

Headquarters: Falls Church, Virginia

Officers: President: Richard A. Viguerie
Executive Vice President: Jim Aldige
Vice President for Public Affairs: Bill Rhatican

Membership/ Mailing List: 4.5 million names listed in direct mail computers

Publications: Conservative Digest, New Right Report, Political Gun News

Affiliates: Committee for a Responsible Youth Politics, Conservative Leadership Youth Foundation, Public Service Political Action Committee

(The following organizations are linked with the Christian and Secular New Right through personnel, policies, and/or projects.)

OLD RIGHT

American Conservative Union

Headquarters	Washington, D.C.
Officers	Chairman: Mickey Edwards (R-Oklahoma) Executive Director: Ross L. Whealton President: Phil Crane (R-Illinois)
Membership/ Mailing List	300,000
Publications	Battle Line, Public Monitor Report
Affiliates	American Conservative Union Education and Research Institute, Conservative Victory Fund

Reagan Campaign

Republican Study Committee

RADICAL RIGHT

American Security Council
Billy James Hargis Christian Crusade
Christian Freedom Foundation
Church League of America
John Birch Society
Liberty Lobby

SINGLE-ISSUE ORGANIZATIONS OR COALITIONS

Anti-Abortion, Anti-ERA

American Life Lobby—"Stop the Baby Killers" Campaign*
Americans for Life*
Concerned Women for America*
Eagle Forum, Stop ERA*
Friends for Life*
Life Amendment Political Action Committee*

*Note: Asterisk represents *direct* participation by Christian New Right figures, participation by Christian New Right Groups in coalitions, and/or the use of Christian New Right resources (e.g., funds, publications) to promote the aims of the organization.

National Pro-Family Coalition*
National Pro-Life Political Action Committee*

Anti-Homosexual

Anita Bryant Ministries—"Save Our Children, Inc."
In God We Trust, Inc*

Anti-"Internal Subversion"

National Committee to Restore Internal Security

Anti-Union

Americans Against Union Control of Government
American Conservative Union—Stop OSHA
National Right-to-Work Committee

Censorship

Citizens for Decency through Law (formerly Citizens for Decent Literature)*
Educational Research Analysis*
Morality in Media
National Federation for Decency—"Clean Up TV" Campaign*

Consumer "Protection"

Consumer Alert, Inc.*

Gun Lobby

Citizens Committee for the Right to Keep and Bear Arms
Gun Owners of America

Pro-Apartheid, Anti-African Liberation Movement

Institute of American Relations

Pro-Pentagon, Anti-Soviet

Coalition for Peace through Strength (American Security Council)

School Prayer

Coalition for the First Amendment*
Leadership Foundation*

Senior Citizens

National Alliance (*not* Council) of Senior Citizens

Taiwan Lobby

American Council for a Free China*
Committee for a Free China
Friends of Free China
"New Flying Tigers" (American Security Council)

BIBLIOGRAPHY

Bellah, Robert N. and Phillip Hammond. *Varieties of Civil Religion*. San Francisco: Harper & Row, 1980

Davis, Charles. *Theology and Political Society*. Cambridge: Cambridge University Press, 1980

Falwell, Jerry. *Listen, America!* Garden City NY: Doubleday, 1980.

Hofstadter, Richard. *Anti-Intellectualism in American Life*. New York: Vintage, 1963.

McLoughlin, William. *Revivals, Awakenings and Reform*. Chicago: University of Chicago Press, 1978.

Marsden, George M. *Fundamentalism and American Culture*. New York/Oxford: Oxford University Press, 1980.

Robbins, Thomas and Dick Anthony. *In Gods We Trust*. New Brunswick NJ: Transaction Books, 1980.

THE FUN-SEEKING MOVEMENT IN CALIFORNIA

by Jean Burfoot

THE MAIN PURPOSE of this paper is to attempt an understanding of the modern fun-seeking movement and its relationship to the formation of new religious movements. The fun phenomenon has been heralded by several social theorists. Wolfe has suggested that we are in the middle of a "Happiness Explosion"[1] with emphasis on fun, joy, and pleasure.[2] This phenomenon is particularly prevalent in California.

It will be argued that fun seeking has much in common with what, in a less secular age, could be referred to as an outbreak of ecstatic religion. According to Huizinga, fun is the feeling obtained from playful activity, and this varies in intensity from frivolity to ecstacy.[3] The central purpose of this paper will be to examine theoretically those social structural processes characterizing modern Western industrial society, which are believed to produce social actors who seek ecstatic experience beyond the bounds of social action.

Once people step over the boundaries of social meaning and action, they enter the marginal realm of *communitas*.[4] *Communitas* is opposed

---

[1]Wolfe, as quoted by R. Weber in *Journal of Popular Culture* 1 (Summer 1974): 73.

[2]Ibid.

[3]J. Huizinga, *Homo Ludens* (Routledge & Kegan, 1955) 21.

[4]V. Turner, *The Ritual Process* (Aldine Publishing Co., 1969).

to structure. It is "anti-structure," the egalitarian "sentiment for humanity" of which David Hume speaks, representing the desire for a total unmediated relationship between person and person."[5] The mass of liminal people, characterized by the sentiment of *communitas*, provides a pool of individuals who are no longer fully committed to the old social meaning systems. While the existence of a fun-seeking phenomenon may announce the initial ecstatic flight from old social meaning, the existence of a growing realm of *communitas* provides the basis for the creation of new systems of meaning, not least those found in new religious movements.

The remainder of this paper will discuss the theoretical conditions, or Triple Process, leading up to fun seeking; the way in which peak fun experiences heal the rifts produced by the Triple Process; and the future of the fun-seeking energy, with special consideration of the Californian situation.

THE TRIPLE PROCESS

Theoretical Framework for Understanding the Preconditions for the Emergence of Fun Seeking. In this section of the paper, the triple process of differentiation, disenchantment, and alienation will be discussed. Special emphasis will be given to the effects of this process on individual social actors.

Differentiation. With the increase in the division of labor in society, the number of provinces of meaning has drastically increased. The problem of differentiation for social actors is twofold. Increased differentiation expresses the themes of both "too much" and "too little." On the one hand the multiple meanings of specialized fields of activity form a vast panoply of diverse opinion defying unification. On the other hand, individuals become isolated in private, individual provinces of meaning, which they may not fully be able to relate to the rest of society.

Thus, with increased specialization, the social actor is left to balance the uneasy relationship between specialized role meaning and the vast mass of other interpretations of the world. The flooding of the "meaning market" may lead to what Klapp has described as "information overload."[6] Klapp describes what happens to individuals in reaction to the

---

[5]V. Turner, *Dramas, Fields, and Metaphors: Symbolic Action in Human Society* (Cornell University Press, 1974) 274.

[6]O. E. Klapp, *Currents of Unrest* (Holt, Rinehart & Winston, 1972) 236-96.

multiple meanings represented in the media. While he is not directly addressing differentiation per se, he does address the problem of multiple meaning. It thus seems relevant to discuss Klapp's description of reactions to "too much" meaning or multiple meanings in society.

According to Klapp, "the human brain has great powers of abstraction, but is severely limited in channel capacity."[7] Klapp points to Miller's discussion of the magic number seven. "We are able to perceive up to about six dots (marbles, beans, dice marks, musical terms) accurately without counting; beyond this errors become frequent."[8] He indicates that selective meaning systems could keep us from being overwhelmed. However, when information comes thick and fast, without obvious connection of meaning, then problems arise. When there is more information than we can process, this produces a meaning gap. "A person may feel that his life is like a jigsaw puzzle that won't come together, either because pieces are missing or new ones added do not fit."[9]

Without an all-encompassing meaning system to unite the diffuse meanings emerging from the division of labor, it is thought that social actors may experience this fragmentation as an overload of information. As Klapp points out in relation to societies with information overload, "the chances are good that a member will be in a chronic state of cognitive dissonance. He finds it difficult to pull himself together, close wounds, repair the fragmentation of his thoughts, tastes, and symbols."[10] Information overload produces a meaning gap, and a meaning gap, is a "hiatus, a vacuum, or a fragmentation of meaning, which separates people of the same society."[11]

Thus, in summary, it is suggested that differentiation produces a fragmentation of meaning which results in a vast number of interpretations of the world. As there is no overall system that unifies these multiple meanings, exposure to the multiple world views is experienced as an overload of information. This, in turn, can produce chronic cognitive dissonance among those who can find no way to put the self or society back together into a meaningful whole.

---

[7]Ibid., 267.

[8]Ibid., 268.

[9]Ibid.

[10]Ibid., 275.

[11]Ibid., 289.

Differentiation may be regarded as the prime mover in the Triple Process: the original force in the separation of meaning, feeling, and action. Disenchantment results from the separation of rational and irrational elements of meaning and activity. Alienation results from the separation of conception and execution produced by the division of labor.

Disenchantment. Weber warned us that growing disenchantment would accompany a social world characterized by bureaucracy as a dominant form of institution. As Gerth and Mills point out, "The extent and direction of 'rationalization' is thus measured negatively in terms of the degree to which magical elements of thought are displaced, or positively by the extent to which ideas gain systematic coherence and naturalistic consistency."[12]

Insofar as there has been an increase in bureaucratization, or rationalization, the "irrational" elements of meaning have been displaced from social action. People are chosen for and maintain office, not because of personal attributes associated with charisma, but because they have acquired qualifications measured by rational criteria such as examinations. Also, because of fixed rules of role content and interaction within a bureaucratic system, social actors have lost the ability to be creative.

Both of these aspects, the exclusion of irrationality and the fixed nature of role content, can be seen in Weber's ideal typical description of bureaucracy:

> Office holding is a "vocation." This is shown, first, in the requirements of a firmly prescribed course of training, which demands the entire capacity for work for a long period of time, and in generally prescribed and special examinations which are prerequisites of employment. . . . It is decisive for the specific nature of modern loyalty to an office that, in the pure type, it does not establish a relationship to a *person*. . . . Modern loyalty is devoted to impersonal and functional purposes. . . . [Also] there is a principle of *fixed* and official jurisdictional areas which are generally ordered by rules, that is, by laws or administrative regulations. . . . The regular activities . . . are distributed in a *fixed* way as official duties.[13]

Thus, typically, the bureaucratic system disallows emotion within and between roles. Relationships are not between feeling people but between functional rational offices. The ability to obtain personal meaning from these roles is thus reduced. The vehicle of feeling, which is

---

[12]Gerth and Mills, *From Max Weber* (Routledge & Kegan, 1948) 51.

[13]Ibid., 196-99.

capable of linking social structure to social action, thus producing consequent meaning for the individual, has been removed as irrelevant in the bureaucratic structure. As Weber pointed out, the rational, calculating systems of thought that underlie bureaucracy deny the importance of any approach that asks for a "meaning of inner worldly occurrences."[14] Thus, meaning derived from feelings is not regarded as legitimate in this system of rationality.

The fixed nature of role content and interaction within the bureaucratic system means that social actors cannot "play" with roles or the social system. "The bearing of man has been disenchanted and denuded of its mystical but inwardly genuine plasticity."[15] This lack of plasticity is further supported by Sennet's comments in "The Fall of Public Man." According to Sennet,

> A person cannot imagine playing with the facts of his position in society, playing with his appearance to others, because these conditions are now part and parcel of himself. . . . To lose the ability to play with social life depends on the existence of a dimension of society which stands apart from, at a distance from, intimate desire, need and identity. . . . Modern man (has) become an actor deprived of his art.[16]

There can be no hope for change in the bureaucratic machine, which Weber aptly described as "the iron cage of bureaucracy." According to Weber, the bureaucrat is "only a single cog in an ever moving mechanism which prescribes to him an essentially fixed route of march."[17] Thus, there is an inability to play with the fixed roles of bureaucracy. At the same time, the expulsion of the personal, emotional content of roles reduces the possibility of creating new, personal meaning, through the expression of feelings. Thus both the fixed nature of bureaucracy and the inability to equate feeling with social action may serve to render this fossilized, emotionally colorless social system personally meaningless. In other words, social actors in a bureaucratic world will become disenchanted. This may lead to boredom, when the social world is experienced as banal—a process described by Klapp:

---

[14]Ibid., 351.

[15]Ibid., 148.

[16]R. Sennet, *The Fall of Public Man* (Alfred A. Knopf, 1977) 267.

[17]Gerth and Mills, *From Max Weber*, 228.

> The very efficiency of technology in the mechanical sense becomes a thrust of noise, intrusion, coercion and boring sameness (banality), which threatens the meaning of the communication system and hence of society itself.[18]

Banality, Klapp contends, arises

> whenever communication networks and social experience are (1) unduly repetitive, offering nothing new—"I've heard all that before"; (2) artificially fabricated and packaged . . . ; (3) shallow in various senses—not permitting depth exploration, meditation; too impersonal; too rapid change; unimaginative matter-of-factness; (4) stereotyped, false as images; (5) hypocritical; (6) low in personal input: requiring little involement, giving all the answers and leaving nothing to do.[19]
>
> A psychological definition might be that banality is a restriction of awareness, of which the main symptom is boredom as a kind of frustration . . . a lack of payoff to imagination, hope, identity and the human spirit.[20]

Thus rational, bureaucratic organization is capable of producing disenchanted, bored individuals who experience the social system as banal. Bureaucratic roles can provide no personal meaning because of the lack of emotional content in roles. Also, the fixed nature of the system, which provides no opportunity for playful human creativity, denies the hope for future change within that system.

Alienation. The problem of alienation for individuals in modern, Western, industrial society, is closely related to the problems of differentiation and disenchantment. In capitalist society, there is not only a general division of labor separating people with specialist skills, but also, according to Marx, a specific division of labor between the capitalist ruling class, with power over ideas in society, and the working class who are meant to execute those ideas. This division of labor is fixed in the bureaucratic system which complements modern capitalism. Social actors in this system are alienated. They cannot fulfill themselves and are therefore alienated from their true selves because the ability to be creative, combining conception and execution in productive social action, is denied them. In capitalist society, the ruling class controls the means of production. Thus, "the activity of the worker is not his spontaneous activity. It is another's activity, and a loss of his own spontaneity."[21] According to

---

[18]Klapp, *Currents*, 300.

[19]Ibid., 348.

[20]Ibid., 347.

[21]Bottomore and Rubel, *Karl Marx—Selected Writings in Sociology and Social Philosophy* (Watts and Co., 1956) 170.

Marx, the inability of social actors under capitalism to perform free creative production produces damaging psychological results. The worker "does not fulfill himself in his work but denies himself, has a feeling of deep misery, not of well-being, does not develop freely a physical and mental energy, but is physically exhausted and mentally debased."[22]

The alienation resulting from the division of mental and material labor in capitalist society, produces still further problems. The ruling-class power over ideology has made it possible to create mythologies which can produce still further frustrations for social members. The American myth that "everyone can make it" (and its extreme emphasis on achievement orientation) sharply contrasts with the stark reality that not everyone can "make it." Individuals are forced to experience feelings of frustration and failure that are by-products of the alienating division of mental and material labor.

Alienation, or the powerlessness which comes with the separation of conception and execution, can be found, of course, in any social role. This more general alienation can be permanent or merely a transitional phase. However, it is felt that the more specific division of mental and material labor in capitalist society produces a situation in which a large number of social actors are alienated from their work and from their true selves on a more permanent basis.

The Triple Process—a Summary. The Triple Process, as outlined above, produces problems for individual actors. Differentiation produces fragmentation of meaning and the possibility of information overload, leading to meaning gap. The individual may not be able to pull the self and society back together into a meaningful whole. At the same time, this process may continually isolate individuals from each other because of the lack of a shared meaning element.

Disenchantment, as a reaction to increasing bureaucratic organization in society, may be seen as a process in which the possibility for personal satisfaction and meaning within the social framework decreases. Bureaucracy, because of its lack of expression for human feelings, and the fixed nature of its organization, is impotent in providing meaning for social actors. Thus, the social actor begins to experience society as banal. Society is no place for the investment of feelings or hope for future change within that system.

---

[22]Ibid., 169

Alienation, produced by gaps between conception and execution in social action, is particularly important in capitalist society because of the class division of mental and material labor. The worker is alienated from his or her true self because he or she cannot combine conception and execution in spontaneous, creative production.

In many ways, the Triple Process may be seen as a process which separates the individual from society. Each part of the process, in some way decreases the possibility for alignment of meaning, feeling, and action. This process thus reduces the possibilities for fulfillment for human beings within the social system.

THE HEALING POWER OF FUN

Healing the Self. When discussing the healing power of fun, it should be pointed out that the object to be healed is the self, or the identity of individual social actors. Weber, in discussing "The Iron Cage of Bureaucracy," seemed pessimistic about social actors within such a cage. Marx discussed alienation and its effects on social actors within the capitalist system. What neither of these authors appeared to recognize was that satisfaction for the self may not always be found within the boundaries of a social structure. In fact, if there is no satisfaction for the self, in terms of alignment of meaning, feeling, and action within a social structure, it seems reasonable to search for satisfaction elsewhere. As Ralph Turner notes, "such concepts as alienation and anomie tell only where the self is not. . . . Why should the self be lodged in work?"[23] Indeed, why should the self be discovered in any institutional context? Turner's answer is that "over the past several decades substantial shifts have occurred away from an institution and toward an impulse emphasis"[24] in realization of the self. This shift in satisfaction for the self corresponds to the progress of the Triple Process, previously outlined.

Thus, if there has been a shift away from satisfaction of the self through "institution" to satisfaction through "impulse," what does "impulse" provide that "institution" does not? It is thought that fun seeking represents an attempt at satisfaction through "impulse" and that satisfaction through "impulse" heals a self which can only be experienced

---

[23]Ralph Turner, "The Real Self: From Institution to Impulse" *American Journal of Sociology* 81:5 (1976): 997.

[24]Ibid.

in a dissected form, if experienced through "institution," as characterized by the Triple Process.

The use of the term "healing" seems appropriate in this context. A healing process puts things back together that have been broken or nonaligned. Healing makes things whole again. In terms of meaning, a synonym for healthiness is defined as a shared meaning element. Healing the self can thus be seen as a process that realigns diffuse parts of the self within a shared meaning element, making the person whole again.

Religious and Secular Healing. Before entering a discussion of why fun works in relation to the Triple Process, some consideration of religious and secular healing will be made.

I. M. Lewis, in his discussion of ecstatic religion, has pointed out that ecstatic cults are also healing cults.[25] Healing is achieved by a variety of ritual mechanisms, such as dancing, designed to achieve a catharsis or peak experience that will consequently give the individual a sense of release and cure.[26] The peak experiences discovered in ecstatic religion appear similar to that which can be achieved through strenuous activity in sports, such as running. The running cult, like other new fun cults, offers social actors the chance to be healed and "get it all together." Claims such as "running can cure heart disease" have appeared on the cover of *Runner's World*, along with other claims to the production of fitness and health.

The catharsis associated with religious ecstatic release can also be found in other secular expressions of fun seeking, such as motorcycle riding. In Alt's work on motorcycling as a form of consumerism, he quotes a poem by Perry, written about the ecstatic peak experience in motorcycling.

> To feel the mastery that you alone
> and only you can feel at that moment.
> A slight twist of the throttle and you are off
> with an acceleration that belies the motorcycle's size
> because it can outstrip any car.
> The twist of the hips and the quick weave around a sharp S turn.
> The tingle of leaning over with danger so close yet so remote.
> Gritting the teeth and the urge to roll on the throttle to its
> fullest stop,

---

[25]I. M. Lewis, *Ecstatic Religion* (Penguin, 1971) 91.

[26]Ibid.

to fly off into the sky
right into the clouds and the sun
the feel of the saddle as it gives with every stretch of the road,
the sharp intake of clean cold air
that fills your blood with an exhilaration no other thing can.
Quivering, vibrating, the tautness,
yet the relaxation of your muscles, but at the ready,
quickening to speed faster and faster
until you can sense yourself flying off into space. . . .

Alt states, "For Perry, the motorcycle transmits 'control,' excitement, 'danger,' transcendence, and a mythical sense of spiritual freedom."[27]

It seems evident that both religious and secular forms of ecstasy may provide similar feelings of transcendence and spiritual freedom. They are all expressions of freedom from social constraints. Just how these ecstatic experiences could heal the wounds inflicted by the Triple Process will be dealt with in the following section of the paper.

How Fun Works or "What's in a kick." Both religious and secular ecstatic experiences are associated with some activity involving strenuous play, whether dancing, running, or motorcycling. Fun is the good feeling that comes from this activity. This section of the paper will examine just why each activity should be able to reverse or reduce the effects of the Triple Process.

Lack of Differentiation. As previously noted, increasing differentiation in society will produce an increase in the possible interpretations of the world. This vast number of multiple meanings may be experienced as an information overload, individuals being unable to pull together the jigsaw puzzle meaning of a specialized society into one, unifying meaning system. The self is thus similarly differentiated, action within such a system being divided up into specialist activities which provide no overall meaning.

It is through play activities, or fun-giving events, that the self can be experienced as a whole, As Klapp pointed out, in a differentiated society it is difficult to "feel ourselves deeply . . . as a unity or whole."[28] He suggests that "what many people seem to be striving for in strenuous and dangerous play . . . [is] . . . some kind of ritual by which to prove

[27]Alt, "Leisure, Labor, and Consumption: a Critical Sociology of Reification under Capitalism" (Ph.D. dissertation, Washington University, 1976).

[28]O. E. Klapp, *Collective Search for Identity* (Holt, Rinehart & Winston, 1969) 19.

themselves, some test which requires a person to extend his whole self, not merely play a role."[29]

Thus, activity in the play arena enables the self to be put back together, to be healed. Meaning, feeling, and action are united in undifferentiated play. This can also be shared with fellow players, thus providing the possibility of "getting it together" with other people, and promoting social as well as individual healing. The self and/or the play group can become the basis of unified, as opposed to diffuse, meaning.

In summary, lack of a shared meaning element in modern, differentiated society separates individuals from each other and from their whole selves. By participating in fun-giving activities, the individual may at least get his or her body and mind (whole self) together. This may be the first step in an attempt to "get it all together" at a more macrosocial level. However, in the meantime, a feeling of health or wholesomeness is given in undifferentiated play.

Enchantment. The process of bureaucratization can be seen as one in which the "irrational" elements of feeling are increasingly removed from social action. Also, the fixed nature of bureaucracy allows no room for play or creativity around social action. This process can be seen to produce disenchanted, bored social actors who experience the social system as banal.

The participation in play reverses both of these factors. Feeling or good feeling is not only sought but expected as a consequence of play. Goffman has pointed out that "Games can be fun to play . . . [and actors may] complain about a game that does not pay its way in immediate pleasure."[30] Not only is 'irrational' feeling reintroduced as an intermediary between meaning and action, but the feeling is good feeling. It is through the ritual activities of play that people experience the "emotional intensification and self definition"[31] which, as Klapp suggests, is not easily found in our modern society. Fun-giving activities also produce excitement and make the individual "feel better," in contrast to the banality associated with bureaucratic activity in which feeling is not even considered to be important. Also, action in play frees the actor's creative tendencies, thus providing release from fixed and uncreative bureaucratic roles.

---

[29]Ibid., 34.

[30]E. Goffman, *Encounters* (Bobbs-Merrill, 1961) 17.

[31]Klapp, *Collective Search*, 20.

Huizinga has suggested that "play is enchanting." It is perhaps because play provides the possibility of unifying meaning, feeling, and action, that it is enchanting, as opposed to the disenchantment produced by a bureaucratic world where meaning, feeling, and action have been separated out. Play is the action within the meaning framework of the game, and fun is the feeling produced by the acting out of the game. The ritual providing for emotional intensification thus forms a basis for self-definition which cannot be found in the emotionally colorless "iron cage of bureaucracy."

Lack of Alienation. The fun experienced in play is also a feeling that emerges from the coming together of conception and execution. There is no discrepancy between the ideal formulation of the game and its real acting out. Also, there is no division of mental and material labor, either in personal fun-giving activities or those shared with others in acting out the game. Thus, actors in the play arena are not alienated from the product of their activity or from themselves. The happiness, pleasure, or fun achieved through play activities lies in sharp contrast to the misery which Marx associated with alienated labor.

In summarizing the healing power of fun it can be said that the experience of playful action brings together elements of social action which have been separated out by the triple process of differentiation, disenchantment, and alienation. The social actor is healed, pulls himself or herself together in activity that unites areas of diffuse meaning, "meaning, feeling and action," and "conception and execution."

IDENTITY, MEANING, AND NEW BELIEF

Thus far in this paper, I have suggested that the Triple Process produces a situation in which social actors can no longer find fulfillment for the self in "institutional" activities. It is because the individual cannot pull together meaning, feeling, and action within society, that he or she seeks to transcend these conditions, seeking a variety of fun-giving activities through which to realign meaning, feeling, and action. This activity may be regarded as a search for satisfaction through "impulse" rather than through "institution."

It is my contention that such a situation is an expression of the "elan vital" or "evolutionary life force," through which individuals seek to rid themselves of obsolete social systems that can no longer provide satisfaction for human individuals.

Following the theoretical approach outlined in this paper, one would predict that those individuals most influenced by the Triple Process would be the first to seek freedom through fun-giving activities. The original urge to seek satisfaction for the self through "impulse" rather than "institution" may mark the original departure from commitment to the existing social system. Identity within that social system may no longer be possible. However, once having transcended the constraints of society, this lack of commitment may lead the individual to seek new identity outside that social system. Thus fun seeking may mark the beginning of a search for new and meaningful identity.

For Klapp, changes in identity may be related to leisure choices. Klapp distinguishes between "square" and "deviant" leisure. He hypothesizes that

> "Squares" have a firm identity and are satisfied with the opportunities of the status quo, [while] those with identity problems feel cheated by the status quo, [and are] disdainful of its opportunities and hence search for a new identity along the "trail of kicks." [Deviant leisure thus] is essentially a cultic quest "to find the highest experience and new identity among those who feel cheated." . . . This search for meaningful fun . . . leads from banal forms of amusement to realizing ones: it takes the seeker to offbeat experiences, cults, poses and bizarre drama.[32]

Thus, when fun seeking becomes a search for new meaning, rather than a short-term release from social pressures, the individuals concerned may be said to have left the constraints of social structure, rejected their social roles, and entered the realm of *communitas*. It is thought that those experiencing the greatest pressure from the Triple Process would be the first to cross over the boundary.

Communitas, according to Victor Turner, is opposed to structure. It is anti-structure, on the boundaries and in the interstitial spaces of society.[33] It is an undifferentiated, egalitarian expression of humanity, that takes one out of the divisive constraints of structure. While we associate fun seeking with activities in "play;" it is interesting to note that properties of play and properties of *communitas* converge.

Both play and *communitas* are concerned with activities outside social structural constraints. They are both undifferentiated expressions of humanity, involving the whole person in relation to other whole

---

[32]Ibid.

[33]Turner, *The Ritual Process*.

persons. They both have an antagonistic quality towards social structure. Huizinga pointed out that "play may turn to seriousness"[34] and Victor Turner has commented on *communitas* as a forum for expression of the powers of the weak in society.[35]

Play within *communitas* can result in a new play community. People may develop a sense of being apart together. This provides a basis for bonding and the production of new social movements, which may provide new meaning and identity. The combined properties of new social bonding, and the antagonistic qualities of play and *communitas*, provide a fertile ground for new religious movements; for new versions of society to replace the old and meaningless.

THE FATE OF THE FUN-SEEKING ENERGY: NEW RELIGIONS OR OLD DIVERSIONS?

General. Most of this paper, thus far, has been concerned with the general social structural conditions leading up to the emergence of fun seeking. Before returning to the specific case of California, some consideration will be given to the general fate of the fun-seeking energy.

It was suggested above that the emergence of fun seeking marks the separation of individuals from old systems of social meaning. These individuals may then become free to create or embrace new systems of meaning, such as those found in new religious movements. However, as Lenin pointed out, "the spontaneous element, in essence, represents nothing more or less than consciousness in its embryonic form."[36] Victor Turner was also conscious of the fragility of this diffuse energy. According to Turner, "spontaneous communitas is a phase, a moment, not a permanent condition."[37] What happens to this energy may depend on the social structural elements available with which to shape this emergent force.

Some of the ecstatic energy may find expression in what Victor Turner has described as "ideological communitas."[38] It is in this format

---

[34]Huizinga, *Homo Ludens*, 8.

[35]Turner, *The Ritual Process*, 200.

[36]J. E. Conner, *Lenin on Politics and Revolution* (Western Publishing Co., 1968) 39.

[37]Turner, *The Ritual Process*, 140.

[38]Ibid.

that new religious movements may arise and flourish, giving new identity and meaning to individuals. These formulations emerging from *communitas* represent the return to a human definition of society, as opposed to a societal definition of human beings. However, society struggles to maintain its power and subsume this energy within old social structural constraints. This "normative communitas" may find religious or secular expression. In a less secular age this energy may all have been channeled into forms of ecstatic religion. Today, however, normative communitas may take at least two major forms. There is 'a choice between (1) secular fun activities, encouraged by consumerism, or (2) religious revivalism in which individuals are encouraged to experience rebirth rather than death of the old belief systems.

The possibilities for the creation of new religious movements from the ecstatic energy will depend on two main characteristics: the size of the population in *communitas*, and the relative power of local social structural arrangements which are capable of controlling and subsuming the energy within normative communitas.

The Specific Case: California. My original interest in the fun-seeking movement began in 1976, when I moved from London to Los Angeles. I was immediately impressed by the blatant and widespread Californian thirst for fun. This lay in sharp contrast to my more conservative English environment, in which outbreaks of enthusiasm were still remarkable events.

I attempted to understand the fun phenomenon by looking towards social structural explanations. However, having produced the previously outlined analysis, I was still left with the question, "Why California?"

There appear to be two main factors involved in answering this question. The first factor is concerned with the necessary conditions for the initial emergence of a fun-seeking phenomenon. The second factor is concerned with the ways in which the local environment is capable of shaping this emergent energy. These two factors may, at first sight, seem identical. However, for purposes of analysis, it seems important to separate them. For the potential fun seeker, the social structure provides different functions at different times. At one point it frees, at another point it constrains the individual.

Concerning the social structural preconditions which provide the backcloth for the emergence of fun seeking, it is hypothesized that California is particularly affected by the Triple Process. In most other social arenas, especially in Europe but also in the United States, there are many old institutions still buttressed by traditional meaning systems that oppose and modify the new emergent forms of social structure. Thus, in social arenas with some cohesive history and tradition, the most extreme effects of the Triple Process may be diluted or at least delayed.

California is unique in that it has no dominant and cohesive traditional structures and systems of meaning to oppose the Triple Process. Perhaps the most decisive factor influencing this lack of tradition is the pattern of population migration into California. Since early settlers from the East began to change the Spanish face of California, the state has been swamped with migrants. California has incorporated more migrants than any other state in the last century. One result of this vast increase in population is that traditional social systems, already existing in California, could not control the incoming tide of people. This lack of controlling tradition has meant that there was more freedom to create new social systems, and also that modern social systems, once instigated, would not be so diluted by tradition.

Thus, the California situation is thought to be one in which the effects of the Triple Process are more extreme than in other social arenas. Individuals in California not only experience the fragmentation of meaning produced by differentiation, but also are unable to find any overall cohesive meaning system in local social structural arrangements through which to mend the fragmentation of thoughts, tastes, and symbols. In addition, it is thought that rationalization, and hence disenchantment, may be more pronounced in California. Because of the inherent "newness" of the Californian population, it seems reasonable to suggest that the majority of social institutions would be characterized by modern methods. Thus, new institutions emerging in this bureaucratic age could be expected to be characteristically rationalistic. In other social arenas, where bureaucracy has been superimposed onto older institutions, there may yet remain some tradition involving more personal interaction and more room for creativity. Although California's predominant institutions may be particularly rational and efficient, their boring sameness provides little in the way of personal satisfaction for individuals.

Alienation, also, is particularly relevant to California. First of all there is the general situation of alienating work produced by the division of mental and material labor. However, more importantly, Californians suffer from the secondary effects of alienation. The myth that "everyone can make it" is particularly relevant to California. It is a myth that has drawn migrants from all over the world, as well as from the United

States. Of course, there are rich and successful individuals in California. However, the majority of hopeful new recruits to the Californian dream have to cope with discrepancies between a dreamed concept of success and the inability to execute the dream.

For all of these reasons, it seems that the effects of the Triple Process may be particularly pronounced in California. Thus, following the previously outlined analysis, one might predict that large numbers of individuals, unable to find personal satisfaction within constraining social roles, would seek to escape from them. I believe that the predominant search by Californians for ecstatic transcendence indicates just such a trend.

The emergence of this fun-seeking phenomenon, as previously stated, also means a possible increase in the population of *communitas*. It is from this population that new religious movements may emerge. However, given the ability of social structure to channel the ecstatic energy into conservative forms of normative communitas, it seems reasonable to examine the Californian situation in this regard.

As previously mentioned, the social structural conditions leading up to fun seeking may also be seen as social structural conditions that are able to shape the emergent fun-seeking energy. It is hypothesized that, just as the lack of tradition in California means that the undiluted Triple Process produces a higher than average number of fun seekers, so also will this lack of tradition shape the future of the fun-seeking potential in California. It seems reasonable to suggest that the lack of a cohesive meaning system in California might mean that there is less likelihood that all the ecstatic energy might be channeled into religious revivalism. The inability of California to control the incoming tide of population has meant that new institutions, including new religious movements, have evolved and maintained their identities within the Californian community.

New religious movements seem to have flourished in the early days of flight into *communitas*, that is, in the 1960s. However, in today's conservative climate, these radical or left-wing communitas movements appear to be taking a back seat, while conservative or right wing normative communitas movements emerge in increasing numbers. Of course, some religious revivalism has emerged in California. However, remembering the characteristic "newness" of the Californian population, it does not seem surprising to note that characteristically modern forms of normative communitas have emerged. Thus, while the undiluted Triple Process may, on the one hand, produce increasing numbers of fun seekers, it also provides an unfettered, bureaucratic capitalism, from which consumerism emerges as the dominant form of normative communitas. Fun within consumerism provides temporary satisfaction for many Californians. Running, motorcycling, and the general fitness craze are examples of some of the more strenuous, ecstatic forms. However, far more Californians are affected in a more general way. Consumer goods are advertised daily, thus giving individuals ideal formulations of goods or goals to strive for. Satisfaction or fun for these individuals is achieved when their buying power enables them to bring ideal and real together by purchasing the advertised object.

However, like all right-wing movements, the channeling of energy into normative communitas often can be seen as a final effort to save a dying social system. Although these secular forms of normative communitas exist, the Triple Process continues to free more and more social actors from commitment to the old social system. Also, while some people may find temporary satisfaction within normative communitas, the fact that these actors have no meaningful social identity still remains problematic. As Victor Turner pointed out, normative communitas is still dangerous.[39] In addition to this, and more importantly, forms of normative communitas, (such as fun within consumerism), which are intricately attached to social structure, can only survive as long as that social structure continues to be effective.

In summary, it is hypothesized that this right-wing, secular form of *communitas* is merely a temporary trend. Although some energy may be diverted into religious revivalism, the lack of cohesion among traditional forces suggests an inability to completely control the emergent force. Thus, it seems that when the secular forms of normative *communitas* can no longer be supported by social structure, the way will open, yet again, for the increase of new religious movements. It is thus hypothesized that, with increasing economic difficulties accompanying the growing problems of capitalism, California will again be the first social arena in which new religious movements, along with other ideological forms of *communitas*, will provide us with new vehicles of meaning through which to transcend the constraining bonds of twentieth-century social structure.

---

[39]Turner, *Dramas, Fields, and Metaphors*, 245.

ESOTERIC "NEW RELIGIOUS MOVEMENTS" AND THE WESTERN ESOTERIC TRADITION

by Geoffrey Ahern

IT IS ATTEMPTED here to give a perspective that can explain why esoteric "new religious movements" have arisen. (An important preliminary will be to define "esoteric.") By outlining the esoteric past, this paper will lead up to the suggestion that the sociological growth of esoteric "new religious movements" in the West varies with and is predominantly caused by the relative plausibility of esoteric cosmology. When the latter has been culturally available and, for macrocultural reasons, the plausibility of alternative, more orthodox cosmologies has declined, there have been esoteric "waves" or fashions.

In this brief paper it is not possible to distinguish the social structure of esotericism from that of "mysticism" (which will be defined), to consider those variants of esotericism and mysticism that cultivate individuality, to show the necessary connection between esoteric cosmology and esoteric social structure, to compare East with West, and to use the development of consciousness as a perspective that underlies all the foregoing. What will follow is merely an aspect of a much fuller analysis I have made elsewhere.[1]

[1]Geoffrey Ahern, *Sun at Midnight: The Rudolph Steiner Movement and the Western Esoteric Tradition* (Wellingborough UK: Aquarian Press, 1984).

WHAT IS "ESOTERICISM"?

The widespread use of "esotericism," meaning private religious experience, must be distinguished from that which is known as the "Western esoteric tradition." The latter, the concern of this paper, includes gnosticism, Hermeticism, alchemy, cabalism, Rosicrucianism, (Mme. Blavatsky's) Theosophy, and Anthroposophy.

Esoteric systems are often inchoate and loosely and comprehensively syncretistic. In studying Anthroposophy I frequently found myself, like Bottom unwillingly caught in Titania's bower, wishing I had "wit enough to get out of this wood." One method of getting out of the wood that I have found helpful is to make a sharper distinction than is perhaps usual between "mysticism" and "esotericism." (This is not merely an ideal-typical distinction since many systems are fully esoteric and there are many examples of mysticism without esotericism.)

The type of mysticism that seeks a unifying spiritual experience seems to be, usually, a necessary but never sufficient feature of esotericism. Mysticism seems to require no specific cosmology: it may be theistic, deistic, or atheistic; Christian, Buddhist, or connected with science fiction; it seems it can be interpreted in terms of almost any *Weltanschauung*. Alternatively, it seems it may be experienced ontologically yet accompanied by cognitive incomprehensive and epistemological confusion.

Mysticism is usually a necessary feature of esoteric cosmology because esoteric paths to the sacred are based on a U-turn of consciousness in which the seeker, if all eventually goes well, experiences a higher unity. In esotericism, unifying mystical experience becomes, typically, an aspiration that is doctrinally enshrined (though there may well be membership, such as the ascriptive, which does not attempt to make this doctrinal aspiration a personal experience). But Western esotericism goes further than mysticism because it explains mystical experience in terms of a special cosmological pattern. This is discernible despite the differences between particular esoteric systems.

Humankind is perceived, in esoteric thought systems, as a *microcosm* of the universe or macrocosm. Humankind is of the same spiritual essence—or essences—as the cosmos. Thus in the semi-esoteric system of Paracelsus[2] the clod from which the first man was created was a

---

[2]See, for example, "Paracelsus and the Neoplatonic and Gnostic Tradition," *Ambix* 8, no. 3 (October 1960).

microcosmic compound of mystic "salt," "sulphur," and "mercury." In Anthroposophy[3] man is considered to be comprised of "etheric," "astral," and other spiritual bodies that are parts of the cosmos itself. Esotericism reduces the separation between inner and outer, moving from private symbolism towards literalness. To know and experience oneself as a microcosm is salvation. Since cognitive and experiential abilities are necessary for this, esoteric systems often relativize salvation on a gradual scale.

With this lessened sense of separation between man and not-man there seems to go a perception of *materialism* as evil. Materialism seems usually to be the negative organizing principle of esotericism. Sometimes there is an explicit spiritual monism: here the reality of the material or finite is denied, and in this relativizing there tends to lurk a concealed dualism. Thus the quasi-esoteric system of Christian Science seems to deny the reality of physical treatments for illness yet makes the physical treatments real by prohibiting them. Sometimes there is a more explicit dualism whereby the finite world is accorded more reality but separated cosmologically from the spiritual. (Full dualism, as in Manichaeism, seems to be relatively infrequent.) It becomes as Shakespeare's Prospero intoned: "These our actors were all spirits and are melted into air, into thin air."

Fully esoteric systems seem to have a cosmogony and gradualist eschatology which, underlying the profusion of individual differences, follow a similar pattern. The pattern is that *all that is finite has proceeded from spirit and will return to spirit*. (Hence the main evil of materialism.) It is not just—as in Christian orthodoxy—that humanity has been created by God and may return (without apotheosis) to God's presence. In fully esoteric cosmology, *all* (or nearly all) has proceeded from and will return to spirit. The finite world, as in Anthroposophy, is often deemed to have materialized from rhythmic planetary emanations from a pristine spiritual unity (or pleroma). Sometimes an evil creator (or demiurge), perhaps identified with the Jehovah of the Old Testament, is considered to have materialized from the unity of original spirit.

---

[3]For references to Anthroposophy, see Rudolf Steiner, *Occult Science*, trans. G. and M. Adams (London: Rudolf Steiner Press, 1972).

COSMOLOGICAL PLAUSIBILITIES: ORTHODOXY VERSUS ESOTERICISM.

Now that esotericism has been defined as a cosmology and distinguished from mysticism, it becomes more meaningful to relate the occurrence of Western esotericism since the establishment of Christian orthodoxy to macrocultural cosmological plausibility. The esoteric tradition in the Middle Ages, in the Renaissance, and in Rosicrucianism in the early seventeenth century are touched on very tentatively and briefly before considering modern esotericism.

Cosmological plausibility can be seen as the dominant variable that explains why people are not just mystical but add the cognitive component peculiar to esotericism. The latter's adoption appears to belong to the emergently or pluralistically sociological. A predisposition, for example, as the result of genetic factors, might be presumed to arise in more or less equal proportions for each generation; if so, genetic predisposition is not a sufficient explanation of the occurrence of esoteric "waves" or fashions.[4]

The plausibility of Christian orthodoxy itself, as the Nag Hammadi finds have made clearer,[5] appears to have been wrested from rival, esoteric versions of Christianity. These gnostic systems seem to have been syncretisms of Hellenic thought and Neoplatonism, Egyptian influence, and later mystery religions, such as Orphism and the Pythagorean cult, astral Babylonian religion and perhaps (as possibly in Basilides' system) Indian influence. But after the centralization of spiritual authority in the church and its bishops, the esoteric tradition, which was at least implicitly antiauthoritarian, seems to have been suppressed in the West for most of the following millennium.

ESOTERICISM IN THE MIDDLE AGES AND RENAISSANCE

Much of medieval *mysticism* seems to have expressed itself within the cosmological structure of Catholicism. Thus Meister Eckhart is said to have stressed that there was an unmeasurable difference between God and man and then to have been doctrinally horrified by the charge of heresy

[4]I have argued in my book (see n. 1) that variations in predisposition are more likely than not to follow from sociological assumptions about the emergence of society.

[5]See E. Pagels, *The Gnostic Gospels* (London: Weidenfeld and Nicolson, 1980) and Hans Jonas, *The Gnostic Religion: The Message of the Alien God and the Beginning of Christianity* (Boston: Beacon Press, 1958).

brought against him at the end of his life.[6] Perhaps such mysticism, arising out of dissatisfaction with the ministrations of the church, reflected social tension.

But some of the educated elite within the church were also influenced by an *esoteric* threat to the church's cosmological structure. The eleventh- and twelfth-century compilation by Albertus Magnus and others of alchemical thought from Arabia, Egypt, and China did not deal simply with the *aurum vulgi* of transformation of lead into gold for commercial profit; there was esoteric significance because for many adepts the turning of lead into gold involved an analogous inner transformation in the spiritual state of the human microcosm.[7] The ultimate aim was for union with transcendent totality, or with the *unus mundus*. Such magical practices in Christendom, had to be clandestine; as did the revival of Cabalism,[8] or rabbinical *gnosis* and Neoplatonism in Provence (later twelfth century), and in Spain, especially in Gerona (first part of the thirteenth century).

As Christian orthodoxy grew more tolerant during the Renaissance Cabalism became less secret. It was synthesized by Pico della Mirandola, and Agrippa, and other magicians with the loosely esoteric collection of treatises known as the *Corpus Hermeticum*.[9] These treatises were attributed to Hermes Trismegistus, who was identified with Thoth, the Egyptian god of wisdom. This synthesis of the *Cabala* and the *Corpus Hermeticum* was itself joined by Paracelsus[10] to the magical practices of alchemy. Though Christocentric, his synthesis was semi-esoteric, retaining much of the *Genesis* orthodoxy, including that of male priority, but understanding the human being as a microcosm.

A late Renaissance magus such as John Dee, who derived much of his thought from Paracelsus, could practice magic without danger only in a few, generally Protestant, Christian cultures. Also, this esotericism,

---

[6]R. B. Blakney, *Meister Eckhart, A Modern Translation* (New York: Harper Torchbooks, n.d.) xiv, xxi, xxiv.

[7]Titus Burchkhardt, *Alchemy: Science of the Cosmos, Science of the Soul*, trans. W. Stoddart (Stuart and Watkyns, 1967).

[8]Gershom Scholem, *Kabbalah* (Jerusalem: Keter Publishing House, 1974).

[9]F. A. Yates, *Giordano Bruno and the Hermetic Tradition* (London: Routledge, 1964).

[10]J. Jacobi, *Paracelsus: Selected Writings* (London: Routledge and Kegan Paul, 1951) 27-73, 87-118, 241, 287.

though it was central to many of the best contemporary minds, appears to have been available only to those—such as Jesuits and Rosicrucians—who were on the most sophisticated margins of Catholic and Protestant plausibilities. Possibly it sometimes amalgamated with indigenous pagan survivals, as Shakespeare's *Tempest* suggests, since Sycorax, Caliban, and Ariel were already on the mysterious island before it was discovered by the unworldly Renaissance magus, Prospero, in his leaky boat.

ROSICRUCIANISM

Serious Rosicrucianism seems to have derived from John Dee's synthesis of Paracelsus and the Cabalist-alchemical tradition. According to Yates in *The Rosicrucian Enlightenment,*[11] Rosicrucianism was strongly opposed to the spirit of the counter-Reformation. Its fashion in the 1620s in Bohemia may be explained through a Hussite-Protestant religious liberalism, the temporary suspension of oppression and the prior presence of a Hermetic-Cabalist tradition. Its failure to make much lasting impact may be partially explicable through Catholic reactionary suppression and, assuming Yates's thesis to be correct, the emergence from its matrix of the different thought form of "science." This, ironically, was of course to lead to the Enlightenment and especially later to the anti-esoteric plausibility of scientific materialism.

Through freemasonry there was some eighteenth-century esoteric influence, as in, for example, the libretto of *The Magic Flute*; also, romantics such as Goethe, Coleridge, and Blake have esoteric resonances. But the plausibility of the *deus ex machina*—whereby fundamentalist Christianity could more or less be reconciled with the increasing emergence of scientific materialism and the cosmos discovered thereby—seems to have reduced Renaissance esotericism to relatively superficial fashionable outbreaks.

ESOTERICISM AND MODERNITY

The esoteric revival which started in England with the Societas Rosicruciana in Anglia in 1865 and later, with Mme. Blavatsky's Theosophy, seems to have been connected with the rise of scientific materialism. As a result of its influence Christian fundamentalism seemed implausible, yet there

[11]Ibid., 268, 270-72, 273, 277.

was intuitive revolt against the *machina* that was contemporarily dispensing with the *deus*. A *fresh* numinosity was sought.

The revival's main manifestations, Theosophy and, later, Anthroposophy, popularized nonorthodox Christian numinosity. Theosophy was ostensibly derived from Eastern religions and became plausible to some through an exotically oriental vocabulary. However, there is evidence that much of its core derives from the Western esoteric tradition,[12] especially its syncretism by Eliphas Levi in the 1870s.[13] Anthroposophy was avowedly Christocentric, but its tradition of reincarnation may have derived from recent translations of Eastern thought and not, as claimed, from Lessing's revival of the Western Pythagorean tradition. Anthroposophy was largely a German-speaking revival of the Western esoteric tradition, and it also esotericized Goethe; it is much more intellectual, earnestly complex, and thoroughly comprehensive than Theosophy, which seems mainly to have appealed to Anglo-Saxons.

This esoteric "wave," unlike Rosicrucianism and earlier Hermetic-Cabalist thought, seems to have repelled most of the best intellects of the time. Perhaps this was partly because of its strenuous syncretism of world religions that had been made available by nineteenth-century scholarship. There is a forced reductionism to spirit that often appears to be culturally degenerate and to be a vehement protest and defense against scientific materialism; there may be analogies with the increased complexities of later Neoplatonism in its defense of Hellenic paganism against Christianity: thus Iamblichus syncretized every known pagan deity into his system.[14] Max Müller thought that nothing had discredited the study of Buddhism as much as the Theosophical book *Esoteric Buddhism*.[15] The devotees of this esoteric revival seem generally to have been from an urban and middle class environment and relatively educated, but they were more poetically than intellectually minded. Thus the magical- and Western-minded Hermetic Order of the Golden Dawn was associated with the "Celtic Twilight" movement and some of the best literature of the modern period, including the poetry of W. B. Yeats.

---

[12]For a detailed analysis (though written for the polemical purpose of exposing Mme. Blavatsky as a plagiarizer) see W. E. Coleman's appendix C. to V. S. Solovyoff, *A Modern Priestess of Isis* (London: Longmans, Green and Co., 1895) 353-66, esp. 365.

[13]Mervyn Jones, "The Rosicrucians," in *Secret Socieities* (London, Aldus, 1967) 144, 147.

[14]*Encyclopaedia Britannica*, 10th ed., s.v. "Neoplatonism."

[15]R. F. Gombrich, *Precept and Practice* (Oxford: Oxford University Press, 1971) 54.

This esoteric fashion seems to have faded out since the First World War even though mysticism, as suggested by Troeltsch, seems to have increased. Proportionately fewer relatively educated people seem to have reacted radically against the scientifically established cosmos. Perhaps this is partly because its plausibility has been more popularly secure. A hundred years ago Darwinian evolution was still publicly establishing itself, often appearing to be in outright opposition to Christianity, and the geological death knell to a literal interpretation of the *Genesis* creation story had only recently tolled; biblical literalism was not so much a part of history that its occurrence should seem remarkable, unlike the 1980s. Esotericism seemed to many a convincing third way out. Scientific materialism then was perhaps penetrating to about the same level of culture that the mystical suggestiveness of neo-Darwinism, relativity, and the "principle of indeterminacy" are today.

Furthermore, the esoteric plausibility structure then could probably more easily syncretize scientific materialism around its spiritual monism or "spiritual science." Developments in the scientifically established cosmos in the early twentieth century have probably made it more indigestible by esotericism, even for vague and poetic minds. (The scientific cosmos, however, seems to have become increasingly amenable to mysticism.) The progressiveness and teleology of much of pre-First World War evolutionary thought was more easily assimilable to fully esoteric systems where the purpose of the cosmos is a linear development of consciousness and cyclical self-apotheosis. It was probably easier then than now to stress an idealist qualitative difference between human beings and animals: as late as 1910 an anthropologist wrote that with the controversial exception of *Pithecanthropus* no bones had been found definitely bridging the gulf between man and "lower" creation and that anthropology had probably reached the limit of discoveries in that direction.[16] Also, since geological and astronomical time spans were then much shorter, it was easier to conceive of the present solar system as one of those emanations that are often part of the esoteric cosmos.

Thus the general plausibility of the scientifically established cosmos, if not of scientific materialism, probably makes an esoteric system today seem to the conventionally educated not just unnecessary but also to oppose the "facts" established by the early twentieth century (or even

---

[16]Quoted by A. Brodrick, *Man and His Ancestry* (Hutchinson, 1960) 104.

contemporary) scientific fraternity. The mysticism of today, where it seeks unity, appears to focus on a vague perennial philosophy that falls far short of esotericism. It is perhaps more of an affirming intuitive response in the face of the pessimism engendered by the modern collision of culture with culture, where "mere" scientific method seems to many to reduce humanity to a machine or worse. Idealistic man-centered esotericism can hardly adopt the definition of the human being that states that he is the only species to eat his own kind.

ESOTERICISM AND "NEW RELIGIOUS MOVEMENTS" (NRMs)

Esotericism today seems to appeal to only a tiny minority of those educated intellects that have closely studied the scientific cosmos in an academically accredited way. This tiny minority perhaps includes followers of Eastern esotericism, devotees of Ouspensky, Anthroposophists, magicians, alchemists, cabalists, and astrologers; more conceptually, followers of what de Chardin called his "new religion,"[17] which seems to have esoteric features; and, more conceptually still some adepts in the new physics. What are the chances of these or analogous esotericisms appealing more generally to the high calibre of mind that earlier was drawn to the Hermetic-Cabalist tradition?

My main speculation is that the predominance of mystical *psychological* interpretations, especially of depth psychology, makes more likely the survival of scientific plausibility without adoption of an esoteric system. Depth psychology generally reduces the cosmology in esotericism to the experiential; the cosmology is typically reduced to the "psyche" only (though not "only" the psyche). This mystical approach allows esotericism to be satisfied as a partial truth; yet because it is made internal only, it does not threaten the sway of scientific cosmology.

This can partly be illustrated even through the tradition of depth psychology which is perhaps most spiritual and esoteric. Jung based his system on Darwinian evolution and so his archetypal theory is grounded in a matter-bound biological model. Admittedly, Jungian thought seems to have some analogies with (fairly dualistic) gnosticism, for while the Jungian creator of the world (or demiurge) is the scientifically established

[17]Quoted by F. L. Baumer, *Modern European Thought* (London: Collier Macmillan, 1977) 450; also see p. 451.

cosmos; and this is perceived generally as an emergent reality[18] there is yet an underlying suggestion that it is derived from a *unus mundus* of spirit. There is some microcosmic/macrocosmic resonance. This is increased by the presentation of the system, which in its ambiguity is very close to experience; the esoteric aspect is also hinted at by epistemological contradiction, since Jung sometimes declares that the numinous is not potentially knowable and other times affirms that it is.

The sway of the *psychological* interpretation that makes the numinous internal—and so mystical—applies much more strongly to the more rationalist schools of depth psychology, such as the Freudian. A microcosm/macrocosm link would surely be interpreted by these as "projection" or, severely, as the psychological heresy of "anthropomorphism." Only a few fringe schools of depth psychology, such as the later Reichian or Laingian, may have originated with esoteric features and in the latter case this is probably by default. Thus I suggested that esotericism cannot become more academically and culturally respectable unless traditional depth psychology also becomes proportionately perceived as invalidly distinguishing between the knower and the cosmos. Depth psychology is perhaps developing in this direction and so may itself produce increasingly esoteric systems. For example, Jungism's archetypal understanding of the alchemical *unus mundus* has very recently been synthesized by a writer with the new religious possibilities of superspace and quantum and relativity physics generally:[19] here the model is not just Darwinian and biological but also transcendent.

If depth psychology consolidates without developing in an esoteric direction I suggest that esotericism will remain almost entirely marginal, with only a few minor and uncoordinated features being part of the cosmology of the most of the most educated people. Most esotericists and esoteric NRMs will then tend to be interpreted developmentally in terms of a "band" of cultural evolution.

The earliest edge of this developmental "band" in any event corresponds broadly to the starting point of self-separation, with considerable symbolization and even abstraction, that is generally necessary to estab-

---

[18]For example, J. Jacobi, *The Psychology of C. G. Jung*, 8th ed. (London: Routledge and Kegan Paul, 1968).

[19]See C. Curling, "Physics and Psyche," *Harvest, Journal of Jungian Studies* 26 (1980): 62-72.

lish an esoteric cosmos: it is broadly where an "anthropological" society becomes "sociological" (or where Durkheim's "mechanical solidarity" becomes "organic"). Thus the Orphic rites in the ancient Mediterranean came to be less identified with locality and more abstractly expressed in mythological terms.[20] The participants were sufficiently removed from nature to adhere to the motto of *semo semi* or "the body a tomb": they had become less and less locals and more and more educated cosmopolitans with the means to travel. They presumably wished to reduce their self-division, moving from the "trap" of symbolization to a literal identity with the cosmos.

The latest edge of this developmental "band," in cultural terms, would probably be interpreted as where the psychological insight of making the numinous internal begins. Depth psychology thus would be perceived as being a culturally more advanced development from esotericism, taking on where it leaves off. Some gnostic sophisticates after the birth of Christ and a few alchemists would probably be included in the "more advanced" band of depth psychology since they also propounded the truth of internalization. The esotericism at the end of the last century might be understood as the final esoteric fling into general Western culture, developing after the urban renewal of shamanism or spiritualism and yielding before the insight of internalization.

But perhaps the plausibility of depth psychology will continue to edge towards the threshold of esoteric cosmology, reinforcing other trends in that direction. In this case making the numinous internal might, in centuries to come, be seen as an insight that is overstressed at the end of a tradition of "ethical prophecy," such as that of Christian orthodoxy. The linear development of "monotheism with a human face,"[21] or Christian orthodoxy, will then be perceived as having imposed a particular illusion, the overly rigid distinction between finite and infinite, history and God, known and unknown. Depth psychology, which started with these "illusions," will in this case be perceived as an important, perhaps central part of the cultural exit towards making esoteric cosmology more plausible; in

---

[20]See N. Smart, "The Mysteries," in *Secret Societies*, ed. N. Mackenzie (London: Aldus Books, 1967) 84-92.

[21]See D. Martin, "Can the Church Survive?" in *Tracts against the Times* (London: Lutterworth Press, 1973) 184.

this event, depth psychology will have contributed to the sociological growth of esotericism, the growth of future esoteric new religious movements.

SUMMARY

In this paper, the attempt has been made to study the sociological growth (or decline) of esotericism in Western culture in terms of the increase (or decrease) of the macrocultural plausibility of esoteric cosmology. Though it has not been possible in this brief paper to give the analysis I have made elsewhere, it has been suggested that in the West the plausibility of esoteric cosmology is the predominant influence on the sociological growth or decline of esotericism. More attention has been paid to modernity (especially to depth psychology) than to the past. It has been suggested that future development in depth psychology will relate most significantly to any future increase in esoteric cosmology and so, of esoteric movements.

A COMPARISON OF ANTI-CULT MOVEMENTS IN THE UNITED STATES AND WEST GERMANY

by Anson D. Shupe Jr.,
Bert L. Hardin,
and David G. Bromley

THIS ESSAY examines the organized reactions to new religious movements, or "anti-cult" movements (hereafter ACMs), in the United States of America and the Federal Republic of Germany during the 1970s and early 1980s with the intent of generating a more abstract understanding of countermovement dynamics. The two countermovements display distinct differences in size, ability to mobilize official state sanctions, popular participation, and popular reaction. These differences, we maintain, can be directly linked to characteristics of the two countries' separate traditions of religious and cultural pluralism and of their respective church/state relations. A basic assumption of the analysis that follows is that the sociocultural environments within which social movements emerge and expand prescribe not only social movements' options for strategies of mobilizing key resources (such as members and finances) but also prescribe the range of possible countermovement reactions. This means that from the viewpoint of an emerging or coalescing countermovement, its own strategies of reaction and its ideology will be significantly influenced by the movement(s) that it opposes, as well as by the traditions, laws, and conventions of the larger society. At a phenomenological level, it suggests that a society's cultural traditions, the latter's pluralism or homogeneity, and so forth, will determine the very definitions and labels of "heresy" in addition to imposing limitations on the countermovements' attempts to deal with "heresy."

The concrete question we will deal with here, out of which we will attempt to extract broader implications, is this: Why has West Germany, with a fairly small activist anti-cult interest group movement and fewer members of new religions, witnessed the *larger* formal institutional (governmental and religious) response, while the United States, with its considerably larger activist anti-cult interest group movement, has witnessed much *less* formal institutional response? Obviously the answer is tied to the two countries' respective religious traditions, church/state relations, and popular tolerance for alternative lifestyles, and it is in terms of these three dimensions that we shall discuss each country's anti-cult movement before concluding with some comparative statements.

THE AMERICAN ANTI-CULT MOVEMENT

Elsewhere we have treated the American ACM with detailed descriptive and conceptual analyses (see, for example, Shupe and Bromley, 1982; Shupe, Spielmann and Stigall, 1980; Shupe and Bromley, 1980, 1979; Bromley and Shupe, 1979). Here we mention only the broadest parameters of the movement and of American society in order to permit a comparison with the less researched West German situation.

The American ACM is composed almost entirely of three categories of participants: (a) a small number of deprogrammers (who are not really organized into any corporate structure, acting rather as individual entrepreneurs or *ersatz* therapists on a sporadic basis);[1] (b) families of new religions' youthful adherents (principally their parents), joined together in local and regional interest group associations (which in turn now form a loose national coalition); and (c) sympathetic religious groups (denominational, interdenominational, non-denominational evangelical) already existing or created expressly for the purpose of opposing new religions.

---

[1]In this essay we shall assume that readers have followed enough of the "cult" controversy to be familiar with anti-cult terms often used such as "deprogramming" and "mind control." Deprogramming, that is, the alleged liberating removal of hypnotically implanted thought patterns from the minds of new religions' members in a sort of psychological exorcism, is used by American anti-cultists to refer to a variety of activities ranging from discussions between parents and offspring on the telephone that induce a reconsideration of religious commitment to the much-publicized coercive kidnapping/internment practices. The public, and indeed most scholars and civil libertarians, generally are concerned only with the coercive version of deprogramming, and it is in that sense that we use the term here.

The latter religious groups have generally refrained from directly sponsoring attempts to mobilize government intervention in dealing with new religions for several reasons. First and foremost, they are acutely aware of the sensitivity over separation of church and state. Second, in some cases their own pasts include records of persecution when they themselves were minorities in American society. Finally, there is a lack of consensus among such groups as to whether the state can solve problems that are ultimately connected with notions of theological orthodoxy and "error." Thus their efforts have been directed more at lending moral support to anti-cult associations, not only in counseling but also in criticizing the new religions' various theologies and thus denying them legitimacy. Deprogrammers as well, aside from occasional appearances at mostly unofficial hearings by outspoken individuals such as Ted Patrick, Joe Alexander, Sr., and Galen Kelly, have not led the lobbying fight to persuade legislatures and executive officials to pass resolutions, conduct investigations, or consider adding or amending laws. Their legal marginality has made them of dubious value to anti-cult associations coming before law-makers, and both the hazards and demands of their occupation (for example, lawsuits and imprisonment, high mobility and irregular employment) permit them fewer resources to invest in lobbying activities. Their primary function in the ACM has always been to provide direct vigilante-style recourse for frustrated families unwilling to await the outcome of legislative debates or the exhaustion of their offspring's idealistic zeal, and as such, they can be understood as attacking merely the symptoms rather than the sources of new religion's expansion. Thus, in the United States it is really only the anti-cult associations, mostly composed of families, that have engaged in efforts to obtain government involvement in the controversy.

Despite a decade of lobbying, the fruits of the anti-cultists' labors have not been terribly impressive. The most success has been achieved at the local level, where local sheriffs and other law enforcement officials, less concerned with complex constitutional issues, have tacitly authorized cooperation with local ACM groups by harassing fundraisers of groups such as the Unification Church and the Hare Krishna sect or by "looking the other way" during deprogrammings, and where local municipalities have tightened up zoning and solicitation ordinances to restrict the new religions' immediate operations. In many cases, however, even at this level, groups such as the Unification Church have successfully challenged overly restrictive or unreasonable ordinances, often taking certain key regional bureaucracies to court to set an example for neighboring areas (see Bromley and Shupe, 1979: 323-24).

Anti-cultists have generated more sympathy at the state than at the federal level. Beginning in the mid-1970s individual state assembly persons and legislators began introducing resolutions to create investigating committees to look into "cult activities." Many of these were symbolic, ineffectual gestures in response to local constituents active in the ACM that were then pigeonholed in committees without ever having been considered by the full legislatures. Some state legislators and executives did appoint committees (for example, New York, 1975; Vermont, 1977; Texas 1977) or consider legislation, such as the New York State Assembly which voted down an amendment to the state's penal code which would have made starting or operating a "pseudoreligious cult" a felony (New York, 1977), but in general little was obtained by the ACM from these relatively token actions except a sense of short-lived satisfaction for anti-cultists and a heightened anticipation of more concrete actions to come. After the tragedy at Jonestown, Guyana, in which over 900 members of Jim Jones's People's Temple sect died, a new flurry of state legislative action and ACM lobbying began and has continued to the present. A number of states once again considered holding hearings (for example, Illinois, 1979; New York, 1979; Pennsylvania, 1979; Connecticut, 1979) or *did* hold them. A bill making it possible to obtain temporary writs of conservatorships over legal adults involved in unconventional religious groups defined as "cults" (the list of "cult" characteristics closely mirrored ACM allegations against the Unification Church) passed both the House of Representatives and State Senate in the New York State Assembly in 1980 but was vetoed in the final stages by the Governor, not out of antipathy toward the bill's intent but rather because of legal technicalities (New York, 1980). Such state-level activity continues into the 1980s (though it has also been vigorously opposed by groups such as the National Council of the Churches of Christ in the U.S.A. and the American Civil Liberties Union).

The federal level, where anti-cult associations are merely one small voice amid an enormous variety of competing interest groups, has witnessed the least legislative and executive response to ACM lobbying. One reason is that the anti-cultists, due to limited resources and the fact that they form a relatively small national constituency, have faced numerous obstacles of time and expense in bringing their case to the attention of many federal officials. Only recently has a full-time ACM lobbying office been established in Washington, D.C. Past lobbying efforts were sporadic and issue-focused, as when an attorney with lobbying experience was retained by a coalition of anti-cult groups to visit Congressional offices and urge Representatives to cite Unification Church leader Daniel Fefferman in contempt of Congress for his refusal to cooperate on all inquiries during the 1977 "Fraser committee" investigation of "Koreagate" (see U.S. Government, 1978). Another reason for the ACM's past lack of success at the federal level has been the generally higher sensitivity of federal officials to the constitutional implications of legislation and investigations. A further reason can be found in the watchdog activities of the American Civil Liberties Union and the National Council of the Churches of Christ in the U.S.A., both of which have lobbied for years on behalf of First Amendment concerns.

Appeals have been made repeatedly by both rank-and-file anti-cultists as well as by sympathetic congresspersons to the U.S. Attorney General and to Presidents to begin investigations of new religions, but without success. President Jimmy Carter explicitly rejected such initiatives in his public comments following the Jonestown incident in late 1978:

> I don't think we ought to have an overreaction because of the Jonestown tragedy by injecting government into trying to control people's religious belief [sic] and I believe we also don't need to deplore on a nationwide basis the fact that the Jonestown cult—so called—was typical of America because it's not [*Fort Worth Star-Telegram*, 1 December 1978].

Up to the present there have been only three notable, direct ACM-prompted actions taken by any branch of the federal government. The first was an unofficial public hearing in February, 1976 in Washington, D.C., chaired by Kansas Senator Robert Dole. Approximately 400 anti-cultists from across the nation agreed to limit complaints to the Unification Church and spent two hours listing these to Dole and a panel composed of other congresspersons and federal officials. The meeting provided an unprecedented opportunity to the ACM for visibility—itself a momentous enough event to encourage ACM proponents to form the first of several unsuccessful attempts at constructing a national coordinating organization—but it generated no further social control actions from Washington. That it was, from the bureaucrats' point of view, like so many similar state-level hearings an exercise in "commission politics" (Lipsky and Olson, 1968)—a symbolic "cooling out" of constituents—is obvious from frequent disclaimers made by Dole during the hearing. For example, he told participants in the audience,

> I want to emphasize that . . . it is not a Congressional hearing, it is not any kind of investigation, it is not a public speech-making forum, and above all it is not a debate between opposing points of view. . . . I would remind everyone one more time that we are not taking any testimony and no one is under oath. Moreover, nothing that is said or done is to be interpreted as a prejudgement or stamp of approval by the legislative branch on anything. . . . Inquiries will be referred to the relevant agency for a more complete, written response. Obviously, there are some areas that simply do not lend themselves to open discussion. Moreover, there are others that might require extensive deliberation before a meaningful reply can be offered [CEFM, 1967: 6].

The second ACM-initiated direct federal action was a second public hearing in 1979 following the Jonestown tragedy, again chaired by Senator Dole. This time, representatives of the American Civil Liberties Union, the Unification Church, and other anti-ACM spokespersons were permitted to voice their concerns. The anti-cult participants essentially recapitulated their arguments of three years earlier, the only new element being the horrific undeniable example of Jonestown which some claimed to have anticipated. Despite their ominous warnings of dire massacres and future bloodbaths, effective (or even token) federal action, legislative or otherwise, was not immediately forthcoming.

Indirectly, perhaps, the second "Dole hearing" *did* help promote the third and most recent federal-level action. As of late 1980, Representative Richard L. Ottinger of New York, who had been a vocal, pro-ACM participant at the 1979 "Dole hearing," announced his intention to submit to Congress in 1981 a temporary conservatorship bill in many ways similar to the one considered by the New York State Assembly bill in 1980. Ottinger indicated in one private communication (Ottinger, 1980) his sympathies for the ACM viewpoint when he wrote:

> I think you underestimate the violation of rights of individuals subjected to incredible pressures by the cults. In fact such pressures can be so great as to result in Jonestown type tragedies. The abuse cannot be made unreachable under the cloak of religion.

The ultimate fate of Ottinger's bill is not known at the time this paper is being written. While its passage in either house of Congress is doubtful, it represents the most concrete step toward federal-level action directed against new religions yet seen in the United States.

In sum, the response of public officials to American ACM concerns and lobbying efforts has, as of 1981, been tepid at best. Jonestown inspired a number of state hearings and investigations, but anti-cult groups (as determined by a reading of their current newsletters and other literature) clearly do not believe that their goals have been achieved, and the continued, even prosperous, presence of groups such as the Hare Krishnas and the Unification Church suggests the same conclusion. Thus far, legislative activity has been uniformly ineffectual. Three facts in American legal-religious culture account for the lack of direct governmental response:

American Religious Tradition. American religion's most distinguishing characteristic is its lack of a dominant religious group and, consequently, its cultivation of a "gentlemen's agreement" among major denominations that they all possess enough legitimacy to merit each other's tolerance, if not cooperation. This includes a deemphasis on "poaching" members from one another through overly aggressive interdenominational proselytization, relying on self-initiated switching and sexual reproduction for member growth. Meanwhile members of these churches are expected to show commitment through active church attendance, other forms of participation, and voluntary contributions. While there exists a range of "legitimacy," from mainline to more sectarian groups, nevertheless, several centuries of inter-group competition have fostered a pragmatic acceptance of pluralism. Thus, at the same time that new religions have been variously condemned theologically (for example, for Jewish and ecumenical Christian critiques of Unification Church "post-Christian" theology, see Rudin, 1976; Cunningham et al., 1977), religious groups have been noticeably reluctant to call for full governmental intervention. Some of the more sectarian groups (for example, Jehovah's Witnesses), themselves not long ago the victims of political discrimination and/or societal persecution, are particularly sensitive to minority rights and have lobbied against possible governmental anti-cult action. There is undoubtedly also the general, unexpressed suspicion that once a government review of unconventional religions begins, the limits of such an examination may never be clearly set and will thus threaten *all* religious groups' hard-won pluralistic co-existence as well as state-granted privileges (such as indirect subsidies through tax exemptions).

Church-State Relations. Although the earliest colonists on the eastern seaboard of North America often established state-supported churches, a number of rather sacrosanct traditions have since evolved that make American government's support of or interference in the internal affairs of religious groups an action the thought of which politicians abhor almost as much as do church leaders. Clearly the separation of church and state affairs is a situation whose understanding rests on America's pluralistic religious traditions and status quo relations. Support and training for clergy is strictly sectarian-denominational—that is, private—as is funding. The guarantee of religious freedom in the Constitution's First Amendment, while technically limited to a group's beliefs rather than to its actions, invariably becomes (in an operational sense) generalized to many actions as well. Thus government, in particular the federal government, has shown a marked reticence even to consider investigating religious groups unless irrefutable evidence is available to show deliberate fraud or danger to the public interest. Even mail-order churches which ordain as clergy anyone for a modest fee—even owner's pets—have flourished despite close monitoring by the Internal Revenue Service. The close interweaving of belief and practice has proven difficult to unravel and presents a "can of worms" to officials. The fact that there is usually some group that disapproves of some other group also gives officials pause before they intercede in what may be merely internecine conflict. Legislators, whose primary operating principle is compromise, probably sense what political scientist Richard E. Morgan (1968: 128-29) concluded about the infusion of politics with religious fervor:

> When religious identifications and beliefs are at the root of a political struggle it is extremely difficult to compromise the matter through the normal political bargaining. . . . While some difference-splitting is done, the ideological component tends to be distressingly large.

Tolerance of Alternative Economic Life-styles. One important factor in the lack of general societal and political response to young American adults who indefinitely abandon conventional career trajectories is the purely localized impact of their deviance. In a society that is an only partially developed welfare state, with a system of higher education that permits entry into most parts of it literally anytime throughout an individual's life cycle, and an immense, diversified economy, the social consequences of a relative minority of young adults who "drop out" of the mainline occupational/educational structure and opt for a utopian/ascetic life-style is minimized. Idealistic youth turning to religion, even if unconventional, seems hardly a crisis equal to the international and economic problems impinging on the average citizen's consciousness—particularly after the fears of the 1960s that many youth were being recruited into dangerous subversive and revolutionary movements or drifting into a hedonistic drug culture, and considering the fact that some of the so-called "cults" cannot be clearly distinguished from the domain of sectarian Christianity. The absolute number of such youth involved in new religions is currently unknown but likely to be small, adding to the relative indifference of the general public to the "cult" controversy on a day-to-day basis. For these reasons the greatest impact of young adults joining unconventional religious groups falls on their individual families. However much such personal decisions disrupt their relatives' lives and frustrate their private hopes and expectations, such conversions are still perceived by public officials as largely a domestic, individualized affair. While the ACM has of late become more adept at trying to persuade state and federal officials otherwise, the "cult menace" still rates rather low on the national agenda of social problems—insofar as it is perceived as occupying a place there at all.

THE WEST GERMAN ANTI-CULT MOVEMENT

It is misleading to speak of an "anti-cult movement" in the Federal Republic of Germany, at least on a scale resembling the movement in the United States. Instead, it may be more appropriate to refer to the reaction against new religions as "anti-cult sentiment." The shift in terminology is in no way related to the effectiveness or political visibility of the German anticult phenomenon—on the contrary, in some respects the German anti-cultists have been more effective than their counterparts in the United States. However, instead of there being any "mass" of organized individuals reacting to social strains who then somehow join together in a concerted effort to achieve a goal, there is a relatively small clique of individuals who hold more or less key positions within important organizations (particularly the Protestant Church), who have an effective communications system, and who have ready access to the media. These individuals are able to mobilize the anticult sentiment, or at least speak for it. There is little or no organized "mass" of people behind them (unlike the American situation), although some of them speak in the name of their parents' organizations and indeed they may well reflect the values and attitudes of a great portion of the society when addressing some matters. Thus, in contrast to the United States the parents' organizations, insofar as they exist other than on paper, serve more *as legitimation for the actions of several key individuals than they reflect any widespread parental unrest.* For example, the founders of the first (and still the most active) anti-movement group were three members of the clergy (two Protestants, one Catholic; one of whom is a prolific author of anti-cult tracts), the wife of one of the clergymen, a lawyer, and *one* couple who had a child in the Unification Church.

The key individuals alluded to above speak with the authority of their affiliated organizations (for example, church-sponsored youth organizations or specially church-created sect research positions) yet represent more conservative stances than the larger church groups. Although these key anti-cult individuals do not represent a broadly based movement, they have been successful in drawing agencies of the federal and state governments into public debate about the new religious movements, more so at least than has been the case at the national level (and often the state level) in the United States. These agencies now distribute materials as a part of their perceived responsibility to "enlighten" the public. These materials heavily reflect anti-cult sentiment, that is, that many of these new religions (usually undifferentiated, just as the American anti-cult movement lumps together a variety of disparate groups under the umbrella label of "cults") pose a real threat to youth and/or the general society. This is an important point because the German government has a constitutional responsibility to protect the family institution and the youth of the nation.

The federal agency most active in the debate over the religions has been the Ministry for Youth, Family, and Health. For example, between 1 July and 15 November 1978 this agency supported a pilot study to locate, view, and evaluate the materials produced by various new religious movements, and to collect and review official research results about the groups in question. Ironically, one of the conclusions of this study was that little or no research approaching social science standards has been undertaken in Germany with regard to new religious movements. German social scientists, in fact, have shown a surprising lack of interest in such phenomena, perhaps because they call for such an applied, policy-oriented perspective. Yet, where social scientists (for the most part) fear to tread, theologians/clergymen/investigative journalists have taken up the banner and flooded the literary marketplace with assorted "pop" analyses that contain much of the brainwashing/mind control ideology, complete with lurid stories told by apostates of new religions, similarly available in American bookstores.

Other state agencies or bodies which have considered the debate over new religious movements and produced policy reports include the Ministries of Labor, Health, and Welfare (*Soziales*) in the state of North Rhein-Westphalia, the Ministry of Welfare (*Soziales*), Health, and Sport in the state of Rheinland-Pfalz, and the Standing Committee for Culture and the Committee for Welfare (*Soziales*), Health, and Family Policy of the Bavarian Senate. Far too many youth affiliate branches of religious, political, and social organizations have become involved (in disseminating anti-cult information, debating the "cult" problem, and so forth) to list them here. However, in addition to legislative bodies and committees that have been heavily influenced by concerned clergy, the West German status quo religious establishment (composed almost entirely of the Protestant [Lutheran and Calvinist] and Catholic churches) has a powerful advantage in resisting and discrediting new religious movements. Religious education is part of the formal school curriculum, and these two mainline bodies cooperate closely with the state in shaping its content (which currently is colored by a good deal of anti-cult sentiment). These mainline bodies also cooperate with the state in influential organizations such as the *Aktion Jugendschutz* which has as one important function watchdog activities to protect youth. Given such influence, it is understandable that public opinion of the new religious movements is low and that there is considerable public support for state intervention on this issue (see *Ministerium für Soziales, Gesundheit und Sport*, State of Rheinland-Pfalz, 1979 for one poll illustrating this sentiment).

In sum, the federal and state governments in West Germany have not been as reluctant as their American counterparts to take a more aggressive role in debating the new religious movements "problem" (despite the fact that the West German anti-cult movement is minimal), and public opinion would seem to support them in their concern. An inspection of the nation's religious traditions, church-state relations and tolerance of alternative economic lifestyles may indicate why.

German Religious Tradition. The Federal Republic of Germany, in comparison to the United States, has in recent decades remained in a condition of religious calm rather than ferment, at least from the perspective of the masses. Most Germans belong to one of the two church groups: the Catholics (approximately forty-five percent of the population) or the Protestants (that is, Calvinist and Lutheran, approximately forty-four percent of the population). The remaining eleven to twelve percent of the population either belong to the "Free Churches" (for example, Baptists, Methodists, Mormons) or have no church affiliation. Almost all church members are baptized as infants and confirmed as children. Adult attendance, except for rites of passage such as marriage and funerals, is minimal. If anything, religious fervor and extreme commitment are suspect. Conversion as it is described in the literature relating to new movements (that is, not just the mere administrative act of changing the religious affiliation on one's identification card) is virtually unknown. Conversion is a matter for theologians to discuss, but the average person on the street does not understand conversion either in terms of his/her own experience or in his/her experience with others. Nor is there any "electronic church" or media vogue of evangelists for Germans to develop models of conversion. The absence of much religious pluralism or sectarian demands for high-intensity religions have rendered conversion phenomena until recently fairly exotic. Most people (eighty-nine percent) are born into one of the two major church traditions and remain nominal members until death.

Thus when the average German is confronted by a zealous member of some new religious movement, he/she has little alternative to a coercive persuasion model for interpreting what has happened to this individual. Religious fervor is perceived as fanatical and pathological, and words like "psycomutation" (borrowed from outspoken psychiatric professionals like John Clark and Margaret Singer in the American anti-cult movement) and "soul-washing" are used to describe the transformation. Its cause is located in some presumed failure on the part of social institutions such as the family, the schools or the churches. Conversion, in other words, is an unfamiliar phenomenon to most Germans and therefore is *a priori* considered problematic.

Church-State Relations. Church-state relations in the Federal Republic of Germany are very different from those in the United States. Following the lines of an older, ecclesiastical model, they help explain why officials in the government are much less reticent to become involved in the current controversy. Clergy are trained in publicly supported institutions and teach religious education in public schools. The state collects a church tax from citizens (approximately ten percent of an individual's income tax), which further adds to the tension between certain new religious movements and the average German when the latter is approached by religious fundraisers. A church-goer may in addition give to the collection plate, but there is little established precedent for private support of religion.

Thus clergy are much more accustomed to dealing with the government and to working closely with officials in areas of mutual concern. It should be noted, however, that the government at both federal and state levels in Germany is *not* concerned with matters of heresy but rather with the social welfare of German youth and their families.

Tolerance for Alternative Economic Life-styles. Earlier we described the "localized" impact on American families of young persons "dropping out" of the conventional economic order to live or work communally with a new religious group. In West Germany the impact is viewed as considerably wider. Apart from the alarm caused by the perception that increasing numbers of youth are becoming disenchanted with the values and opportunities of German society, there is the concern that their failure to contribute to the society's social welfare system could, if enough persons became involved in "cults," have serious future effects. Germany's social welfare system is both comprehensive and expensive. Retirement payments are very high, unemployment insurance is very good, and medical insurance is obligatory. To make this social welfare system work there is a complex system of mutual obligations with the state acting as guarantor. For example, there is what is referred to as the *implicit generation contract*, that is, that the young people moving into the labor market will help to pay the costs which the state incurs in taking care of the old age population. Thus a person who does not work and pay into the social security system not only is diminishing his/her own maximum possible benefits (or not making even him/herself eligible for a benefit), he/she is not living up to the obligations to those who now are receiving benefits. He or she may become a burden on the state. This is further complicated by the fact that legally the family of origin remains a family through the life of the individual. Of course, at the age of majority the child is no longer forced to accept the control of the parents, but mutual obligations binding on all members of the role set continue to exist. This means that if a child past the age of majority becomes dependent upon the state and if the parents are still alive and are not also wards of the state, then the parents must at least share with the state the burden of the child. In other words, if an adult "child" "freaks out" after a visit to a guru and has to receive long-term medical aid and is not insured, the state guarantees that he/she will receive the aid. But the state may then turn to the parents and request compensation. Thus, the charge that the new religions are not socially responsible if they do not provide medical insurance for their members who are not employed in conventional jobs and who spend all of their time in the mission work of the new religion is often heard. The impact of this argument is possibly more understandable when one considers the present population pyramid of West Germany. The birth rate has dropped drastically in recent years, and there is a fear that the "generation contract" will eventually become burdensome enough without "cultists" contributing to the problem.

In sum, tolerance for the alternative lifestyles which many new religious movements require of members is low in West Germany. This factor may even be said to override concerns that youths have been brainwashed into joining such groups and therefore may suffer long-term psycho-physical impairment.

CONCLUSIONS

The greater official response to new religious movements by the Federal Republic of Germany in comparison to the United States situation has not simply been a case of the latter country being considerably larger and therefore slower to mobilize than its European counterpart. Nor is it simply the case that one country has an abundance of research to inform public policy while the other does not. (Indeed, the United States has had an abundance of behavioral science research—much of it admittedly contradictory—on new religious movements in recent years while there has been an undeniable paucity of similar research in West Germany.) Rather, we have argued that in the past few years the Federal Republic of Germany has witnessed greater official response to the new religions controversy than has the United States because of three distinct but related factors: (1) the two countries' respective religious traditions (pluralistic-sectarian versus more ecclesiastical); (2) church-state relations (relative separation versus relative cooperation); and (3) tolerance for youth engaged in alternative lifestyles (a difference, as we noted, closely tied to economic and demographic factors). The United States has witnessed a larger *unofficial* reaction or citizens' movement along the lines of interest group politics that has had as its major goal the prompting of *official* repression of various new religions. In West Germany, where church-state relations manifest less tension and the political economy is more centralized, there has been less need for such a social movement. Matters of religion that in the United States are considered a "sacred cow" foster a "hands off" attitude among public officials that is not easily overcome. After a decade of intense lobbying the American ACM is only now having an impact on legislators. In the West German welfare state, on the other hand, such matters fall within the legitimate domain of social welfare and become more accessible for government investigation and intervention. There the need for unofficial reaction to stimulate official action is considerably less.

But social movements and their relations with their environments can manifest fluid change. In the two years following Jonestown, for instance, anti-cult activity in state legislatures in the United States increased dramatically. It may well be that in the 1980s the United States will see a good deal more meaningful governmental involvement in this controversy and that our analysis will only explain the lag between the beginning of the American ACM and official responses to its grievances. The United States, in other words, may soon "catch up" with West Germany in terms of formal governmental involvement with new religious movements. Such a development poses some interesting, larger questions about institutions and the mobilization of power in decentralized and centralized political economies. From the perspective of developing a theory of social control, it may be that the processes that lead to repression in two societies that differ as do West Germany and the United States will arrive ultimately at the same end point. Ten years hence we shall be in a better position to evaluate such a hypothesis.

REFERENCES

Beckford, James

1981 "Cross Cultural Comparisons of Anti-Cultism." Paper presented at the B.S.A. Sociology of Religion Study Group, Lincoln Conference, 10-16 April 1981.

Bromley, David G., and Anson D. Shupe, Jr.

1979 *"Moonies" in America: Cult, Church, and Crusade*. Beverly Hills CA: Sage.

CEFM (Citizens Engaged in Freeing Minds).

1976 *A Special Report. The Unification Church: Its Activities and Practices*. Vols. 1 and 2. Arlington TX: National Ad Hoc Committee, A Day of Affirmation and Protest.

Connecticut.

1979 Proposed Bill No. 7337, Committee on General Law: "An Act Concerning Establishment of a Commission to Investigate Activities in Connecticut of the Rev. Sun Myung Moon and the Unification Church of America." Hartford CT: State Assembly.

Cunningham, Agnes, J. Robert Nelson, William L. Hendricks, and Jorge LaraBraud

1977 "Report: Critique of the Theology of the Unification Church as Set Forth in Divine Principle." Issued by the National Council of the Churches of Christ in the USA, Commission on Faith and Order.

Hardin, Bert and Günter Kehrer

1982 "Some Social Factors Affecting the Rejection of New Belief Systems," in Eileen Barker, ed., *New Religious Movements: A Perspective for Understanding Society*, Lewiston NY: Edwin Mellen Press.

1978 *Bericht über eine wissenschaftliche Vorstudie im Beriech der "Neuen Jugendreligionen."* Report prepared for the German Federal Ministry for Youth, Family, and Health, Tübingen.

Hardin, Bert

1981 "Causes and Consequences of Social Dissension of Young People: with special consideration of new religious movements. The German Contribution to the International Survey." Report presented in an international workshop on Causes and Consequences of Social Dissension of Young People. Sponsored by the European Center for Social Welfare Training and Research Center for Social Welfare Training and Research. Munich, 31 March-3 April 1981.

Illinois

1979 "House Resolution 121." Springfield IL: General Assembly.

Lipsky, M., and D. J. Olson

1968 "On the Politics of Riot Commissions." (Discussion Paper, Institute for Research on Poverty) Madison: University of Wisconsin.

Ministerium für Soziales, Gesundheit und Sport, State of Rheinland Pfalz.

1979 *Jugendliche in destruktiven religiosen Gruppen: Bericht der Landesregierung Rheinland-Pfalz über die sogenannten neuen Jugendreligionen.*

New York
1980 "Assembly Bill 11122-A, An Act to Amend the Mental Hygiene Law, In Relation to Temporary Conservator," introduced by Howard L. Lasher et al. Albany NY: New York State Assembly (25 March).

1979 "Public Hearing on Treatment of Children by Cults." (Transcript.) Albany NY: New York State Assembly 9-10 August; reprinted by the American Family Foundation, Inc.

1977 Proposed Bill AB9666-A (Section 240.46) "Promoting a Pseudo-religious Cult." Albany NY: New York State Assembly (5 October.)

1975 *Final Report on the Activities of the Children of God to Hon. Louis J. Lefkowitz, Attorney General of the State of New York.* Albany NY: Charity Frauds Bureau.

Ottinger, Richard L.
1980 Working Draft of a Bill to Provide for the Appointment of Temporary Conservators. Washington DC: U.S. House of Representatives (1 October.)

Pennsylvania
1979 House Resolution No. 20. Harrisburg PA: General Assembly of Pennsylvania.

Rudin, A. James
1976 "Report: Jews and Judaism in Rev. Moon's *Divine Principle.*" New York: American Jewish Committee, Inter-religious Affairs Department.

Morgan, Richard E.
1968 *The Politics of Religious Conflict.* New York: Pegasus.

Shupe, Anson D., Jr., and David G. Bromley
1982 *A Documentary History of the American Anti-Cult Movement.* New York: The Edwin Mellen Press.

1980 *The New Vigilantes: Deprogrammers. Anti-Cultists, and the New Religions.* Beverly Hills CA: Sage.

Shupe, Anson D., Jr., Roger Spielmann and Sam Stigall
1980 "Cults of Anti-Cultism." *Society* 17 (March/April): 43-46.

Texas
1977 Resolution (H.S.R. No. 35) passed by the House of Representatives' Committee on Criminal Jurisprudence. Austin TX. (10 May).

United States.
1978 *Investigation of Korean-American Relations* (Report of the Subcommittee on International Organizations of the Committee on International Relations, U.S. House of Representatives). Washington DC: U.S. Government Printing Office.

Vermont.
1977 "Fraudulent and Criminal Practices of Various Organizations in the State." Montpelier VT: State Senate (January).

THE "CULT PROBLEM" IN FIVE COUNTRIES: THE SOCIAL CONSTRUCTION OF RELIGIOUS CONTROVERSY

by James A. Beckford

INTRODUCTION

IN THE GLOBAL VILLAGE that supposedly characterizes the present world system the village store is probably owned by a multinational corporation; the village policeman has been trained by the CIA in countersubversion tactics; and the village school teacher has graduated in standard Spock Studies. But what of the village priest? Where does she fit into the picture? She has become the Parsonsian pontiff of the Central Value System—including integration through the liturgy of latency. But does the *Gesellschaft* team always beat *Gemeinschaft* 1-0 in the village football match?

The peace of this rural idyll is occasionally shattered by wandering merchants, the cunning-men of the cults—peddlers of paradise who carry on a subversive trade. They trade in transcendence—a ticket to multiple realities. These Freddy Lakers of religion, mysticism, and human potential offer cut-price consciousness expansion or standby-seats to salvation. And, of course, there are special student discount schemes. The rumor of angels, the still small voice, is almost drowned out by the roar of the lemming, and the sounding brass in the cult coffers is sweet to the believer's ear.

But rescue from the cults is at hand in the shape of the twin pillars of the Central Value System—money and medicine—and the Pied Pipers of instant salvation find themselves facing the protectionist lobby. They are accused either of consumer fraud or of the illicit practice of medicine. For wealth and health are firmly sewn up in the Global Village. The struggle for a piece of the market in religion is the topic of this paper.

Folk-wisdom about new religious movements, or "cults,"[1] would have us believe that they are multinational businesses operating in a standard fashion in different countries. But I want to argue that this is a misleading picture. It fails to take account of the widely varying conditions within which the movements have to operate and, more particularly, it fails to recognize that "cults" are constituted as different kinds of problems in different countries.

Despite the plethora of recently published studies of new religious movements in the West,[2] little or no attention has been paid to the ways in which these supposedly standardized monoliths have been received in different places. We know that efforts to win new members and to improve the material base of their operations are often modelled on the American example. And we know that there is considerable interchange between countries not only of ideas and techniques but also of personnel. Members of both high and low status are frequently moved from one country to another in order to distribute human resources where they are needed most urgently. This practice is, of course, common to many multinational enterprises. Yet, until recently, no comparative research had been conducted into the differential reception given to new international religious movements. The main aim of this paper is to present the preliminary findings of a project[3] designed specifically to examine ways in which the operations of various so-called cults have been affected by the sociocultural and legal frameworks of five countries: the USA, the United Kingdom, France, the Federal Republic of Germany, and Japan.[4]

---

[1]The term "cult" is probably the most widely used expression in everyday English for referring to new religious movements which have been at the center of controversies in the West for the past decade or so. The best-known movements include the Unification Church, the Church of Scientology, the International Society for Krishna Consciousness, the Children of God (now the Family of Love), and the Divine Light Mission. There are enormous differences among them, but for the purpose of understanding the public response to new religious movements it is essential to preserve the sense of a perceived unity.

[2]Good surveys of the literature are available in Robbins, Anthony, and Richardson, 1978; and Wallis, 1978.

[3]I am grateful to the Nuffield Foundation for a grant enabling me to conduct research into anti-cult sentiment.

[4]A more intensive analysis of the situation in the Federal Republic of Germany and France is contained in Beckford, 1982.

The topic is potentially vast in scope, so this paper will concentrate solely on the conditions that have helped to ensure that, in different ways, the new religious movements have been conceptualized as dangerous or threatening.[5] Even with this qualification, however, there will not be space to consider in detail the processes whereby in each country the movements have been turned into a problem or vilified. I shall only be able to point out the very general differences among countries in respect of their construction of the "cult problem." For this purpose I shall suggest that the UK and the USA represent one type of response (the "Anglo-Saxon"); France and Japan represent a different type; and the Federal Republic of Germany represents a midpoint between these two distinct types of response.

THE UK AND THE USA: VOLUNTARISM

Since the main themes of the public response to new religious movements in the UK and the USA have been discussed elsewhere (Beckford, 1979; Shupe and Bromley, 1981a and 1981b; Shupe, Hardin, and Bromley, in this volume), what I shall call the "Anglo Saxon" response will only be sketched here. It has two main themes: psychologization and construction of religion as deviance. Both of these themes constitute new religious movements of many kinds as a problem for individuals first and foremost.

In the first place there is a virtually automatic disposition among many people in these two countries to consider the attraction of new religious movements as nothing other than a matter of individual psychology—and abnormal psychology at that. Attention is focused in this perspective on what happens in the minds of the movements' recruits. What goes wrong? Or, how was the mind manipulated and weakened? The focus is therefore on a series of before-and-after contrasts which can be schematized as follows:

BEFORE	AFTER
Clear-thinking	Brainwashed
Autonomous	Manipulated
Critical	Uncritical
Private	Exposed
Balanced	Fanatical
Family-minded	Family-indifferent

[5]It is unfortunately impossible in analyzing anti-cultism to avoid repeating potentially defamatory allegations about new religious movements, so I must make it clear that my intention is not malicious.

These psychological oppositions are deeply rooted in everyday assumptions about the boundaries of the "normal" person in cultural, social, and legal institutions. Thinking about the so-called problem of new religious movements is dominated by them in casual conversations, courtroom argument and social scientific discourse.

A second widespread disposition in the UK and USA is to argue that, since "cultists" exceed the limits of psychological normality, they should be subject to appropriate social control mechanisms. There may even be grounds for believing that a process of deviance-amplification is at work as a result of the application of a "deviant" label to new religious movements. Certainly attempts have been made to counteract three particular manifestations of the supposed deviance, namely, the abandonment of control over private property, the forsaking of courses of education and training, and the rejection of family ties. Hostile sentiments towards new religious movements are most easily aroused in connection with these alleged deviations from normality, and the mass media have accorded them great prominence.

Given that the "cult problem" is widely seen in the UK and the USA as an expression of deviant individual psychology, anti-cult sentiment is diffuse and not easily mobilized in collective movements. Propaganda against new religious movements is therefore couched in terms which treat their recruits as victims of circumstances or of their own psychological weaknesses. Harrowing accounts of the suffering experienced by recruits and their relatives are used as threats that the same problems could befall anyone without warning.[6]

This "accidental" aetiology of membership in a new religious movement has the effect of blocking interest in the actual teachings and practices of the movements. The problem is simply not located in this area at all: it lies in the manipulative methods whereby "destructive cults" allegedly identify and amplify individual psychological weaknesses. A further implication of the individualistic and accidental aetiology of membership is that little or no consideration is given in the UK and the USA to the contribution that new religious movements *as collectivities*

---

[6]See, e.g., the following headline in a British magazine for teenagers: "The Enemy: the Family. Its Mission: Total Manipulation of Body, Soul & Mind. Victims: Today—You! Tomorrow—the World! 19 Brings You A Story of Faith, Hope And Insanity—the Dark, Destructive, Side Of the Moonies," *19* (January 1980): 33.

might make to cultural or social change. Nor is there much enthusiasm in Anglo-Saxon anti-cult circles for attempts to understand the sociocultural context within which new religious movements have operated. In this way the "cult problem" has been kept separate from consideration of other social and cultural problems.

Anti-cult groups in the UK and the USA are highly vocal but not very influential. This is primarily because they have purveyed an individualistic and accidental "theory" of cultism and, therefore, have failed to join forces with, or draw on the resources of, already existing networks of interest groups, pressure groups and lobbies which might have lent the anti-cult campaign a wider significance. As it is, anti-cult groups have approximated to the form of associations of "victims and their relatives," and this has made it correspondingly difficult for them to mobilize public opinion on a large scale. Even those groups with a readily available religious or confessional identity have failed to achieve widespread support for anti-cultism within their own denominations.

The anti-cult response in the UK and the USA has been strictly voluntaristic and largely separate from other moral concerns and campaigns. With the exception of a small proportion of religiously motivated participants, the vast majority of supporters are people who have been personally affected in various ways by new religious movements and who see the main problem in individualistic and psychological terms. Consequently, anti-cult strategies have tended to be pragmatic and *ad hoc*. The groups have found it relatively difficult to gain access to official authorities at all levels of the state. But in the USA groups of the "concerned citizens" type have been successful in helping to prepare and support numerous law suits against new religious movements and on behalf of deprogrammers. In the UK, however, activities have centered on counseling affected individuals and on disseminating information. Other points of significant difference between anti-cultism in the UK and the USA include the scale of the perceived "cult problem," the volume of litigation concerning new religious movements and the extent of professional deprogramming (the practice of removing people from movements, initially at least, against their will). Although no reliable accounts of the number of people involved in new religious movements are available in either country, there is no doubt that American members outnumber their British counterparts by a wide margin. The scale of anti-cult activity is correspondingly greater in the USA. In particular, the number of anti-cult groups, the public visibility of their operation and their extensive involvement in litigation all indicate that American anti-cultism, though activated by concerns very similar to the preoccupations of the British, is virtually of a different order of magnitude. And one of the closely associated differences between the situations in each country is that professional deprogrammers have been far more active in the USA than in the UK. In fact, deprogramming on a professional basis has been attempted on only a handful of occasions in the latter. This all points to the conclusions that the temper, frequency and volume of anti-cult activity are much higher in the USA; but the underlying assumption that recruitment to new religious movements is achieved by the deliberate inducement of psychological deviance is common to both countries. This shared assumption is matched by a shared form of strictly voluntary, pressure-group activity on the part of "concerned citizens."

FRANCE AND JAPAN: ORGANICISM

There is an affinity between the individualistic and psychological voluntarism of Anglo-Saxon anti-cult groups and the pluralism which has characterized the religious life of the UK and the USA in modern times. The distinctive complexion of the "cult problem" in those countries has been brought about in conditions reflecting pluralism and a relatively high degree of religious toleration. I now wish to contrast this picture with the conditions affecting anti-cult sentiment in France and Japan, two countries characterized in part by a relatively homogeneous religious culture and by the persistence of strong attachments to the traditional family form. Despite the evidence of recent transformations of many traditional structures I believe that it is still justified to refer to the religious cultures of France and Japan as "organicist" insofar as they successfully evoke feelings and notions of socioreligious wholeness, integrity and uniqueness.

The dominant response to new religious movements in France has been very much in line with the earlier response shown to such Protestant "sects" as the Salvation Army, the Jehovah's Witnesses, the Brethren, and the Mormons. All are suspected of undermining the natural, organic order of French society; and all are characterized as *dissidences*. The main objection to dissident religion is not psychological and is not centered on the sufferings of individual "victims." Rather, it is based on the cultural-cum-political charge that they are somehow closed off from the rest of society and are therefore a dangerous threat to national integrity. The most authoritative French study of new religious movements consequently treats old and new sects alike as "politicoreligious sects . . . captivating a young generation which has gone adrift, with the lure of the craziest utopias" (Woodrow, 1977: 12). To the extent that attention is paid in France to the psychological effects of new religious movements they are set in a wider context of the conspiracy which they allegedly represent against prevailing social order.

A closely allied feature of the peculiarity of the "cult problem" in France is that the theme of conspiracy is reinforced with accusations about the supposedly totalitarian aims and methods of cult leaders. This is clearly illustrated in the following extract from a document published by Les Associations de Défense de la Famille et de l'Individu (ADFI), France's main anti-cult organization:

> It is time to understand how our children are, in good faith, being manipulated, blinded and subjected to a sect as if they were slaves. They cannot see the secret aims of their organization and, anyway, they are not allowed the time for reflection nor the material opportunities to understand what kind of a plot is being hatched around them. They fail to realize what an evil role they are being surreptitiously made to play against the national interest.

Added to the accusations of conspiracy and totalitariansim is a note of xenophobia which further reflects the organicist character of the French response to new religious movements:

> The problem [of cults] is serious enough for the government and our elected representatives to take the necessary steps to prevent the nation from suffering a dictatorship which would be all the more terrible for being the work of foreigners with an outlook different from our own. (ADFI, 1977: 17-18 my translation)

It is not difficult to see that these charges go far beyond the scope of the kind of accusations leveled by British and American anti-cultists at the allegedly self-interested confidence trickery of some cult leaders. The altogether more radical and alarmist tone of French anti-cultism derives from the perception of new religious movements as a serious and orchestrated threat to the former unity and integrity of national culture.

The character of French anti-cultism can only be understood when account is taken of the politicoreligious scandal surrounding a small Franco-Belgian sect called The Three Holy Hearts in the early 1970s. It was run by Roger Melchior, whose doctoral dissertation at the University of Louvain on "Terror as a System of Domination" seems to have provided the basis of its practice. The full details of the scandal cannot be examined here (see Lecerf, 1975), but it clearly raised very serious issues about what one of its critics claimed to be "the fragility of the defenses of major institutions confronting schemes for infiltration which are cleverly conducted by mini-churches in search of legitimacy" (Baffoy, 1978: 55).

ADFI is a federally structured, partly voluntary, and partly subsidized organization that, while remaining critical of the French government's apparent lack of concern about the alleged dangers of new religious movements, has received grants from the Ministry of Health and has the support of a number of legislators. In its origins it was composed very largely of the relatives of "cult victims" but it quickly gained the support of various individuals and agencies in the Catholic Church, with the result that it is now more broadly based than its British and American counterparts. One of the reasons for ADFI's prominence and credibility is that is has been successful in persuading journalists to take anti-cultism seriously by situating it in a more overtly political context than has happened in any other Western country. The twin themes of conspiracy and cover-up are the *leitmotiv* in its recurrent argument that France must be vigilant against would-be subversive and totalitarian cults.[7]

The cultural and social differences between France and Japan are enormous, but the two countries share a formally similar image of themselves as organic wholes. Of course, the detailed, symbolic representations of societal wholeness and integrity are entirely distinctive, but their respective responses to the new religious movements which have become active in the West in the past two decades display some notable parallels. In the following treatment of the Japanese case I shall have to supply a disproportionate amount of background information in order to acquaint the Western reader with the outlines of recent religious history in Japan.

Since the early nineteenth century Japan has given rise to hundreds and hundreds of so-called New Religions, most of which have actually been syntheses of ancient Buddhism, Shinto, and folk-religion. Only since 1945 has real freedom of religion been enjoyed, and the postwar period has seen the consolidation of massive New Religions of various kinds. There are, for example, the energetic lay Buddhism of the Soka Gakkai; the syncretistic salvationist Buddhism of the Rissho Kosei-kai; the ascetic this-worldliness of Tenri-kyo; the aesthetic neo-Shinto of Ōmoto; and

[7]See, e.g., Facon and Parent, 1980; and Leduc and de Plaige, 1978.

the so-called "businessman's religion" of Perfect Liberty Kyodan (for summaries, see McFarland, 1967; Offner & Van Straelen, 1963; Earhart, 1970).

Each of these movements has, in distinctive fashion, welded its followers into a cohesive, active, and self-conscious "clan" that provides them with a highly salient and novel means of self-identification. The processes of urbanization, social mobility and rapid modernization of the spheres of work and family relations are said to have created a vast market for religious experimentation and for the basic realignment of religious loyalties (Morioka, 1975). As the New Religions have matured, so the traditionally tolerant and pragmatic attitude of the Japanese in religious matters has been eroded to some extent.

The Japanese constitution of 1947 is modeled on the American in respect of its guarantee of the freedom of religion and the separation of church and state.[8] This was insisted upon by the American authorities at the conclusion of the Second World War, and the deliberate undermining of traditional loyalties to highly localized Shinto shrines or Buddhist temples seemed appropriate to an age of greatly increased geographical and social mobility. The initial flowering of so many diverse religious movements in the late-1940s received unofficial encouragement from the American forces of the occupation who probably believed that religious pluralism would be a healthy antidote to unhealthy fascistic patriotism.

What could not have been foreseen, however, was that the initial *élan* of some movements would be maintained for at least thirty years. The result has been that religious loyalty has again emerged as a dominant source of identity, morality and motivation for many Japanese. But this time the formerly national focus has been largely replaced by a series of occasionally conflicting kinds of clan-loyalties which cut across regional and social status divisions. And since some of these movements have become immensely stable, powerful and all-inclusive in their scope, the situation is beginning to approach that of the Dutch and Belgian "pillarization." The largest movements can now provide their members with cradle-to-grave care and protection (see Hambrick, 1974; and Shimazono, 1979). In the words of Nishio,

---

[8]For an instructive account of the political background to the controversy about the Soka Gakkai's close connection with a political party, see Ingram, 1969.

> the individuals brought into the large-scale, complex organization of a new religion can feel they are persons who are cared for; but at the same time, from the standpoint of the organization, they can act with group discipline to accomplish the specified goals of organization. (Nishio, 1967: 783)

Small, regular discussion groups ("Hoza" in Rissho Kosei-kai, and "Zadankai" in Soka Gakkai) are the organizational vehicle or mechanism for promoting the feeling of belonging within the massive organization characterizing these two movements in particular. Other movements have functional equivalents.

The Soka Gakkai is virtually unique in having a special relationship with a political party—the Komeito ("clean government party."). The two organizations were declared formally separate in 1970 in order to forestall some of the hostile responses displayed by left-of-center opinion to what was seen as an unhealthy alliance between politics and religion. But the fact remains that Komeito, with its persisting affinity with Soka Gakkai's ideals and with the electoral support of a large proportion of the movement's members, is able to exercise considerable power in the Japanese Diet. And this is the most important source of public disquiet about its activities.

A similar kind of disquiet is also felt about the Unification Church (UC) which is the only new religious movement with extensive operations in the West to have prospered in Japan. It was here that the Rev. Moon enjoyed his first successes in a mission field. Beginning in 1958, only four years after the UC's official foundation in the Republic of Korea, the movement has achieved great recruiting success, among the student population in particular. It now has a membership of at least 20,000 people. There are strong and frequent suggestions in the Japanese press that the whole movement is nothing but a front for anticommunism; there are suspicions that it was financed at least in the early days by political and industrial interest groups of the extreme right-wing; its alleged implication in the "Koreagate" scandal in the USA aroused indignation in Japan; and there are rumors that various attempts to have its progress checked have been blocked at the highest levels of government.

In short, the "problem" of the UC in Japan is seen in basically political terms. On the one hand it is accused of corruption and underhanded tactics, and on the other there are fears that it may attain the monolithic dimensions of the Soka Gakkai and thereby aggravate an already delicate political situation. Indeed, the combination of these two accusations makes the UC a natural target for liberal indignation. Matters are only made worse by the widespread scorn among the Japanese for anything Korean.

No official investigations[9] have been conducted into new religious movements in Japan since 1945, and there are good grounds for believing that the extensive involvement of the larger movements in such areas as social welfare and education is welcomed by governments which are reluctant to expand the public provision of services which would amount to a Welfare State in some other advanced capitalist countries. Care of the sick, the young and the aged is left very largely in the hands either of the family or of the company. It may be no coincidence, therefore, that members of the New Religions are drawn disproportionately from groups falling outside the bounds of the traditional sources of welfare, that is, isolated pensioners and families with young children whose income derives from self-employment, service industries or marginal and unstable occupations.

Opposition to the New Religions has been muted, although in its early days the Soka Gakkai acquired notoriety for its robust methods of recruitment. To some extent the desire to control them was weakened by the realization that the competition among the new movements was so intense that they seemed to keep each other in check. But in 1951 Rissho Kosei-kai formed an association whose aims included the formation of an alliance against the Soka Gakkai which was blamed for bringing all other New Religions into disrepute. The Shin Nippon Shukyo Dantai Rengo-kai (Federation of New Japanese Religious Organizations) grouped together about eighty movements which collectively endorsed and supported candidates in general elections as well as maintained communication among themselves. The competition with the Soka Gakkai actually led to violence in some districts in the 1967 elections, and the mass media held out the prospect of a religious war (Shukyo Senso) of attrition (see *Asahi Shimbun*, 22 January 1967). But the separation of the Soka Gakkai from Komeito in 1970 reduced the danger of outright intersectarian conflict. Nowadays, a certain amount of sniping takes place in their respective newspapers, but the main movements are probably more

[9]It should be added, however, that there were congressional hearings on the specific charges that Rissho Kosei-kai had permitted potentially lethal faith-healing practices and had been involved in illegal possession of land where its headquarters now stand.

worried about their stagnant membership statistics than about competition with others.

Opposition to the UC, the only "cult" in the Western sense to have made an impact in Japan, has been growing stronger since the early 1970s. The reasons for this are related to some basic values and structural features of modern Japanese society.

First and foremost is a deep-rooted suspicion of anything closely connnected with Korea. Since the Rev. Moon has been accused of being an agent for the Korean CIA and has been implicated in "Koreagate" in the USA, the strength of liberal opposition has increased. His movement is accused of being an attempt to further Korean interests by underhanded methods. This theme is prominent in mass media exposés of the movement. At the personal level these feelings are translated into the view that association with the UC is "shameful" and brings dishonor on the family. This is even extended to the complaint among anti-cultists that many hostile parents cannot bring themselves to admit publicly that their child has joined a Korean religious movement. The fear of shame therefore prevents the anti-cult campaign from accelerating (interview with vice-president of anti-UC association). It also helps to explain why few ex-members of the UC joined or supported the campaign.

A second source of resistance to the UC is the way in which it is felt to usurp the functions and status of the family. This is particularly acute with regard to the practice of allowing the movement to select marriage partners independently of the family's preferences: for even in the highly mobile and urbanized sectors of Japanese society weddings still play a major role in consolidating long-term relations between whole families.

A third and allied objection to the UC is that it sends abroad about 700 of its Japanese members each year, and this is widely felt to be an intolerable affront to the value of family unity and family-centeredness. But compared with the orientation of many Western critics of the UC the Japanese regard the disruption of courses of higher education with relatively little anxiety. This reflects the relatively low prestige of higher education institutions and qualifications in Japan. More disturbing to the Japanese is the disruption of traditional relations with sources of potential patronage and lifelong employment.

Fourth, the UC has become an object of suspicion because it is associated with politics in a country where politicians generally have low social prestige. There is a pervasive feeling that the success achieved by the movement in a short period of time could only have resulted from compromises and deals with people in political power. The fact that the student recruiting wing of the UC, J-CARP, was apparently allowed to operate without hindrance on some university campuses, for example, is cited as evidence of collusion in high places. The same is true of the belief that a highly critical report from the Japanese Bar Association has been suppressed on orders from a government minister.

When comparisons are made with anti-cultism in other countries, one is struck by the relatively insignificant weight given in Japan to the argument that recruits are gained by brainwashing or psychological manipulation. Indeed, psychological concepts are virtually absent from the public and private discourse about movements such as the UC and the New Religions. A journalist who has published several books on the UC reported that only one piece of research had been attempted into accusations of brainwashing in Japan, but that even this project had never been completed (private communication).

Another prominent theme of Western anti-cultism which is virtually lacking from the Japanese counterpart is any sense of indignation about the connection between wealth, power, and religion. Since the connection appears to be more acceptable in the eyes of the Japanese, neither the UC nor the New Religions have been consistently criticized for their money-making endeavours or the occasionally luxurious life-style of their leaders.

My research in Japan brought to light only one recognizable anti-cult organization, the Association of Parents of Victims of the Unification Church, which has several branches at the prefectural level as well as a national headquarters in Nagoya. Approximately 200 people are affiliated with it and participate in its main activities of lobbying politicians, collecting information, and disseminating its propaganda. Its resources are meager, and its impact on Japanese public opinion is negligible compared with that of its counterparts in, for example, the UK, the USA, France, and the Federal Republic of Germany.

If the level of anti-cultism in Japan appears to be surprisingly low in view of the size and visibility of various New Religions, the reason probably lies in the fact that very few of them recruit individual young adults and remove them from their jobs, colleges, or families. Rather, the New Religions are composed mainly of family units, and members are encouraged to retain their secular employment with the obvious exception of the large numbers of full-time employees of the movements. In this respect, then, the vast majority of New Religions are considered not to represent a serious threat to any of the country's most important social institutions. For this reason among others it is questionable whether "New Religions" is an appropriate designation for movements that have provided merely novel means of expressing traditional beliefs, values, and social relations. These considerations therefore help to explain the comparative weakness of anti-cult sentiment in general and the antipathy shown towards the UC in particular.

The public response to new religious movements of the Western "cult" type in France and Japan can be termed "organicist" in the sense that in both countries, albeit to different degrees and in different respects, it is dominated by a concern to protect a formerly unitary and cohesive religious culture. Both countries have, until quite recently, displayed virtual monopolies in the field of religion, and the family institution has been strong in them. Therefore, it is not surprising that the advent of some new religious movements should have appeared to threaten the traditional order in religious and family matters, even though these institutions had already been greatly reduced in prestige and privileges. It also seems appropriate that, against a background of a formerly unitary culture, the "cult problem" should be regarded as the outcome of an organized conspiracy by evil forces to subvert a normally and naturally good social order. In these circumstances, then, the "cult problem" is seen in largely social and cultural terms as an insidious threat to the integrity of the French and Japanese nations, and as such it cannot be kept separate from political considerations.

THE FEDERAL REPUBLIC OF GERMANY: RETICULATION

A detailed consideration of the multifaceted "cult problem" in the Federal Republic of Germany would occupy far more space than is available here, but thanks to the pioneering analyses of Hardin (1980), of Kehrer (1980), and of Hardin and Kehrer (1982) it will be possible to present a summary picture of the situation. The task is also made easier by the fact that many of the parties involved in the problem from different points of view have published their own sophisticated analyses of it. In general, the discourse about new religious movements is more varied, analytical, and (above all) self-reflexive in the Federal Republic than in any of the other countries considered in this paper.

The most salient point in the German literature is that, in a country characterized as being in "stable equilibrium between the two major churches" (Kehrer, 1972: 191) and as displaying a high degree of moral consensus (Schmidtchen, 1972), the readiness of large numbers of young, well-educated people to join new religious movements is widely perceived as disaffection from prevailing social values. In fact it is regarded as an aspect of the same "flight from reality" which is blamed for student rebellions and political terrorism. This was clearly articulated by the Federal Council for Youth:

> Terrorism may be legitimately considered as the extreme behavior of a tiny, isolated group of young people, but there are many indications—which have so far largely failed to attract attention in public discussion—that terrorism is only *one* form of the numerous variants on youth withdrawal from our society. Other symptoms of the sickness of social, political and cultural life are apathy, the flight into drugs or alcohol, the turning to youth sects and suicide. (Fetscher, 1979: 115-16; emphasis original; my translation)

The link with terrorism has also been explored seriously in more specialized analyses of the so-called youth religions (see, for example, Haack, 1979, and Müller-Küppers & Specht, 1979).

The other major theme of anti-cult sentiment in the Federal Republic concerns the allegedly harmful effect produced by youth religions on the willingness of young Germans to complete courses of education and to embark on careers (Shupe, Hardin, and Bromley, in this volume). While this is far from being unique to Germany it is more than usually powerful in that country because of the special resonance that this theme has for so many social institutions. Hard work and the determination to prepare adequately for a career are highly prized in the ruling circles of the State, the Civil Service, provincial governments, political parties, trades unions, educational institutions, and churches (see Almond and Verba, 1963; Fürstenberg, 1974; Dahrendorf, 1965). The strength of consensus on this point has implications for the organization of anti-cult campaigns.

In particular, it means that anti-cult interests have been able to make common cause with a wide variety of groups whose general concern is for the "protection of youth." For, given that new religious movements were defined as primarily a youth problem, and given that the widely accepted aetiology of the problem specified its relation to the wider "flight from reality," there was a natural affinity between the interests of youth protection and anti-cultism. The main practical implication of this affinity is that specifically anti-cult groups have found it easier to obtain a public hearing for their cause in the Federal Republic than in other countries. A ready-made network of communications and personal sympathies was available to diffuse the main message about the alleged dangers represented by youth religions and to lay the foundation for practical resistance to them.

Resistance to new religious movements in the Federal Republic is based in an impressive variety of religious, political, social, governmental, and consumer-protection bodies. The extraordinarily intrusive role of the Federal Ministry of Youth, Family and Health in providing moral and material support to anti-cult causes helps to explain the effectiveness of the intricate network. For it serves as a source of legitimation and a clearinghouse for ideas and initiatives originating in diverse interest groups. This is clearly evident in its own 23-page brochure on Youth Religions in the German Federal Republic (*Die Jugendreligionen in der Bundesrepublik Deutschland*) that was published in 1980 and distributed under the aegis of many anti-cult groups. The minister's foreword locates the brochure in the context of her responsibility to "protect" young people and their families from all kinds of "dangers." She pinpointed the psychic damage that is allegedly caused by the "dubious" practices of youth religions, and she offered her support to parents of cult members. At the same time as endorsing the view that cult membership is part of a "flight from reality" the Ministry's brochure encourages law-enforcement agencies to act effectively against new religious movements which appear to break existing laws concerning the use of public places for recruitment, the solicitation of donations from the public, the issue of fraudulent promises, and the use of force against a person's will.

The objection that a federal ministry should play no part in suppressing religion in a country whose constitution guarantees freedom of religion is met with the argument that, first, some cults have forfeited their constitutional privileges by their commercial activities, and second, the privileges are available only on condition that religious groups observe the codes of contemporary morality (*"soweit sie sich im Rahmen gewisser übereinstimmender sittlicher Grundanschauungen der heutigen Kulturvölker hälten"*).

The most tangible expression of the Federal Ministry of Youth, Family and Health's involvement in combating the spread of new religious movements is the financial assistance that it has made to the most influential anti-cult organization in Germany, namely, the Campaign for Spiritual and Psychical Freedom (*die Aktion für geistige und psychische Freiheit*). This organization is the closest equivalent to the "parents' groups" of the UK and the USA, but it differs from them primarily in the amount of influence that it is able to wield with public authorities and, conversely, in their readiness to aid it. There are good relations between this organization and sympathetic agencies in the major churches such as the Catholic "*Aktion Jugendschutz*" and the prolific author of anti-cult works on behalf of the Evangelical Church, Pastor Haack. Relations are also good with anti-cult interests in other countries and with medical doctors and psychiatrists who support the "flight from reality" explanation of adherence to new religious movements.

Finally, mention must be made of one unique feature of anti-cult activity in the Federal Republic. This concerns the energetic and extensive campaign waged by a consumer protection agency specializing in the field of private education, *Aktion Bildungsinformation* (ABI), against the recruitment practices of the Church of Scientology. It has won at least fifteen legal cases against Scientology for alleged infringements of the law relating to recruitment in public places, and its 130-page book *The Sect of Scientology and its Front Organizations* is regarded in anti-cult circles as a model of reasoned criticism. It is entirely in line with the reticulate character of anti-cultism in the Federal Republic that the publications of ABI should be widely distributed and promoted by sympathizers in political and religious groups as well as in provincial and federal government.

The best way to summarize the character of German anti-cultism is to emphasize the central preoccupation with the protection of young people from forces which are felt to threaten their morality and their motivation. More specifically, new religious movements are depicted as a further threat to the long-term stability and viability of a pluralistic democracy beset by problems of apathy, withdrawal and terrorism. In consequence, the "cult problem" is not confined to small, voluntary groups of cult members' parents or to ex-members: it is actually taken up and shared by many diverse organizations, some with governmental support. The network of such groups is intricate and effective, so that the visibility of the public debate about new religious movements is greater than in most other countries. Needless to say, questions about religious freedom and the extent to which illiberal "cults" can be tolerated in a liberal democracy are highly prominent in the Federal Republic of Germany and peculiarly pertinent to the country's political well-being.

CONCLUSIONS

Consideration of the fortunes of new religious movements in five countries leads to three general observations.

First, the character of the "cult problem" varies with social, political, and cultural circumstances. The way in which a new religious movement is received by a host society clearly depends on far more than simply its own teachings, values and practices. It may also achieve "insertion" in society (Séguy, 1977) in a variety of ways in spite of an apparently uniform or standardized set of procedures imposed by a central agency. The mutual interaction between new religious movements and their host societies has been one of this paper's main topics. Second, the social "vehicles" of anti-cult sentiment and practice vary from country to country in form and intensity. Some are purely voluntary and *ad hoc*, whereas others are grafted on to official or semi-official agencies and make common cause with existing interest groups. Consideration of new religious movements in one country alone underestimates the potential scope of disquiet about them.

Third, critics and opponents of new religious movements rarely concern themselves with the contributions that the movements might be trying to make to change in culture and patterns of social relations. Accusations of religious intolerance and bigotry are invariably dismissed as irrelevant. Rather, anticultism is usually focused narrowly on the short-term behavioral consequences of recruitment to, and involvement in, new religious movements.

This paper has merely tried to document some general aspects of the processes whereby the "cult problem" is constructed in five different countries displaying three types of anti-cultism. Further research is required to refine the analysis and, in particular, to investigate the social sources of support for anti-cult groups and their members' ideological sympathies. At the same time, it is important to learn more about the response of new religious movements to the specific forms of opposition that they encounter. Above all, a dynamic and interactive approach to these phenomena must be maintained.

REFERENCES

A.B.I.
n.d. *Die Scientologie-Sekte und ihre Tarnorganisationen.* Stuttgart: ABI e. V.

A.D.F.I.
1977 *Etude comparative de deux idéologies.* Rennes, 1977. Mimeographed.

Almond, G. and S. Verba.
1963 *The Civic Culture.* Princeton NJ: Princeton University Press.

Baffoy, T.
1978 "Les sectes totalitaires." *Esprit* (January): 53-59.

Beckford, J. A.
1979 "Politics and the anti-cult movement." *Annual Review of the Social Sciences of Religion* 3:169-90.

1981 "Cults, Controversy and Control: a Comparative Analysis of the Problems Posed by New Movements in the Federal Republic of Germany and France." *Sociological Analysis* 42, 3:249-264.

Dahrendorf, R.
1965 *Gesellschaft und Demokratie in Deutschland.* Munich.

Earhart, H. B.
1970 *The New Religions of Japan. A Bibliography of Western-Language Materials.* Tokyo: Sophia University.

Facon, R., and J. M. Parent.
1980 *Sectes et Sociétés Secrètes Aujourd'hui. Le Complot des Ombres.* Paris: Lefeuvre.

Fetscher, I., ed.
1979 *Jugend und Terrorismus.* Munich: Juventa Verlag.

Fürstenberg, F.
1974 *Die Sozialstruktur der Bundesrepublik Deutschland. Ein soziologischer Überblick.* Opladen: Westdeutscher Verlag. Third edition.

Haack, F.-W.
1979 *Jugendreligionen. Ursachen, Trends, Reaktionen.* Munich: Claudius Verlag.

Hambrick, C. H.
1974 "Tradition and modernity in the New Religions of Japan." *Japanese Journal of Religious Studies* 1:2-3:217-52.

Hardin, B.
1980 "Rückzug in der Innerlichkeit? Jugendsekten als moralischen Alternativerlebnis." Mimeographed.

Hardin, B., and G. Kehrer.
1982 "Some social factors affecting the rejection of new belief systems." in E. V. Barker, ed., *New Religious Movements: A Perspective for Understanding Society.* New York: Edwin Mellen.

Ingram, P. O.
1969 "Soka Gakkai and the Komeito. Buddhism and political power in Japan." *Contemporary Religions in Japan* 10:155-80.

Kehrer, G.

1972 "Germany: the Federal Republic." 189-212 in J. J. Mol, ed., *Western Religion.* The Hague: Mouton.

1980 "Kirchen, Sekten und der Staat. Zum Problem der religiösen Toleranz." Mimeographed.

Lecerf, Y.

1975 *Les Marchands de Dieu. Analyse Socio-Politique de l'Affaire Melchior.* Brussels: Complexe.

Leduc, J.-M., and D. de Plaige.

1978 *Les Nouveaux Prophètes.* Paris: Buchet/Chastel.

McFarland, H. N.

1967 *The Rush Hour of the Gods. A Study of New Religious Movements in Japan.* New York: Macmillan.

Morioka, K.

1975 *Religion in Changing Japanese Society.* Tokyo: Tokyo University Press.

Müller-Küppers, M., and F. Specht, eds.

1979 *Neue Jugendreligionen.* Göttingen: Vandenhoeck und Ruprecht.

Nishio, H.

1967 "Comparative analysis of the Rissho Koseikai and the Soka Gakkai." *Asian Survey* 7:776-90.

Offner, C. B., and H. Van Straelen.

1963 *Modern Japanese Religions, with Special Emphasis on their Doctrines of Healing.* Tokyo: Rupert Enderle.

Robbins, T., D. Anthony, and J. T. Richardson.

1978 "Theory and research on today's 'New Religions'." *Sociological Analysis* 39:2:95-122.

Schmidtchen, G.

1972 *Zwischen Kirche und Gesellschaft.* Freiburg: Herder.

Séguy, J.

1977 "Les sectes comme mode d'insertion sociale." 293-316 in *Eglises et Groupes Religieux dans la Société Française.* Strasbourg: Cerdic Publications.

Shimazono, S.

1979 "The Living Kami Idea in the New Religions of Japan." *Japanese Journal of Religious Studies* 6:3:389-412.

Shupe, A. D., Jr., and D. G. Bromley.

1981a *The New Vigilantes: Deprogrammers, Anti-Cultists and the New Religions.* Los Angeles: Sage.

1981b "Apostates and Atrocity Stories: Some Parameters in the Dynamics of Deprogramming," 179-215 in B. R. Wilson, ed., *The Social Impact of New Religious Movements.* New York: Rose of Sharon Press.

Wallis, R.

1978 *The Rebirth of the Gods? Reflections on New Religions in the West.* An inaugural lecture, the Queen's University, Belfast, Northern Ireland.

Woodrow, A.

1977 *Les Nouvelles Sectes.* Paris: Seuil.

PARTICIPATION RATES IN NEW RELIGIOUS AND PARARELIGIOUS MOVEMENTS*

by Frederick Bird
and William Reimer

SINCE THE MIDDLE of the 1960s a large number of New Religious and Parareligious Movements have either been established or have greatly expanded the numbers of their adherents. A number of observers have produced studies of these movements, usually focusing on one, two or several movements. Many have attempted to explain the significance of these movements by referring to them as a religious revival (McLoughlin, 1978); as an example of experimental religion (Wuthnow, 1978); as an expression of political disenchantment (Tipton, 1977); or as the emergence of a new humanism (Westley, 1978a, 1978b; Bellah, 1976). In this paper, we will analyze these movements and examine their significance by looking at the characteristic rates with which people have participated in these movements. We will be raising and answering four questions:

- What percentage of the adult population have ever participated in these movements?
- What is the typical form of their participation?
- Are there any significant characteristics of those who have participated?

*This paper was published in the *Journal for the Scientific Study of Religion* (March 1982).

• Are there any differences among participants in relation to the kinds of New Religious movements in which they have been affiliated?[1]

In brief, survey data collected in Montreal indicate that a surprisingly high proportion of the adult population has participated in New Religious and Parareligious Movements (somewhere between one-fifth and one-fourth of the population), but that most persons who do participate become involved only for a short time and then drop out. While there is a core of persons who have become committed members of these groups, the typical participant is a transitory affiliate. In relation to social and economic status, participants are more likely to be younger, unmarried, and middle class, but the differences here are not dramatic. There are more marked differences with regard to life-style variables, where participants are much more likely to have gotten high on psychedelics and to have gotten involved with astrology and the *I Ching*. In relation to all these variables, participants in those types of movements herein labeled as countercultural devotional, differ more decidedly from nonparticipants than did other participants. Moreover, countercultural devotional participants were much more likely to have changed their religious identification and to have been involved in several of these groups. However, while participants in countercultural devotional groups more nearly correspond to the stereotyped public image of cult members, they represent only a very small proportion of persons who have become involved in New Religious and Parareligious Movements.

We collected data in Montreal in two surveys—one conducted in 1975 and another in 1980. This survey data will be compared with a survey conducted in the San Francisco Bay area. The first survey was completed by 1,607 adults who were in the process of registering for classes, mostly evening classes, at Concordia University. Since most of those registering were taking evening classes, already held full-time jobs, and were in their late twenties, thirties, or older, this sample was clearly not typical of most undergraduate student bodies. However, compared to the adult population of Montreal as a whole, this sample was much more likely to be anglophone, somewhat more likely to be single, more likely to

---

[1]Research for this paper was made possible in part by several research grants from the Quebec Ministry of Education. The authors would like to thank the following persons for helping to gather data cited herein: Susan Bernstein, Paul Schwartz, Elizabeth Sandul, Ann McManaman, and Shaarda Himes. We would also like to thank Frances Westley for a careful reading of this paper.

hold middle-class occupations, and much younger in age (see appendix). In spite of these limitations, the sample has considerable utility. The survey permitted us to question a large number of present and former participants in New Religious Movements outside the context of their own groups and to compare their responses to a large number of persons who had never participated in these movements. The sample allows us to compare participation rates between groups and to analyze characteristic features of participants. The sample is less reliable as a gauge of the absolute level of participation in these movements as a proportion of the adult population as a whole. The survey does permit us to make educated estimates in this regard, however, both by comparing our data with that collected elsewhere and by taking into consideration the likely biases of the sample. In 1980 this survey was supplemented by a census of participation rates in nine selected movements as reported by the movements themselves. Here we recognize that self-reported membership statistics are not without value but must be treated as estimates that are likely to be inflated. Given the absence of rigorous data with regard to participation rates in New Religious Movements, these surveys provide an initial basis for examining the characteristic forms of this participation.

OVERALL PARTICIPATION RATES

Considering the quite divergent views about New Religious Movements, it is not at all clear what kinds of groups and associations ought to be included under this label. Some seem to associate these movements largely with Eastern religions; others insist on including a wide variety of human potential groups; and many would include groups like the Self-Realization Fellowship, Theosophists, Baha'is, and Spiritualists that have existed in North America for several generations. We have adopted a fairly broad definition (see Bird and Reimer, 1976; Bird, 1979). Our focus has been a wide variety of movements that since the middle 1960s have greatly expanded their numbers; that exist apart from exclusive Christian and Jewish denominations; and that use rites and symbols traditionally associated with religions even though many are quite secular by their own understanding.[2] We, therefore, have included within the

[2]These movements correspond as a whole to what Sydney Ahlstrom has referred to as the emergence of "Harmonial Religions" in the late nineteenth and early twentieth centuries with their similar interest in health, the use of science, and mystical meditation.

rubric "New Religious and Parareligious Movements" groups like Tai Chi and Transcendental Meditation, both of which use traditional religious imagery and techniques, and both of which consider themselves to be generally secular in orientation. The leaders of both of these groups often defend their practices by citing traditional Taoist and Hindu wisdom. We also have included groups like the Charismatics or Neo-Pentecostals as well as the Spiritualists, because both have recently greatly expanded their population appeal in spite of a much older history, and both exist as supplements rather than competitors to the organized, denominational patterns of American religion. Furthermore, we have included a number of new therapy movements—groups like est, ARICA, Scientology, Psychosynthesis, and Silva Mind Control—because in their symbolism and ritual, in strikingly similar ways, they seek to give birth to a reservoir of sacred power within each person (compare Westley, 1978, 1979).

Using this broad definition of New Religious and Parareligious Movements, we may observe that the overall rates of participation in these movements is surprisingly high (see tables 1 and 2). In Metropolitan areas like San Francisco and Montreal, somewhere between a fifth and a fourth of the adult population have at one time participated in these movements. In the San Francisco Bay area survey, conducted in the early 1970s, twenty-one percent of the adult population had participated in a variety of groups identified in responses to the questionnaire. This questionnaire excluded from consideration a number of groups we would argue ought to be listed—groups like Spiritualists, Other Eastern, other Buddhists, Divine Light Mission, Other Therapy groups, and some Martial Arts groups like Aikado and Tai Chi that have explicitly religious aspects. If these groups had been added to the survey form, it is reasonable to assume that the overall level of participation would have been higher since the level of participation in these excluded groups has been significant both in the Bay Area and in Montreal. It seems reasonable to assume that the participation rates in New Religious and Parareligious Move-

(Ahlstrom). There are several noticeable, differences: (1) unlike the previous emergence of Harmonial Religions, the contemporary New Religious Movements largely have not formed distinct, exclusive denominations like the Christian Scientists, Unity, or Science of Mind; (2) unlike the movements of Harmonial Religion, among contemporary New Religious and Parareligious Movements there are far more movements that are not related to the traditions of orthodox Christianity because they are derived from Buddhist, Hindu, Taoist, Moslem, or unorthodox Christian traditions.

ments for the Bay Area then would have been higher. The Montreal survey listed a wider range of groups. By oversampling a somewhat younger, better educated population, this survey no doubt also oversampled those persons more likely to participate in New Religious Movements. If these biases were reduced, then we would expect a significant decline in the reported participation rates, probably down to about eighteen to twenty percent of the adult population. While these participation rates may seem to be higher than expected, the significance of this fact cannot be judged without further examining both the characteristic forms of this participation and what kinds of groups succeed in gaining the largest numbers of affiliates.

TABLE 1

Participatory Rates in New Religious and Parareligious Movements

	Montreal Survey (1975)	Bay Area Survey*
Participated in One Group	22.8%	13.0%
Participated in Two Groups	5.5%	5.0%
Participated in Three Groups or More	3.4%	3.0%
Total Participants	31.7%	21.0%
Sample	1,607	1,000

*As reported in Wuthnow, 1976, table 13-2 (p. 275).

PATTERNS OF PARTICIPATION

The typical adherent of these New Religious and Parareligous Movements momentarily establishes a peripheral, transitory relationship to these groups and then drops out. These terms must be explained.

It is possible to distinguish between two forms of participation. According to a membership pattern, a person joins an exclusive religious group that assumes he will not belong at the same time to other competitive religious groups, or he joins a group to which he commits a large proportion of his time, feelings, and identification even though the group does not necessarily require exclusive loyalties. Such memberships become a major source of meanings, values, and norms for individuals involved. All New Religious Movements have succeeded in winning a membership-like commitment from numbers of persons, who assume

TABLE 2

Rates of Participation in Various New Religious and Parareligious Movements

	Montreal Survey	Bay Area Survey
Western Devotional		
Charismatics	1.9%	6.0%
Jesus Groups	--	2.5%
Campus Crusade	--	2.9%
Other Western	3.1%	--
Countercultural Devotional		
Spiritualists	3.1%	--
All Buddhist Groups	2.3%	--
Zen Buddhists	--	2.6%
Baha'i	2.0%	--
Divine Light Mission	1.2%	--
All Other Eastern	4.0%	--
Krishna Consciousness	--	1.6%
Apprenticeship/Discipleship Groups		
Yoga	12.3%	7.9%
Transcendental Meditation	6.7%	5.3%
Scientology	.8%	1.1%
est	--	1.5%
Synanon	--	3.1%
Other Therapy	4.9%	--
Martial Arts	6.0%	--

leadership in these groups and/or who devote themselves to these groups with an intense religious fervor. Such "committed members" provide the core or central cadre for these movements. In some movements—like the Divine Light Mission, or the Zen Center, or Nichiren Shoshu Sokagakkai or the Unification Church—the groups are largely constituted by such persons. In many movements where there are also other forms of affiliations, special names exist to identify these "committed members" as

Members, Instructors and Siddhis, celibates and householders, and regulars.

According to a more peripheral or transitory form of affiliation, persons do not become members as such of these movements. Rather they are students who are enrolled in a specific, time-limited class in yoga or Tai Chi or Silva Mind Control; or they are clients who have once upon a time made use of an offered service like palm reading or spiritual counseling; or they are initiates who have at one time been given instructions in personal, private practice of meditation; or they are persons who attended occasional festivals or retreats put on by Krishna Consciousness society or a Charismatic cadre; or they are curious and intrigued audiences witnessing a Spiritualist Medium. Affiliates may attend these classes, festivals, counseling sessions, and meetings with an occasional but regular sequence. They may engage in private spiritual practices from time to time. However, in terms of their religious membership, they either belong to a regular parish, congregation, or synagogue, or to none. These various New Religious and Parareligious Movements may continue to exert influence on their moral outlook, but they have not committed themselves to them as part of an ongoing membership. In many cases, they are explicitly instructed that they may make whatever use they wish of the techniques or knowledge they learned in these movements.

There are various examples of this pattern of loose affiliation. Thus, the local Krishna temple in Montreal includes sixty-six adult members, but some 250 people regularly attend their Sunday open houses and many more, including many traditional Hindus, attend their periodic celebration of Hindu holy days. Most yoga and therapy groups provide courses for hundreds of students, who take classes but never accept the invitation to become more closely involved. While some Charismatics belong to specific prayer groups, many simply attend periodic retreats, luncheon meetings, occasional prayer services established by a core of committed members. Thousands of persons who have been initiated into Transcendental Meditation or have had their palms read by a Palmist/Astrologer make no attempts to pursue a closer connection with these groups. In the recent census of nine New Religious Movements in Montreal, ninety-five percent of the 29,000 persons participating in nine groups surveyed would be classed as affiliates rather than members of these groups.

The dropout rate from New Religious and Parareligious Movements is extremely high. According to the Montreal Survey seventy-five and one-half percent of all those who had ever participated in these

TABLE 3

Types of Participation in a Selection of New Religious and Parareligious Movements in Montreal (1980)

	Numbers of Affiliates*	Numbers of Members*	
Krishna Consciousness	800	66	(householders, celibates)
Spiritual Healing Church	200	36	(regulars)
Le Jourdain (Charismatic)	1,500	310	(staff plus an estimate of those most directly involved)
National Research Institute for Self-Understanding (Palmistry)	3,950	50	(staff, meditators, members)
International Meditation Institute	200	90	(core, regulars)
Transcendental Meditation (those ever initiated)	14,725	275	(instructors, Siddhis)
Integral Yoga Institute	300	56	(premonastics, monastics, close members)
Sivanada Yoga (on mailing list)	7,000	204	(staff, regulars)
Sri Chinmoy Followers	70	25	(initiated)

*Participation data as reported by groups themselves.

movements were no longer participants.[3] Thus in Montreal current participants represented only eight and four-tenths percent of the total sample. This high dropout rate is significant, but it is not necessarily an indication of complete disenchantment with these movements. The figures may represent failure of members to become involved in the first place. Furthermore, when we examine the dropout rate for particular groups, several complex factors seem to be involved (see table 4). One, a high dropout rate is presumed by a number of yoga and therapy groups that view themselves as providing classes and not soliciting members. A high turnover rate is characteristic of groups like Baha'i and the Spiritualists, both of which stage regular meetings for the public from which they

[3]These figures are almost exactly the same as those estimated by Buddhist groups with regard to their own dropout rates (Layman, 1978), 30.)

expect to gain a few but not many new regular participants. High dropout rates are to be expected from groups like Transcendental Meditation, which provide few ongoing communal supports for initiates. Finally, high dropout rates are to be expected from groups like Divine Light, Scientology, Dharmadatu, and Nichiren Shoshu which make excessive demands on adherents. These high dropout rates mean that the typical adherent has only a transitory relationship to these groups.[4] While his transient adherence may not be without significance—as the transient involvement with a therapist may deeply affect a client—it is likely that the typical participant will be influenced by many other factors unrelated to these movements.

TABLE 4

Dropout Rates for Various New Religious and Parareligious Movements

	Total Number of Persons Who Have Ever Participated	Total Number of Current Participants	Dropout Rates
Transcendental Meditation	96	43	55.2%
Martial Arts	96	32	66.3%
Buddhist Groups	37	13	64.9%
Other Western	49	16	67.3%
Charismatics	31	10	67.7%
Therapy Groups	78	25	67.9%
Other Eastern	64	18	71.8%
Spiritualists	50	13	74.0%
Divine Light	20	5	75.0%
Yoga Groups	196	46	76.5%
Baha'i	32	6	81.2%
Scientology	13	0	100.0%

[4]The high dropout rate from these New Religious and Parareligious Movements means that the actual number of persons who still consider themselves to be affiliates is probably less than half the number of those reported by the group themselves. The

FACTORS RELATED TO PARTICIPATION

SES Variables. In comparison to the adult population in general, participants in New Religious and Parareligious Movements are more likely to be younger, single, female, and middle class. The differences are not marked and are more likely to be dramatic for the participants of particular groups than for participants in general. The most significant variation between participants and nonparticipants is that the former are much more likely to have experimented with divination arts like astrology and with psychedelic drugs.

Participants were significantly more likely to be unmarried than were nonparticipants. Whereas one in four participants were married, forty-three percent of nonparticipants within the Montreal sample were married. As several observers have commented, single and divorced persons are more likely to become involved in these groups because the absence of family commitments renders them somewhat more available for entering into other kinds of commitments (Glock, 1963; Lofland, 1966; see table 5).

Participants were somewhat more likely to be younger in age but the variations here were not significant (see table 6). The most dramatic differences seem to be between groups. According to the 1980 census of memberships, there was a marked difference between three groups—Transcendental Meditation, Krishna Consciousness Society, and the International Meditation Institute—that attracted fifty-five percent of their adherents from persons under thirty and six other groups, who attracted only about twenty-six percent of their adherents from the same age group (see table 7). The latter groups—including Spiritualists, a Palmist, two yoga groups, a Charismatic group, and Sri Chinmoy Followers—by their own report were more successful in attracting persons between the ages of thirty and fifty. It is not at all clear that New Religious and Parareligious Movements primarily or especially attract young persons. It is more likely the case that interest in these movements is related to a historic, generational shift in religious orientations, that initially in the late 1960s attracted young persons in greater proportions

---

movements themselves report a steady increase in the number of persons who have become involved with them. By their own reports, the total number of participants in nine groups surveyed was twice as large in 1980 as in 1975. However, given the high rate of disaffiliation, we suspect that actual numbers of participants—whether as members or affiliates—has not grown measurably.

but that has subsequently attracted persons from all age groups. It is interesting that the most recent data, from 1980, indicates a somewhat higher participation rate for persons over thirty than did the 1975 survey.

Overall, participants in these movements do not vary markedly in gender from nonparticipants. However, some movements are much more attractive to women and others to men. Men participate in larger proportions in the countercultural devotional movements—groups like Divine Light, Buddhists, Other Eastern Groups—and in martial arts. By contrast women participate in larger numbers in yoga groups, therapy groups, and Transcendental Meditation. Overall, these variations do not appear significant (table 5).

Moreover, there is no significant difference between participants and nonparticipants with regard to their current occupational class. To be sure, some particular New Religious Movements, like some traditional denominations, have proven to be significantly more successful in recruiting middle-class or working-class participants. For example, the Charismatics and the Spiritualists, by their own report, have a much larger proportion of working-class participants than the yoga groups or Transcendental Meditation.

We also know that some groups, like Krishna Consciousness and Divine Light, have been especially attractive to persons whose careers in education and employment are uneven and/or at a lower scale than their parents.[5] One of the more intriguing findings in this regard is the fact that current participants in these New Religious Movements are much more likely to hold middle-class occupational positions than both nonparticipants and former participants and much more likely to be upwardly mobile. The difference between present and former participants is marked (see table 8). It seems reasonable to conjecture that the success of current participants in their occupations is matched by their comparative success within the organization of these movements. It is possible that many have remained in these movements because the movements themselves rewarded them for their achievements in group-sponsored activities.[6]

---

[5]This statement is based on a random sample of core members undertaken in Montreal in 1974 and 1975.

[6]These findings should be considered tentative because the sample as a whole seems to be overweighted with persons of higher occupational class and because of the small number of cases (N=21) who are males, over 25, and present participants of these groups.

TABLE 5

Gender and Marital Status of Participants

	Percent Women	Percent Married	N
Sample as Whole	47.8%	38.0%	1,600
Countercultural Devotional	36.1%	25.7%	202
Western Devotional	35.4%	26.6%	79
Apprentice/Discipleship	58.1%	26.7%	465
Martial Arts	28.1%		96

TABLE 6

Age of Participants

	Under 25	25 to 34	35 plus	N
Present Participants	38%	46%	15%	130
Former Participants	45%	45%	10%	372
Nonparticipants	39%	45%	16%	1,084

0 = .0477 (Wilcoxon's signed ranks test, coefficient of differentia).

Life-Style Variable. Compared to nonparticipants, present and former participants in New Religious and Parareligious Movements are significantly more likely to have experimented with astrology, divination, and psychedelic drugs. Those persons who have had their charts cast by an astrologer or have consulted the Chinese book of divinization, the *I Ching*, are twice as likely to have been participants in these movements as persons who have never done so. Nearly a third of current adherents of these movements have had their astrological charts cast and gone through the ritual practice of seeking wisdom from the enigmatic wisdom of the *I Ching*. In both cases, such practices signify an involvement with divination arts that extends beyond that of the casual horoscope reader (see table 9). Involvement with these divination practices does signify an experimental attitude, as Wuthnow has argued (Wuthnow, 1976). We suspect that the relationship between involvement in New Religious Movements and divination arts is even stronger. After all, the divination arts are sources of wisdom, originating from long, revered traditions that claim to be as reliable as, if not more reliable than, the wisdom

TABLE 7

Age of Participants in Selected Groups
(as reported by groups themselves)

	N	Under 25	25-29	30-39	40-plus
Groups A Krishna Consciousness, Transcendental Meditation, International Meditation Institute	15,170	25.1%	30.0%	29.1%	15.0%
Groups B Spiritual Healing Church, le Jourdain, Palmist, Integral Yoga Institute, Sivanada Yoga, Sri Chinmoy	10,870	7.2%	18.7%	46.0%	38.9%

TABLE 8

Occupational Status of Participants
(males, 25 years old or older)

	Percent with higher-class occupations*	Percent whose fathers had higher-class occupations*	N
Current Participants	90.5%	52.4%	21
Former Participants	62.9%	66.7%	55
All Participants (past and present)	71.1%	63.2%	76
Sample as a Whole	67.0%	52.6%	297

*Higher-class occupations: professional, technical, managerial, proprietors; lower class occupations: clerical, sales, service, craftsmen, labor, other.

derived from the orthodoxies of science and rational philosophy. They provide an irrational, magical inspiration that often comes clothed in science-like expositions and craftsman-like attention to details. They provide quite personal and private sources of guidance and insight which are alternative to those offered by traditional denominational religious and moral systems. Like most New Religious movements, their wisdom is articulated in language that deviates from the ordinary vernacular language of common sense. Like most New Religious Movements, wisdom is here gained through what amounts to a ritual-like experience rather than from discursive expositions (see Bird, 1978).

Persons who have used marijuana or LSD three or more times are also twice as likely to have become participants in New Religious Movements than persons who have either never used these drugs or used them less intensely (see table 9). Given the high dropout rate from these movements, experimentation with drugs seems to be correlated with experimentation with religious movements and experimentation with divination practices. Participants in New Religious Movements do seem to evidence an experimental attitude at least with regard to these kinds of personal activities. However, what is in common between participants in New Religious Movements, users of psychedelics, and users of divination arts is a specific kind of experimental attitude in which persons seek to have specific nonordinary, self-reassuring experiences, often by faithfully adhering to ritual-like guidelines. After all, there are special cultic forms for dropping acid, for consulting the *I Ching*, for meditating, for sitting Zazen, for Sufi dancing, for receiving the Holy Spirit, and for chanting.

TABLE 9

Use of Drugs and Divination Arts

	Percent who have had chart cast by Astrologers	Percent who have consulted I Ching	Percent high on marijuana (3 times plus)	Percent high on LSD (3 times plus)
Present Participants N 133	31.4% (42)	21.1% (36)	40.6% (54)	19.4% (25)
Past Participants N 370	23.2% (86)	18.9% (70)	38.1% (141)	15.3% (57)
Nonparticipants N 1056	11.8% (125)	5.5% (58)	22.4% (238)	6.6% (70)
	x^2=51.42	x^2=97.57	x^2=43.70	x^2=40.00
	P = .000	P = .000	P =.000	P = .000

PARTICIPATION RATES IN DIFFERENT KINDS OF MOVEMENTS

New Religious and Parareligious Movements have assumed varied forms. For comparative purposes it is possible to distinguish between four types of movements, identified heuristically in terms of the relationship between the participants and whatever the group itself considers to be the ultimate and revered source of power and well-being (see Bird, 1979; 1978). For some this sacred source is conceived of as a self-transcending, omnipresent reality—a God, a spiritual realm, a sacred principle to which participants devote themselves. Such movements may appropriately be identified as devotional (see Smart) because of the central role of congregational practices of devotion. Such movements ordinarily seek members more than affiliates, converts rather than interested students.

Among such devotional groups, it is necessary to distinguish further between those which remain in accord with the prevailing religious beliefs of denominational religion—groups like the Charismatics, the Jesus groups, the Lubavitcher movement—and those which adopt beliefs that are antagonistic. The latter would include movements that adopt Buddhist, Hindu, or Moslem belief—like Nichiren Shoshu or Shinran Buddhists, Divine Light or Krishna Consciousness, or Sufi groups—as well as groups with distinctive beliefs of their own at considerable variance from denominational beliefs—like the Baha'is or the Spiritualists. By making this distinction between Western devotional and countercultural devotional groups, we can thereby distinguish movements which self-consciously seek to reinforce and bolster prevailing beliefs of traditional denominations and other movements which directly challenge and counter these beliefs.

In a third kind of movement, the ultimate, revered, source of personal power and well-being is conceived as existing in individualized form in the deepest recess of each person (see Westley, 1978). These movements believe that there is not one universal source to which all are directed but that sacred power exists in each person. People participate in these movements in order to gain the skills and knowledge necessary for them to learn how to gain access to this indwelling energy and intelligence. Like sorcerers' apprentices, they seek to gain mastery over these extraordinary powers by following the example of those more skilled in these arts. These movements are appropriately referred to as apprenticeship groups, since class-like settings for instruction are characteristic. Apprenticeship-like relationships are found in a wide variety of human growth groups and parareligious movements like est, ARICA, Silva Mind Control, and Psychosynthesis.

In a fourth kind of movement participants seek not so much to make contact with an extraordinary source of power and well-being as to harmonize their lives with the sacred ways of nature or the cosmos. What is necessary for such harmony is discipline. Participants seek to discipline their minds and bodies by practicing meditation in a variety of forms from sitting motionless to being in movement in keeping with stylized forms. Discipline is learned by subjecting oneself as a disciple to one who has achieved self-mastery and harmony of mind and body. Yoga groups, Tai Chi groups, Vedanta meditation groups, Zen centers may all appropriately be referred to as discipleship movements because in all participants seek this kind of self harmony through disciplined forms of meditation (Smart; Eliade).

Discipleship and apprenticeship movements differ in several significant ways. Largely, apprenticeship groups utilize ideas and practices developed in North America or Europe from transcendentalism, occult traditions of wisdom, gnosticism, and transpersonal psychology. In contrast, discipleship groups are largely based on assumptions derived from religious traditions of Buddhism, Hinduism, and Taoism. However, both share the assumption that individuals may gradually enhance self-mastery by developing certain psychic skills. Both provide classes for large numbers of affiliate participants. In many cases, both envision themselves as providing spiritual and psychic opportunities which are neither competitive nor complementary but supplementary in relation to the traditional denominational religion. For the purpose of analyzing this survey data, we have combined discipleship and apprenticeship movements together.

When we examine the participation rates for various New Religious and Parareligious Movements, the most striking fact is that the overwhelming majority of participants have been involved either with Western devotional groups or with discipleship/apprenticeship groups. According to the Bay Area survey nearly nine of ten participants were involved in these groups; the number was slightly smaller in Montreal (see tables 2, 10). The somewhat smaller participation rates for these groups in Montreal reflect the fact that among the anglophone population of the city in 1975, various Western devotional groups like the

Charismatics, Jesus groups, and Campus Crusade were not very developed.[7] What is noteworthy is the low level of participation in those kinds of countercultural devotional movements, that have received the most public notoriety because they seem most directly to challenge prevailing religious ideas and conventional life patterns. In contrast, the various Western devotional and discipleship/apprenticeship groups that enjoy exceedingly higher participation rates largely support prevailing religious and moral values. The Western devotional groups do so quite intentionally and in this sense represent another expression of the tide of revivalism that periodically has arisen in North American history. The apprenticeship/discipleship groups reinforce what might be described as a modified achievement ethic, in which emphasis is not so much placed on self-mastery in economic affairs or politics as in the private, personal sense of well-being and accomplishment.

Participants in countercultural devotional movements differ from other participants and nonparticipants in relation to several factors. Overall they seem to participate in these movements with greater excess. In relation to factors already analyzed, they are more likely to have consulted an astrologer or used psychedelic drugs repeatedly than participants in other movements. They are also more likely to have participated in a number of different New Religious and Parareligious Movements. Three-fifths of the participants in these movements have been involved as well in at least one other New Religious Movement and two-fifths have been involved in a total of three or more groups (see table 11). More than other present participants, and especially more than past participants, current adherents of countercultural devotional groups correspond to the model of the religious shopper. Rather than simply dropping out, as most participants of New Religious and Parareligious Movements have done, these adherents of countercultural devotional groups have sought out another group more to their liking. Markedly more than the participants in any other New Religious Movements, involvement in these groups has led adherents of countercultural devotional movements to change their religious identification. Almost all the participants in New Religious and Parareligious Movements continue to identify their religious affiliation as being the same as their mothers (table 12). In

---

[7]The Charismatics have grown rapidly in numbers during the late 1970s in Montreal, especially among the francophone population.

sharp contrast, three-fifths of the current members of countercultural devotional groups indicated that their religious identification differed from that of their mothers because it was "other" or because it involved an identification with more than one religious tradition.[8] It is reasonable to argue that for many of the participants in these countercultural devotional groups their involvement has for them an intense religious significance. After all, their involvement leads many of them to identify themselves as having a religious affiliation other than that to which they were exposed as children. Moreover, their involvement is closely linked with a belief that what is especially attractive about their group is its ideas. Over half isolated their group's ideas as being what they found initially most attractive in comparison to proportions half as large for adherents of other movements. It is interesting that fifty-six percent of current adherents in apprenticeship/discipleship groups were initially attracted to these groups by more pragmatic considerations about claimed results and practices of these movements, in contrast to twenty-seven percent for the countercultural devotional groups.

The position of current participants in countercultural devotional groups is far from typical. The overwhelming majority of participants in New Religious Movements do not change their religious identification, have not participated in any more than one such movement, and participate in these groups on account of their practices, claimed results, and/or the other people who are involved. The typical participant has not consulted the *I Ching* and has not used LSD. Although correlations exist with such factors, they are far from definitive. It is clear that persons from quite varied backgrounds enter these movements. Adherents of countercultural devotional groups correspond more closely to a popular stereotype of what so called "cult followers" are like. But these adherents are atypical of the much larger numbers of persons who have participated in these movements.

CONCLUSIONS

This examination of participation rates in New Religious and Parareligious Movements leads to several general conclusions. While the participation rate in these movements, as defined herein, is comparatively high,

[8]The findings on Transcendental Meditation are interesting in this regard: in spite of the group's claim to be nonreligious, a large number of the participants in our sample felt it necessary to list their religious affiliation as "other" or "several" rather than listing only the religious affiliation of their mothers.

TABLE 10

Participation Rates in Different Kinds of Movements

In the following kinds of movements:	Percent of total number of participations (Montreal)	Percent of total number of participations (Bay Area)
Countercultural Devotional	26.1%	12.1%
Western Devotional	10.4%	33.1%
Apprenticeship/Discipleship	63.5%	54.8%
Total:	100.0%	100.0%
N:	748	345

N.B.: The number of Participations exceeds the number of participants because some persons were members of more than one group.

TABLE 11

Percent of Participants Participating in Three or more or Two or more New Religious and Parareligious Movements

	Three Plus	Two Plus	N
Countercultural Devotional	40.4%	61.9%	203
Western Devotional	25.0%	43.7%	80
Apprenticeship/Discipleship	25.6%	49.2%	465

TABLE 12

Percent of Current Participants Who Have Adopted A Religious Identification Different From Their Mothers

Countercultural Devotional	62.0%
Western Devotional	27.0%
Apprenticeship/Discipleship (except TM)	14.5%
(Transcendental Meditation)	32.0%

N.B.: This question was considered only for respondents whose mother's religious affiliation was Protestant or Catholic.

the ratio of persons who continue to be adherents of these movements is exceedingly low. For most persons their participation was temporary and involved them only in the periphery of these groups. It is impossible to conclude that such an involvement is without much significance for the individual. It is possible to argue that the significance would be different were typical participants to become involved members of these movements. This kind of temporary, peripheral affiliation may become increasingly characteristic for many traditional as well as new religious groups.

In relation to their age, social class, family status, and gender, participants vary somewhat from the adult population in general. However, these differences do not seem to be marked enough to argue that these variations can account for participation rates. Clearly younger and single persons can more easily make commitments to new organizations and activities, whether they involve evangelical religion or yoga groups.

As Wuthnow and McLoughlin have argued, the increasing interest in these New Religious and Parareligious Movements represents an historical, generational shift in values and religious orientation (Wuthnow, 1978; McLoughlin, 1978). In assessing the significance of the increased participation in these nonorthodox forms of religion, it is necessary also to recognize an even greater increase of interest in traditional forms of evangelical and pentecostal religion as well as in a wide variety of human growth groups and popular therapies (Kelly, 1972; Bach, 1971). It is tempting to attempt to discover some general characteristics shared by these various movements, such as, for example, their almost universal attention to feelings of personal well-being. The significance of this resurgent spirituality and therapeutic interest, however, probably lies in its variety rather than its commonality. What is evident is a new kind of pluralism in which hosts of heterogeneous organizations, institutes, prayer groups, radio ministries, encounter groups, and meditation classes have emerged and exist alongside, often in tacit cooperation with, traditional forms of denominational religion.

If one were to attempt to characterize the increasing interest in these various "new" "para," Pentecostal, and evangelical religious movements in a phrase, it might aptly be referred to as religion and the rise of magic. If we assume a broad, anthropological approach toward defining magic, then we would include under this rubric a host of activities including divination, nonmedical healing, exorcising, communication with spirits, shamanistic practices to gain power, the cultivation of trance-like states, and the chanting of sacred names. These kinds of activities are widely evident in the resurgent spirituality of both New Religious Movements and many Pentecostal groups as well as the ritual-like use of psychedelics, and the fascination with astrology. If magic refers to sacred techniques for gaining power and well-being—and this is the way both Weber and Malinowski used the term—then there is much evidence for an increased interest in magical practices. Of course, the term magic is not broad enough to cover many of the activities of New Religious and Parareligious Movements; much of what takes place would more appropriately be described as an increasing popular interest in mysticism, in orthodox forms of Buddhist and Hindu religion, in evangelical religion, and in therapy.

The phrase "religion and the rise of magic" is offered to suggest a historical argument by contrasting the period beginning in the mid-1960s to the period of the Enlightenment in Europe beginning in the late seventeenth century. Keith Thomas examined this latter period in England and wrote a study entitled *Religion and the Decline of Magic* (Thomas, 1971). What was noticeable about this period both in England and in France was the systematic way in which many traditional spiritual and magical practices lost their appeal (Despland, 1981). These practices, which had previously enjoyed the tolerance if not support of the churches, included divination, nonmedical healing, exorcising, communication with spirits, shamanistic practices, the cultivation of trance-like states, and the chanting of sacred names. For much of the period since the Enlightenment these "magical" practices have remained out of popular favor. However, the same kind of practices, together with a renewed interest in mysticism, have recently gained considerable interest, as the high rates of participation in New Religious and Parareligious Movements make evident. Characteristically, as with traditional magical practices, persons establish a transitory, affiliate relation with those sponsoring such activities. Typically, participation in these magical practices involves a particular kind of experimental attitude, in which one ventures one's luck by following ritual-like sacred forms.

Thomas's hypothesis about the reason for the decline of "magic" with the Enlightenment offers a hypothesis for the increasing interest in New Religious and Parareligious Movements since the middle of the 1960s. He argued that the major factor that led to a disenchantment with magic—a disenchantment favored by the well-educated clergy—was not an increasing belief in science nor was it a marked rise in the standard of living. Both of these followed later. Rather, Thomas argues that magical practices of quite varied forms lost their enchantment as the population in general gained an increased confidence, born of their rationalized religious convictions, that they could shape the contours of their own lives, that they could measurably affect their own destinies. It is reasonable to argue that the increasing, new enchantment with a wide variety of magic and mystical practices during the 1960s and later has arisen as that confidence has in turn declined.

REFERENCES

Ahlstrom, Sydney

1972 *A Religious History of the American People*. New Haven: Yale University Press.

Bach, Kurt

1972 *Beyond Words: The Story of Sensitivity Training and the Encounter Movement*. Baltimore: Penguin Books.

Bellah, Robert

1976 "New Religious Consciousness and the Crisis in Modernity" in *The New Religious Consciousness*, ed. Charles Y. Glock and Robert N. Bellah. Berkeley: University of California Press.

Bird, Frederick, and William Reimer

1976 "A Sociological Analysis of New Religious and Para-Religious Movements" in *Religion in Canadian Society*, ed. Stewart Crysdale and Les Wheatcroft. Toronto: Macmillan of Canada.

Bird, Frederick

1978 "Ritual and Charisma in New Religious Movements." In *Understanding the New Religions*, ed. Jacob Needleman and George Baker. New York: Seabury Books.

1979 "The Pursuit of Innocence: New Religious Movements and Moral Accountability." *Sociological Analysis* 40:4 (1979): 335-46.

Despland, Michel

1981 "Comparative Religious Ethics: Early Modern European Problems." *Journal for Religious Ethics* (1981).

Eliade, Mircea

1957 *Yoga*. Princeton: Princeton University Press.

Glock, Charles Y.

1967 *To Comfort and to Challenge*. Berkeley CA: University of California Press.

Kelley, Dean

1972 *Why Conservative Churches Are Growing*. New York: Harper and Row, 1972, 1977.

Layman, Emma

1978 *Buddhism in America*. Chicago: Nelson-Hall.

Lofland, John

1966 *Doomsday Cult*. Englewood Cliffs NJ: Prentice-Hall.

McLoughlin, William G.

1978 *Revivals, Awakenings, and Reform*. Chicago: University of Chicago Press.

Malinowski, Bronislaw

1978 *Magic, Science, and Religion*. New York: Doubleday (Anchor), 1954, 1978.

Smart, Ninian

1968 *The Yogi and the Devotee*. London: Allen and Unwin.

Thomas, Keith

1971 *Religion and the Decline of Magic*. London: Weidenfield and Nicholson.

Tipton, Steve
1977 "Getting Saved from the Sixties." Ph.D. dissertation, Harvard University.

Westley, Frances
1978a "The Cult of Man: Durkheimian Predictions and New Religious Movements." *Sociological Analysis* 39:135-45.

1978b "The Complex Forms of the Religious Life: A Durkheimian View of the New Religious Movements." Ph.D. Dissertation, McGill University.

Wuthnow, Robert
1976a *The Consciousness Reformation.* Berkeley: University of California Press.

1976b "The New Religions in a Social Context" in *The New Religious Consciousness*, ed. Charles Y. Glock and Robert N. Bellah. Berkeley: University of California Press.

1978 *Experimentation in American Religion: The New Mysticisms and Their Implications for the Churches.* Berkeley: University of California Press.

APPENDIX

Age and Occupational Characteristics of 1975 Sample

Percentage of Respondents in Various Age Groupings

Age Groupings	**Montreal Survey**
16 to 24	40.8%
25 to 34	55.9%
35 to 44	10.3%
45 plus	4.0%
N	1607

Percentage of Respondents in Various Occupational Groupings

	Montreal Survey
Professional, Technical, Managerial, Proprietor	53.0%
Clerical	23.5%
Sales	5.0%
Other: craftsmen, service, laborer	19.5%

STRATEGIES FOR SURVIVAL: SECTARIAN EXPERIENCE IN THE THIRD REICH

by Christine E. King

THE PROTESTANT and Catholic churches in Nazi Germany, while living on borrowed time, were, because of their size, safe from the danger of immediate and sudden closure by the government. While there were areas of petty annoyance and some members suffered for their views and their private resistance to the horrors of the Nazi state, the majority not only survived the regime untouched, but also gave tacit or open support to the regime as a bulwark against communism and atheism.

The story of the *Kirchenkampf,* or the churches' struggle with National Socialism, is a complex one and it is clear that response to the Nazi regime varied, both at institutional and individual level. The Roman Catholic Church was party to a concordat signed by the pope and Hitler in July 1933, and there was a certain amount of official support for the program of the government. Opposition came about at a private and individual level from both laymen and priests, but was not part of official church policy. The hierarchy sought, on the whole, a *modus vivendi* and Catholic priests, for example, were to be seen blessing the German troops about to reoccupy the Rhineland in 1935.

Attitudes within the Evangelical churches were sharply polarized. The "German Christians," supported by an ever-growing number of Protestants, embodied the principles of "positive Christianity" espoused in Nazi party circles. This group rejected the Jewish elements of Christianity; thus the whole of the Old Testament was discarded, as was the work of the "Rabbi Paul" who had "corrupted" the noble and Aryan ideals of Jesus. Hitler, the German Christians preached, had risen, sent from God, to cleanse and restore Christianity in its true form to Germany. The German Christians, whose ideas were publicized in their famous Sports Palace Rally in Berlin in 1933, called themselves the Storm Troopers of Christ and became so vocal and extreme in their views and aroused such opposition from mainstream Christians that the Nazis were forced to withdraw their initial toleration. Nevertheless, the German Christians remained active within the Evangelical churches and continued both to win converts and to influence the churches' thinking.

On the other hand, some Evangelicals found themselves in bitter opposition, less to the party's general program and more to the change in church government being planned by the regime. These Christians, both clerical and lay, found a home within the Confessing Church, founded as a direct response to National Socialist interference in church government. The stance of this group, while primarily that of conservatives resisting change in their church structure, came to include criticism of Nazi policies in general, and it is from their ranks that Dietrich Bonhoeffer came.

It is clear from public speeches and private policy statements that the aim of National Socialism was the ultimate destruction of the churches. Even though there were some within party ranks who saw Hitler's and Goebbels's frequent use of Christian language and symbolism in speeches as a sign that the churches, suitably nazified, would be allowed to survive, they were few.[1] Meanwhile, for practical reasons, the major churches had to be tolerated and were treated with a mixture of conciliation and scorn. At the local level there were harassments and even the persecution and murder of priests and pastors who used the pulpit for other than "nationalist" causes. The churches would be allowed to survive, for the time being, but only insofar as their members accepted National Socialism and the implications of living in a National Socialist state. Most did.[2]

For sectarian groups within the Nazi state, the situation was more complex. If the major reasons for allowing the churches to survive were

---

[1]See, for example, the comments of Franke and von Papen at the Nuremberg Trials: *Trials of the Major War Criminals before the Nuremberg Military Tribunal* (London, 1947) 1:60-61.

[2]For a bibliography of the discussion of the church struggle, see Otto Diehn, *Bibliographie zur Geschichte des Kirchenkampfs* (Göttingen, 1959).

practical, and related to their numbers and influence, the numerically small sects had little ground to stand on. Indeed, an examination of government discussions on religious groups which took place early in 1933 suggests that a total closure of sects was thought to be desirable, if not inevitable. For, while the party in 1933 had no clearly defined policy towards the sects, it nevertheless had a considerable suspicion of the political connections of sectarians. Moreover, anti-Christians like Reinhardt Heydrich and Martin Bormann worked ceaselessly for the closure of the sects and offered powerfully presented arguments to support their case. Sectarians, it was said were "fanatics" and "troublemakers," likely to provide a hiding place for dissidents. They have contacts, it was explained, with Marxists and Communists[3] and they "exploit and trick the German Volk."[4] Most significant, perhaps, was the evident desire that the party be seen to flex a few muscles in the direction of Christianity. The sects were not universally closed down; however, a number of small groups were banned, and some of the larger groups found themselves fighting for their survival.

Fifty or so small sects are mentioned in Gestapo reports as worthy of attention, and by 1937 the majority of these were banned. Their closure was justified in a variety of ways; the B'hai group was banned because of its "pacifist and international teachings;"[5] others, like the Church of the Kingdom of God, were banned for having "bolshevik connections."[6] Some leaders were imprisoned;[7] others went into exile; and the majority of the groups, from the Bavarian Druids[8] to the Mazadaznan movement, willingly ceased their activities. These small groups attempted no opposition or resistance to closure: they made little or no protest; attempted no kind of legal redress; and, while a few continued to meet secretly until discovered by the Gestapo, there were no serious attempts made to continue missionary work or to keep the groups alive.

---

[3]J. Neuhausler, *Kreuz und Hakenkreuz* (Munich, 1946) 363, 375ff.

[4]Ibid.

[5]Bavarian State Archives, Munich, Rd s-PP(11B) 4030/37.

[6]Ibid., 11 E2-244/215; Regierungszeiger Ausg. 343/343, 8 December 1936, nr. 1587.

[7]The leader of the group, Liebe Vater habe du Dank, Fürst Sela, for example, was imprisoned in 1937. Sela had founded the group at the end of the First World War, believing himself to be the reincarnation of Elijah.

[8]Bavarian State Archives, B. nr. 18105/35 I 1B.

Several of the larger sects, however, found themselves in a position to negotiate or to fight for their continued existence. The implications for an understanding of the Nazi state of this apparent about-face are discussed elsewhere.[9] The concern of this paper is the response made to National Socialism by five of these groups, and a preliminary examination of the factors that determined their behavior, considering the influence of theology, history, and the nature of a group's organization. Consideration is given to the question why these five chosen groups should have responded in such very different ways to the challenge of a totalitarian state.

The groups chosen for this study—the Jehovah's Witnesses, the Mormons, the Christian Scientists, the Seventh Day Adventists, and the New Apostolic church—all enjoyed, at the time of the Nazi seizure of power, a similar and relatively sheltered position under the Weimar constitution. All were registered as religious societies and thereby were granted certain tax advantages. Since the new regime was deliberately vague about its intentions regarding the exact status of the Weimar law in the Third Reich, the legal position of these religious societies was unclear. The sects appear to have been optimistic, pointing to the party promises of freedom of worship and anticipating little trouble , it would seem, in spite of the fate of the smaller sects whose closure was already being implemented and reported in the Nazi press.

The leaders of the sects doubtless saw in the apparently cordial relations between the major churches and the new regime an echo of their own fate. The small groups they—with the government—saw as troublemakers, and their closure was welcomed. Not only the comparatively large membership of the five groups but also their general reputation as upright citizens would, it was felt, save them.

In this general hope they were mistaken. While these groups were larger numerically than the fifty or so small sects whose activities were banned, their overall membership was considerably less than one per cent of the population.[10] (The Evangelical and Roman Catholic Churches between them included some sixty million of the sixty-five million Germans.) Indeed, the largest of the groups discussed here, the New

---

[9]C. King, "The Case of the Third Reich," in Eileen Barker, ed., *New Religious Movements: A Perspective for Understanding Society* (Lewiston NY, 1982).

[10]*Statistiches Jahrbuch für das deutsche Reich, 1933* (Berlin, 1933); and Bavarian Police and Gestapo Reports.

Apostolic Church, had in 1933 an approximate membership of only 250,000. Seventh Day Adventism claimed some 36,000; the Witnesses, 20,000. The Mormon membership was close to 17,000, and Christian Science, for which figures are not available, was by far the smallest.[11] In numerical terms, therefore, these groups hardly counted as more significant than the small and banned groups.

Moreover, what the sectarians saw as evidence of their respectability—their honesty, and good citizenship—was hardly seen in these terms by the Nazis. While these five groups were not, at least on the surface, tinged with the "white rubbish" of spiritualism or any of the weirder, enthusiastic outpourings of some of the fringe groups, they were nevertheless sectarian and by this very fact presented an ideological challenge to the Nazi state. They were, by definition, unacceptable—less for their teachings and more for their exclusiveness—for the fact that they could not, at first sight, be easily contained within the "coordination" policy of Nazism. Under *Gleichschaltung,* all areas of German life were to be absorbed within the totalitarian state. Significantly predating the acceptance of similar notions by the British government, the Nazis claimed to cover every citizen's life from cradle to grave. Not just welfare, however, but education, labor relations, family life, individual and public belief, both political and ideological, were to be included under the umbrella of what was not just a new political system but an all-embracing way of life. The sects, by their very existence, challenged these assumptions in a way in which the major churches—willing on the whole to accept the trappings of Nazism—and the small sects—accepting closure—did not.

In the brief pause while the government considered its approach to these groups, the sects all took immediate action and in the first few months of National Socialist rule each formulated a policy that was to inform its behaviour throughout the twelve and one-half years that the thousand year *Reich* lasted.

One may advance a typology of the response of the sects. Of the five considered—and with the exception of a small schism of the Adventist Church to be considered below—only the Jehovah's Witnesses resisted the regime. They fought tooth and nail and as a result one-half of their number was imprisoned and one-quarter executed. The Witnesses

[11]Ibid.

refused, on theological grounds, to give allegiance to the new state, whether by the Hitler salute, by taking part in elections, or by enlisting. They insisted that the only reason that they could not accept citizenship of the Third Reich was that they were already citizens of God's kingdom and could not serve two masters. Similarly, they could not fight in the German army, not because they were pacifist, but because they were already enlisted in God's army and were to fight for Him at Armageddon. Such a stance had caused no problems under the liberal Weimar rule, but it was not difficult to see that it might in the new totalitarian regime. However, the Witness position was intransigent. Polite at first, they soon came to identify the regime not only as hostile to Jehovah's people, but as intrinsically satanic, noting clearly in their literature not only the persecutions they were suffering, but also the Nazi atrocities against the Jews and against other German citizens.[12]

Two groups with influential American connections, the Christian Scientists and the Mormons, made it clear, very early in 1933, that they would use whatever international influence they held, in order to ensure their safety in the New Germany. What is more, this policy was most effective. Christian Scientists thus were not harassed until America's entry into the war, and even then, while under a ban, members were treated with none of the severity the Witnesses experienced. The Christian Science Church had already indicated that it would respond favorably to Hitler and National Socialism and members in Germany were urging the *Monitor* to take a positive approach to the new government. In September 1933, this was stressed by a visiting group of influential international Christian Scientists and sympathizers who were able to exert pressure on the government. The visiting party, among whom was Lord Astor, not only secured an interview with Minister of the Interior William Frick in order to discuss the fate of the sects, but also gained a rare interview with Hitler. The American ambassador to Germany, William Dodd, had indeed already been cabled by the State Department

[12]See, for example, the highly graphic and satirical cartoons published in the Jehovah's Witness journal, *The Golden Age* 18 10 March 1937. These cartoons describe "the New Germany" where the "tourist" will "watch stormtroopers violate womanhood and debauch German Youth," "hear the sweet strains of Nazi propaganda," "tour our whip factory and get a souvenir 10 pf per welt," and "finally join our expert Jew-baiters and assert your pure Aryan blood." The latter "attraction" is accompanied by a drawing of a man on a gallows.

in Washington alerting him to watch out for the safety of Christian Science groups.[13]

The Mormons had found in National Socialism some echoes of their own teaching. Their program of genealogical research, undertaken for the purposes of posthumous baptism, was facilitated by the new availability of records occasioned by the search for Aryan ancestry. The Mormons thus were able not only to pursue their own work with zeal, but also, *en route,* to demonstrate their Aryan lineage. Members were commended by their government for their enthusiasm in this crucial area of Nazi racial policy.[14] Other aspects of this policy were acceptable to the church, for, at the time and until quite recently, no black could hold priestly office in the Mormon church; and there are theological arguments to explain the differences and—it is implied—inferiority, of certain races. The general Nazi stress on "clean living," on the family, and on nationalism, hard work and discipline were well received in Mormon circles. Relations with the government thus rested not only on the American influence exercised on the Mormons' behalf, but on deeper grounds. Cultural and sporting links were forged, and the presence of Mormon missionaries as referees and coaches in basketball at the 1936 Olympics perhaps may illustrate the nature of the relationship that grew up between the sect and the Nazis. This relationship even survived a quite serious incident in which three Mormon young men were found to be working in the underground. Such a discovery probably would have meant harsh reprisals for any of the other groups, but the assurances of the church officials that the boys were working alone and the excommunication of one of the boys after his execution served to prove Mormon loyalty and trustworthiness.[15]

Two German-centered groups, the Seventh Day Adventists and the New Apostolic Church responded in yet another way. Neither had the scale and type of influence abroad of the Mormons or Christian Scientists, so both were forced to employ a different strategy. Both thus stressed the nationalist and conservative leanings of their membership and, while promising to promote Germany's cause and good name to brethren abroad, stressed the essentially indigenous nature of their organization.

[13]William Dodd, Jr. and Martha Dodd, eds., *Ambassador Dodd's Diary* (London, 1945) 54.

[14]West German Mission MSS History, 31 December 1945; quoted by G. Scharffs in an unpublished doctoral dissertation, Brigham Young University, 1969, 111.

[15]Secret Memorandum, 2nd Senate, *Volksgerichthof,* 8Ji27142-2M141142.

Each was able to absorb into its teaching elements of National Socialism with comparatively little difficulty. For the New Apostolic Church this process involved few contradictions, since members of the church had supported the Nazi party even before it came to power.[16] The Adventists were more vulnerable to investigation and more open to charges that their teaching was inimical to Nazism. They had, for example, special links with Judaism. Compromises were made, however, and the government was persuaded of the loyalty of church members to the ideals of National Socialism.[17] The "Sabbath" while still celebrated on Saturday, changed its name to "rest-day." Sabbath schools became "Bible Schools" and words like "Zion" were obliterated from the liturgy, while teaching in general was "purified from the Jewish spirit." Even the Jewish birth of Christ came under debate, and some suggested that Christ was "no Jew" and "belonged to no nation," while others claimed that "Christ was a Jew, but rejected the corruption of His own people."[18] Similarly, in what for Adventists are important areas of Christian work—welfare and health—compromises were made and members were taught to accept, for example, the new sterilization laws, even if these appeared at first sight to run counter to teaching.[19] Adventist welfare services were handed over to and absorbed into the state welfare scheme and it was accepted without question that many of their former clients—gypsies, Jews, down-and-outs—were no longer to be served.[20]

Thus the five groups demonstrated a variety of responses. In terms of success, the Mormons and Christian Scientists rate most highly. The

---

[16]Bavarian State Archives, BayHSTA, Reichstaathalter 638, December 1933.

[17]"Denkschrift" to the Ministry of the Interior, Berlin, 20 December 1933.

[18]See, for example, *Der Adventbote* 45:3 (1 February 1939).

[19]D. M. Ulbrich in *Staat und Kirche* 24:1 (1933). See also an article in *Soziale Arbeit,* reprinted in *Gute Gesundheit* 37:4 (1934), which states that sterilization was "the only protection for a people from the decline of their race." Others—see *Gute Gesundheit* 37:4 (1934): 170-71—suggested that the state include even more categories of the sick in the program, thereby saving the state money.

[20]Note that, interestingly, the Adventists added one further category to the state list of "undesirables," the Seventh Day Adventist Reform Movement members, since they were seen to uphold "un-German" views. In the light of the discussion below on the stance of this group against the Nazis, this addition is significant. Indeed, as early as 1933, leaders of the mainstream Adventists had, in clarifying and defending their position before the state authorities, directed police attention to the schism as a dangerous and potentially hostile group with whom they wished to be dissociated.

Mormons alone were scarcely watched and experienced the very minimum of difficulties. Christian Science also was efficient in its use of its friends, for its survival until 1941 without any real difficulties was against a background of pressure from the Nazi press and within party circles that it be banned.[21] Gestapo documents even make the rare admission that it was simply and solely international influences and the *Führer's* desire to keep friendly with America and Britain that saved this potentially dangerous group from persecution. The two "German" churches were also successful in their own way, with their influence operating at local and national rather than international levels. Members were presented as respected and valuable citizens, often holding office in local government, rather than extremists likely to oppose the regime. Their prayers were offered for Hitler and his praises were sung.[22] In some ways this was a more naive approach, but it was in its own way, a successful one. The Witnesses' behaviour stands outside any comparison with these four groups, although they too, in 1933, had imported American lawyers to guard their rights after some property was seized. However, even in what were intended to be conciliatory talks with the government, the Witnesses expressed their position neither in the politically sophisticated language of the Christian Scientists or Mormons, nor in the grovelingly laudatory language of the other two groups, but in heavily and uncompromisingly religious terms, stating that their duty was to Jehovah and that all who opposed them in this, their divine role, were to be named as oppressors and to be resisted.[23]

When looking for some theories to explain the variety of responses made to National Socialism, it is reasonable to examine the theology of the groups concerned. At first sight, however, significant similarities between the groups seem to outweigh their differences. All five groups, for example, based their teaching to a greater or lesser degree on the Old Testament and all saw the Jewish nation as fulfilling a special role in the history of man's salvation. All had elements of millennial teaching and adventist expectation, again to varying degrees and with different emphases. Each of the five groups, whatever the response of its members

[21]*Blitz,* 16 June 1937.

[22]See, for example, the words of the New Apostolic Church on the text—"A wise regent"—noted in Bavarian State Archives, December 1933.

[23]*Jehovah's Witness 1974 Yearbook* (Pennsylvania, 1973) 136ff.

to the Nazis, interpreted the coming of the new regime in religious, even eschatological language.[24] Admittedly this ranged from the prayers of the Adventists welcoming the "new saviour of Germany" to the Witnesses' condemnation of the regime as "satanic;"[25] nevertheless all saw history and politics in broadly theological terms.

Perhaps, then, differences in the nature of a group's organization and leadership might inform the different approaches? For example, did a politically sophisticated Mormon leadership direct the opinions of its brethren towards support of the regime, while Witness leaders led their members into opposition? While there is an element of truth in this suggestion, it does not totally explain the nature of the responses made. Why should the leadership of a particular group be sophisticated politically? Is it not likely that the leadership was reflecting rather than directing general opinion? If this is so, again there are significant similarities between the groups. All members of the five sects would have been able to echo National Socialism's attacks on Communism and anarchy, all would have seen themselves as traditionalists in areas of morality and behavior and all—although the Witnesses with some reservations—would fit the category of political conservatives.

If there are similarities in theology, at least in areas that were likely to come under scrutiny in Nazi Germany, so also were there broad similarities in the way in which the groups were organized. All had international links and three of them—significantly, groups that shared very different fates, the Mormons, the Witnesses, and Christian Scientists—had strong links with the United States. These three groups all had to adjust when ties were severed because of the war and all three coped in various ways, reestablishing links rapidly when the war was over. All the groups had some kind of central government, although the influence of this body was considerably stronger for the Witnesses and Mormons than for the others. The Witnesses, who had possibly the most centralized and authoritarian structure, also, however, like the Mormons, had a local organizational structure with a German leadership. Theological interpretation for all five groups came from the central authority, although there were degrees of personal choice and interpretation, with Christian Scientists, for example, making private and individual choices on whether to fight in a war or not.

---

[24]Bavarian State Archives, December 1933.

[25]See, for example, *The Golden Age* 18 (10 March 1937).

The leaders of the sects, both in Germany and, for the three American-based groups, in the States, all reacted in a similar way to the Nazi seizure of power. All attempted to negotiate their position with the new government; all were prepared to use contacts and legal help if necessary. Thus even in patterns of formal response, there were similarities. Each of the groups' leaders compiled some kind of document outlining their position and sent this to the authorities. None ignored the new regime; all hoped to convince the Nazis of the value of their position, even though this ranged with the different groups from support to neutrality.

Although it is possible to outline major and important differences between the sects in theology and organization, their similarities in areas which might have been considered suspect by the Nazis were significant. Thus an explanation for the vast variety of responses must be sought elsewhere. It is not enough simply to say that Witnesses refused to fight for Germany and consequently suffered, since Adventists also believed that to fight was wrong and that to work on the Sabbath, a fact of army life, was a contravention of a basic divine instruction. Thus, not belief, but the way in which a group was willing to amend its beliefs becomes significant. If a group can show itself willing not only to adapt and amend teaching to fit political thinking and demands, but to do so with apparent sincerity, then it is likely to be able to make the kind of adjustments needed for survival in a totalitarian society. Moreover, this ability is both reflected in and is an example of a kind of political awareness and wordly sophistication required by any group aiming to survive and be tolerated within a potentially hostile political environment.

Those who were tolerated all gave evidence of some of these characteristics and these may provide some of the ingredients necessary for survival. Thus, the Mormons, Christian Scientists, the Adventists, and the New Apostolic Church all demonstrated a degree of political involvement; all their members voted, were prepared to hold local or national political office and saw nothing contradictory in being politically active and in belonging to their own religious group. Indeed, participation in civil affairs may be seen as directly encouraged by the Mormons, Christian Science, and New Apostolic churches in particular. All saw themselves as good citizens, respectable and respected, anxious to be seen as Germans, rather than as sectarians. All tried—and to a certain extent succeeded—to conform to acceptable images of citizenship. Thus when the demands made on a good German citizen were that he support the new regime, these sectarians conformed, behaving less like sectarians and more like the conservative German citizens they claimed to be.

Whatever the direct social composition of the four sects in question, and this varies considerably, all had what might be called a middle-class leadership, articulate and with the necessary skills and connections to make immediate appeal to the government in 1933. Moreover, the groups embodied many middle-class ideals, seeing, for example, wordly success and respectability as desirable aims. These ideals are evident in the welfare work of both the Mormons and the Adventists, where the aim is not charity but self-sufficiency, and where the Protestant work ethic dominates. Perhaps most clearly, Christian Science demonstrates elements of this middle-class approach to life evident in all four sects. The Committee on Publications, a watchdog office set up by the Mother Church in Boston in every country where there are branch churches, embodies the alert, articulate concern of the group to be understood and tolerated in society. Its officers are appointed for the very process of negotiation with the authorities and the public, and its general guidance, together with the high educational and social level of many members, allowed the groups in the Third Reich to maintain such a low-key profile that even after it was banned in 1941, meetings could be held without undue trouble. Not only were the members willing and able to make necessary adjustments, but the Committee on Publications was alerted to any possible difficulties long before they arose. Christian Scientists, like the Mormons, it will be remembered, had secured their initial toleration by the unashamed use of influential contacts.

Such a world view leads to a political sensitivity that is in itself a survival characteristic. Mormons, for example, had experienced some persecution and litigation in the early years of their missionary work in Germany. Nevertheless, within a short while, they had learned from this experience, were undertaking vast public relations campaigns, and by the time the Weimar Constitution was established they were able to point to a good war record and to establish sporting and cultural links with the authorities—for example, sending a choir to entertain in state prisons.[26] Such a response to a potentially dangerous political situation, given the Mormons' predisposition to adapt and given their experiences in nineteenth-century America, is perhaps not altogether surprising. This

[26]Early in the 1920s, for example, a Mormon choir was invited to perform at Hamburg state prison.

same willingness to learn and adapt was evident in the clear desire of the Mormon church in 1933 to be seen as not opposing Nazism.

From this political sophistication and willingness to compromise, demonstrated by the four sects during the Nazi period, came an ability to amend teaching to fit a new and emergency situation. Adventists thus were willing to change their emphasis on the Old Testament, even though it is a crucial element of their teaching, and in the name of survival they did so not only willingly but in the apparent conviction that such changes were not only justifiable but right. It is interesting to read the postwar literature of these sects, some of which attempts to come to terms with what is described as a "capitulation before the spirit of the times." Thus, a fusion of the practical ability to survive with the theological flexibility which allows significant changes in teaching to be introduced informs the response of the four survivor groups in the Third Reich.

The case of the famous nonsurvivors of the Third Reich, the Jehovah's Witnesses, supports this interpretation. They, in contrast to the other four, are nonworldly in the sense that they do not seek the approbation or the rewards of the material world and do not consider themselves to be members of it. They are political "neutrals" since they belong already to another world—God's. They have none of the material, middle-class aspirations of the others. They do not seek or offer compromises. They are unlikely to attract middle-class members since what they offer is a denial of the traditional values of the world. Even their leadership, while articulate and ready to negotiate with the authorities, talks not in the politically sophisticated language of the others, but, as has been noted, in an uncompromisingly religious tone.

The experience of persecution and litigation in Germany which the Witnesses shared with the Mormons was, for this group, not a learning experience, but a confirmation of their world view. This world view is rooted not in a political awareness but in a theological system and the unwillingness of the Witnesses to bend the knee in worldly matters is a reflection of their self-contained and tight theology. Any compromise would undermine the whole structure of their religious thinking, thus they are not just unwilling to compromise, but are unable to, since compromise on the smallest matter would mean that the whole structure of their world would be put at risk. To serve in the army, to vote, or to give the Hitler salute would have meant a recognition of the claims of this world as dominant over the claims of God. To serve the state would be to serve Satan, and thus the believer would be outside his own community and alienated from his basic ideological paradigm.

The sects most likely to resist a totalitarian regime, therefore, are the most conservative and unyielding in their belief systems. A comparison might be made here between the resistance of the Witnesses to the Nazis and the stance of the Confessing Church. Both resisted any interference in their organization or any alteration of their beliefs—and it was not from the liberal theological school of German Christianity that the Confessing Church came, but from among the conservatives. While some liberals were able to see the rejection of the Old Testament as part of the "demythologizing" process, and to see "positive Christianity" as a radical and relevant reinterpretation of Christianity for the modern age, the conservatives in the Confessing Church resisted changes of any sort, especially when imposed from outside.

The political stance of the Witnesses can be seen as a feature of their basic theological conservatism, but also as more than simply a function of theology. The rigidity of stance was a result of a complex mesh of socioeconomic, historical, and theological factors. Thus a theological system such as that of the Seventh Day Adventists may suggest certain patterns of behavior—for example, strict Sabbath observance or refusal to kill—but for historical reasons the adherents of that sect may develop in ways that allow them to deviate from the pure model of their theology. This kind of willingness to blur the edges may be seen to develop the more materially successful and worldly a body becomes. Rigidity, on the other hand, results from the disappointing life experiences of the membership, tempered by their theologically all-embracing world view. Thus the Witnesses' lack of material success was accompanied by a lack of sophistication that made them more likely to remain true to "pure" principles, interpreted for them by a central authority.

The case of a small schismatic Seventh Day Adventist group provides further empirical support for the thesis that what determines the political survival of a sect is its willingness or lack of willingness to compromise theologically. The Seventh Day Adventist Reform Movement broke away from the mainstream in 1916, seeing as an unacceptable compromise the group's attitude toward members' involvement in the First World War. A small and separatist group, the Reform Movement remained outside the demands and rewards of the material world until the coming of National Socialism forced their hand. Their response was clear; they refused to compromise in any way and were persecuted bitterly on a scale that may be compared to the treatment received by the Witnesses. The Reform Movement demonstrates that it is not theology, but the flexibility of that theology that determines a response to external challenges. The Witnesses and the Reform Movement each remained true to their original teaching and found themselves victims of a totalitarian state simply because they presented an opposing totalitarian challenge. Like the Jehovah's Witnesses, the Adventist Reform Movement continues to be persecuted and to work underground in the USSR while the mainstream Adventist Church long ago came to a satisfactory compromise with the Soviet government.

NEW RELIGIOUS MOVEMENTS AND MENTAL HEALTH

by Wolfgang Kuner

INTRODUCTION

NEW RELIGIOUS movements often have been accused of being harmful to the mental health of their members by psychiatrists (Clark, n.d., 1977 a, 1977b, 1978a, 1978b, 1979; Galper, 1976a, 1976b, 1977; Singer, 1978, 1979) and the public, while contradictory literature (Galanter, 1978a, 1978b, 1979; Galanter/Buckley 1978; Ungerleider/Wellisch 1978, 1979) has widely been ignored. It has mostly been neglected, however, that all findings published so far are based on rather small samples, and in some cases (for example, Clark, Galper, Singer) focused on ex-members alone. In order to assess the mental status the Minnesota Multiphase Personality Inventory (MMPI) was administered to German members of the Unification Church (UC), the Children of God/Family of Love (CoG) and Ananda Marga (AM). A total of 517 persons were interviewed (271 women, 246 men): 303 (=58.6%) of the UC (171m/132f); 42 (=8.12%) of the CoG (19m/23f); 47 (=9.1%) of AM (15m/32f); and 125 (=24.18%) students (66m/59f). The means for age and time of membership are shown in table 1.

The MMPI is a multidimensional, objective, standardized personality inventory that elicits a wide range of self-descriptions from a test subject and provides in a quantitative form a set of evaluations of the subject's personality status and emotional adjustment. Each test subject is asked to answer 566 items either "True" or "False" as they apply,

TABLE 1

Age and Time of Membership by Sex

	AGE (in years)		TIME OF MEMBERSHIP (in months)	
Groups	**Female**	**Male**	**Female**	**Male**
CoG	23.5	25.1	28.4	43.7
UC	26.4	26.5	50.5	50.8
AM	21.9	23.7	15.3	26.3
Control group	22.3	22.7	-	-

although the subject may also indicate that some of the items do not apply (see Dahlstrom et al., 1972a, 3ff.). The inventory consists of 14 basic scales:

Basic Minnesota Multiphasic Personality Inventory Scales

Scale Name	Abbreviation	Code Number	No. of Items
Validity Scales			
Cannot Say score	?		
Lie	L		15
Infrequency	F		64
Correction	K		30
Clinical Scales			
Hypochondriasis	Hs	1	33
Depression	D	2	60
Conversion hysteria	Hy	3	60
Psychopathic deviate	Pd	4	50
Masculinity-femininity	Mf	5	60
Paranoia	Pa	6	40
Psychasthenia	Pt	7	48
Schizophrenia	Sc	8	78
Hypomania	Ma	9	46
Social introversion	Si	0	70

(Source: Dahlstrom et al., 1972a, 4.)

Validity scales are designed to evaluate (1) the utility of the test in general for this particular assessment, (2) the acceptability of a particular set of data from a test subject, and (3) certain personality traits. From clinical scales a test subject's main personality characteristics are derived (see Dahlstrom et al., 1972a, 166).

RESULTS

MMPI Scale Configurations. The profiles of validity scales and clinical scales scatter within the range of "normality": the test results are valid and none of the groups shows a profile indicating "mental illness." Altogether, the members of the three new religious movements achieved "better" scores than the control group of students; their life seems to be one of less psychic stress and fewer worries. The degree of this "relief effect" seems to be correlated with the extent of disregard for society.

The members of the New Religious Movements are of similar but not identical personality types. In common they reveal narcissistic traits and need for social appreciation. Similar male and female characters can be found in AM and, to a smaller extent, in the UC. The resemblance of CoG men and CoG women is limited to basic traits. Categorizing the belief systems into "biblical" and "Eastern," one probably would expect a similarity of followers within the same category and a marked difference from those of the other. This is actually not the case: it is not the members of UC and CoG who show a resemblance but those of CoG and AM on one hand, and UC members and students on the other. This seems to indicate that belief systems do not play a dominant role in the process of conversion and should rather be regarded as an ideological correlate when a new way of life, a new way of production and reproduction, is to be established and/or maintained (see Kuner, 1979, 1980; Galanter, 1978; Stark/Bainbridge, 1980).

Although the average profiles scatter within the range of "normality," there were some respondents who scored beyond. Table 2 shows the numbers and percentages of those who achieved elevated scores on three or more scales ("clinical cases"). There is no statistically significant difference, except for a lower rate of UC women compared to the student control group.

A rate of twenty-two percent male and twelve percent female UC members scored beyond the upper limit of the L-scale. Elevated L-scores indicate that the respondents are hardly willing to talk about themselves in a frank and self-critical way, and to admit foibles and mistakes (on a simple level). Since the L-scale is used as a measure of validity, elevated scores imply that the clinical-scale scores should be higher than computed. Looking at the wording of the L-scale one finds that at least five out of

TABLE 2

Number and Percentage of Persons with Elevated Scale Scores on three or more Scales

Groups		Elevated Scores n	%
CoG	F	1	5
	M	1	4
UC	F	4	2
	M	11	8
AM	F	2	13
	M	1	3
Control group	F	6	9
	M	3	5

fifteen items could be answered deviantly because of the UC members' way of life and belief system.

This, of course, is contradictory because there is either defensiveness and respondents try to create a favorable impression (that is, the answer is deviant from reality) or they answer in a frank and open way (that is, according to their—in this case, deviant—reality).

> Valid elevations [of the L-scale, wk] in the high to markedly elevated ranges are most likely to be generated by subjects who are honestly describing themselves. They tend, therefore, to be overly conventional, socially conforming, and prosaic. Some of the descriptions actually correspond to their habitual patterns of behavior while other features of their test answers reflect their poor insight and limited self-knowledge. That is, they may be highly religious and moralistic individuals who rigidly control any overt expression of anti-social or unethical impulses. At the same time, studies of these test subjects also indicate that they may be expressing some of these tendencies without being aware of the impact that their behaviour may have upon others or without recognizing their own motives and purposes. Thus, elevated L-scale values are likely in test subjects who are ministers, reformers, social activists, or evangelical missionaries (Dahlstrom et al., 1972a 158).

Following these guidelines the elevated L-scores can be interpreted as (1) an extreme identification with the UC's religious activities and doctrines, and (2) a test taken without defensiveness or trying to create a favorable impression. (3) These members strongly align their needs and behavior with the group's normative pattern and "use" the movement as a substitute for superego deficits.

Correlation between Scale Scores and Time of Membership. Only a few statistically significant linear correlations between scale scores and time of membership exist. In general the amount of variance explained is less than ten percent, that is, the impact of the variable "time of membership" on the variation of scale scores is rather weak. A significantly positive correlation between the L-scale and membership in the UC and AM (women) lends support to the assumption that the movements take over superego functions in the long run. Longtime membership seems to exert a resocializing influence of which the negative correlation between disregard for social customs and mores and UC-membership is a statistically significant example. No significant linear correlations were found between elevated scale scores ("clinical cases") and time of membership. A series of students' t-tests was run in order to scan for differences in time of membership between respondents scoring beyond 70t ("clinical cases") and those scoring within 40-60t ("sane cases"). It was found that the longer the membership lasted the higher the probability was of achieving a 40-60t score.

CONCLUSIONS

So far no figures have been found that lend support to the public image of "cults that destroy their members' mental health" or of the movements being "a pool of mentally ill youngsters." On the other hand, there is evidence of the occurrence of severe psychic trouble in connection with membership in new religious movements.

I would like to propose two basic explanations:

(1) A small number of "mentally upset" people unconsciously regarded the movements as a kind of "therapeutic group," joined them, could not be treated properly because of lack of professional competence, and finally dropped out in a worse psychic status.

(2) As has been mentioned before, the scale configurations reveal strong narcissistic traits. Because of an unfinished mother-child dyad this personality permanently tries to reestablish this (lost but not outgrown) kind of symbiosis. Additionally there is a rejection of the dependence on parental authority. This combination results in a condition of psychic stress. The family-type character of the new religious movements offers a potential of identification and melting, an adequacy to these symbiotic needs and the possibility to untie the existing dependence on parental

authority by submitting to a new, stronger one. As long as the symbiotic relationship remains in existence, psychic well-being may result; and as soon as the narcissistic person "grows up," that is, leaves the needs of this kind of symbiosis behind, he/she may break the relationship without severe psychic troubles. Should the symbiotic attachment be vigorously broken from the "outside," however, psychic troubles (their strength depending on the strength of the attachment) may occur. This sort of cutoff seems to apply to most of the "clinical cases" reported: parents having their child "rescued" or groups having turned out members. It must be assumed that here the psychic "costs" of a vigorous cutoff have been described, an artificially created "schizoid" status of two worlds to live in: the former symbiotic attachment still anchored in the individual's psyche and not outgrown, and a new nonsymbiotic world suddenly forced upon the (ex-)member.

As has been shown earlier only a small number of members seems to have strong symbiotic needs to identify strongly and to substitute superego deficiencies. On the other hand only a limited and comparatively few parents try to fight the new religious movements and/or force their children back. The question is why some parents do while others do not, or why some children do while others do not. If it is correct that these very members do have symbiotic needs (narcissistic personality), then their parents (in particular, mothers) will also have such needs. Had the mother enabled the child to overcome that stage of mother-child attachment, the symbiotic needs and resulting compulsion to satisfy them permanently and thus to reproduce this very relationship would have disappeared. That is to say, the psychic structures of mother (parents) and child do correspond and are just two sides of the same coin (see Moeller, 1980; Kursbuch, 1979). Hence one could argue that some of the parents, too, are shown to have strong narcissistic (symbiotic) needs. Parental descriptions concerning the child before his/her conversion often read: "most intelligent, creative, but sensitive as well; best in class, very critical, most artistic, and so forth" (see Aktion, 1978). It is not very difficult to see that the children contributed to their parents' self-esteem to a considerable extent, functioning as a means of narcissistic self-satisfaction. The loss of the child must therefore have been an offense to the parental narcissistic psyche and has been acted out in "fighting" the new religious movements.

Since it can be assumed that only the most narcissistic parents compensated in this way a specific social dynamic is brought into action:

the most narcissistic parents try to get their most narcissistic children back. Since these ex-members, however, are the ones that had most identified, hence most changed during membership, it becomes clear how the public image of the new religious movements has got its particular shape. It is the children that had most changed (because of being most narcissistic) who are presented to the public by the most angry (because of being most narcissistic) parents—thereby offering appropriately exotic stories to a press that lives off selling sensations.

SUMMARY

The MMPI profiles of members of three new religious movements scatter within the range of "normality." There is no evidence of a general "mental disturbance" in terms of clinical psychology. In general there are no significant linear correlations between time of membership and scale scores. Longtime membership seems to have a resocializing and "therapeutic" effect. The number of "clinical cases" found within the movements proportionately equals the number found within a student control group. The members have similar but not identical types of personality revealing narcissistic traits. It must be assumed that mental problems of ex-members were produced not by living with a group but by suddenly and violently breaking up the relationship between the member and the group. The public image of the new religious movements has most likely been shaped by a small number of the most narcissistic (and hence militant) parents and most narcissistic ex-members (and hence "Zombie-like" followers) in a kind of "cooperation" with a mass media which is interested in sensations.

REFERENCES

Aktion für geistige und psychische Freiheit—Arbeitsgemeinschaft der Elterninitiativen

1978 *Dokumentation über die Auswirkungen der Jugendreligionen auf Jugendliche in Einzelfällen.* Bonn.

Clark, John G.

N.d. ***Investigating the Effects of Some Religious Cults on the Health and Welfare*** *of Their Converts.* n.p.

1977a "Destructive Cults: Defined and Held Accountable." Address presented to National Guard chaplains, Minneapolis.

1977b "The Noisy Brain in a Noisy World." Paper presented to New Jersey Psychological Association.

1978a *The Psychophysiology of Religious Conversion.* n.p.

1978b "Untersuchungen über die Auswirkungen einiger religiöser Sekten auf Gesundheit und Wohlergehen ihrer Anhänger." *Praxis der Kinderpsychologie und Kinderpsychiatrie* 27.

1979 "Der künstlich gesteuerte Wahnsinn." In Müller-Küppers/Specht, 1979.

Dahlstrom/Welsh/Dahlstrom

1972a *An MMPI Handbook*, vol. 1. Minneapolis.

1972b *An MMPI Handbook*, vol. 2. Minneapolis.

Galanter, Marc

1978a "The 'Relief Effect': A Sociobiological Model for Neurotic Distress and Large-Group Therapy. *American Journal of Psychiatry* 135:5.

1978b "Religious Conversion: An Experimental Model for affecting Alcoholic Denial." Paper presented at the Medical-Scientific Conference, St. Louis.

Galanter/Buckley

1978 "Evangelical Religion and Meditation: Psychotherapeutic Effects." *Journal of Nervous and Mental Disease* 166:10.

Galanter et al.

1979 "The 'Moonies': A Psychological Study of Conversion and Membership in a Contemporary Religious Sect. *American Journal of Psychiatry* 136:2.

Galper, Marvin

1976 "Adolescent Identity Diffusion and the Extremist Religious Cult." Paper presented at the Annual Meeting of the Western Psychological Association, Seattle.

Kuner, Wolfgang

1979 *You gotta be a baby oder Happiness flutsch flutsch. Eine Untersuchung zu Charakter, Genese und sozialen Ursachen einer den sogenannten "Jugendreligionen" zugeordneten sozialen Bewegung, der Kinder Gottes* (Familie der Liebe). Tübingen: Unveröffentlichte MA-Arbeit.

1980 "Die neuen religiösen Gruppen in der BRD: Interpretationen und Realität." In Graff/Tiefenbacher, *Kirche—Lebensraum für Jugendliche.* Mainz.

Kursbuch
1979 *Sekten* 55.

Moeller, Michael-L.
1980 "Von der Sektenkritik zur Selbstkritik." See Kuner, 1980.

Müller-Küppers/Specht, eds.
1979 *Neue Jugendreligionen.* Göttingen.

Singer, M.
1978a *Psychologie Heute* 8.

1978b "Therapy with Ex-Cult Members." *National Association of Private Psychological Hospitals Journal* 9.4.

1979 See Müller-Küppers/Specht.

Stark/Bainbridge
1980 "Networks of Faith: Recruitment of Cults and Sects." *American Journal of Sociology* 85:6.

Ungerleider, J. T.
N.d. *The New Religions: Insights into the Cult Phenomenon.* n.p.

Ungerleider/Wellisch
1978 *Cultism, Thought Control and Deprogramming—Observations on a Phenomenon.* n.p.

1979 "Coercive Persuasion (Brainwashing), Religious Cults and Deprogramming." *American Journal of Psychiatry* 136:3.

MAKING THE WORLD WORK: IDEAS OF SOCIAL RESPONSIBILITY IN THE HUMAN POTENTIAL MOVEMENT

by Steven M. Tipton

LIKE MOST HUMAN potential and therapeutic movements, Erhard Seminars Training (*est*) sees itself as communicating epistemological, psychological, and psychosomatic facts about human existence, not teaching religious beliefs or ethics; and doing so via experience, not ideas. "The Training isn't a set of precepts or concepts or notions; it isn't anything we tell people," explains Werner Erhard, *est's* founder. "It is the experience that the person has of himself."[1] The analysis to follow will suggest that *est* is practically important to at least some of its participants, particularly 1960s youth, for the system of moral norms, values, and attitudes it transmits to them.[2]

---

[1]*Est,* "Werner Erhard: 'All I can do is lie," an undated reprint of an interview published in the *East-West Journal* (September 1974):2.

[2]For a fuller development of this thesis, see my *Getting Saved from the Sixties: Moral Meaning in Conversion and Cultural Change* (Berkeley, Los Angeles, London: University of California Press, 1982), chapter 4, from which this paper is drawn. This material appears here by permission of the original publishers. Data used in this paper comes from taped formal interviews averaging three hours each with twenty 1960s youths who are *est* graduates, done in the San Francisco Bay Area in 1975-1978; and from informal interviews with thirty others done over a year's participant-observation, during which period the writer took the *est* training and two "graduate seminar series," and worked as an *est* volunteer. Youths formally interviewed averaged 32.3 years of age in 1980, were equally divided by sex, and were all Caucasians. Fourteen of the twenty held B.A. degrees, of whom seven also held advanced degrees. Fourteen of the twenty did white-collar work, one, blue-collar; four were professionals, and one a law student. Two of the twenty were

Est describes itself as an "educational corporation" that trains its clients "to transform their ability to experience living so that the situations they have been trying to change or have been putting up with clear up just in the process of life itself."[3] The standard training program takes over sixty hours spread across four days on two consecutive weekends, and it costs $350. A single "trainer" delivers the program to groups of 200-250 persons, who are mostly urban, middle-class young adults, employed in white collar jobs, unmarried, and uninvolved in any religious

---

married and another four were divorced. Six of the twenty were living with someone when interviewed; four were regularly dating one person; five were dating more than one person; three dated only occasionally. Fifteen of the twenty had lived with someone for at least several months in the past, and only two were still living with their first such partner. None were affiliated with a conventional church; twelve had been involved with at least one spiritual or therapeutic discipline. Eighteen of the twenty had used marijuana; fourteen LSD. All reported using drugs less often now than in the past. Nine had been in political demonstrations; none were active in politics at present. Eleven of the twenty had lived communally; three now did so. Fifteen of the twenty had worked irregularly since school; three were now unemployed, one by choice. This sample appears representative of 1960s youth involved in *est*, as depicted in Robert Ornstein, Charles Swencionis, Arthur Deikmar, and Ralph Morris, *A Self-Report Survey: Preliminary Study of Participants in Erhard Seminars Training* (The *est* Foundation: San Francisco: 1975), 25-27, 34-36, 59; supplemented by Ornstein et al. data sets in file SYS8, 10/11/74, Variables W29-88, deposited in The *est* Archives, San Francisco. This survey data of *est* graduates as a whole shows that, compared to the larger population, they number proportionately more young adults and fewer persons under twenty or over forty, more divorced and fewer married persons, more women and fewer men. Persons 25-34 comprise 46.7% of *est*'s clientele and 19% of the San Francisco Bay Area population, a ratio of 2.45 to 1. They comprise only 12.3% of the U.S. population according to the 1970 census. Caucasians make up 88% of *est*'s clientele; blacks, 1.3%. Nearly 90% of all graduates began college; only 57% graduated. Most graduates (some 70%) work primarily with other persons in white-collar jobs, not with abstractions as technically specialized professionals or with physical objects as laborers. Almost two-thirds of all *est* graduates are now unmarried (62%); more than a quarter have never been married; another quarter are presently divorced or separated, a rate three times that of San Franciscans and seven times that of Americans generally. Some 26.7% of *all* graduates, four of ten ever married, have gone through such breakups within the year before or after taking *est*. One of three *est* graduates is affiliated with a conventional religious denomination, but less than one of ten participates weekly. Among those 25-34 in *est*, conventional religious affiliation is virtually nonexistent, but many of them are involved in "new age" spiritual and therapeutic disciplines such as macrobiotics, yoga, TM, aikido, and encounter groups, which they tend to continue after the training. Some 40% of *all* graduates had used marijuana, and 14% had used LSD: since *est*, 50% reported using less marijuana, and 56% reported using less LSD. Data regarding *est* and its graduate population as a whole, if not otherwise cited herein, come from staff communications and records of *est*'s Office of Research, San Francisco.

[3]From "What is the purpose of the *est* training?" a pamphlet published by *est*, no. 680-3 (13 January 1976), San Francisco.

denomination. *Est* trained some 220,000 persons through 1979. Their mean age was then 33.7, with 1960s youth (those aged 25-34) comprising nearly half the total. In the San Francisco Bay Area, where *est* is based, one out of every nine college-educated young adults has taken the training and became an "*est* graduate.".

Controversy over *est's* ethic grows sharpest in discussions of its implications for social and political responsibility. Youthful graduates usually disapprove radical politics and liberal reformism of 1960s vintage as inevitably vain attempts to force persons to change or to "help" them, instead of accepting them as they are and "creating the space" for them to transform themselves abreactively. What sort of concrete social activity is implied by the latter ideal? Graduates' views vary in reply. Some justify exemplary responsibility for oneself and for the others with whom one normally interacts as sufficient. Most point to participation in *est* itself as the most effective contribution one can make to the future of American society, namely the transformation of its members and institutions in *est's* image. The growing number of educators, doctors, therapists, clergy, and other professionals who have taken the training, along with special training sessions offered in schools, prisons, and local governments, are pointed to as indications that progress toward such institutional transformation is already underway. Traditional forms of political participation and voluntarism are supported as secondary ways of "taking responsibility for the system, since you created it the way it is." Graduates often cite *est*'s nonpartisan voter registration drive among its members as an example of the latter sort of social concern, along with its "Hunger Project." Since 1977 the Project has "enrolled" several million persons and raised millions of dollars to publicize the idea that it is now possible "to end world hunger in twenty years."[4]

One young graduate, a veteran of antiwar demonstrations and campus politics during the late 1960s though he was never arrested or affiliated with any radical political organization, characterizes his past and present political involvement in terms of *est*'s idea of responsibility:

---

[4]See "*est*," *The Graduate Review* (September 1977): 2; also, "The Hunger Project, A Shift in the Wind," *The Hunger Project Newspaper*, May 1978; and "The Hunger Project: It's Our Planet—It's Our Hunger Project," a ten-page brochure, published in May 1978, p. 5. Through 1980 the Hunger Project enrolled 1.7 million persons and raised $5.7 million, according to *est* trainer K. Anbender, personal communication, 1981.

Q: During the 1960s where did you stand on radical politics?
A: I was for it. I demonstrated. I marched on Washington in 1968 at Nixon's inauguration. You know, "There ought to be a Revolution. Off the President. Kick the sonuvabitch out. Change the system. It's worthless, junk it. Let's take over, and start a whole new thing."

Q: How did you see American society in the 1960s?
A: I always pointed the finger at the system. "This is wrong. That's wrong." I blamed the establishment, while I played the victim. I never took responsibility for anything. I wasn't responsible for the rules, I wasn't responsible for the laws. I wasn't responsible for the Vietnam War. I wasn't responsible for politics. I didn't own any of that s. . . . I didn't take responsibility for my choices. There I was trying to make the world work, and my own life didn't work. I couldn't even make a commitment to be on time before the training.

Q: How does the system look to you now?
A: Totally different. Now I feel that the system is perfectly fine. What doesn't work is the people, because they don't take responsibility for it. Now I'm taking responsibility. I'm assisting [as a volunteer at *est*]. I'm gonna vote, because the system's set up to vote and it's my system, so I'm gonna take responsibility for it and vote.

Q: What's responsibility then?
A: Owning my choices. Being more active, dealing with the system *in* the system, under the system. To me what's most important is conscious awareness, awakening. First you have to take responsibility for yourself, and from there it's an easy step to taking responsibility for the people around you and the whole system.

The radicalism of the 1960s, which blamed and opposed the established sources of political power for conditions of social injustice, is now interpreted as self-righteous abnegation of one's own responsibility for these conditions. The graduate sees this to be especially hypocritical in view of his own irresponsibility in his personal life. He sees participation in *est* and cooperation with conventional politics at present to mark acceptance of responsibility for the existing social system. Its failures are due not to institutionalized structural conditions nor the concerted efforts of particular interest groups or classes, but to the universal unwillingness of individuals, first of all oneself, to take *est*'s kind of responsibility for themselves and the society as a whole. Typically, the young graduate has shifted from an attitude of outright alienation from the established social order during the 1960s to mediated identification with it at present, from activities of overt political opposition (more hip than radical in tenor) to modest participation. His present position is grounded less in any new faith in the established order than in commitment to *est*'s ideology of therapeutic change through abreactive acceptance, and the promise *est* offers for the society's transformation from the inside out.

During the 1960s young *est* graduates shared the countercultural perception that American society was fundamentally wrong and in need of change. They usually subscribed to the hip view that America's "screwed up values," more than its social structure, were to blame for its problems, which were approaching solution through cultural changes already underway. Many youths sympathized with political activists, some accepted radical diagnoses of what was wrong, why, and how it was to be changed. But virtually none committed themselves to enacting any such programs of change.[5] "I hung on the sidelines and watched the political game," concedes one. "I was interested but I wasn't ready to play it." *Est*'s picture of society accounts for the futility of the hip vision of a psychedelic utopia, while retracing its postmillennial shape in more conventional colors.

Est agrees that American society is fundamentally faulty, but it blames the individual graduate. The trainer stresses,

> When you see why your lives don't work, you'll see why this whole f. . . . . . country doesn't work. Look at General Motors. That's the best this country can do. And look at one of their f. . . . . . cars. It's a piece of s. . . ! I'm not blaming GM. I'm blaming you for being so stupid that you think it works. . . . Sure, you *understand* all the problems, you *want* things to get better. But not if it costs *you* anything, not if *you* have to take responsibility for it.[6]

The country is criticized for "not working," just as its corporate representative is criticized for the inefficiency of its machinery, not for its mode of ownership and operation, its political influence, or ecological impact. Such criticism leads to the conclusion that what must be done is to make the system work by accepting it as it is, acknowledging oneself as its cause, and participating in it according to its rules. Political activists failed in trying to make the system over by resisting it, blaming others for

---

[5]If we define the committed political activist by such indices as leading or regularly participating in radical political activity, being arrested for so doing, belonging to a radical organization, mastering the formal ideology, resisting the draft, or filing for CO status, then none of those formally interviewed could be classified as a committed activist. Of thirty or so additional graduates informally interviewed, only one, a civil rights worker and CORE member in the early 1960s (now turned massage teacher) would qualify, the case of *est* graduate Jerry Rubin notwithstanding. Seventeen of twenty interviewees reported sympathy during the 1960s with the view that American society seemed fundamentally in the wrong; only four of these persons accepted a full-blown radical political analysis of what was wrong, and none acted on it.

[6]R. McNamara, day 1, San Francisco "A" *est* training (September 1975).

causing it, and dropping out of it, all according to their own rules. "How did the War end, anyway?" the trainer demands. "Did the kids running around with their little banners end it? No! All they did was get everyone else pissed off at them. What ended it was millions of ordinary people in this country going to the polls and voting it out."[7] *Est* argues that the paradox of its psychological theory of change ("Trying to change an experience makes it persist; accepting it and being with it makes it disappear.") applies as powerfully to social institutions as to the individual mind. By heeding it first with themselves, then others, then everyone, individuals can "transubstantiate" social institutions, altering their essence while leaving their structural accidents unchanged. Thus psychodynamics defines both the mode and sequence of social change.

Est presents itself as an agent of societal transformation whose success will, in Erhard's phrase, enable "the institutions of man to deliver on their promises." "What I want is for the world to work," he says. "The organizing principle of *est* is: *Whatever the world is doing, get it to do that.*"[8] *Est* is already acting to this end along two avenues. First, it is transforming an ever-increasing number of individuals, who will eventually make up a "critical mass" of the entire population, triggering its transformation by a chain reaction. A longtime *est* volunteer reports that

> there's a cumulative effect from graduates changing personally. They create the space for other people to get it. It's Werner's intention to give the training to forty million people in America, which would be like a critical mass. Everybody will be giving the training to everybody else just by living with them day by day.

By transforming individuals *est* is transforming society conceived as a collection of individuals. In this postmillennial vision no heroic efforts by a small elite of morally perfected Christians or enlightened Buddhists, "clear" Scientologists, or the like will be required to remake American society after it has been destroyed by divine or ecological catastrophes. Instead, the new age has already dawned and is now advancing, its continuous progress charted by the swelling curve of *est*'s mass membership.

In the process of its numerical growth *est* is "creating a context" to transform society, in America and around the world, just as its Hunger

---

[7]R. McNamara, day 3.

[8]William W. Bartley III, *Werner Erhard: The Transformation of Jack Rosenberg* (New York: Clarkson Potter, 1978) 221.

Project is "creating a context" to end world starvation. Project literature makes clear that "the process by which a context is created is communication and enrollment, communication and enrollment, communication and enrollment;"[9] while *est* points out that "numerical growth and international trainings represent, however, only one dimension of *est*'s development as a force for transformation in the world."[10]

Second, *est* is transforming the larger society's institutions of socialization—educational, therapeutic, medical, legal-penal, religious, governmental, and familial. They will take over the training's functions as their members assimilate its ethic, eventually permitting *est* itself to wither away. Erhard states that "the real thrust and goal of *est* is to put *est* in education. *Est* will cease to exist somewhere along the pike. We've already begun to make inroads, we've already made good plans, we've demonstrated our effectiveness to the world, people will listen to us. We are starting to get into the education system."[11] Although *est* has yet to win over any institutional establishment, its pre-1976 graduates already included nine percent of all "educators" in the San Francisco School District.[12] The University of California has offered academic credit for a course on "the *est* experience: Implications for Educators," with the training as a prerequisite. A California state college has given credit for the training itself, conducted on-campus.[13] *Est*'s advisory board includes a score of distinguished doctors and professors, including educators who have formerly been president of Oberlin College, chancellor of the University of California at San Francisco and HEW assistant secretary, and a Harvard Business School assistant dean. It also includes entertainers John

---

[9]"The Hunger Project, It's Our Planet—It's Our Hunger Project," 5.

[10]*Graduate Review* (July 1978): 16.

[11]*Est*, "Werner Erhard: 'All I Can Do Is Lie,' " 5.

[12]*Est* has had mixed success with professionals, winning the loyalty of some individuals, notably clinical psychologists and M.D.'s, and the interest of others, but not the approval of any professional establishment. *Est has* won over substantial elements of the middle echelons of certain educational, business, and administrative institutions, in which its ethic is particularly applicable. At the end of 1975 *est* claimed 8.83% of all "educators" in the San Francisco Unified School District among its graduates. R. C. Devon Heck and J. L. Thompson, *San Francisco Magazine*, January 1976, 22.

[13]Robert W. Fuller and Zara Wallace, *A Look at est in Education* (San Francisco: *est*, 1975) 62-63.

Denver, Valerie Harper, Suzy Chaffee, and a vice-president of the National Broadcasting Company.[14]

Asked about *est*'s potential for transforming American institutions, a young graduate replies with confidence, "It seems like it could happen. *Est* is growing faster than anything else and graduates are strategically located. *Est* doesn't make anything else wrong, so it can get along with anything. It doesn't give you any answers, so its answers can't be proved wrong. It just gives you a more open, useful viewpoint." The utility of *est*'s ethics for bureaucratic work and social relations, the psychological content of its doctrine (high on epistemology, low on cosmology), and its streamlined delivery (weekend scheduling without "touchie-feelie" or religious props) do indeed make *est* more appealing across the range of secular middle-class life than such human potential competitors as Scientology and Arica, let alone conservative Christian or neo-Oriental religious movements.

Est's modest millennialism fits the social situation of its young graduates. Compared to their counterparts in Christian sects and neo-Oriental ashrams, they have dropped back in closer to the middle of mainstream work and personal life. In fact, they had not dropped out so far nor burned their bridges back so drastically in the first place. They did not use drugs so heavily, reject school so vehemently, nor so commit themselves to countercultural careers as drug dealers, rock musicians, hustlers, artists, craftsmen, communards, or political activists. Nonetheless they shared countercultural hopes whose disappointment was not painless for them. *Est*'s ethic has responded to the frustration and helplessness felt by college-educated youths now stuck in white collar jobs within the system they had hoped to change. Says one resignedly,

> When I look at what we're doing in the world, it makes me feel helpless. There's nothing I can do about it, except accept it. *Est* has shown me that's OK. At least after training I felt a big burden of guilt removed toward people who were having problems, whatever they were, because I got that *they* were responsible in a way.
>
> *Q:* Why do you think it looked different to you in the 1960s?
> *A:* We were all going to college then. The real world was outside. You could be outrageous, because you didn't have to deal with it. In college everyone was young like me. They all did dope like me, wore long hair, and pointed out there at "them," the ones who were screwing everything up.

---

[14]*Graduate Review* (June 1978): 15-17.

> But then when I got out and started working as a salesman, I found myself being one of "them." I wanted to get more for my efforts, you know, get ahead. . . . I guess I'd gotten my hands dirty, so I wasn't so interested anymore in sitting around trying to figure out if it was left-wing dirt or right-wing dirt. [*laughing*] I found out you can't worry about saving the world. You have to just live your own life.

While it represents a reaction to cooled-off political and tightened economic conditions in America since the 1960s, this shift of outlook—from seeking to understand the society to surviving in it, from making it over to making one's way in it—cannot be separated from the subject's age-related shift of position in the society: from studying in an age-segregated youth setting while being supported by others to working in an age-integrated adult setting to support oneself.

Following the line of such shifts of position, *est*'s ethic has also sustained hopes for social change, outside the context of radical or liberal politics, in a form compatible with a conventional career and lifestyle. A graduate seeking his first job as a corporate lawyer doing pro bono environmental work on the side suggest how closely *est*'s ideology suits his own situation:

> When I was an undergrad I was involved in mildly radical politics. The War was a great rallying point for me, although I couldn't swallow the revolutionary rhetoric. I was coming from the place of "What you're doing, America, is wrong. You can't do that. It's evil." Which was absolutely ineffective. I was flailing around with my eyes closed.
>
> Now instead of saying, "No, no, no," I say, "Yes, you're doing that." I'm seeing and dealing with what is, instead of wishing it were different. I'm coming to a place of acknowledging how things actually work, what the facts are, whether I like it or not, because it is what it is. It's not right or wrong.
>
> In the past few years I've become more involved in my relationship to myself, the people around me, the earth. Social concern is there, but it's not the big issue. It's a question of putting it on a smaller scale, trying to change the energy instead of resisting it. *Est* is like that. It's less defensive and more accepting than the radicals. And it's very centered and clear about where I am individually. You can accept opposition and not feel threatened about it. You can communicate with other people and see the world through their eyes, and then maybe you can do something better. It's like Werner saying,
>
> The way it is
> is enough.
> Who you are is enough.
> The only thing you have to do
> is be.[15]

---

[15]*Est* "Special Guest Seminar" announcement, 13 February 1976.

I feel OK with a wait-and-see position on *est* and society, since I already see so much value in *est* for individuals.

For many who have come of age in the 1960s, *est*'s ethic of taking responsibility for the existing social order while pursuing one's own interests within it sounds sensible and straightforward. For many of their elders, once caught in the middle between the establishment and the kids, *est* has opened up a new middle ground. An older businessman reflects on what *est* has meant to him:

> Where once I saw a bloated capitalist, an exploiter of the masses, now I see a man in a Lincoln.
>
> Where once I saw radical, hippy freaks, now I see four bearded men in a battered van. . . .
>
> When I had to understand everything, I didn't understand anything. When I needed to judge, I had no standards of my own. . . . When I knew what the world was supposed to be like, that's the way it was, whether I liked it or not, and I usually didn't.
>
> Since *est,* the world can be any way it wants. Fine with me. Here I am, then, with a wife who pats me on the leg, customers who want more work than I have time to do. I ride along the freeway and kids flash the peace sign, girls wave, and two guys in the back of a pickup truck offer me a beer.
>
> So I don't understand it.
>
> So what?[16]

A social world that could not be understood or justified before, now can be accepted. A society that could not be changed through politics, can now be "transformed" through *est.*

The ambiguity of *est*'s notion of moral responsibility derives ultimately from its binocular axioms, which are radically individualistic on one side and monistic on the other. *Est* posits that each individual is the cause of all his experience, and it prescribes an attitude of responsibility as the acknowledgment of this fact. Construed dualistically (by distinguishing subject and object, I and other, instead of fusing them into one universal existence), this view can be generalized to mean that each and every person is "totally at cause" and therefore totally *and exclusively* responsible for his own situation and its difficulties. If *A* is subject to some difficulty, then by definition *A* willed it so. This inference can be used to excuse anyone else from seeking to alter the external conditions of *A*'s predicament, since *A* alone is seen to have caused them and to have the capacity to change them. Now if *A* is a self-indulgent and self-

---

[16]*Graduate Review* (June 1976): 11.

defeating individual whom others have sought to help, only to be exploited and resented, this diagnosis of the situation is easy to accept as factual. More to the point, if *A* is the trainee himself in face-to-face relation to a lover, friend, family member, or work associate, this diagnosis may usefully motivate him to take the initiative to act to improve his situation, regardless of its factual accuracy. If, however, *A* is an individual or group relatively deprived of power to act on their own behalf by external conditions (whether social position, race, gender, physical handicaps, or the like), then this diagnosis appears not only inaccurate but outrageously tolerant of social injustice and human suffering, according to *est*'s critics. They view *est* from a liberal-humanist or Judeo-Christian vantage point, from which they perceive a laissez-faire individualism, stripped now of even half-hearted attempts at liberal reform or Christian charity. Disillusioned by the frustrated efforts of 1960s radicalism and liberalism, the middle class in this view has turned inward to self-realization and interpersonal intimacy with each other in ways compatible with staying on the job and working toward incrementally greater socioeconomic status. Meanwhile the less advantaged continue to pay a disproportionate price for the existing order, and the more advantaged continue to enjoy its disproportionate profits.

More sophisticated adherents of *est* reject its characterization as a leading version of "the new narcissism," arguing that an exclusively individualistic construction of its concept of responsibility is mistaken. They offer, first, a social-psychological expansion of the concept, and then a monistic universalization of it. First, the individual is totally responsible for his own experience, and that experience includes all the other persons with whom he interacts. As a social self, then, each individual is totally responsible for everything that happens to others in relation to himself and, in relation to one another. If another person feels sad, angry, dominated, or whatever in relation to *A*, *A* is responsible for it. Second, *est* posits that while each individual experiences himself as a discrete "mind," he exists ultimately as a "being" coextensive with all existence, conceived monistically. Therefore, each individual has "caused" and "created" every other person and everything that exists; and each individual is consequently responsible for everything and everyone else.

Est's small staff and core of veteran volunteers, in contrast to its mass clientele, often interpret *est*'s ethic as deriving entirely from the "transformation of self" they take to be the training's essence. As Erhard defines it,

> transformation is *the self as the self,* the self as the context of all contexts, everything/nothing. The self itself is the ground of all being, that from which everything arises. The self is pure context, it is everything/nothing, it is pure space. And out of the self emerges a manifestation of it. That is, the self (context) *is complete;* the self manifests itself by *being complete,* and the manifestation is process or content.[17]

In other words, *est* shifts one's sense of self from the dualist's discrete ego to the monist's universal being. Echoing Zen Buddhist distinctions between small mind and Buddha-mind or small and Big Self, *est*'s distinctions between mind and being, self and Self, content and context, position and space all rely on this dualist-to-monist shift for their meaning. So do Erhard's replies to his social critics:

> It is clear that people who think that transformation leads to narcissism and cuts you off from other people are confusing the "self" with a [dualist-realist] position, a body, an ego, an individual. The true experience of the [monist] self takes you out into the world to express the self.[18]

This monistic universalization of individual identity and moral responsibility takes form as an ethic of "service" to all humanity which is often cited by Erhard in public statements of his own intentions and *est*'s mission in society, He states:

> In *est*, the organization's purpose is to serve people, to create an opportunity for people to experience transformation, enlightenment, satisfaction and well-being in their lives. And to create an opportunity for people to participate in making the world work and to contribute to the lives of others. That's the purpose of *est.* [19]

Formal description of this service ethic, though sketchy, vaguely resembles the Bodhisattva ethic in Zen Buddhism, in which feelings of universal compassion and acts of exemplary service flow from monistic identification with all living beings.

Neither the *est* training nor its graduates elaborate this ethic of service in any systematic detail. They do often allude to it in connection with their appointed role of "assisting" others and *est*'s role in sponsor-

---

[17]*Graduate Review* (November 1976): 3.

[18]Ibid.

[19]Ibid.

ing the Hunger Project. To what extent *est* or its graduates enact this ethic and with whom remains a question open to debate, although *est*'s social critics see monistic universalization of responsibility for social problems as obscuring their particular causes and dissolving focused efforts to resolve them. For example, while Erhard states that "ultimately, the Hunger Project is about transformation of Self as Humanity—about making the world work,"[20] a critical food expert counters, "it's probably collected more money in the name of hunger and done the least about hunger than any group I can think of." He adds,

> Anyone who has real concern about hunger has to have some understanding and concern for social justice in developing countries, about existing inequitable structures, about rapid population growth. I can't see the Hunger Project doing anything about this.[21]

Its critics see *est* depoliticizing such issues by dissolving their social structure and moral substance into pure consciousness, thereby salving the conscience of its naive if well-meaning recruits and harnessing their volunteer efforts to the end of *est*'s own numerical growth and legitimation.[22]

The ambiguity of *est*'s ethic follows from its axiomatic assumptions. These axioms inform *est*'s understanding of ethical evaluation, and fit with the social situation of its graduates. *Est* interprets moral judgment as a function of the individual's subjective tastes, which are not subject to rational justification. And it issues no act-specific moral rules of its own comparable to the Christian's Commandments or the Buddhist's precepts. "We are not a source of rules. *Get it!*" insists a staff member. In the absence of any such rules, personal preference and self-interest tend to determine action more freely. Consciousness of the relativity of one's own

---

[20]*Graduate Review* (September 1977): 5.

[21]Lester Brown, director of the Worldwatch Institute, quoted in Suzanne Gordon, "Let Them Eat *est*," *Mother Jones* (December 1978): 52.

[22]Such critics point to the Project's first-year budget: 57.6% ($518,000) went to pay for a nationwide tour by Erhard to present the Project to graduates, the media, and the public; another 26.6% ($238,000) went to produce Project literature and films; 15% ($135,250) went for the Project's own administrative, organizational, and miscellaneous expenses. This left 0.8% (7,500) to support other hunger organizations that actually feed people. Critics also point to reports of nongraduate Project volunteers being pressured by its *est*-trained staff and assistants to take the *est* training. (See Suzanne Gordon, "Let Them Eat *est*"; also, Mac Margolis and R. Hornung, "An Idea on Every Plate," *Nightfall* (October 1978): 15-22. Cf. the sources cited in note 4 above.

tastes and openness to the asserted interests of immediately present others function to make *est*'s contractual ethic relatively feasible in interpersonal affairs.

On the larger social and political scale, where others are not so immediately present or equally empowered to assert their interests, countervailing considerations of justice and noninjury may be discounted as mere expressions of taste or personal preference. Where a certain agent does not accept the empirical assumption that following conventional social rules invariably results in his own interest being best served, other parties can exert no moral persuasion over against his empirical assessment. They can only seek to sanction him so as to cause him to revise his assessment of the personal consequences following on rule breaking.

Similarly, one may ask what happens if certain of the rules of society themselves appear to one group, *A,* to work systematically to their disadvantage and systematically to advantage another group, *B*? Faced with this question, a young graduate trained as a lawyer declares:

> OK, they [the disadvantaged] aren't experiencing choice right now. *And* they actually chose what they got. They couldn't have gotten anything but what they chose. "Could have" denies reality, like "should have" replaces it with guilt. Let's just talk about "was, is, and will be," or better yet, just "is." If they choose what they got, then they can move on. If they keep bitching about it, they're stuck with it forever.

To be sure, the disadvantaged group, *A,* receives a promise of social change modeled on therapeutic abreaction ("choose, and move on"). But this line of response can also allow the advantaged group, *B*, to discount *A*'s perception as purely subjective and their appeals to justice as mere expressions of personal preference. Invoking *est*'s own version of Locke's "tacit consent" to the social contract, the advantaged may counterclaim, "What you got is what you actually chose. The rules are just the rules. There are no reasons for them. Besides, since they govern the society you joined, you agreed to them beforehand, even if you don't get to vote now. So follow the rules."[23] Unless disadvantaged group *A* is somehow residually empowered to demonstrate empirically to advantaged group *B* that

[23]Compare, for example, one of Werner Erhard's aphorisms: "Life is a ripoff / when you expect to get what you want. / Life works / when you choose what you got. / Actually what you got is what you chose. / To move on, choose it." From Erhard, *Up to Your Ass in Aphorisms* (San Francisco: *est,* 1973), an unpaginated booklet.

changing the rules will better serve *B*'s own interests, then apparently arbitrary or unjust rules remain as they are. In areas of social action where laws and regulations do not reach or, worse, reach in and operate unjustly, we are left without moral leverage to do anything about it.

An *est* graduate responds to the preceding line of criticism from the standpoint of *est*'s ideas of responsibility and the social contract:

> *Q:* How do you respond to people who see *est* being selfish and authoritarian in a way that looks to them like political fascism?
> *A:* I grant that the training itself is an authoritarian, "law and order," "Werner knows best, so do what he says" setup. But you enter into it as a contract aimed at giving you what you want. And I don't see that authoritarian side of the training being held up as a model for society.
> In *est* the majority doesn't make the rules. In the society it does, and *est* supports the majority making the rules by participating in the system, since it's your system. You created it, so you're responsible for it.
>
> *Q:* What about the radical who claims *est* is really only holding up the status quo and helping the middle class adapt to it?
> *A:* I just don't feel like *est* is an adaptation. It's not repressive; it's *ex*pressive. When you accept the way it is and go with it, then it gets better. If you didn't have power before, you can get it. Not just power over your own individual life, but power in the system. You become the cause, instead of staying at the effect of it. Adaptation is saying, "Well, that's fate. It's determined," which is like being at effect.
>
> *Q:* How does that power work? Is it mostly power to change the system or to move up in it? I mean, when you go with it and it gets better, who does it get better *for*? Yourself? Other people who've already got a piece of the action, or everybody?
> *A:* For everybody, I'd say, but I'm not sure I follow you, not if you're saying some people actually have more power because of class and money. I used to think that choice was impossible because it was conditioned by that kind of thing. And even more by random events and all the choices you've already made. That's what psychology's all about. It all depends on whether your mother dropped you on your head. You're programmed. Well, *est* accepts that. Everybody's a total robot. That means everybody can be totally free, too. If I accept it, then I'm free to choose. Now I know I can pick myself up by my boot straps, even if I don't always choose to do it. Before I thought people couldn't do it. Maybe their bootstraps were damaged in infancy or they were lower class and didn't have any.
>
> *Q:* OK. What's the difference then between going with it and going for yourself? The radical sees *est* telling people that if they change their attitude and put out, they can do a little better for themselves than they're doing now and feel better, too, without changing the basic setup.
> *A:* Well, I think that's precisely where we have to start, since that's where we are now. The Revolution hasn't come, and a lot of the people who threw in with it are just the worse for wear now. Werner has talked about beginning with ourselves and coming from service. Forty million people down the road we're gonna see some big changes.

> Aspen [Colorado] is a small example of what can happen when you get enough people in one place who've done the training. They're people with power, too. Twenty percent of the year-round population, the entire town council, the police chief. When people share the same experiences and assumptions and vocabulary from the training, you get a very high level of communication and agreement. That enables graduates to work together very powerfully.
>
> I experience *est* being concerned with how the society is, although it doesn't talk that much about what the society will look like in the future.
>
> *Q:* Wouldn't the radical say maybe that's because *est* doesn't have any model for the future except more of the same?
> *A:* Maybe so, but that's missing the whole point between transforming something and trying to change it.

Est advocates a form of "responsible" social participation to a white middle-class constituency that constitutes the rule-making majority of a society shaped by contractual agreement. It conceives the process of social change according to the paradoxical model of psychological self-transformation. Abreactive transformation appears to be a dynamic category distinct from mere adaption to existing social conditions, whose psychological analogue is repression. Social power derives from psychologically generated personal power. It is contractually exerted toward a utopia suggested more by a hip yet conventionally chic and thriving ski resort than by a communal religious sect or ashram.

Insofar as graduates' social participation is predicated on an ethic of subjectively defined self-interest, one can question how responsive they can be to the moral claims of other smaller and less powerful groups that lie beyond the interpersonal pale of face-to-face communication with them and the possession of interests shaped by social experience specific to the middle class. *Est* rests its ideological rebuttal, first, on the utilitarian assumption that mutual advantage and optimal societal conditions result from the psychologically rational pursuit of self-interest by each person; and the individualist assumption that each person is equally empowered to engage in it. A graduate writes, "Dear Werner, This week while driving around I realized that the world is shaped in such a way as to allow everyone to be on top of it at any given time."[24] The invisible hand extends its reach from the economic to the social-psychological sphere, contractually creating bureaucratic regulations that benefit each and every agent as impartially as do traffic lights. Second, *est* professes a supplementary ethic of compassionate service based on the monistic

---

[24] *Graduate Review* (June 1978): 22.

identification of each individual with every other by reference to the universal "being" they all share. "Transformation of Self as humanity" will make the world work.

Although *est*'s picture of reality may be highly conceptual for a popular movement, it is not a conceptual system, either in its eclectic development or in its presentation in the training. Its plausibility depends less on its philosophical logic than on the experienced power of the training itself in tandem with the social situation of the trainee. Youth of the 1960s who have taken the *est* training span the middle class in their social background and usually hail from the cities and suburbs of major urban areas. Typically, they identified themselves as members of the counterculture while going to college and for several years afterward, often living during this time in modestly hip, dropout style. Now they have come of age and dropped back into the white-collar work force. Consolidating a career and a "relationship" have become their abiding concerns, both of which call for interpersonal fluency and emotional self-management in their white-collar singles milieu. They call, too, for an end to manifestos of radical social change. The need to make it in the world subdues the aspiration to make it over.

Est's ethic responds to the predicament of 1960s youth strongly exposed to the expressive values of the counterculture and conventional private life, yet now faced with the instrumental demands of adult middle-class social and economic life. Its psychologized reintegration of expressive and utilitarian moral ideas also appeals, with differently felt emphases, to older graduates moved by the same contrary cultural impulse. *Est* defines what is intrinsically valuable in self-expressive categories consonant with countercultural ideals. Then it uses these personally fulfilling and expressive ends to justify the routine work and goal achievement of mainstream public life. "Work hard and achieve your goals in order to feel alive and natural," *est* advises in effect. This formula justifies 1960s youth in dropping back into middle-class economic and social life. And it motivates them to lead this life effectively, with an eye to inner satisfaction as well as external success. It also explains these youths' felt difficulty in continuing to be gratified by a countercultural life-style that did not fulfill residual middle-class expectations of social status, material comfort and stability, respectable work, emotional security, or the specifically ethical requirement that one must *deserve* feelings of well-being by virtue of first having achieved certain goals.

The counterculture's expressive ethic suited 1960s youth experimenting with the possibilities of alternative states of consciousness and community in the expectation of a utopian social order to come. Its surrender was brought on by the disappointment of these expectations due both to changes in the society over a decade and to changes in the sort of life-projects that passage from youth to adulthood implies. *Est* has eased this passage and this surrender of one ethical outlook for another. Making the world work through *est* makes sense to the white-collar adult seeking self-fulfillment and still hoping for a better world, yet needing to consolidate a career and interpersonal relationships within the existing social order.

RECRUITMENT STRATEGIES, IDEOLOGY, AND ORGANIZATION IN THE HARE KRISHNA MOVEMENT*

by E. Burke Rochford, Jr.

Studies of recruitment to social movements have focused mainly on the social psychological reasons for joining or the interaction between members and prospective recruits. This paper examines the interrelationship between recruitment strategy, ideology, movement structure, and external social forces in the development of the Hare Krishna movement. A survey of over 200 Hare Krishna devotees shows that opportunistic exploitation of local conditions, rather than ideology or structure, has been responsible for the growth of the Hare Krishna movement in the United States.

WHY PEOPLE ACT collectively has long been a subject of debate among scholars. Yet not until the 1960s, when collective movements became prominent in the United States, did sociologists begin to take a special interest in why some people join movements while others do not. A variety of social psychological attributes were identified to explain why people join movements bent on changing society and/or hearts and minds of their adherents, including: alienation (Judah, 1974; Seeman, 1959, 1975), the search for meaning (Klapp, 1972), deprivation (Davies,

---

*Revised version of a paper presented at the Sociology of Religion Conference on the New Religious Movements, April 1981, Lincoln, England. Appeared in *Social Problems* 29:4 (April 1982). The author thanks Jean Burfoot, Robert M. Emerson, Roderick Harrison, Melvin Seeman, Ralph Turner, and three *Social Problems* reviewers for their comments. Correspondence to: Department of Occupational Therapy, Medical College of Virginia, Virginia Commonwealth University, MCV Station, Richmond, Virginia 23298.

1971; Glock, 1964; Gurr, 1970), tension (Lofland and Stark, 1965), personal problems (Stark and Bainbridge, 1980), and troubles (Rochford, 1978). Common to all these theories is the belief that people with personal troubles join movements to alleviate their sources of distress.[1]

Critics of this perspective argue that many people experience tension, alienation, and other troubles, yet few join movements (Lofland, 1977); Snow and Phillips, 1980; Snow et al., 1980; Turner and Killian, 1972; Wood, 1974). Contact with somebody offering an alternative ideology and/or way of life is essential, as Snow et al. argue:

> However reasonable the underlying assumption that some persons are more susceptible than others to movement participation, that view deflects attention from the fact that recruitment cannot occur without prior contact with a movement agent. The potential participant has to be informed about and introduced into a particular movement (1980:789).

This perspective focuses on how people make contact with participants in a movement, and vice versa. Differential recruitment is seen in interactional and relational terms, rather than cognitive and social psychological terms.[2]

Movement contact is not a random event. Rather, movements develop recruitment strategies for reaching out and contacting prospective recruits. Such strategies are usually seen as emanating from a movement's ideology (Freeman, 1979; Garner, 1972; Wilson, 1973). Yet Snow et al. also suggest that recruitment strategy is strongly influenced by a movement's organizational structure:

> Movements requiring exclusive participation by their members in movement activities will attract members primarily from public places rather than from among extramovement interpersonal associations and networks. Movements which do not require exclusive participation by their members in movement

---

[1]Of course, social movements are only one way of dealing with personal troubles; political activity and psychotherapy are others. See Lofland and Stark (1965) and Richardson and Steward (1978) for discussion of the general orientations used to deal with felt problems; and Emerson and Messinger (1977) on the micropolitics of trouble.

[2]Lofland and Stark (1965) and Snow and Phillips (1980) have shown that cult-affective bonds and intensive interaction are essential to the conversion process. I argue that similar relational factors are likewise crucial to the influence process and the decision to join a particular movement. Barker (1980:394) reports that most potential recruits attended one of the Unification Church's programs in Britain because they were seeking some kind of truth, or because they had an "interest in or curiosity about the person who has talked to them."

activities will attract members primarily from among extramovement interpersonal associations and networks, rather than from public places (1980:796).

I propose that under certain conditions recruitment opportunities and associated recruitment strategies can themselves shape movement ideology and organizational arrangements. In particular, I argue that as external social forces change, a movement's recruitment strategies, ideology and organization also change. In this paper I examine the inter-relationships between recruitment strategy, ideology, movement structure, and external social forces through a study of the growth of the International Society for Krishna Consciousness (ISKCON), popularly known as the Hare Krishna movement.[3] ISKCON's recruitment strategies have been tailored to local conditions rather than tied to the movement's ideology or structure. Such opportunism has played an important role in the development of ISKCON by helping to shape its ideology and structure.

METHOD AND DATA

This paper relies on three sources of data:

(1) I observed the Los Angeles ISKCON community over a five-year period, taking part in day-to-day activities, conducting formal and informal interviews, and on several occasions living in the community as a new recruit and taking part in the Bhakta program for neophyte members.

(2) I reviewed the scholarly literature on ISKCON (Daner, 1976; Johnson, 1970; Judah, 1974; Pilarzyk, 1978), as well as Goswami's (1980) inside account. These sources were supplemented by numerous interviews and conversations with some of the first Krishna devotees.

(3) I conducted a non-random survey of six ISKCON communities in the United States in 1980. Data were collected from 214 adult devotees in Los Angeles, Denver, Chicago, Port Royal (a farm community in Penn-

---

[3]ISKCON is a movement originating in India that is dedicated to spreading Krishna Consciousness throughout the world. The aim of the Krishna devotee is to become self-realized by practicing the bhakti yoga process: chanting the Hare Krishna mantra and living an austere life-style which requires avoiding meat, intoxicants, illicit sex, and gambling. At its height in the early 1970s, ISKCON had approximately 5,000 members throughout the world. This case study of ISKCON focuses only on its growth in the United States. For a discussion of the movement's historical roots in India, see Judah (1974).

sylvania), New York, and Boston. Response to questionnaires[4] ranged from nearly 50 percent for the large communities (Los Angeles and New York) up to more than 90 percent for several of the smaller communities. Based upon estimates by devotees in the movement, my sample represents approximately 10 percent of the total ISKCON population in the United States.

TYPES OF CONTACT WITH ISKCON

There are four general types of contacts between prospective recruits and a movement: (1) self-initiated contacts, where an individual seeks out a movement and/or its representatives; (2) contacts made with movement members in public places; (3) contacts made through social network ties

TABLE 1

Mode of Recruitment by Year of Entry

Year Entered ISKCON	Devotee Networks[a]	Non-Member Networks[b]	Public Places	Other[c]	Total
1967-1971	29%	7%	54%	10%	100% (40)
1972-1974	16%	33%	38%	13%	100% (44)
1975-1976	18%	26%	46%	10%	100% (50)
1977-1978	23%	40%	31%	6%	100% (35)
1979-1980	30%	12%	40%	19%	101% (43)
Mean Percent	(23%)	(23%)	(42%)	(12%)	(100%) (212)

NOTES:

[a]Devotee networks are contacts leading to membership initiated through social ties with persons who are already ISKCON members.

[b]Non-member networks are contacts initiated with movement sympathizers which lead to persons taking up membership with ISKCON.

[c]Contacts coded as "other" include being picked up hitchhiking by ISKCON members, visiting a Krishna community for a school project, and meeting the devotees at an anti-nuclear rally. Since only six percent of the devotee respondents indicated that they initiated contact with the movement on their own (i.e., attended a Sunday feast at a local temple or read ISKCON's literature) we have grouped them in the "other" category.

---

[4]Among the issues addressed by the questionnaire were: how devotees first made contact with ISKCON and/or Krishna Consciousness; factors and circumstances which attracted devotees to the movement and influenced their decision to join; devotee involvements in other social movements prior to ISKCON; and devotee current commitments to ISKCON and Krishna Consciousness.

with friends, acquaintances, and family members who belong to a movement; and (4) non-member network ties where movement sympathizers influence persons in their sphere of social relations to join a movement. Sympathizers are those "who believe in or agree with the goals of a movement or movement organization, but who do not devote any personal resources to it" (Snow et al., 1980:789).

While social ties have played a prominent role in recruiting people to new religious movements (Bibby and Brinkerhoff, 1974; Gerlach and Hine, 1970; Harrison, 1974; Snow et al., 1980; Stark and Bainbridge, 1980),[5] recruitment to ISKCON is an exception. Judah's (1974) study of the San Francisco ISKCON community in the early 1970s found that two-thirds of the 63 devotees sampled made their initial contact with the movement in encounters with other devotees in public places. Only three percent made contact through pre-established social ties. Snow et al. (1980) found only one of the 25 ISKCON devotees they interviewed in Los Angeles and Dallas had been recruited by a former acquaintance.

In contrast, my survey reveals that both social network ties and encounters in public places have been crucial in recruiting new members to ISKCON. Table 1 shows nearly half of the devotees made contact with ISKCON through a social tie with ISKCON members or sympathizers, while 42 percent made contact in public places.[6] Table 1 also reveals historical changes in the contact process. Approximately one-third of the recruits joining prior to 1971 first learned about ISKCON from a friend or family member who had been previously recruited. Devotee network influences declined in importance after 1971, but again became a major source of recruits after 1977. Between 1972 and 1978, non-member networks increasingly became a major source of recruitment.

Table 2 shows recruitment patterns varied widely with locale, as well as over time. The Los Angeles community has expanded mainly through social network ties, while other communities have had greater success

---

[5]The importance of social network ties have also been noted for traditional religions (Stark and Bainbridge, 1980); nonreligious groups and movements (Leahy, 1975; Sills, 1957): job contacts (Granovetter, 1973); seeking an abortionist (Lee, 1969); the diffusion of medical innovations (Coleman *et al.*, 1966); seeking psychiatric treatment (Horwitz, 1977); and the mobilization of political support (Scheingold, 1973).

[6]Sixty-seven devotees surveyed had multiple contacts with Krishna Consciousness prior to joining ISKCON. I coded cases where social ties were involved along with other forms of contact (e.g. public places, self-initiated, or other) as either devotee or non-member network, because the social tie ultimately led to the decision to join.

recruiting in public places.[7] These variations suggest that ISKCON's recruitment strategies are determined locally and not by either ideology or organizational structure. As the following analysis of ISKCON's growth and development shows, leaders and members of the movement have been sensitive to the settings in each of the communities where ISKCON has expanded, developing what must be seen as opportunistic recruitment strategies.

TABLE 2

Mode of Recruitment by Community Where the Devotees Joined ISKCON

Community	Devotee Networks	Non-Member Networks	Public Places	Other	Total
Los Angeles	40%	33%	20%	7%	100% (30)
New York	28%	14%	42%	16%	100% (43)
San Francisco*	13%	0	88%	0	100% (8)
Denver	13%	9%	65%	13%	100% (23)
Boston	21%	16%	47%	16%	100% (19)
Other ISKCON Communities in U.S.	14%	39%	39%	9%	101% (65)
ISKCON Communities in Foreign Countries	31%	15%	39%	15%	100% (26)
Mean Percent	(23%)	(23%)	(42%)	(12%)	(100%) (214)

NOTE:

*Despite the small number of respondents in the present survey who joined ISKCON in San Francisco, these data generally correspond to those collected by Judah (1974:162).

THE SOCIOSPATIAL DIMENSIONS OF ISKCON'S RECRUITMENT STRATEGIES

ISKCON began modestly in New York City in 1965. A.C. Bhaktivedanta Swami Prabhupada, or "the Swami" as he was known by his followers,

---

[7]While Judah (1974) does not say where the devotees in his survey joined, we assume the vast majority did so in San Francisco, since only a handful of Prabhupada's disciples relocated from New York City. Snow et al's (1980) data is more difficult to interpret: they do not report where the devotees they interviewed joined and we cannot make an accurate inference, since by the mid-1970s many had moved to communities other than those in which they had joined.

came to New York from Calcutta on the instruction of his spiritual master to spread Krishna Consciousness to the Western world. With no organizational backing or followers to help him begin his Hare Krishna movement, Prabhupada first tried to gain a following among the elderly on New York's West Side. Unsuccessful, he turned to the youth living on the Bowery on the Lower East Side. As one of his early followers explained:

> I think most of the teachers from India up to that time had older followers, and sometimes wealthy widows would provide a source of income. But Swamiji changed right away to the younger people. The next thing that happened was that Bill Epstein [an early follower of Prabhupada] and others began talking about how it would be better for the Swami to come downtown to the Lower East Side. Things were really happening down there, and somehow they weren't happening uptown (Goswami, 1980:66).

Most of the Swami's early followers were musicians and bohemians that lived in or frequented the Bowery (Goswami, 1980:72). Their interests in Prabhupada were often far from philosophical: many were only interested in fitting Krishna Consciousness into their own life-style:

> Persons were coming to see what Prabhupada was doing so they could incorporate it into their own ways. Some who were into drugs saw what Prabhupada was doing in those terms. Others like myself were more impersonalist (in their philosophy) and were looking to see what the Swami was saying in terms of this. I mean, a lot of people came because of the music. People came for a lot of different reasons but not because they understood what Prabhupada was doing and what the philosophy was about. I didn't know what Prabhupada was about. I mean, we understood about one-millionth of what Prabhupada was saying (personal interview).

Prabhupada recognized that his early followers were not interested in forsaking their life-style to become Krishna conscious. He did not try to restrict their activities, and did not insist that followers give up meat, intoxicants, illicit sex and gambling. Nor did he require them to live with him in his temple. The majority of his followers continued to live and work in the surrounding community and helped to support the temple through their earnings. Only a few of the most downtrodden ever lived with Prabhupada in the temple, and next to none of them stayed on to become his disciples (Goswami, 1980:124). ISKCON at this time had few spiritual practices or programs which in any way restricted the Bohemian life-style of Prabhupada's followers:

> You have to remember that [in these early days in New York] there was only the chanting, kirtanas [music and dancing], the Swami, and prasadam [spiritual

food]. That was all, it was a simple process not complicated and culturally involved like it is now (personal interview).

Given the structural openness of ISKCON in those first days in New York and the availability of social networks as a means to disseminate information about the movement, we would expect that social ties would serve as the primary means of recruitment. Indeed, during Prabhupada's first year in New York City he initiated nineteen disciples; of the fourteen for which information is available (Goswami, 1980), eight met Prabhupada through network ties. Only six encountered Prabhupada or his disciples on the street or in nearby Tompkins Park where they chanted. Public chanting as a recruitment strategy was not well developed at the time.

ISKCON changed radically after it moved its headquarters in 1967 to the emerging "hippie" mecca, the Haight-Ashbury district of San Francisco.

> During the first week of the new year a letter arrived from Mukunda [one of Prabhupada's first disciples in New York]. He had rented a storefront in the heart of the Haight-Ashbury district, on Frederick Street. "We are busy converting it into a temple now," he wrote. And Prabhupada announced: "I shall go immediately." Mukunda had told of a "Gathering of the Tribes" in San Francisco's Haight-Ashbury. Thousands of hippies were migrating from all over the country to the very neighborhood where Mukunda had rented the storefront. It was a youth renaissance much bigger than what was going on in New York City (Goswami, 1980:270).

Haight-Ashbury was a fertile environment for ISKCON's recruitment efforts; during its first two years in San Francisco, an estimated 150 to 200 persons were converted (Johnson, 1970:4).

The location of the new temple brought potential recruits literally to the doorstep.

> The large scale dislocation accompanying the migration of young people to the Haight-Ashbury created *a large, continually walking gathering of unattached persons*. Several members noted that they had first discovered the Krishna Consciousness movement by accident—by walking by the temple or hearing the mantra performed in the park. . . . The immediate area around the temple was characterized by extensive foot-traffic compared to other sections of the city. Below the large "Hare Krishna" sign on the outside of the temple was a smaller placard which states: "Stay High All the Time, Discover Eternal Bliss" (Johnson, 1970:13 emphasis added).

Cavan (1972:94) similarly observed that the Haight-Ashbury in the late 1960s was crowded with youth taking part in the hippie practice of "just being," that is, meandering "through the day, caught up in no particular thing and in the company of no particular person."

With public places providing such an abundance of potential recruits, chanting parties were sent into the streets of the Haight-Ashbury and nearby Berkeley to spread Prabhupada's message. These encounters between the devotees and hippies were central to ISKCON's expansion during this early period. Social network ties yielded relatively few converts in San Francisco: Prabhupada's first disciples had only recently relocated from New York, and the majority of those recruited in Haight-Ashbury had weak social ties in the community.

The Unification Church (UC) experienced similar problems in trying to recruit through social networks when it first moved from Oregon to San Francisco in the early 1960s:

> In San Francisco [the church] was unable to grow for a considerable time because its members were strangers lacking social ties to potential recruits. Indeed, some new recruits continued to come out of the original Eugene [Oregon] network. Only when the cult found ways to connect with other newcomers to San Francisco and develop serious relationships with them did recruitment resume. But in relying on befriending lonely newcomers, the Moonies were unable to grow rapidly. New members did not open new social networks through which the cult could spread (Stark and Bainbridge, 1980:1379).

Unlike the UC, ISKCON had a readily available source of potential recruits when it moved to San Francisco. Rather than waiting to establish social relations within the community, the devotees took to recruiting on the streets outside the temple—an option not available to the UC several years earlier.

While the environment in San Francisco encouraged recruiting in public it also shaped the emerging structural arrangements within ISKCON. In New York, the structure of the movement had been fluid and open to surrounding worldly influences. Indeed, it was this relative openness that helped ISKCON grow prior to moving to San Francisco. Only after the move did a more closed, communal structure develop. Many of the young people joining ISKCON in San Francisco had only recently migrated to the area and hence were without stable or permanent residence in the area. Given the living situation of these hippie recruits, ISKCON's communal structure emerged as a means to hold those attracted to Krishna Consciousness.

EXPANSION AND ADAPTATION

ISKCON's San Francisco organization served as a model for devotees who were deployed to other cities to establish Krishna temples and recruit new members. But while a closed communal structure emerged in each of ISKCON's communities, it was modified to meet local opportunities for recruitment. For example, the socio-spatial environment encountered by ISKCON when it moved into Los Angeles in 1970 was quite different from that of Haight-Ashbury. Rather than locating in Hollywood or the Venice Beach area, where countercultural youth of Los Angeles could be found in large numbers, ISKCON established its community in a middle-class residential area. This environment offered few opportunities for the devotees to confront people, and especially youth, on the street around the temple. While chanting parties were sent out into the community, they had little success in persuading people to come to the temple and participate in the Krishna life-style. Thus, the ISKCON community in Los Angeles focused their recruitment efforts on the friends and family of existing members. Unlike recruits in San Francisco, most of those recruited in Los Angeles were from the local area. Being well-connected socially, the devotees used these ties to disseminate information about the movement and recruit new members.

While there were local variations in ISKCON's structure, the Krishna life-style in general afforded few opportunities for maintaining contacts with the outside society. Isolation was accelerated in the early 1970s as ISKCON came under attack by deprogrammers and other opponents of cults. Social ties with persons outside the movement increasingly came to be seen as sources of potential trouble, rather than as possible avenues of recruitment (Rochford, 1976). During this period, and up until Prabhupada's death in 1977, ISKCON was more closed to the outside society than at any other time in its North American history. Growth was sustained only by the proselytizing of movement sympathizers.

THE ROLE OF MOVEMENT SYMPATHIZERS IN THE RECRUITMENT PROCESS

As a movement becomes more structurally closed and members concern themselves exclusively with its activities, recruitment through pre-established social ties becomes more difficult. If adherents are cut off from their previous social relationships, a movement must disseminate information about its mission in other ways. Snow et al. (1980: 796) argue that movements like ISKCON, which demand total commitment from members, are "structurally compelled" to recruit new members in public. While this may be true for core adherents, who live within the context of the group, a larger body of movement supporters also contribute to the recruitment process. Table 2 shows that as ISKCON became increasingly closed to society, it relied on movement sympathizers to promote its cause and encourage potential recruits to seek out ISKCON. While devotees continued to have some success recruiting in public places, the relative importance of movement sympathizers in the recruitment process grew significantly.

Little or no research has been done on the role that movement sympathizers play in the recruitment process. Snow et al. (1980) discuss why sympathizers do not participate in movement activities, but they did not consider the role of sympathizers in influencing others to participate. Yet many devotees first learned about ISKCON through a friend or relation who, while not a member of ISKCON, was nevertheless knowledgeable and sympathetic toward the movement and/or its philosophy. Two devotees who responded to my questionnaire described how they first made contact with ISKCON:

> My father received a book from a devotee in the airport and brought it home. He told me to read it and try chanting Hare Krishna. He brought me to various temples and was also interested in Krishna Consciousness.

> I studied religious studies with a noted religious scholar who is actively involved with ISKCON. I also had student friends in his courses who were likewise familiar with the philosophy and/or had been to an ISKCON temple.

Other devotees reported that, while they first made contact with the movement in a public place, it wasn't until they were introduced to the movement by a non-devotee friend that they seriously considered ISKCON:

> I first saw the devotees chant at city hall in 1968 and I took an invitation card [to the Sunday feast]. The next Sunday I went to the feast. I didn't like it much but through the years I didn't mind the devotees as much and would sometimes look at their literature. In 1971, a friend took me twice to the temple, and I enjoyed the food and friendship very much. I joined right after that.

> I encountered the devotees on the street a few times but was very *unimpressed.* Later some friends of mine [who were not involved with ISKCON] took to chanting and influenced me. Six months later I joined the movement.

While most sympathizers have no direct ties to ISKCON, some people were recruited only after making contact with a former devotee.

> One blooped devotee [former ISKCON member] came and got a job where I was working as an electronic technician. He introduced me to Krishna. He took

> me to the feast a number of times and encouraged me to chant and be more serious about becoming Krishna conscious. He had a family, a wife and four kids, and I was very attracted to them because of their higher consciousness and activities.

Non-member networks can be important to the recruitment process in more direct ways as well. Several devotees first came to the Krishna community at the urging of a friend or spouse who also joined. In some instances, the non-devotee initiating the contact could be seen as a movement sympathizer. Other cases seem less clear:

> I married a man who had previous contact with the devotees and who wanted to become a devotee himself. We joined together one year later.

> My friend took me for dinner at the temple and we both became involved. As it turned out we joined together and will probably be married.

As the above responses to my questionnaire suggest, potential recruits can come into contact with a movement in ways other than through direct contact with core adherents. As a movement grows and becomes more visible within society, indirect means of contact can become increasingly important. Furthermore, as adherents defect from the movement they may become vehicles by which others come into contact with the movement's ideology and lifestyle.

TABLE 3

*Percent of Devotees Who See Their Community as More or Less Open to Outside Worldly Influences**

Community	More Open to Outside Influence	Less Open to Outside Influence	Neither	Total	
Los Angeles	53%	0%	47%	100%	(45)
New York	27%	9%	64%	100%	(44)
Boston	31%	8%	62%	101%	(13)
Chicago	28%	11%	61%	100%	(18)
Denver	7%	3%	90%	100%	(29)
Port Royal (Farm Community)	15%	23%	62%	100%	(13)
Mean Percent	(30%)	(7%)	(63%)	(100%)	(162)

Note:
*Includes those devotees who have been in the movement for more than one year.

RECENT CHANGES IN ISKCON'S RECRUITMENT STRATEGIES

As a movement develops in a cultural setting, its relationship with the surrounding society changes. In the extreme cases, a movement may become institutionalized, and thereby no longer be a social movement at all (Messinger, 1955; Turner and Killian, 1972; Wilson, 1973; Zald, 1970). Usually, the changes are less dramatic and affect only certain ideological and structural features of the movement.

By the mid-1970s, ISKCON was declining as a social movement. Few recruits were being attracted, and Prabhupada's death in 1977, with the resulting politicization of ISKCON, resulted in an exodus of many long-time Krishna devotees.[8] In response to these developments, ISKCON'S ideology and organizational structure changed. Many ISKCON communities relaxed their communal structure and membership criteria, and opened themselves to influences from the outside society. As evidence of the trend: (1) Relationships with non-devotees outside the community are becoming more common. One-fourth of the devotees surveyed said they had close friendships with persons outside the movement. (2) Thirty percent of devotees surveyed felt that their community was "more open to outside worldly influences" than during their early days in ISKCON (Table 3). Only seven percent felt that the community in which they were residing was now less open to outside influences. (3) In those communities where social networks have served as a rich source of recruits (for example, Los Angeles and New York), devotees are both more involved in nondevotee relationships and see their community as more open to outside influence.

Since 1976, the Los Angeles ISKCON community has been the most open to influences from the surrounding urban environment. Automo-

---

[8]With Prabhupada's death ISKCON was reorganized in 1978. Prabhupada reportedly appointed 11 of his closest disciples as gurus just prior to his death. Each guru was placed in charge of a particular "zone," responsible for initiating new disciples to Krishna Consciousness and overseeing the affairs of ISKCON communities in his territory. Within a year following Prabhupada's death, however, ISKCON faced serious succession problems as many long-time ISKCON members challenged the legitimacy of the gurus to lead the movement. Many of these devotees are now overtly questioning the appointment of the gurus claiming that Prabhupada, in fact, never appointed them to their positions. This continuing debate within ISKCON has led to factionalism, splintering, the defection of many long-time devotees from ISKCON and the purging of others by the leadership (Rochford, 1982).

biles, televisions, furniture, newspapers, and weekly news magazines have become commonplace within the community. An attempt by the leaders to purge these objects, especially television, in 1980 was largely unsuccessful. A number of Los Angeles devotees hold jobs outside the ISKCON community, and an increasing number are living on the outskirts of the community where they are less under the control of the leaders.

TABLE 4

Mode of Recruitment by Year Entered ISKCON for the Los Angeles Community

Year Entered ISKCON	Devotee Networks	Non-Member Networks	Public Places	Other	Total
1969-1971	33%	0	69%	0	(100%) (3)
1972-1976	27%	47%	13%	13%	(100%) (15)
1977-1980	58%	25%	17%	0	(100%) (12)
					(30)

In keeping with Los Angeles' image throughout the movement, devotees in other ISKCON communities refer to it as "Loose Angeles," implying that devotees there are too involved in the activities of the dominant society ("Maya") and are therefore not adhering to the Krishna Consciousness process. The temple president of one of ISKCON's communities in Texas accounted for the large fringe community of former, or marginal, ISKCON devotees in Los Angeles by pointing to the lack of preaching in that community:

> There is a definite reason for the growth of the fringe community in L.A. The fact is that the householders who are living out there simply have it too easy. They are too comfortable. There is no emphasis on going out and preaching, distributing Prabhupada's books. This movement is based upon preaching. Without maintaining the proper preaching attitude one loses touch with Krishna Consciousness and falls into the fringe. Let them emphasize the preaching like they do in other [ISKCON] communities and all this nonsense will go away. That is the essence of this movement (personal interview).

The structural openness of the Los Angeles community in recent years has increased recruitment through devotee network ties. As table 4 shows, devotee networks have become more important than movement sympathizers in the recruitment process in Los Angeles.[9]

This emphasis on network recruitment seems likely to grow with ISKCON's recent decision to try to build a congregation of "patron members" and "life members" whose commitment to Krishna Consciousness and ISKCON varies from mainly financial support to more or less regular participation. This strategy, aimed at recruiting "part-time" devotees, was summed up by a devotee of nine years:

> If [potential recruits] can only accept five percent, fine, then we should encourage them so that they can accept more, make more progress. If a man drinks beer but has some feeling for Krishna Consciousness then we should attempt to increase his feeling, not discourage him because he drinks. In the past we would have criticized, now that we have matured we see the need to encourage part-time devotees. We now need to build up our congregational devotees, encourage them. In this way we can spread Krishna Consciousness (personal interview).[10]

While there are a number of young persons becoming patron members of ISKCON, there are also a growing number of "life members," usually immigrants from India, who contribute financially toward ISKCON's support. In Los Angeles, the local East Indian community uses the ISKCON temple each Sunday to worship and take part in the vegetarian feast. Their involvement is for the most part limited to these Sunday services.

Thus, as the boundaries between ISKCON and the dominant social structure have broken down, recruitment through social networks has once again become possible—just as it was during ISKCON's early days in New York City. ISKCON communities continue to become more structurally open, and as public recruitment declines due to the demise of countercultural areas like Haight-Ashbury, we expect that recruitment will increasingly occur through pre-established social ties.[11]

---

[9]Recruitment in the New York and Boston communities has also shifted away from public places toward devotee networks.

[10]The Unification Church has made a similar attempt to build a congregation of less committed members. Barker (1980:393) reports that since 1978 there has been a growing number of "Home Church" members in Britain: "These are people who accept the truth of the Divine Principle but who remain associate members living at home rather than devoting their whole lives to the movement."

[11]ISKCON's declining ability to recruit in public has also been affected by recent changes in the devotees' use of these settings. After Prabhupada's death public places were used more as financial centers where organizational commodities such as candles, records, candy and other products were sold as a means to maintain ISKCON financially. Since public places now serve as settings where customers are sought rather than prospective

SUMMARY AND CONCLUSIONS

No social movement emerges with a fully developed ideology, set of goals, or organizational structure (Turner and Killian, 1972). These evolve as the movement develops and expands within a cultural setting. From tenuous beginnings in New York, ISKCON's ideology and structure took shape as the movement began to attract committed adherents in Haight-Ashbury. But neither the movement's religious beliefs and practices, nor its life-style, determined its recruitment strategies as it spread through the United States in the 1970s. Instead, the success of ISKCON's communities depended on the ability of devotees to adapt recruitment strategies to specific, local socio-spatial environments. In order to take advantage of the local lines of access, ISKCON's communities modified the movement's structure and ideology. Thus, analysis of ISKCON's expansion suggests that there is no fixed linear relationship between ideology and structure on the one hand, and the recruitment strategies devised by a social movement to assure its growth on the other.

The growth and expansion of ISKCON highlights two additional issues:

(1) Opportunism lies at the heart of efforts by world-transforming movements to recruit new members to their cause. Such movements see social change as resulting from recruiting and converting the masses to their values and way of life (Bromley and Shupe, 1979). Hence, leaders and members alike face considerable pressure to recruit more persons into the movement. But despite the importance placed on recruitment within world-transforming movements, there are external constraints which limit their ability to win new converts. All world-transforming movements challenge the values of the prevailing social order. Growing awareness of these movements' objectives often generates a public reaction which restricts their access to legitimate avenues of promoting their cause and recruiting new adherents. If the movement is seen as peculiar, as is the case with ISKCON, these lines of access may be further curtailed (Turner and Killian, 1972). The resulting dilemma posed for world-transforming movements necessitates that they become opportunistic. While my findings demonstrate ISKCON's opportunism, a similar pattern has been discovered in other world-transforming movements, such

recruits, recruitment is of secondary importance. For a more detailed discussion see Rochford (1982).

as the Unification Church (Bromley and Shupe, 1979; Lofland, 1966), the Children of God (Davis, 1981), and Nichiren Shoshu (Snow, 1976, 1979).

(2) My analysis of differential recruitment processes has identified the potentially critical role of movement sympathizers. This study further suggests that movement sympathizers can be instrumental to the growth of *exclusive* movements. Given the intense and total commitment demanded of members in exclusive movements, many who come into contact with such movements remain outside the organization despite their attraction to its ideology. Conversely, for less demanding and inclusive movements like Nichiren Shoshu (Snow, 1976), persons with an equal degree of sympathy would probably be granted formal membership. As a result of these differing membership criteria, I expect that member networks are more critical to the expansion of inclusive movements, while non-member networks are more critical to exclusive movements. Furthermore, as an exclusive movement becomes structurally more open to the outside society, and more inclusive in its membership, the role of network ties in recruiting will change toward a greater reliance on member networks.

REFERENCES

Barker, Eileen
1980 "Free to choose? Some thoughts on the Unification Church and other new religious movements." *Clergy Review* 65:365-68, 392-98.

Bibby, Reginald W. and Merlin Brinkerhoff
1974 "When proselytizing fails: An organizational analysis." *Sociological Analysis* 35:189-200.

Bromley, David and Anson Shupe Jr.
1979 *Moonies in America: Cult, Church, and Crusade*. Beverly Hills: Sage.

Cavan, Sherri
1972 *Medical Innovation: A Diffusion Study*. Indianapolis: Bobbs-Merrill.

Daner, Francine
1976 *The American Children of Krishna: A Study of the Hare Krishna Movement*. New York: Holt, Rinehart and Winston.

Davies, James
1971 *When Men Revolt and Why*. New York: Free Press.

Davis, Rex
1981 "Where have the Children gone?" Paper presented at the Sociology of Religion Conference on New Religious Movements, Lincoln, England. April.

Emerson, Robert and Sheldon Messinger
1977 "The micro-politics of trouble." *Social Problems* 25:121-34.

Freeman, Jo
1979 "Resource mobilization and strategy: A model for analyzing social movement organization actions." Pp. 167-89 in Mayer Zald and John McCarthy, eds. *The Dynamics of Social Movements*. Cambridge, Mass: Winthrop Publishing.

Garner, Roberta Ash
1972 *Social Movements in America*. Chicago: Rand McNally College Publishing Co.

Gerlach, Luther and Virginia Hine
1970 *People, Power and Change: Movements of Social Transformation*. Indianapolis: Bobbs-Merrill.

Glock, Charles
1964 "The role of deprivation in the origin and evolution of religious groups." Pp. 24-36 in R. Lee and M. Marty, eds., *Religion and Social Conflict*. New York: Oxford University Press.

Goswami Satsvarupa dasa
1980 *Planting the Seed*. Los Angeles: Bhaktivedanta Book Trust.

Granovetter, Mark
1973 "The strength of weak ties." *American Journal of Sociology* 78:1360-80.

Gurr, Ted
1970 *Why Men Rebel*. Princeton, NJ: Princeton University Press.

Harrison, Michael
1974 "Sources of recruitment to Catholic Pentecostalism." *Journal for the Scientific Study of Religion* 13:49-64.

Horwitz, Allen
1977 "The pathways into psychiatric treatment: Some differences between men and women." *Journal of Health and Social Behavior* 18:169-78.

Johnson, Gregory
1970 "Counterculture in microcosm: A study of Hare Krishna in San Francisco." Unpublished paper, department of sociology, University of California, Berkeley.

Judah, Stillson
1974 *Hare Krishna and the Counterculture*. New York: Wiley.

Klapp, Orrin
1972 *Currents of Unrest*. New York: Holt, Rinehart and Winston.

Leahy, Peter
1975 "The anti-abortion movement: Testing a theory of the rise and fall of social movements." Ph.D. dissertation, Syracuse University.

Lee, Nancy H.
1969 *The Search for an Abortionist*. Chicago: University of Chicago Press.

Lofland, John
1966 *Doomsday Cult*. Englewood Cliffs, NJ: Prentice-Hall.

1977 "Becoming a world-saver revisited." *American Behavioral Scientist* 20: 805-19.

Lofland, John and Rodney Stark
1965 "Becoming a world-saver: A theory of conversion to a deviant perspective." *American Sociological Review* 30:862-74.

Messinger, Sheldon
1955 "Organizational transformation: A case study of a declining social movement." *American Sociological Review* 20:3-10.

Pilarzyk, Thomas
1978 "Conversion and alternation processes in the youth culture." *Pacific Sociological Review* 21:379-405.

Richardson, James and Mary Stewart
1978 "Conversion process models and the Jesus movement." Pp. 24-42 in James Richardson, ed., *Conversion Careers: In and Out of the New Religions*. Beverly Hills: Sage.

Rochford, E. Burke, Jr.
1976 "World view resocialization: Commitment building processes and the Hare Krishna movement." Masters thesis, University of California, Los Angeles.

1982 "A study of recruitment and transformation processes in the Hare Krishna movement." Ph.D. dissertation, University of California, Los Angeles.

Seeman, Melvin
1959 "On the meaning of alienation." *American Sociological Review* 24: 783-91.

1975 "Alienation studies." *Annual Review of Sociology* 1:91-122.

Sheingold, Carl
1973 "Social networks and voting: The resurrection of a research agenda." *American Sociological Review* 38:712-28.

Sills, David L.
1957 *The Volunteers.* Glencoe, IL: Free Press.

Snow, David
1976 *The Nichiren Shoshu Buddhist movement in America: A sociological examination of its value orientation, recruitment efforts, and spread."* Ann Arbor, Michigan: University Microfilms.

1979 "A dramaturgical analysis of movement accommodation: Building idiosyncrasy credit as a movement mobilization strategy." *Symbolic Interaction* 2(2): 23-44.

Snow, David and Cynthia Phillips
1980 "The Lofland-Stark conversion model: A critical reassessment." *Social Problems* 27:430-47.

Snow, David, Louis Zurcher, Jr. and Sheldon Ekland-Olson
1980 "Social networks and social movements: A microstructural approach to differential recruitment." *American Sociological Review* 45:787-801.

Stark, Rodney and William S. Bainbridge
1980 "Networks of faith: Interpersonal bonds and recruitment to cults and sects." *American Journal of Sociology* 85:1376-95.

Turner, Ralph and Lewis Killian
1972 *Collective Behavior.* Englewood Cliffs, NJ: Prentice-Hall.

Wilson, John
1973 *Introduction to Social Movements.* New York: Basic Books.

Wood, James
1974 *The Source of American Student Activism.* Lexington, MA: Lexington Books.

Zald, Mayer
1970 *Organizational Change: The Political Economy of the YMCA.* Chicago: University of Chicago Press.

SUBGROUPS IN DIVINE LIGHT MISSION MEMBERSHIP: A COMMENT ON DOWNTON

by Frans Derks
and Jan M. van der Lans

IN AN ARTICLE in the 1980 winter issue of the *Journal for the Scientific Study of Religion*, Downton presents an "evolutionary theory of spiritual conversion and commitment." He differentiates twenty-seven steps in the conversion process and in the growth of commitment to Divine Light Mission ideology. In this article we do not criticize Downton's theory, although we think it problematic to identify as many stages as he did. We only want to point out that Downton's group of respondents differs in at least one important way from Divine Light Mission members we have interviewed, and that this difference has some important theoretical implications.

Although Downton does not give exact information on his data, we may infer some characteristics of his respondents from his theoretical model and from data in *Sacred Journeys* (Downton, 1979). They may be typified as young people—mean age 23, range 19 to 29 years (Downton, 1979: 229)—who were disillusioned with conventional values and religion as a result of participation in the counterculture. The use of psychedelic drugs gave them some hints of a spiritual reality that attracted them. Slowly they came to identify themselves in spiritual terms. "An image of themselves as 'spiritual seekers' became the outward feature of a new ego-ideal" (Downton, 1980: 385-386). They created a spiritual ego-ideal and self-image. However, because of their unrealistically high spiritual ideals, they became doubtful about their capacity to realize this spiritual self without the help of a teacher or guru.

Through contacts with Divine Light Mission members, they heard about the movement. They were struck by the differences between their own unsuccessful attempts to live the spiritual life and the sense of joy, peace, and commitment in the behavior of members. This behavior made them open to accept the movement's problem-solving perspective and influenced them to join the movement. They did so, and at that moment their locus of identity shifted from their ego to their spiritual self. Because Divine Light Mission equates the spiritual self with God and with Guru Maharaj Ji, this shift implied surrender to the guru. They became "devotees" and increased their investments in, and sacrifices for, the movement. Their final sacrifice is "mortification of the ego," because it implies a total modification of identity. It is the final stage of surrender that results in total adherence to the movement.

Although we agree with Downton's conception of conversion as a gradual process requiring a continous intensification of commitment, we think that he is not correct in treating his respondents as one uniform group.

From Downton's line of thinking we infer that his respondents experienced a growing disillusion with conventional values and religion through participation in the counterculture and through the use of psychedelic drugs. This seems to hold for all his respondents—at least, he does not state the contrary. In contrast, we were able to distinguish two subgroups within our group of Divine Light Mission respondents: those who joined before 1975 (n=10) and those who joined after that date (n=9). The former fit very well with Downton's description of the former drug-consuming participant in the counterculture. The latter do not; they were in no way dropouts from society. On the contrary: their educational and job-careers were quite normal. Hardly any of them ever used drugs, and most of them did not feel alienated from society. Their reasons for joining, and in fact their whole life-histories and the way in which they became affiliated, differed considerably from those who joined earlier. Many pre-1975 converts gave as a reason for joining that they could not imagine themselves becoming what they called "responsible members of society." Many post-1975 converts mentioned personal problems (for instance, loneliness), or the impossibility of expressing their religious feelings through participation in the existing, traditional, religious institutions.

These changes in membership characteristics coincided with organizational and ideological changes within the movement (which are extensively described in Downton, 1979: 185-210). After 1975 the movement appealed to a different kind of person, because it came to emphasize other elements in its ideology. The pre-1975 members had joined the movement because they had been attracted by Divine Light Mission's Hinduistic ideology that offered them an opportunity to legitimate their already existing rejection of the Western utilitarian world view. However, in 1975 there was a schism within the movement. Guru Maharaj Ji's mother did not approve of his marriage to his American secretary and dismissed him as the movement's leader. The American and European adherents did not accept his dismissal and remained faithful to him. The movement split up into an Eastern and Western branch. The Western branch tried to smother its Hinduistic background and started to emphasize Guru Maharaj Ji as a personification of ideology. This change in ideology may be illustrated by the fact that since then, Guru Maharaj Ji's father, Shri Hans, the movement's founder, became less important and was much less referred to in the movement's journal. It may further be illustrated by the differences in initiation policy before and after 1975. Before 1975 it was sufficient to have a desperate longing for "Knowledge" (in the sense Divine Light Mission uses this term); after 1975 one had to accept Guru Maharaj Ji as a personal saviour in order to become a member.

Many pre-1975 members had problems in adapting themselves to this new line of thinking, and some of them left the movement. But many new members were attracted. One of the characteristics of these new members is that they had been very religious in their preadolescent years. In those years their religiosity had been characterized by the experiential dimension; they had felt a warm personal relation with Jesus. But this religiosity had disappeared, partially because they had been taught—by their religion teachers at secondary school—to think in a rational way about religious matters. They lost their capacity for religious experiences, and as a result, the Christian religion lost its plausibility for them. In Divine Light Mission they recognized, during "Satsang," the religious experiences they had had during their childhood. They came to see Guru Maharaj Ji and their relationship with him as a source of continuous religious experience. This made Guru Maharaj Ji much more important for them than he had been for the pre-1975 members.

The research findings on which we based the present comment are supported by observations made by other researchers, to which Downton surprisingly does not refer. This is the more surprising since Downton himself, on the concluding pages of the final chapter of his book, states as his expectation for the future that Divine Light Mission will no longer recruit from the counterculture but from (1) the group of youth who are disillusioned with conventional religion, (2) college students who are traditionally more willing to explore the esoteric and the novel, and (3) those who are disenchanted with other Eastern movements.

In a reply to Nelson's comment on his paper in the *Review of Religious Research*, Tom Pilarzyk states (1979: 110):

> one indication of DLM's slow but increasing differentiation from its youth culture origins is the present shift in its recruitment and membership patterns. Stoner and Parke (1977) also noted this shift in type of religious seekers that have more recently become members, partly due to the movement's new image promoted by its leaders. Present members do remain part of a larger metaphysical cultic milieu but are less likely to be countercultural types.

The passage in Stoner and Parke (1977) to which Pilarzyk refers, reads as follows:

> Once Divine Light proselytized among druggies and dropouts promising a constant high without drugs, much as the Krishnas did. But a contemporary premie recruit is more likely to be a student, musician, artist, lawyer, or teacher—a well-educated man or woman who is, or is destined to become, a solid member of the community (page 34; quoted from the 1979 Penguin Books pocket edition).

Finally, Foss and Larkin in their chapter in Harry M. Johnson's *Religious Change and Continuity* (1979) say that from about 1973, Divine Light Mission and similar groups began to attract persons who had not participated in the counterculture. Although we do not agree with their opinion that these later converts are characterized by their awareness of having a "low exchange value in the sexual marketplace," we think that the fact that Foss and Larkin also differentiate two subgroups in Divine Light Mission membership supports our conclusion that we should not treat Divine Light Mission members as one uniform group—as Downton did.

The findings reported in this comment have some important theoretical implications. First of all, they remind us of the limits of research results in this field. Because these movements are "living" religions, they adapt themselves to societal changes. We should not conclude too soon that by now we know why people join Divine Light Mission or similar movements. We may indeed know why and how people joined in the early seventies, but recruitment and membership patterns may change over time. Obviously explanations that try to relate the growth of these movements to countercultural phenomena (for example, Bellah, 1976; or Anthony and Robbins, 1974) have become less relevant to the contemporary situation. Moreover, these results make us more sensitive to the risks of undue generalizations: there are large inter- and intra-group differences. Second, when movements change their organizational or ideological characteristics or their recruitment tactics, we should incorporate this in our evaluation. The Children of God are mainly being blamed for their use of "flirty fishing" as a deceptive proselytization method although they already existed many years before they "invented" it (and after the fact constructed a theological legitimation). John Lofland's epilogue section to his revised edition of *Doomsday Cult* (1977) is another good example. It may well be that "destructive cults" evolve into highly respected churches, or that "marginal" movements become "integrative" (or vice versa). Third, we formulated that the changes in membership pattern *coincided* with organizational and ideological changes within Divine Light Mission. It is very difficult to find out in which way these changes are related. However it might be very worthwhile to look at other movements and see if similar phenomena happened in them. This will not only be relevant for our understanding of these movements, but also for our theorizing on the dynamics of religious systems in general.

REFERENCES

Anthony D., and Th. Robbins
1974 "The Meher Baba movement: its effect on Postadolescent Social Alienation." In I. Zaretsky, and M. Leone, *Religious movements in contemporary America*. Princeton: Princeton University Press. 479-511.

Bellah, R.
1976 "New Religious Consciousness and the Crisis in Modernity." In Glock, and R. Bellah, *The New Religious Consciousness*. Berkeley: University of California Press. 333-53.

Downton, James V. Jr.
1979 *Sacred Journeys: The Conversion of Young Americans to Divine Light Mission*. New York: Columbia University Press.

1980 "An Evolutionary Theory of Spiritual Conversion and Commitment: The case of Divine Light Mission." *Journal for the Scientific Study of Religion* 19:4:381-96.

Foss, Daniel A., and Ralph W. Larkin
1979 "The Roar of the Lemming: Youth, Post-movement Groups, and the Life Construction Crisis." In Harry M. Johnson, *Religious Change and Continuity*. In Harry M. Johnson, *Religious Change and Continuity*. San Francisco: Jossey Bass Publishers.

Lofland, John
1977 *Doomsday Cult*. New York: Irvington.

Pilarzyk, Thomas
1979 "The Cultic Resilience of the Divine Light Mission: A Reply to Nelson." *Review of Religious Research* 21:1:109-12.

Stoner, Carroll, and Jo Anne Park
1977 *All God's Children*. Radnor PA: Chilton Book Co.

THE ONES WHO GOT AWAY: PEOPLE WHO ATTEND UNIFICATION CHURCH WORKSHOPS AND DO NOT BECOME MEMBERS

by Eileen Barker

IT IS FREQUENTLY asserted that conversion to the Unification Church is the result of brainwashing—that those who become members do so because they have been subjected to some kind of irresistible mind control while attending a Unification workshop. Such assertions do not, however, offer any explanation as to why more than ninety percent of those who attend the two-day introductory workshops in Britain (and most other countries in the West) do *not* end up as UC members. The existence of this large, unconverted majority suggests that there must be a differential susceptibility to the "lure of the cult" and that independent factors (that is, factors brought to the workshop by the guests) must be at least as crucial as the workshop in determining the final outcome.

This paper attempts an analysis of such factors by supplementing the more familiar question, "What are the values, hopes, and past experiences that predispose a person towards becoming a member of the Unification Church?" with the further, complementary question, "What are the factors that 'protect' the vast majority of those who attend Unification workshops from falling victim to the allegedly coercive practices of the movement?" Through a comparison of the joiners and non-joiners in which we are able to hold as a constant the *objective* reality of the workshop situation, we shall be concerned with the *subjective*

*This paper is also to appear in Rodney Stark, ed. *Religious Movements: Genesis, Exodus and Numbers* (Rose of Sharon Press, forthcoming).

experience of the situation as our primary variable. Each individual will be seeing the workshop and the proffered vision of the Unification Church in the light of his predispositions and past experiences. Like most evangelizers, the workshop personnel will be trying as hard as they can to present the beliefs and practices of the movement in the most attractive and appealing light. For some of the guests they will succeed in creating a new *gestalt*, a new pair of glasses with which to see the world, a new vision of reality, a new meaning for existence, a new hope, or a new direction for the future; life in the Unification Church will seem to offer a new security, a new family, a new kind of loving, or a new sense of identity. But for others all that the Unification evangelists will be seen to be doing is (to borrow the phraseology of one vociferously eloquent informant) "spewing out a load of boring old cod's wallop."

PARTICIPANT OBSERVATION AND QUESTIONNAIRE RESPONSE[1]

During the course of my five-year study of the Unification Church I attended numerous workshops. On these occasions one of my first self-appointed tasks was to try to predict which of the "guests" were likely to become members, or at least to continue to a further workshop. I would make notes categorizing them as "probable," "possible," or "no-way." At first I failed rather miserably. I found, for example, that the argumentative young man who kept slipping outside for a quick smoke and whom I had classified as "no-way" would continue to the next stage, while the quiet, neatly dressed girl whom I thought looked rather a likely prospect would not continue. After some time, however, I developed a remarkably high

---

[1]The research upon which this paper is based has been carried out with funds from the Social Science Research Council of Great Britain, to whom I wish to express my gratitude.

Further details of the methods employed in this study (participant observation, in-depth interview, and questionnaire) can be found in "Confessions of a Methodological Schizophrenic: Problems Encountered in the Study of Rev. Sun Myung Moon's Unification Church," *Institute for the Study of Worship and Religious Architecture Research Bulletin* (University of Birmingham, 1978); or "The Professional Stranger: Some Methodological Problems Encountered in a Study of the Reverend Sun Myung Moon's Unification Church." Open University Course Media Notes for D207: An Introduction to Sociology, Open University, 1980; or "Der professionelle Fremde: Erklärung des Unerklärlichen beim Studium einer abweichenden religiosen Gruppe," in *Das Entstehen einer neuen Religion: Das Beispiel der Vereinigungskirche*, Gunter Kehrer, ed. (Kosel-Verlag, Munich: 1981).

rate of predictive accuracy. My trouble was the prediction rested (and to some extent still does) on a subjective feeling or recognition that I found difficult to verbalize—even to myself. I eventually did decide, however, that the intensity of interest, or curiosity, shown by the guest in what was going on was one of the most important variables—irrespective of whether this took a positive or a negative form. The most effective "protection" undoubtedly seemed to be apathy, lack of interest, or boredom.

The next question then became why, when we were all listening to the same lecture, were some sitting on the edge of their chairs, listening with fascination, excitement, disgust, or disbelief to every word, while others were lost in a day dream, gazing out of the window or glancing at their watches every five minutes? What were the different personalities, the different interests, the different experiences that were responsible for these different reactions?

Obviously, the people who turned up at a workshop were not representative of the population as a whole, nor, presumably, as not all of them became members were they likely to share all the characteristics of those who did join. It seemed rational to assume that some sort of initial "natural selection" procedure would already have taken place. Workshop attenders seemed, for example, to share with the members some easily recognizable characteristics with respect to such variables as age and social background. I had already compared Church members with a control group of people who were not members but whom I had "matched" for age and social background. Perhaps, I hypothesized, those who came to the workshop would form a group that occupied an *intermediate* position. As, for example, the members were disproportionately male and from Catholic homes, might the workshop group contain more males and Catholics than the general population, but fewer males and Catholics than the Unification Church? If, for example, one were to find that two-thirds of the members had considered a particular goal or value to be of great importance while only one-third of the control group had done so, might we expect roughly half of the workshop group to consider the goal or value to be of great importance?

Neither informal chats nor participant observation would supply the data necessary to test such hypotheses. Larger numbers and a more systematic comparability were needed. From application forms for workshop attendance in the London area during 1979 I was able to code for computer analysis the sex, occupation, date of birth, religious background, and nationality for 1,017 two-day workshop applicants. In addition to this information, by checking through various other lists and membership application forms, I was able to trace the "Unification careers" of these thousand or so persons. The careers were short-lived for the majority—there were more who left before the end of the initial two-day course than there were eventual converts. Roughly a third of the applicants went on to a seven-day workshop and about a fifth to a twenty-one-day course and just over half of these then declared that they would join, although in fact they did not all do so. Out of the original thousand, a *maximum* of fifty (nineteen of whom were British) were full-time members of the church by 1981. This number had dropped to a maximum of thirty-six by March 1982. This is probably an overstatement as it includes several people who had returned to their own countries saying they would join the church, but about whom no record of continuing membership was available. The maximum number of affiliated members was sixty-six persons (forty-eight by March 1982)—this figure including nine (six by 1982) Home Church members (who live in their own homes and follow an independent occupation but profess to accept the teachings of the Church) and seven (six by 1982) CARP members (students who are continuing their studies at a university of other place of further education and usually living with other CARP members in a center—CARP standing for Collegiate Association for the Research into Principles).

In other words, by the end of 1980, of all those who had been sufficiently interested in the Unification Church to start a two-day workshop in the London area during the previous year, no more than five percent were full-time members and no more than seven percent were still affiliated with the movement. By March 1982 the percentage of survivors was a maximum of three and six-tenths percent for full-time members and four and eight-tenths percent for all affiliated persons.

In order to obtain further information about the workshop applicants I persuaded the Church to allow me to use the addresses on the forms to send out a six-page questionnaire to the two-day applicants. This elicited a response of 136 questionnaires (only 131 of which were worth coding) eight letters, and six telephone calls, and an inquiry addressed to a colleague checking whether I was really a Church member who had got hold of the University of London stationery.

In an attempt to gauge how representative the respondents were of all the workshop attenders the information on the application forms of those who filled in questionnaires was compared with the information on the forms of the entire applicant population. These data were then subjected to a chi-square significance test. Except in the case of nationality, those who had filled in the questionnaire did not differ significantly from the applicants as a whole. In other words, in much the same way as the vast majority of randomly selected samples would faithfully reflect the total population, questionnaire respondents reflected the total population of the two-day workshop applicants with respect to such variables as sex, age, religion, and occupation. There was, however, some bias in favor of British and Irish respondents when the nationalities of the two groups were compared. This could be accounted for largely by the fact that questionnaires were not sent to the majority of overseas addresses, and that people from overseas tend to be a fairly transitory population while they are in Britain—two thirds of the hundred or so envelopes that were returned unopened were addressed to people with "foreign-looking" names. This suggests that what bias there was could be explained by factors that were external to the person concerned rather than by his subjective response to the Unification Church. It is also true, however, that it would be more difficult for those whose mother tongue is not English to fill in the questionnaire (two of those questionnaires that were uncodable were so because of language difficulties).

However encouraging it is to learn that there is little significant bias in characteristics that are known, it is, of course, a bias in the characteristics that are *not* known which will always be of concern to those who have to work from samples. It must be admitted that this could well exist. It was reassuring, however, that the sample did contain a wide spread of reactions and "types" of respondents that seemed to reflect the range of reactions and types with which I had become familiar through talking to individuals at workshops. Neither the opponents nor the proponents, neither the caring nor the indifferent, were necessarily put off responding. Furthermore the ratio of the non-joining to the joining-and-still-some-sort-of-a-member respondents (100:7), which reflected the ratio for the workshop applicants as a whole pretty accurately, was another reassuring sign.

Just because of this last fact, however, there were not enough respondents who had joined to provide a sufficiently large basis for a statistically significant comparison with the nonjoiners. Accordingly further questionnaires were sent to all those Church members in Britain who had joined during 1979 or 1980. The final total of 217 usable questionnaires came from sixty-four people who were currently full-time members, eleven Home Church members, thirteen CARP members, twenty-five persons who joined and then left the movement, and 104 who never joined.

FIRST CONTACT WITH UNIFICATION CHURCH

For the majority of those who go to a workshop the first contact they have with the Unification Church will be a meeting in the street or other public place. However, a quarter will be introduced to the movement by a friend or a relative, and the rest will usually have been contacted in their homes by a member knocking on the door. Those who became Home Church members were most likely to have been contacted in their own homes or by a relative (usually a son or daughter) but, generally speaking, those who were introduced to the movement by a friend or relative were the least likely to end up by joining, and they were also the people who, were they persuaded to try out a seven- or twenty-one-day workshop, were most likely to drop out before the end of the course. One also found the highest rate of antagonism expressed towards the movement by those introduced to it by friends, the most positive feelings being expressed by those who had first made contact in the street or a public place. This would seem to suggest that a "friendship network" explanation as to why people join a new movement is not particularly cogent in the case of the Unification Church in Britain. While a friendship with a member may temporarily overcome the preliminary "natural selection" process which filters out the vast majority of nonjoiners at the point of first contact (so that they do not even agree to attend a workshop), the suasive powers of the workshop are not as effective on those selected by friends as they are on those who have agreed to attend because of other factors which, presumably, have a greater "resonance" with *their* (rather than a friend's) predispositions.

The myth that UC members track their prey with attractive members of the opposite sex is not borne out by the British data. All the 1017 application forms gave information about the person who had first contacted the applicant and analysis of these showed that opposite sex contacts were almost exactly balanced by same-sex contacts.

In answer to a question as to why they agreed to go to a workshop, a third of the respondents who were to join (and almost half of those who were to join and then leave) said they were actively seeking the truth and hoping to find it. Only a fifth of the nonjoiners gave such a reason. While the joiners (and leavers) were slightly more likely to say that they thought the lectures might be interesting than were the nonjoiners, the latter group was more likely to say they were curious about the members or had nothing better to do. Around one in ten of leavers and nonjoiners said it was the insistence of the members which made it hard to refuse to go to the workshop.

Over half of the respondents said that they had known that it was the Reverend Moon's Unification Church before agreeing to go to the workshop (the percentage was higher among joiners, including leavers); but several of those who said they had not known added a rider to the effect that they had not realized that it was the Reverend Moon's movement although they had been told it was the Unification Church. Half of the respondents said that they had not heard about either the Unification Church or its members before they first went to a Church center. Only three percent reported having heard anything good about the movement (and I suspect that this had been from members). Almost everyone else who had heard anything had heard negative evaluations. Very few factual details were known (this pattern of only having picked up a negative evaluation with little or no factual information mirrored the responses given by my control group), but it may seem rather surprising that half of those who had heard anything had heard that the church brainwashes people.The interesting fact was not that they had heard this but that they had been *prepared to attend a workshop* with this information.

As might be expected, those who were to join the movement tended to declare that their experience did not substantiate what they had heard; but a third of the nonjoiners also said that they had found what they had heard to be untrue; a further one-third said they had found it only partly true; and the final third said it was either true, or mostly true.

SEX, AGE, AND CLASS

In an earlier article[2] I demonstrated how, by controlling for age, sex, and social class, one could increase the statistical density of Unification church

---

[2]"Who'd Be a Moonie? A Comparative Study of those who join the Unification Church in Britain," in *The Social Impact of New Religious Movements*, Bryan R. Wilson, ed. (New York: Rose of Sharon Press, 1981).

Other papers resulting from the study include "Living the Divine Principle: Inside the Reverend Sun Myung Moon's Unification Church in Britain," *Archives de Sciences Sociales des Religions* 45:1 (1978): 75-93; "Whose Service is Perfect Freedom: The Concept of Spiritual Well-Being in Relation to the Reverend Sun Myung Moon's Unification Church in Britain," *Spiritual Well-Being*, David O. Moberg, ed. (Washington DC:

members from one-thousandth percent to four-hundredths percent of the British population. In other words, within the category of middle-middle-and upper-middle-class males aged between the ages of twenty-one and twenty-six the chance of finding a member of the movement is roughly forty times greater than it is in the general population. Of course, we would still be a long way from identifying the members (and we would be leaving eighty percent of the British members out of the search), but we would have been able to narrow the field down enough to make it pertinent to ask how far the composition of workshop attenders reflected a selection in the direction of the church's population with respect to these variables.

When we look at the sex distribution we see that the selection of roughly two males to every female has already occurred by the time people come to a two-day workshop. Men are more likely to leave immediately, women being more prepared to wait at least until the end of the course. It might also be noted that although fewer women than men join, those women who do join are more likely either to leave immediately or else to stay longer than the men. (Nearly all those who become student [CARP] members are male.)

As with sex, the main selection for ages seems to have been carried out before the guests arrived for the workshop. Like the members, workshop attenders tend to be in their early twenties, but they are not so tightly concentrated—it appears that those who are to join the movement are especially "ripe" around the age of twenty-two or twenty-three. While it is sometimes argued that these people are particularly impressionable because of their youth and therefore most likely to fall victim to mind-control techniques, a histogram clearly shows that the nonjoiners are not only those who are older than the joiners, they are also those who are younger. The short-term leavers, however, do tend to be slightly older than the joiners who stay in the movement for a longer period. There are several possible reasons for this. It may be that, being older, they find it easier to assert themselves and so leave once they have to face the reality

University Press of America, 1979) 153-71; "Free to Choose? Some Thoughts on the Unification Church and Other New Religious Movements," Part 1, *Clergy Review* (October 1980): 365-68, Part 2 (November 1980): 392-98; "Who Draws the Lines Where?", *Intermedia* 9:2 (March 1981): 12-14; "Resistible Coercion: The Significance of Failure Rates in Conversion and Commitment to the Unification Church," in *Conversion, Coercion and Commitment in New Religious Movements*, Dick Anthony, Jacob Needleman, and Thomas Robbins, eds. (forthcoming).

of Unification Church life; it may be that they are the ones who are the "professional joiners and leavers" and have grown old trying out all sorts of life-styles without success; it may be that a significant proportion of members who are still in the movement will in fact leave when they, too, reach that age.

Again it looks as though initial selection procedures seem to have been at work on the social class of the potential member before he or she reaches the workshop, the majority coming from the middle classes. There is, however, an interesting further selection that is to take place after this initial stage. This is observable if one does not make the distinction according to a crude manual/non-manual division, but according to degrees of responsibility and the kinds of values that are associated with the father's occupation. A higher proportion of joiners than nonjoiners come from the upper-working classes which contain skilled workers, often in positions of considerable responsibility. Over twice as many nonjoiners as joiners have fathers in the more routine nonmanual (lower middle-class) occupations; but nonjoiners are also twice as likely to have come from the *upper* middle classes. Leavers are the only group that had (just) a majority of fathers in manual occupations, forty-eight percent coming from the middle or lower-middle classes. Fathers of nonjoiners are more likely than joiners' fathers to have come from occupations that were concerned with making money (such as the stock exchange).

PROTECTIONS AND PROPENSITIES

In several ways it would seem that the nonjoining group contains *both* a subgroup that is "protected" from joining because it does *not* possess certain characteristics embodied in the Unification population, *and* a subgroup that possesses these characteristics to a *greater* degree than the members. While the workshop does gather in those who are more predisposed towards Unification Church beliefs and practices than the general population, if the characteristics get beyond a particular stage/strength/level then they acquire what the economists would call a negative marginal utility. We have already seen, for example, that while youth is an important predisposing factor, the youngest cohorts are less rather than more likely to join.

This negative marginal utility factor is even more obvious among those who join and leave within a short time than it is among the nonjoiners. It is as if those who are the candidates most likely to be susceptible to the Church's suasion, according to proponents of the brain washing/mind-control thesis, are indeed the ones selected at the initial stages from the general population, but they are also the ones who are subsequently rejected by, or will themselves reject the Unification environment. This is, for example, apparent in the degree to which the workshop guests could be classified as religious "seekers" (thirty percent nonjoiners; fifty percent leavers; forty-five percent continuing members).

It is probable that the greatest protection against conversion for a guest in a European Unification workshop is atheism. (This is less clearly the case in California where the lectures given by the "Oakland Family" have not been so obviously based on the theological tenets of Unification thought.) Among the questionnaire respondents none of the full-time joiners (eight percent of the nonjoiners) said that they definitely did not believe in God at the time they went to the workshop, and only six percent (eight percent of the leavers and eighteen percent of nonjoiners) coded "not really." Two-thirds of joiners and one-half of nonjoiners had "definitely believed in God." The leavers as a group held the strongest belief.

Although denominational differences between joiners and nonjoiners do occur, the most important factor seemed to be that the Christian tradition—perhaps accepting the Bible as a source of revelation—while not exactly a necessary condition, is at least conducive to joining in England. The small number of Jews and Muslims who come to the workshops tend to leave before they finish. Hindus are slightly less inclined to do so, their comments suggesting that they see many ways to God and for some the *Divine Principle* might be described as "acceptable" rather than the truth. The overweighting of Catholics in relation to the wider society which is found in the Unification Church is reflected among the workshop attenders but this is not an overweighting if one (a) takes church membership, rather than nominal affiliation, as a reference group, and (b) takes into account the nationality of the workshop attenders (and, more especially, that of their fathers). In other words, it is coming from a Catholic country and being actively involved with religion that would seem to be more pertinent "selectors" than Catholicism per se, the apparent "protection" offered, relatively speaking, by Church of England membership being more traceable to the loose use made of that label than to any particular characteristics of Anglican dogma or practices.

The non-joining group contained more people who never went to church during childhood or (less markedly) during the period before attending the workshop than either members or the control group which, it will be remembered, consisted of persons "matched" with members on such characteristics as age and social background but who had had no personal contact with the movement. But there were a few more nonjoining workshop attenders than control group participants who attended frequently in early childhood. Respondents from *all* the groups in the study expressed disillusionment with established religious institutions, but this did not mean that they might not still have been trying to find something in a church as a considerably larger proportion (of full-time joiners in particular) were attending a place of worship more frequently than the general population.

Of the workshop questionnaire respondents, joiners were the least likely, and leavers the most likely, to have "shopped around" different organizations or movements before attending the workshop. Nonjoiners had the highest percentage of respondents trying out secular movements, especially political ones (in which members tended not to have been particularly interested).

All the respondents were asked to assess the extent to which they thought important, and were actively seeking a set of nine different values. Few people put a "high standard of living" high on their list of priorities, the leavers valuing it least of all. "Success in their careers" was most important for the nonjoiners but it was also very important for the majority of the control group; (that is, the group that I had earlier "matched" with Unification Church members but that, unlike the workshop group, had had no contact with the movement); neither leavers (in particular) nor members valued their careers so highly—though a few had valued them very highly indeed.

"Better relations" were important and sought after by all groups but least by the leavers and the nonjoiners and most by the control group; an "ideal marriage" was sought after less by nonjoiners than by joiners, leavers or the control group. Members and especially leavers claim to have been more actively seeking and to have considered "improving the world" more important than either nonjoiners or the control group. For all groups "control over one's own life" was the most important and most sought after of the values. This was particularly so for leavers (fifty-eight percent), slightly less so for the control group and members (forty-nine percent) and least so for nonjoiners (thirty-three percent). Both "spiritual fulfillment" and "understanding God" were, quite markedly, most important for the leavers, then for the members, then for the nonjoiners, and least important for the control group.

The greatest discrepancy between the groups showed up when they were asked to rate the importance of "something but don't know what." The majority of members claimed to have considered this very important and to have been actively seeking it at the time of attending the workshop—a considerable, but smaller, proportion of the leavers made a similar claim. Although a third of the nonjoiners said it was important and they were seeking it, more of them were likely to agree with the vast majority of the control group that they did not think about it at all (and probably thought the question rather daft). This might suggest the hypothesis that some of those who were to become members could go to a workshop with an already existing gap waiting to be filled—in other words, society has already done some "brain*washing*" but has not offered anything with which to fill the vacuum it has created. It may be that while not just anything can be "poured into" the void, those who are to leave have a slightly clearer idea of what it was they were seeking than had some of the members

Next to atheism, it is possible that the most effective "protection" against the lure of the Unification Church is having a stable or permanent relationship with another person. The majority of people in all the groups were most likely to spend their leisure time with a few close friends (rather than by themselves or in a large group). While Unification members were slightly more likely than the control group to have spent their time by themselves, the nonjoiners and especially the leavers were even *more* likely than the members to have been isolated in the period six months before the workshop. In their subjective (retrospective) assessments of happiness during that period members as a group were less likely to have been very happy than were the members of the control group at the time of filling in the questionnaires. Nonjoiners also tended to have been happier than the members (Home Church members in particular said they had been unhappy). Leavers were the least happy of all the groups during their childhood and adolescence.

Considering the youth of the respondents, it was hardly surprising that over thirty percent of all groups said that they enjoyed either excellent or good physical health. Full-time members were most inclined to claim that their health was now excellent, although slightly more of them had suffered some sort of illness in the past. Leavers had the poorest health.

The number of those who reported any kind of psychiatric problem was small in all groups, by far the highest percentage (twenty-two percent) being in the group of immediate leavers. Next were the nonjoiners (sixteen percent), then the Home Church members (twelve percent), then full-time members (five percent). None of the CARP members reported having had any such problems. Most of the cases were of a mild depression; only ten respondents to the workshop questionnaire said their illness had been severe enough to seek medical help; seven of these were nonjoiners, two immediate leavers and one became a full-time member. In the earlier comparison I had made between a far larger number of "established" members and the control group, fourteen percent of the members and twelve percent of the control group had reported some history of psychiatric problems; this had been severe in the case of six percent of the members and seven percent of the control group.

On another, albeit highly subjective, level the research assistants who coded the questionnaires were asked to give an overall impression of each respondent. Four-fifths of the members and half of the nonjoiners and the leavers were placed in the "nice ordinary boy/girl next door" category; five percent of the members, fifteen percent of the nonjoiners, and eight percent of the leavers were typecast as "mildly peculiar"; four percent of the nonjoiners, three percent of the leavers (no members) were coded "psychopathologically peculiar"; and five percent of the members, four percent of the nonjoiners, and sixteen percent of the leavers were seen as "rather sad and pathetic."

The respondents were far more educated than the general population, over half of all the groups having been educated up to or beyond the age of twenty. Leavers tended to have been educated either for less or for more time than the members or the nonjoiners, but they were less likely to have had further education at a university. As a group, members got better grades than the nonjoiners or leavers, but the nonjoiners could be subdivided into those who did slightly better than the average member and those who did considerably worse. The leavers tended to have the poorest grades and to be the most individually erratic in their results.

Over half the members (fifty-nine percent) and nonjoiners (fifty-three percent) and sixty-four percent of the leavers were qualified for some sort of job. Most frequently the qualifications for all groups, but particularly for leavers, were of a lower professional type (such as school teacher or nurse), but within other categories nonjoiners were more likely to have clerical-type or semiskilled manual qualifications while the joiners (members and leavers) were more likely to have "lower technical" or responsible manual skills. Exactly a third of the nonjoiners, slightly fewer joiners, and slightly more leavers were not either students or in paid employment at the time of attending the workshop. The nonjoiners (forty-one percent) and the leavers (forty percent) were more likely than those who were to become full-time members (twenty-three percent) to have been students at the time of the workshop, but of course nearly all those who were to become CARP members were already students. At the time of the workshop the members had been the least and the leavers the most settled retrospectively, but prospectively short-term leavers were the least and members the most settled—that is, leavers were likely to have had settled jobs in the past but to have been uncertain about their future, while members were slightly more likely to have had definite career prospects ahead of them.

Thus far I have attempted to indicate some of the already existing differences between those who, as a result of attending a workshop were to become members, those who were to join then leave, and those who were not to join at all. Some of these differences were described in comparison either to characteristics of a control group of similar age and background or to characteristics of the British population as a whole. Further quantitive findings have been reported elsewhere.[3]

In the next section an attempt will be made to indicate the range of subjective experiences of the workshop participants by quoting some of their comments, most of which were written in response to "open questions" in the questionnaire.

THE WORKSHOP EXPERIENCE

The number of guests at a workshop will range from one to thirty or possibly even more at a "peak" period such as summer or Easter vacations. Most frequently there are between eight and twelve guests and then, on the Unification Church side, there will be a lecturer and his assistant and perhaps two other members of staff and two more members

[3]See especially "Who'd Be a Moonie" and "Resistible Coercion" (details in note 2). See also *Moonies* (Oxford: Blackwell, 1984).

who will be in charge of domestic arrangements, including the kitchen. The guests may be accompanied by the person who first introduced them to the movement, but this is by no means always the case. A brief schedule for a two-day workshop is given in appendix 1.

The intention in this section being to inject a qualitatively subjective flavor into the paper in order to illustrate the diversity of the workshop experiences, no attempt will be made to assess the quotations for objective accuracy—indeed to do so would be to miss the whole point of the present exercise. But, bearing in mind the methodological dangers of selecting examples for descriptive purposes, an indication of the relative frequencies of the different kinds of assessments made in response to some precoded questions is to be found in the tables in appendix 2.

From these tables it will be noticed that while the lectures were an important and appreciated factor for the joiners (including those who were to leave) there was less enthusiasm from the nonjoiners. Among the nonjoiners who employed the "other" category for what they like best, four percent said they liked nothing, five percent said they liked everything, and indeed most of the remaining "other" answers reflected the diversity of subjective experiences by frequently having their counterpart in the "other" response given by someone else to the question asking what they liked *least* about the workshop. Thus for quite a few people the food seemed to be the high point of their stay, while for others it was the major source of complaint; while one nonjoiner could write that he had particularly liked the "eccentric modes of behaviour, for example, running across the common at 6:45 before breakfast and listening to Beethoven over lunch," another would write that

> the childish games went on and nobody could refuse to do things whether they were asked to sing or dance and were all made to feel like children. But my character will not allow me to do these things and I became unpopular. The members would say I was typical English and that [I] did not know how to enjoye [*sic*] myself but I could see everyone making fools of themselfs [*sic*].

It was pretty clear from responses to the open questions that the primary assessment of the workshops rested upon the respondents' evaluation of the truth of the Divine Principle. There were a few nonjoiners who said that they thought that Unification theology was the truth but that they did not feel they were prepared to join. There was, for example, one respondent who said that she had had quite a frightening shock on having what she had come to believe was the truth revealed to her. She wrote:

> I feel that people condemn the UC because they will not admit that what the members say makes sense; probably fear is in most people's minds. The members have answers to all questions, answers that are so real that one does tend to get a little fearful. Most people like to pop along on a Sunday evening and say a few prayers and sing a few hymns and they think they have done their duty. I am the worst culprit, I don't even do that! Most people are not dedicated enough to join this church. Some won't even listen, they are too busy trying to persecute them. . . . I am aware (acutely) of God's presence in my life. I know what I ought to do but I do not do it. It is too much for me to comprehend, I feel. The Unification Church DO know the answers, there is NO doubt in my mind on that, and there are very few things that I can say I am not doubtful about. P.S.: They have not brainwashed me, by the way!

Another respondent, admitting that it was for selfish reasons he had not joined (he had put "not being able to smoke inside" as the thing he had liked least about the workshop), wrote:

> I thoroughly believe in the UC and that the other churches are both ignorant and arrogant towards the UC. The UC has God in their hearts and not just in their mouths.

Many of the respondents felt that they could accept a great deal of the theology but had some doubts about certain aspects of it—particularly the idea that Sun Myung Moon could be the Messiah. One respondent who had agreed to join and then decided not to (partly because of parental pressure) wrote:

> I still think a great deal of them. Although all contact with them is over. They really are lovely people, from all accounts, trying to make a better world. But the question of Rev. Moon comes into it and I cannot accept him; and of course if you can't accept him that destroys the whole argument. Unfortunately with the Moonies it's all or nothing. Which is a shame, as they are wonderful people.

Another respondent agreed to join as a Home Church member but then changed her mind:

> There were parts of the teachings that I felt some doubt about, and felt that to be a UC member I needed to give one hundred percent of myself but I was not willing to do so—my career, and so forth. I think more people should look at UC because some of their ways and ideas are good. When I decided not to join full-time I was not pressured to stay but allowed to do what I wanted to do.

At the other end of the spectrum there were those people who were violently opposed to the movement. There was, for example, the man who had converted to Christianity at the age of fifteen. It had meant something for a little while, he said, "but cooled off as I faced new temptations of sex and drugs and rock and roll which seemed to offer greater excitements and fulfillment." About the Unification Church he wrote:

> The UC is evil. I hate everything about it. I don't blame the members—they are victims of some dark satanic force. I'm glad I was challenged, and was able to resist. People shouldn't be subjected to this sort of thing. We should be free to walk down a street without being emotionally assaulted by these Moon-worshipers.

A Jamaican woman who was lonely and thought that the Unification Church was a debating society where she could have interesting discussions and make new friends dismissed the experience with the words, "I thought it was a load of intellectual claptrap. I couldn't accept the written philosophy. It seemed pseudo-intellectual."

The majority of people, however, were more inclined to show some kind of respect for the status of the teachings, even when they did not accept them. Often the respondents would compare them with other beliefs. One fairly typical response came from a Malaysian who said that he did not continue the seven-day course because he "couldn't find the time. Besides I can't live for seven days with so much holiness." He wrote:

> I find the UC's belief is much more logical than others and had better solutions to some problems. Like others they believe in love and peace. But they certainly try and have a good way of achieving it. Of course I do find some of their "theories" "unbelievable." If you get to *understand* more religions, you'll find it hard to tell which is the truth!!

Another respondent said that he had not continued to the seven-day workshop because it was "too expensive (£15) also tedious to listen to things one could not accept when they would not argue constructively." He commented:

> My impression is divided between my own experiences and the media's "version." My experience has not been wide enough to see the dubious financial base or Moon's politics or the changed character of the estranged children of concerned parents. The Moonies did not seem to have lost their rationality except that they fervently accepted Moon's doctrine. To me an Anglican vicar appears equally irrational except his arguments are based on more serious scholarship and study of the Bible. Apart from this I envy the UC members for not being part of our society like other communes.

A further fairly typical response came from a highly educated Indian:

> UC's beliefs as far as I can judge are nothing new: they contain the good points which are basic to all major religions; however, what they are trying to achieve is to involve people, irrespective of their religious backgrounds, nationality, or

ethnic grouping, which is definitely needed in our modern day world. I believe in good humanitarian aims in general and in overall harmony, but can't accept anything or any principle blindly. Its members are good, sincere, and devoted workers.

Several of the evaluations of the theology gave clues as to the kinds of "protection" with which the respondents might have come to the workshop. There was, for example, the tolerant indifference of the British lapsed Catholic who wrote: "Nothing wrong with it, if you like that type of thing. I was bored." And there were those who were already confirmed in their beliefs—beliefs which could take various forms. There was, for example, a Marxist community worker:

A captalist venture camouflaged in a kind of religious revelation. Mr. Moon thinks of himself as a second Christ which is rubbish. Waste of time.

There was the French atheist:

They are not stupid. I find the ideal of brotherhood fine. But it is difficult to approve such beliefs when you don't believe in any deity. On the whole [the members are] sensible people, agreeable, nice, open to other people's ideas, and so forth. But I wouldn't like to share their way of life. I want to achieve my spiritual fulfilment myself.

There was the seventy-seven-year-old inveterate searcher:

So far Theosophy is the nearest to satisfy me. But I search and keep an open mind on other teachings.

There was the "True Believer":

Boring, very claustrophobic, and I found no truth at all. The truth was not there. In one month they could turn your mind into a cabbage. The members have *no* longer minds of there [*sic*] own. There [*sic*] beliefs are of the mind but not of the hard [*sic*]. The church and its practices is *just* for money. . . . My faith is in God and *Christ said blessed is he who hears my word and keeps it*, and he who keeps the commandments shall have eternal life.

As will already be apparent, many of the respondents found themselves liking or admiring the members, sometimes feeling rather sorry for them, perhaps, but generally acknowledging their commitment and dedication. A few respondents talked of individual members whom they had not liked, and one or two dismissed all members as brainwashed zombies, but the most frequent criticisms leveled against the members were that they were *too* nice and *too* dedicated. One fairly typical comment came from a young woman who had a relative in the Church:

> Well, the members are nice people and most of them, like [X], are truly believers in the beliefs, but who knows what there is behind the organization? . . . Why are they so kind? Too kind. . . .

Another respondent was put off by the general lack of realism he found:

> I think that its beliefs are too "positive" to have any significance on the everyday life of today. Their values and practices cannot possibly be relevant to present-day society. The members seem to me to be on cloud nine trying to escape reality on the whole! To me they are too "nice" and "good" and "obliging" for me to be able to relate to them as real people.

Then there was the African who had only been in the country for three months and said he had not really fitted into the society and (despite the fact that he had heard that the Unification Church was "a sect not unlike the Rev. Jim Jones's catastrophe in Guyana") had agreed to go on the seven-day course because he "got bored staying at home and it was a chance to see places outside London and live on a farm." He got as far as starting the twenty-one-day course but did not finish it because:

> it was too much time to waste on a thing the essence of which I don't agree with and I got bored with the lectures.
>
> I don't agree with their teachings or the methods employed; they stress too much on making people feel guilty and since they dogmatically believe in their principle the people themselves become boring to talk to.
>
> The members themselves are nice and fraternal people but rather boring and uninteresting to talk to because they are enthusiastic about one subject only—their Divine Principle.

Some respondents reported feeling rather hurt or disappointed that they seemed to be unable to continue a friendship with a member once they had said that they were not going to join, but many others reported that they still kept in touch with one or two, often claiming to maintain a deep, spiritual relationship with their Unification friends. One fairly extreme case was that of the Briton who confessed:

> I must be honest that I fell in love with one of the members and had decided that I had met the perfect match. Even though I am extremely anti-Unification Church I still keep in touch with her in her own country. It is my conclusion that she, being involved in the church, has moved away from her family and therefore comes more to rely on the Church. After a recent program on the Church I got in touch with her, trying to tell her the truth, but to no avail.

A more commonly cited experience was:

> Within two weeks of my becoming acquainted with one of its members I realized that my hope of making friends on a social basis was quite unrealistic.

> Since this was the reason I had agreed to go to the workshop, I decided fairly quickly that I could not benefit from its superficial overflow of joy for mankind. Most of its members were so happy on the surface that people like me were forced to adopt a cynical attitude if only because it was impossible to reconcile what we had heard from the press with our present experiences. In spite of this initial turn-off I was still very impressed by the dedication of many of its members. I still receive regular letters from the person who introduced me to the church—all the way from [Africa]. Instead of sending stereotype forms asking you to contact them they send very personal messages about their hopes, fears, and spiritual desires. This very positive attitude towards thinking about themselves—and the fact that many of them travel worldwide to spread their news—really does deserve my admiration, even if I do not agree with everything they say.

A not atypical comment from a woman who had joined and then left was:

> In a nutshell, the UC members are basically good and sound people being totally led up the garden path. If the spiritual energy expounded by these people was channeled into a Christian movement (instead of "fake Christian" movement) the world would truly benefit from their work.

The longer-term effects of the workshop experience are examined in the next section, but some examples might be given here to illustrate the range of more immediate emotional responses elicited by the Unification Church. The most disturbing account of a respondent's reaction was not as the result of a workshop experience but came from a woman who had joined and then left. She wrote:

> When I went to London to work about two years ago, I became very interested in spiritualism. I had always felt there was more to life. Spiritualism answered a lot of questions for me, for example, was God really a condemning God, the true meaning of Heaven and Hell. Man's free will and karma. I also had a deep feeling for Jesus Christ. Who was he really? Was he meant to die? In the [Unification] Church I studied the mission of Christ. The results of the deep study upset me very much. Everything became acutely out of proportion. I felt that man was so evil, that I was better off taking my life than living in this world.

For another woman, who became a Home Church member, the opportunity to talk about the spirit world and life after death brought her feelings of immense relief: "For the first time in my life I have met people who did not think I was strange to talk about such things."

Among the nonjoiners the reactions reported as a result of the workshop ranged from: "I was stunned by being thrown into the outside world again after the workshop. My entire concentration had been in the artificial environment at Greenwich: no papers, television, and so forth," to: "[the workshop] was one of my best spent weekends." As has already been mentioned, several of the nonjoiners found the experience boring, but several others found it highly stimulating. Some people felt irritated and/or frustrated: "They only wanted to tell me what they wanted me to know. I wanted them to tell me what I wanted to know." Others felt gratitude and interest:

> I learned a lot from the two-day workshop. I did not go with the intention of changing my religion [RC] but to help me understand it more. It helped me a lot.
>
> As for "brainwashing" I don't believe it. I was not forced to do anything I did not wish to do.

Several people made a point of saying that accusations of brainwashing were obviously rubbish, but some did say they had felt watched or pressured—for nonjoiners this tended either to take the form of irritation at the members' controlling the environment in ways such as saying what to do when, or not allowing people to ask questions when they wanted to, or else it took the form of concern for guests other than the respondent himself:

> I was terrified by the very young age of many of the people who were being brought to the workshops, youngsters who were easily influenced.

It is from the ranks of those who joined and then left that one is most likely to find a deeper fear of having themselves been influenced: "I wonder sometimes whether my thoughts are my own or whether they are there because they have been put there."

In this section none of the quotations has been made by respondents who were full-time members of the Unification Church at the time of filling in the questionnaire. This is partly because the paper is not about conversion experiences but is more concerned with the subjective experiences of the nonjoiners. It might be helpful, however, for comparative purposes to finish with a couple of brief examples from those who became committed members. First there was the medical student who wrote:

> Right from the start I felt it was the truth. For a long time I asked questions which no one but the UC answer.
>
> I believe that anyone who hears this new truth from God and does nothing about it knowing how much we need help in this messy world needs a good wollop.

Finally, there was the English woman who had been a nun for two and a half years and who said she agreed to go on to a seven-day workshop because:

> After a month from the two-day workshop I was almost convinced it was the truth—after a theological and prayerful struggle with myself. And so I wanted to find out more (so I could decide on further information).

She agreed to go on to a twenty-one-day workshop because, she claims: "After [the] seven-day [workshop] I knew it was the truth." She then agreed to join "because it is the Way, the Truth, and the Light!" Talking about difficulties in relating to many people, she mentioned that she had developed a problem of speaking much too quickly:

> Sometimes I still retain these problems, but already I feel far more free to be myself and to be understood and accepted without barriers.

THE NONCONVERSION EXPERIENCE

Thus far the only consequence for nonjoiners which we have considered to be of note was that they *were* nonjoiners. It would be a mistake however, to assume that the workshop is nothing more than a passing nonevent (although one inveterate seeker did write a letter claiming that he had been to so many of these sorts of things that he was not really sure that he could remember which had been the Unification Church).

Unintended consequences can be as interesting as intended purposes. Nonjoiners may not have become converted to the church, but it does not follow that they were unaffected by the workshop. Indeed, when they were asked whether they felt that they had changed in any way as a result of attending the workshops, a third of the nonjoiners said that they felt they had and a further quarter answered "perhaps." (Not surprisingly, those who had joined and those who had joined and then left were even more likely to claim that they had changed as a result of the experience.)

Well over half the nonjoiners who admitted to a possible change said that they had become more convinced of the truth of some religious belief *other* than that of the Unification Church (for example, "I have become stronger in my Catholic religion"). Twenty-six percent said that this was a *negative* reaction to Unification teachings: "It has made me more aware of false christs as prophesied in 'Revelation' (New Testament) . . . and has made me look at the Bible more closely . . . it has been a marvelous education and confirmation of the one and only true Bible." Twenty percent affirmed that hearing the *Principle* had been a *positive* help in their understanding of their religious beliefs. Twenty-five percent claimed to have actually discovered God or to have been given a renewed experience of God as a result of attending the workshop: "Now [I] have a very firm belief in God"; "I now can talk deeper about God and know more things about him"; "My faith in God has grown stronger"; "[I am] more stable in my religious belief." Disbelief also could be reinforced: "[I now] hate everything to do with religion and my past values and beliefs were greatly strengthened."

Concentrating on more secular changes, fifteen percent of the non-joiners said that they were happier or more contented in some way: "I came out of my depression and no longer take tablets. I am bright and alert as never in my life before"; "More optimistic." On the other hand, eleven percent said that they had become unsettled or unhappy: "Bad-tempered sometimes, unsure of life in general, edgy"; and a further eleven percent intimated that they had learned to be more careful in the future: "Less naive—more cautious about this sort of thing"; "I used to be very friendly and trusting. Now I am more suspicious."

Several people felt that they had improved, having learned how to become better people as a result of the workshop: "I seem to look at things differently. I still pray. I had morals anyway, but they have been upheld even more strongly"; "I feel I can discipline myself much more—and care for more people unselfishly—plus many personal changes."

Many felt that they had become more open-minded or recognized the need for open-mindedness: "Now [I] appreciate more other people's beliefs"; I think a lot more and question most things"; "Opened my mind to religion, but not blinded my view, for I can see both sides of the coin, unlike some who only see one"; "Opened my eyes to unexplored avenues"; "The workshop did not change me to the extent of making me want to join but made me more aware of the need for a greater understanding and a greater fellowship between churches".

One or two said that while they themselves had remained immune, they were worried about those who had not had their strength: "I have not changed. But I have realized how easy it is to influence people with certain ideas." One person was rather unsure as to whether he might or might not have been affected: "what I was told in the lectures subconsciously affecting the way I think perhaps."

So much for the comments of those who did not join. It is hardly surprising that some of those who had joined and then left were forcefully resentful of the effect that the Unification Church had wrought in their lives: "at the time I joined I felt I had something worth living and working for. . . . After I left the workshop, I saw everything from a completely different viewpoint. . . . Everything seemed very evil. . . ." She continued in a letter:

> I would also like to say that I left the movement about five months ago. At first I really didn't think I was going to survive. The Unification Church strips you completely of your ego. You become very frightened of life. I left with [. . . . . .]. He has suffered the same reactions. Since then we both feel more able to cope, although there are of course occasions when we both revert back to this childlike fear and acute depression. Our faith in God and the spirit world have not been completely destroyed.

Another leaver wrote:

> As an ex-Moonie I am not bitter towards the members but astounded, rather, at my own gullibility. I think if I had not left when I did it may possibly have been too late. After making the decision that I had to get out or sink because I could no longer swim with the movement I truly found myself doubting my sanity—even now, after having left six months, I find myself wondering what they will do next!

Perhaps it was more surprising to find that the majority of those who had joined then left still saw the experience in positive terms:

> I (now, because of the UC) believe in God, the Bible, Jesus, spiritualism and the probability that Rev. Moon is what the UC claims him to be. I have a guideline by which to set my life morally and feel more capable of responsibilities of life.

Another person who left wrote "I feel I think more deeply—to a degree I feel my morals are higher." Another wrote that "my view on relationships between people has altered. I find I am trying not to be so self-centered. Perhaps I am still searching to find the truth." Another leaver wrote "I understand better why I should love other people and the need for helping others less well off than me." Finally, another leaver wrote "I became more sensitive generally about life and more open-minded."

Whether or not the respondents have indeed changed in the sorts of ways they claim to have changed, and, if they have so changed, to what extent such changes are indeed attributable to the Unification Church, is not something that the present data can tell us. The responses do indicate, however, that the social context of the workshop might well result in a not inconsiderable variety of influences that affect the subjective experiences (at least) of the participant in ways other than that of ensuring his lifelong membership in the movement—one ironic twist of fate being the possibility that, through the offices of the Unification workshops, more persons are convinced of non-Unification beliefs than are brought to Unification beliefs. It is not inconceivable that the Unification Church's techniques of persuasion are, numerically speaking, less effective in swelling the ranks of the Unification Church than they are in swelling the ranks of other religions.

SUMMARY

The focus of this paper arises from the fact that more than nine out of ten of those who attend a Unification two-day workshop do not join the movement, suggesting that factors *brought to* the workshop by the guests are likely to be the most important determinants of the final outcome.

It was suggested that while a selective process had already been brought into play at the point of initial contact, certain other factors came into operation during the workshop experience. In the case of the British workshop, the greatest "protection" would seem to stem from a boredom with the lectures and a lack of interest in the alternative views and way of life offered by the movement. This in turn would seem to be strongest among those who are uninterested or uncommitted to religious or, more specifically, biblically based answers to personal and social problems. An already strongly held set of beliefs, if unambigiously held, can also offer some, though not as much, protection. Those who already have an established, strong, personal relationship with another person are also likely to be less attracted to the Church. But while certain factors that are frequently presumed to be associated with suggestibility or need (like youthfulness, seekership, isolation, history of psychiatric problems, or boredom) might select people for *attending* a workshop, these were not necessarily precipitating factors for *joining*. Indeed, such factors might have a "negative marginal utility" in that they selected people *out of*, rather than *into* the movement. The variety of subjective experiences of the workshop situation further reinforces the probability that the guests' values or social background, their predispositions and their presuppositions about society, were operating actively in this selection/protection process.

The argument underlying this essay has been addressed to those who wish to insist that conversion to the Unification Church is due solely, or even predominantly, to irresistible, manipulative techniques employed at the workshops. The data challenge such people to answer the question:

How is it that these techniques are so successfully resisted by the ones who got away?

APPENDIX 1

Timetable for Typical Weekend Workshop, United Kingdom

Arrive Friday afternoon or evening. No formal arrangements.

Saturday

7:45 Rise
8:15 Exercise or walk in park
9:00 Breakfast
10:15 Lecture (1)
11:30 Coffee Break
11:45 Lecture (2)
1:00 Break
1:15 Lunch
Afternoon: playing games or taking a walk
5:00 Lecture (3)
6:30 Break
7:00 Dinner
8:00 Singing, entertainment, band, etc.
10:00 Break
11:30 Bed

Sunday

As Saturday morning but often with service rather than first lecture.
1:00 Lunch
Afternoon: short walk
3:00 Final Lecture (5)
4:30 Discussion, and break up for people to go home

APPENDIX 2

Reactions to Two-Day Workshop

(Figures are given in percentages, but do not add up to 100% in (1) as some respondents coded more than one option. In (1) and (2) "everything" and "nothing" were not precoded options, but there were sufficient responses to create a separate category for coding.)

	Non-joiners N x 104	Leavers N x 25	Full-time joiners N x 64
(1) What did you like most about the two-day workshop?			
The lectures	24	57	52
The people	31	11	31
The general atmosphere	34	35	35
Everything	5	4	6
Nothing	5	-	-
Other	9	-	2
(2) What did you like least about the two-day workshop?			
The lectures	43	32	16
The people	15	5	5
The general atmosphere	14	5	11
Nothing	8	26	46
Other	20	31	20
(3) How would you rate your reaction to the following during the two-day workshop?			
(a) *the lectures:*			
You thought they were the truth	9	44	63
Quite a lot of truth, but you couldn't accept it all	40	44	30
Interesting, but you did not accept their truth	43	8	8
Boring and uninteresting	4	-	-
Nothing but a load of rubbish	5	4	-
(b) *the members:*			
Really nice people whom you liked a lot	53	60	84
One or two you liked, others not so much	27	36	13
You found them rather strange and peculiar	18	4	3
You did not like them at all	2	-	-
(c) *the general atmosphere:*			
Friendly and homely	52	68	61
Stimulating and exciting	8	12	31
Quite pleasant, but not really your cup of tea	29	20	8
Oppressive, claustrophobic, frightening	12	-	-

CONTRIBUTORS

GEOFFREY AHERN graduated from Oxford and obtained his Ph.D. at the London School of Economics. His book *Sun at Midnight: The Rudolf Steiner Movement and the Western Esoteric Tradition* is to be published by the Aquarian Press in 1984.

EILEEN BARKER is lecturer in the department of sociology and dean of undergraduate studies at the London School of Economics. She was convener of the British Sociological Association Sociology of Religion Study Group from 1978 to 1981. Her two main research areas are the relationship between modern images of science and religion, and new religious movements. She has written numerous articles, is editor of *New Religious Movements: A Perspective for Understanding Society* (New York: Edwin Mellen Press, 1982), and her book *Moonies* is to be published by Basil Blackwells, Oxford.

JAMES A. BECKFORD is senior lecturer in sociology at the University of Durham, England. His early research interest was in the study of religious sects, but more recently he has completed studies of the processes of withdrawal from authoritarian movements and of the growth of anticult sentiment in several countries. His main publications include *The Trumpet of Prophecy: A Sociological Study of Jehovah's Witnesses* (Oxford: Blackwell, 1975), and "Religious Organization. A Trend Report and Bibliography." *Current Sociology* 21:2 (1973).

FREDERICK BIRD is an associate professor of religion and sociology at Concordia University in Montreal. He is a graduate of Harvard College, Harvard Divinity School, and the Graduate Theological Union, Berkeley. He is currently completing a book on the sociology of Moral Systems.

CARROLL J. BOURG is a professor of sociology and chairman of the department of sociology and anthropology at Fisk University (Nashville, Tennessee). During 1973-1979 he was editor of *Sociological Analysis: A Journal in the Sociology of Religion.* In 1979-1980 he was president of the *Association for the Sociology of Religion.* His current work includes studies of religion and politics, the tensions within the state in Western societies, and the sacred in modern societies.

DAVID G. BROMLEY is professor of sociology at the Virginia Commonwealth University, Richmond, Virginia. He is coauthor with Anson D. Shupe of three monographs on new religious movements: *"Moonies" in America*, *The New Vigilantes*, and *Strange Gods*. He is currently writing a book on religious apostates.

JEAN BURFOOT is a graduate of the London School of Economics and received her M.A. in sociology at the University of California, Los Angeles, in 1980. Her main research interest is in the area of loss and change; the sociologies of humour, and death and dying. She is currently working as a thanatologist, counseling dying patients and their families.

FRANS DERKS graduated in the psychology of culture and religion and became a research assistant in the subdepartment for the Psychology of Culture and Religion of the Catholic University at Nijmegen (the Netherlands). In 1980 he received a grant from the Dutch Government to investigate the problems of disaffiliators from new religious movements.

BERT HARDIN is a United States citizen whose research interests cover the new religious movements, the sociology of beliefs, and the history of sociology in both America and West Germany. He is currently a member of the department of sociology in the University ofTübingen, West Germany.

SAMUEL HILL is a professor of religion at the University of Florida (Gainesville). His special interests are religion in American culture, viewed both historically and sociologically. Recent publications include *The New Religious Political Right in America* (with Dennis E. Owen), Abingdon Press, 1982; and *The South and the North in American Religion*, University of Georgia Press, 1980. A holder of the Ph.D. in Religion from Duke University, he was previously (1960-1972) a member of the department of religion at the University of North Carolina at Chapel Hill.

CHRISTINE KING has an academic background of history and theology and is at present senior lecturer in history at Preston Polytechnic, England. Her publications are in the history of religion and include work on English medieval pilgrimage and, more recently, a book on Christian sects in the Third Reich (Edwin Mellen Press, New York). She is currently involved in launching a research program on the history of religious bigotry in the United Kingdom since 1700, with particular emphasis on sects.

WOLFGANG KUNER studied business administration and then sociology and political science. He gained his doctorate in social science from the University of Tübingen. He was Wissenschaftlicher Mitarbeiter at the department of political science at the University of Tübingen and is currently Wissenschaftlicher Mitarbeiter in the department of sociology and political science at the Pädagogische Hochschule of Heidelberg (West Germany).

JOHN LOFLAND is a professor in the department of sociology at the University of California, Davis. His scholarly works include *Doomsday Cult* (Halstead Press, 1977); *Social Life*, (Wyley, 1976); and *Symbolic Sit-ins*, (University Press of America, 1982). He has served as president of the Pacific Sociological Association, editor of the journal *Urban Life* and chairman of the American Sociological Association's Section on Collective Behaviour and Social Movements.

RICHARD MACHALEK is associate professor of sociology at Trinity University in San Antonio, Texas. His major research interests include the study of theoretical issues in the sociology of religion and the study of religious conversion and related cognitive transformations. His publications appear in the *Journal for the Scientific Study of Religion, Social Science Quarterly*, and *Sociological Theory*. He and David Snow are currently engaged in research on religious conversion.

JAMES McBRIDE is a graduate of Johns Hopkins University (B.A.), the University of Chicago (M.A.) and currently is a doctoral candidate in the field of religion and society at the Graduate Theological Union in Berkeley, California. As a research associate of the Center for the Study of New Religious Movements (Berkeley) he has contributed papers to several publications and has just completed the manuscript of the forthcoming *Theopolis Americana: The Rise of the New Christian Right* with Paul Schwartz.

WILLIAM REIMER teaches in the department of sociology and anthropology at Concordia University, Montreal. He earned his Ph.D. from the University of British Columbia. From 1972 to 1978 he was one of the coordinators for the Study of Religious and Parareligious Groups in the Montreal Area. He is currently conducting research on agricultural communities in Quebec.

JAMES T. RICHARDSON is professor of sociology at the University of Nevada, Reno. He has conducted extensive research into the Jesus Movement and other new religious groups. His many publications include *Organized Miracles: A Study of a Contemporary, Youth, Communal, Fundamentalist Organization* (with M. W. Stewart and R. B. Simmonds), Transaction Books, New Brunswick, 1979.

E. BURKE ROCHFORD, JR. is currently in the sociology department of the University of Tulsa, Oklahoma. His research interests are in the areas of social movements and mental health and illness. For the past six years he has been studying the Hare Krishna movement in America.

PAUL ANTHONY SCHWARTZ is project director of the Center for the Study of New Religious Movements at the Graduate Theological Union in Berkeley, California. His doctoral research in the field of religion and society includes an analysis of the political ideology of the Moral Majority and other new religious movements. With Jim McBride he has recently completed writing *Theopolis Americana: The Rise of the New Christian Right.*

ANSON D. SHUPE is associate professor of sociology at the University of Texas at Arlington and associate director of its Center for Social Research. He received his Ph.D. in sociology from Indiana University in 1975. Since that time he has authored or coauthored five books and over forty professional journal articles.

NORMAN SKONOVD is presently engaged in criminal justice and delinquency research at the California Youth Authority. He recently received a Ph.D. in sociology from the University of California at Davis. His dissertation concerned the process of defection from totalistic religious movements.

DAVID A. SNOW is associate professor of sociology at the University of Texas at Austin. He has conducted research on social movements, religious cults, conversion, crowd behaviour, social interaction, and the self-concept. His publications appear in a range of journals, including the *American Sociological Review, Social Problems, Symbolic Interaction,* and the *Journal for the Scientific Study of Religion.*

STEVEN M. TIPTON teaches sociology and ethics at Emory University (Atlanta, Georgia) and at its Candler School of Theology. He is the author of *Getting Saved from the Sixties: Moral Meaning in Conversion and Cultural Change*, University of California Press, 1982.

JAN M. VAN DER LANS is assistant professor in the department of psychology, subdepartment for the Psychology of Culture and Religion, at the Catholic University Nijmegen (the Netherlands). He has published a book and several articles resulting from his experimental studies into religious experience and meditation.

ANDREW WALKER studied at the Hull, Salford, and London Universities. He is director of the London School of Ecumenical Studies. He has been a lecturer at Manchester University, Chiswick Polytechnic, and the West London Institute where he is still based. He is the author of several articles on Pentecostalism and the philosophy of social science, and a former consultant to the British Council of Churches and the World Council of Churches. He is also a television researcher/consultant and a member of the B.B.C.Ecumenical Board.

INDEX